A Better Life for Half the Price

HOW TO THRIVE ON LESS MONEY IN THE CHEAPEST PLACES TO LIVE

Revised Second Edition

by Tim Leffel

A Better Life for Half the Price

Published by Al Centro Media, Florida. USA.

Disclaimer
The author is not a lawyer, CPA, tax advisor, financial advisor, or doctor. The information presented in this book is a collection of advice. Interviews, and opinions from a person who has lived abroad and many subjects who have done the same, but none of it is guaranteed to be absolutely current and without fault. Nothing in this book should be construed as legal, financial, or medical advice that should be taken without secondary verification.

Prices, tax laws, visa requirements, and exchange rates are in a constant state of flux. Anything written in these pages is subject to change, so always verify key items before basing a life-changing decision on them. All attempts have been made to ensure visa/residency information was correct at the time of writing and to fact-check statistics, but it's especially important to verify this information with your local consulate or embassy—or the people living where you want to live — before proceeding.

Dedicated to the millions of expatriates who made the leap and are already living large for less money.

TABLE OF CONTENTS

Introduction

When we lived in a mid-sized city in the USA, we were blowing through money like it was water flowing through our fingers. Our rent for a not-very-large house or condo in a good school district ranged from $2,000 to $2,300 per month. We had a car payment and insurance to pay monthly. Most of our bills had three digits, from the internet/phone/cable bundle to cell phones for the family to electricity. Since I was self-employed, we were paying 20% of my income for substandard health insurance that came with a $7,000 deductible that was never met. Add in food and all the various expenses that pop up for a family, and we were spending close to $5,000 per month before even counting my business expenses. This for a family that lives a relatively frugal life, shares one car, and isn't very materialistic.

Since the incoming cash flow didn't always match the month's outgoing expenses while running an online business that pays a lot of freelancer invoices and hosting bills, we racked up some debt. Despite all the outward signs of my success other people saw, we were struggling to live a rather simple middle-class life in the second-tier city of Tampa, even though we were earning a fair bit more than the mean U.S. salary of $52,000 a year. If we had been in San Francisco or New York City, we might have been headed to bankruptcy.

There were some fights between my wife and I, some painful decisions on what we couldn't afford to do, and some strains on our marriage that we hadn't dealt with before. I look back on my last two rounds of living in the USA now with a mix of anger and relief. Anger that it's so damn expensive just to get by in the country of my birth, and relief that I'm not there now.

We moved back to Mexico in the nick of time as my daughter headed off to college. Now we are spending less each month total than we had been just on rent and utilities in Florida, even after factoring in furniture purchases, maintenance, and renovations. Instead of struggling to scrape up enough money to go out to eat—or putting it on a credit card—we are now paying cash to go out multiple times a week and we don't sweat it.

Our expenses have dropped by two-thirds, so we can stress less about money and spend time enjoying life instead. We're putting money into savings rather than just hoping to cover the bills. Our income is roughly the same, but our quality of life is drastically better. What we earned before seemed to never be enough. What we earn now buys a life of abundance.

The interesting thing is, it's the same amount of money. Only the address has changed.

The New Reality in the Developed World
As you've probably noticed, getting ahead where you live now is getting tougher all the time. Things are not so hunky-dory for the non-rich in the rich countries of the world these days. You still have boat and train loads of immigrants trying to get into the USA, Canada, Europe, and Australia each week, but for those of us living in these countries, the future does not look as bright as it did for our grandparents. Costs keep rising, wages do not, and only the richest of the rich seem to be seeing their conditions steadily improve.

You basically have two choices if you want to increase your disposable income: you can find a way to earn far more money, or you can dramatically cut your expenses. You know better than me how feasible the first option is for you. For most people, if it were easy to double their income, they would have done it already.

If you stay where you are now, the latter option usually involves a series of painful sacrifices. You have to cut back on groceries, eat out less, downsize your living quarters, sell your car, forgo vacations, forget about enhancing your wardrobe, and basically stop doing any fun activities that aren't free.

There's a better solution though that millions of others have discovered already. You can just move.

Time for a Change of Scenery
If you move from a rich country to a poorer one, you can cut your expenses in half without all those sacrifices. You can live a better life while spending far less for your basic expenses. You end up with more money to spend or save without cutting back on what you enjoy or living more frugally. It's the equivalent of going on a diet without giving up ice cream or cheeseburgers.

This book is your guide to getting from where you are now to the point where you can live a better life for half the price. It shows you which countries are viable in terms of costs and visa requirements for long-term residency. It also gives you a clear look at the pros and cons of each destination. More than 50 expatriates tell their stories here, showing you how much they spend in an average month while also outlining some of the challenges they have overcome.

I also share some of my own experiences. I'm not some desk reporter who hasn't ventured out on my own. I wrote this book from my home office in central Mexico, now my permanent base. In the past, I've lived in Turkey and Korea, as well as the New York City area, Virginia, Tennessee, and Florida. I've been through multiple residency visa applications and renewals abroad and I talk monthly with others doing the same. You can be confident I know more about this subject than most and have reached out to people who are living the dream in other countries around the world. You'll hear from young digital nomads, couples running a virtual business, families with kids in schools abroad, and retirees taking it easy in a warmer, calmer climate.

I've spent time in every country profiled in detail except Georgia (hope to get there soon), plus I've covered many of them in my *World's Cheapest Destinations* book, which is now in its fifth edition. This book should serve you well as an idea generator, move motivator, and guide to how to turn your dreams and desires into reality. I won't be able to answer every question you possibly have in these pages of course, but there are entire books out there on moving to just one country. If you want to explore your options in more depth before making the leap after finishing this book, see the packages with extra info and personal consulting at CheapLivingAbroad.com.

One quick note on current events: yes, I know travel is limited as this book hits the shelves and it may stay that way for a while. Until the world gets the COVID-19 virus under control, you may not be able to just hop on a plane and land in any of these countries. As I release this in late 2020, however, a fair number of them are already open and others will be the following year. This book is meant to be evergreen, so I only refer to the temporary restrictions in passing. Hopefully by the time you read this, the lockdowns will be history.

Now, let's see what it feels like to have twice as much money on hand without having to double your income.

Chapter 1:
Open Your Eyes to a Better Way

Christa Roberts lived in New York City before moving abroad. She loved her apartment on 6th Avenue on the edge of the West Village and right near Washington Square Park, but she spent a whopping $1,300 a month on rent and utilities for her share. "I lived with two friends in a two-bedroom apartment, which we converted into a three-bedroom one by hiring a contractor to come in and build a wall halfway through the living room," she says. "We had a small table that fit two stools and a small L-shaped couch that was in the same room as the railroad kitchen. That was it for furniture. If you can imagine that, you can see that we could provide actual seats for five people, so when we would have parties people would end up standing or sitting on the kitchen counter. All three of the 'bedrooms' fit a double bed (touching three walls) and just enough space to put a yoga mat next to it. My window faced a brick wall."

Then she moved to Thailand's largest city of Bangkok and it was a different story.

"Now I make about half of what I made in NYC. My new 2-bedroom apartment, however, which has a big living room, a small but separate kitchen, two balconies, and bedrooms big enough for king sized beds, costs me a little over $330 total for rent and utilities, including internet. This means that instead of spending half of my salary on regular expenses, I'm spending a fifth. Now I can not only have a travel fund but an actual savings account. Despite making a lot less, I can easily save at least twice as much.

Before, I was always watching my money, especially when going out to dinner. It's nice not having to look at each price on the menu before I order and to not feel stressed out if someone at the table suggests another round of cocktails.

The best part though, is that I can travel a lot more. I recently stayed in a huge share-house with about 20 friends located in a prestigious beach town a few hours outside of Bangkok. It was essentially the same experience I had while going to the Hamptons with friends, but this time I didn't have to sleep on the floor and got to enjoy food from our hired chef who was around all weekend. This trip cost me $100 as opposed to the $500 I used to spend on one weekend in the Hamptons.

In New York, I would save all year to go on a few long weekend trips and then one big trip out of the country per year. Now I can go away every month if I want and am also saving to visit my family this year. Being in a foreign country automatically puts you in a better position to travel internationally and see new places, but financially it's much easier as well."

Right now, while you're reading this, there are a million and a half Americans and Canadians living in Mexico alone. You'll run into plenty of other Brits in Portugal and Bulgaria, and won't have to look very hard to find someone else from Australia or New Zealand in Thailand or Malaysia. The stories and experiences you will read in this book are from real people who are different from you in one way: they took the leap already. They're just a little further along on the continuum than you are, that's all. What makes them different is they picked up and moved.

Moving to another country to enjoy a better life for half the price is not odd, radical, crazy, or dumb. The people around you might say that, or at least think it, but very few who have actually done it will. Often when I asked people what regrets they had or what mistakes they had made, they replied, "I just wish I had done it sooner."

It's Not Your Imagination: Things Are Getting Worse at Home
No matter how you look at it, living in one of the world's economic superpowers is not the easy ride it used to be. The top one percent keep getting richer, while everyone else is having a tougher time finding a good job and holding onto it. That's not just my opinion: it's borne out by statistics and an open-eyed look around at your fellow citizens. In poll after poll, two-thirds of Americans said they are dissatisfied with "the way income and wealth are currently distributed in the U.S." The Council of Economic Advisors in Washington D.C. created "The Gatsby Curve" to plot how well countries are doing with income inequality and the ability of people to move up the ladder to a better life. The USA and UK scored among the worst in the world on both counts. According to the U.S. Federal Reserve, the top one percent in America are worth $36 trillion, which is more than the entire middle class added together. Throw in a pandemic and a second high-unemployment recession and a lot of people are getting left behind in the wealthiest countries in the world.

If you feel like prices keep going up where you live but your wages are not, you're probably right. Over the past 25 years, wages in most developed countries have edged up just 2 – 5% in good years and have declined in bad ones, including 2010 and 2020. In good years, the wage increases have beat inflation barely, but only if you take out categories such as healthcare and education.

Many students are graduating from a good university and finding that all they have to show for it years later is a piece of paper and lots of debt. Even before the worldwide pandemic hit, the number of "under-employed college graduates in jobs that don't require that education topped 20% in the USA, Canada, and Europe. Student debt routinely tops $1 trillion per quarter in the USA.

Meanwhile, housing prices continue to rise in these countries, apart from a few anomalies where newly remote workers are leaving big cities. Many dual-earning couples are paying a third of their income just on rent or a mortgage.

Housing has continued to eat up a larger and larger share of income as rental or purchase prices rise faster than stagnant wages, in all three of these countries. On top of that, healthcare and university tuition costs keep rising far faster than the rate of inflation for Americans, and education that was once completely tax-supported is becoming less so elsewhere. Almost a third of Americans aren't saving any money and are in fact spending more than they're earning every year.

In other words, apart from the billionaires and the politicians who serve them, those of us in "rich" countries are falling further and further behind. According to an Oxfam report from years ago, the combined wealth of the world's 86 richest people was equivalent to the entire bottom half of the world's population—3.5 billion people. Those at the top have done even better in the latest recession since many head up companies that benefited from the lockdowns. The average middle-class wage earner keeps running faster on the treadmill but is not getting any further ahead.

Ask those who have made the move how they feel now and many feel like they've gone from shackled to free economically. Kristen Raccuia left a high-stress, high-cost real estate business in Chicago to move to Penang, Malaysia with her husband and their costs plummeted. "In an average month, not being careful or budgeting, we spend around $2,000 total. Our 3-bedroom, 4-bath apartment of 2,300 square feet has balconies with a great ocean view and we pay $650 per month."

How would things change if you could snap your fingers and cut your expenses in half or by two-thirds? It might actually take a wee bit longer than snapping your fingers, but you do have the power to live a more fulfilling life at a dramatically lower cost just by moving.

It's time for a reboot. Let's reset the equation.

Chapter 2:
How Your Bills Get Drastically Lower in Some Countries

After getting his MBA, Michael Gans had no luck finding the kind of job he wanted in the USA. After getting no response from 100 job applications, he applied for and got a graduate internship in London, in a division of one of the world's biggest investment firms. After having to pay for a full year of housing up front, he had to live on a stipend of 600 pounds sterling a month, which he didn't receive until after working for a month. "I was broke. I had $58 in my pocket upon arrival. I ate lentils and white rice for the whole first month." Transportation is affordable there, but almost anything else costs a fortune. "If you go to Tesco or Marks and Spencer, a cut of meat will be £10. I would say to myself, 'I can have that, but then I won't be able to eat the rest of the week.'"

After getting good experience there, a year later he got a job in San Francisco, which wasn't much better. "I was living in a one-bedroom apartment with a tiny little living room for $1,340. Once you add in utilities and internet it was $1,500. It wasn't even anything very exciting for that price." At his one-year point he started looking around at international jobs and six months later was employed as a financial associate in Delhi, India. After the move, his rent for an equivalent apartment was $247, just a 15-minute walk from his office. He earned less, but his rent and utilities only took up a quarter of his pay, compared to almost half when he was in San Francisco. A 5-mile taxi ride went from $25 to $3. Lunch at a decent restaurant near the office went from $10 to $2.

If you went to India on some kind of luxury tour, you may not have realized how cheap it is there. The same goes for your vacation in the Galapagos Islands of Ecuador, or the high-end resorts of Thailand. There's a huge gulf between what tourists pay and what locals or budget travelers pay.

Ask any backpacker who has traveled around the world what kinds of misconceptions they deal with when talking to friends and family about their travels. One of the big ones is that most people think travel has to be expensive. They can't fathom how you could travel around the world on $50 a day, or that in some countries it could average out to half that amount for two. It simply does not compute for them that there are places with $2 restaurant meals, $10 hotels, and museums that cost a buck.

Most expatriates who have cut their expenses in half without trying awfully hard deal with similar misconceptions. People have trouble believing that a family can live in Mexico for $2,000 or less per month and actually go out more often. Their impressions of Mexico are mostly of all-inclusive resorts, expensive tours, and inflated taxi costs in Cancun or Los Cabos. Their impression of Portugal is a holiday in the Algarve, which might be cheap compared to one on the coast of France, but not half of what they spend just living at home. People comment on my blog all the time that "Thailand is not cheap anymore." Usually it turns out they only stayed at resort area hotels in Phuket and never ate where the locals eat.

There are two vastly different sides to all the countries profiled in this book: the tourist side and the everyday living side. The two have little to do with each other when it comes to prices. The tourist side is priced for foreigners on a short-term vacation budget. The everyday living side is priced for what the local market will bear. The "invisible hand" of economics takes its cue from local wages and the local ability to pay for goods and services. Tourist prices exist in a parallel economic universe, based solely on what visitors from a richer country are willing to pay.

When you move somewhere to become a resident, you generally move from the tourist price universe to the local price universe. And those local prices can cost a tiny fraction of what you're used to. After all, the per capita annual Gross Domestic Product in Australia is more than $55,000. In Nepal it's more like $550. If you earned just half the annual per capita GDP amount in Australia—$27,500—and spent that in Nepal, you'd instantly be among the upper crust. You'd be elite, wealthy, stinking rich by local standards.

Here are the factors that impact your monthly cost of living, from housing to recurring bills to eating out.

Lower Housing Costs
If a typical office job salary where you're moving to is $800 per month, there will be few takers for apartments that cost $1,000 per month. The laws of supply and demand just won't match up. If we assume the average person is paying a quarter of their income on housing, then $200 will be an average rent price. Even at $400, they'd be spending half their salary on rent, so they're probably going to bring in a roommate or wait until there are two earners in the family.

If you waltz into the city earning $2,000 a month from your pension or remote job, you've joined the elites. You won't feel rich at all in Canada or the UK on that amount, but you might where you're headed. You have your pick of the best properties in town. If you spend a quarter of your income on rent, you can afford $500 per month. Unlike where you live now, that will get you a nice apartment in nearly every country featured in this book. If you spend anything close to the going rate of where you live now— where average salaries are much higher—you'll probably be able to afford a mansion or a luxury penthouse.

The same applies to purchase prices, though keep in mind that the percentage of foreigners will have a big impact on real estate. The reason Costa Rica and Belize aren't featured in this book is because a huge percentage of the buyers in prime areas have been foreigners—for decades on end. That has driven up prices to a point where there are few great deals left. It's also the reason you won't find many bargains in the outlier elite areas of cheap countries, such as Los Cabos in Mexico or Punta del Este, Uruguay. To find a real bargain, you need to buy where you're competing with the locals on prices, not with 10,000 other foreigners bringing in the proceeds of a house sale back in their own country.

Lower Utility Costs

Back in 2014, Google bought a little company called Nest for $3.2 billion. What that company does is help you control your home thermostat remotely with a phone app. Why is that such a big deal? Because heating and air conditioning together account for 56 percent of the average U.S. home's energy consumption. If one of the world's biggest companies can help you substantially lower your utility bills, you're probably going to be more than willing to pay a monthly subscription fee.

Or you could just move.

Let's say you move to an "eternal spring" climate place like Boquete (Panama), Medellin (Colombia), Cuenca (Ecuador), or one of the highland Mexican towns like Ajijic, or San Miguel de Allende. You rarely need heat, hardly anyone has air conditioning, so voila—half-price utility bills.

Even if you go somewhere hot and tropical, if you're in a place with regular sea breezes you might find that you need the A/C less than you used to as time goes by and you get acclimated. If nothing else, your utility rate—what you pay per kilowatt hour—is more likely to go down than up. In most countries, power costs are subsidized or at least tightly controlled to prevent rapid spikes.

After all, if nobody can afford electricity or gas in the country a ruler is governing, he's going to have a rebellion or coup on his hands in short order. Every elected official will be blamed and booted out of office.

In general, utility costs have a correlation with the average income in a country. It's not a direct correlation because of policy decisions: in Venezuela gasoline is practically free, in Ecuador it's half price, in Cambodia it's priced at the world market rate, in Europe it's double the market rate because of high taxes. Overall though, electricity costs in Morocco or Thailand are going to be less than in Canada or Denmark. If not, the market will usually find a way to bring costs down for individuals, such as through increased use of cheap solar hot water heaters or ultra-efficient appliances. Your monthly utility bills should decrease, and you'll benefit from lower prices at businesses that use energy too.

Lower Labor Costs
Close your eyes and think of ten services you spend money on where labor is a high percentage of that organization's cost.

Now, imagine what kind of impact it would have if all of the people doing those jobs had their pay cut by two thirds or more.

Wow, that would drastically lower the costs to consumers like you, wouldn't it?

It doesn't really matter which things popped into your mind. It's a very long list to pick from. You can imagine hospitals and plastic surgery, taxis and flights, babysitters and house painters, hotels and water parks. If a person who would be paid $50 an hour where you live now gets $15 an hour where you're moving, that's a massive difference. If a surgeon makes $3,000 a day in your hometown and makes $300 a day where you're going, imagine what that's going to do to your coronary bypass bill.

Where I live in Mexico, you can hire an experienced handyman for around $5 an hour and that's considered good money. The housekeeper cleans our four-bedroom house for the local equivalent of $17. A ten-minute taxi ride across town is $3. A carpenter made us an entire king-sized platform bed frame with built-in drawers, in cedar, for a shade over $300. We get clothing alterations done for a few dollars per garment. In none of these cases have we bargained people down to their minimum: we're paying normal rates or better.

The minimum wage in Ecuador is around $10 *a day*. In Portugal it's only twice that. In Nepal it's less than $1 a day. So, if you pay someone triple the minimum in Cuenca to build you some custom cabinets, the labor part of the cost may only be $30 per day. Taking advantage of this is not exploitation. It's arbitrage. You're using your dollars/pounds/euros acquired where labor costs are high and spending them where labor costs are low. Keep doing this over and over again in your daily life, on nearly every transaction you make, and it's easy to understand how you can cut your expenses in half quite easily.

Lower Food Costs
Here's how Bryan Haines of GringosAbroad.com described his food costs in Cuenca, Ecuador compared with when he travels back to Canada:

"We eat at the food court at Mall del Rio for less than $8 (3 people, with a hearty meal and drinks). We had 3 ice creams on the Halifax Waterfront in Canada, and it was $14. Dinner at McDonalds there is around $30."

Where I live in Mexico, a sit-down "meal of the day" can easily be found for $3 or $4, a tamale on the street is never more than 80 cents, and a fresh-squeezed orange juice is $1 for 16 ounces. A pulled-pork sandwich is $1.55, and I can get four pastries at the bakery for a buck. If we are going to spend more than $10 on seasonal fruit and vegetables at the market, then two of us make the trip to carry it all home.

Think about your last trip to the supermarket and where all those items came from. You may have bought blueberries from Chile, peppers from Mexico, pineapples from Costa Rica, and bananas from Honduras. If you're in the UK, maybe green beans, oranges, and bananas from somewhere in Africa or Asia. Assume the wholesale cost doubled along the way, there were shipping costs, and then the retailer doubled the price again. You're easily paying four times what the cost was at the source. So, when you move to the source and start shopping locally, you'll probably find your food costs are a small fraction of what you paid at home.

There are exceptions of course: coffee tends to follow international export prices for the good stuff and if you want imported products, you're back to the same mark-ups. If you mostly eat what locals of average means eat, however, you are going to eat very well on far less money. This is a good reason, of course, to pick a place where you like the food. If you can't stand Thai food or Vietnamese food makes you cringe, you're probably not going to be happy in Thailand or Vietnam. You'll also spend far more than people who love those cuisines.

Lower Taxes

In many European countries, the tax burden on average individual income can easily reach 50 percent when you add everything together. In the United States the tax burden is significantly lower. Unless you're a multi-millionaire living in a high-tax state like California or New York, you probably don't pay out more than 25 percent of your income. When you look at what corporations actually pay (as opposed to what the rate is in theory), it's well under 10 percent.

These numbers are quite high by developing world standards, however. In a place where the average wage is $10 a day or less, it doesn't make much sense to hit people with an income tax that's going to scrape off a big chunk of that. So almost anywhere you're going to move to from the destinations in the last section of this book, your tax bill will go down. You may need to keep filing and paying in your home country—especially if your income is still from there—but your local bills for property taxes, sales taxes, business license fees, and a million other things will probably be lower than where you left. When you buy something at a store, you're paying sales tax or an IVA, but it's usually included in the price already. It's not an add-on surprise at the end. In many countries this is the main revenue source for the government, so there's not an income tax on top of that.

It's the indirect result of this lower tax bill that matters most in your everyday life, however. If businesses pay less in taxes, they don't have to build a big impact into their prices. If a laborer doesn't have to give 30% of his income to the government, he's going to be far more flexible on what he's charging you for a job. If the license fee to run a street cart is low or non-existent, your street tacos or Thai curry dishes don't have to have that cost built into the product charge. If it doesn't cost an astronomical sum for a taxi license, a cab driver can charge you a much lower fare. This, in a nutshell, is the argument for lower taxes by conservative politicians and pundits around the world. Let the market set rates, with no government interference or influence.

That ignores the other half of the equation, however. Most of that tax money does not go into a black hole or get siphoned off by the corrupt. Most of it builds infrastructure, treats water, educates children, funds safety net programs, and covers defense spending. In the civilized nations of the developed world, taxes fund health care that cures the sick and covers the expenses for a mother to have a baby—for 100 percent of the population. It's an irony that vexes the libertarians that some of the happiest people in the world in surveys live in the countries with the highest taxes. It makes sense though: with a strong safety net and more equality, a lot of daily stress is removed.

So, there's the eternal trade-off: what you give up in taxes, you give up in government spending. That treated water you can drink from the tap in developed countries like the one you were born in? In many destinations covered in this book, you're on your own for drinking water. It's not a given that you can drink what comes out of the tap. The wastewater flowing out of your toilet may not be treated properly either. The local schools might be terrible, with 45 kids in a class going nuts every day. There's probably a public healthcare system, but if you want quality care and good testing equipment, you'll need to pay for private system care. The food inspections may be non-existent or minimal, the regulations weak. The laws that are on the books to protect workers, keep the air clean, and protect the environment may not have enough of a budget behind them to ensure compliance. There are probably not enough police, and the ones that are in place may be easy for criminals to buy off since their pay is so lousy.

Always keep this trade-off in mind when you're ready to go on a tirade about how nothing works properly in your newfound home and how the workers are so lazy in every public service office you have to deal with. You're often getting what you pay for. The good news is, you're paying a lot less—even if you do factor in those five-gallon purified water bottles you have to keep buying.

Lower Medical Bills for Better Care
If you're moving from the USA, lower healthcare costs can present a dramatic change in your expenses. Only three countries spend more per capita than the United States on healthcare, (Luxembourg, Norway, and Monaco), and they have far superior nationalized systems. Those politicians who tell you national healthcare would be a fiasco haven't spent much time living elsewhere. Just ask anyone living in another country if they'd prefer our privatized, profit-oriented system. Unless they're a billionaire with a rare type of cancer that you want treated at Johns Hopkins, probably not.

If you have even two or three prescriptions, you know how much the cost of medicine can impact your budget. Most new medicines are developed in the United States, but the Big Pharma companies certainly don't do their home country citizens any favors. The average cost of heartburn drug Nexium is $215 in the U.S., but $58 in Spain, $42 in England, and $23 in the

Netherlands. It's less than $20 in most developing countries: nobody would buy it otherwise. An anti-parasite medicine that's typically $5 or less in Latin American sells for more than $100 in the USA.

If you have to actually go visit a doctor or stay in the hospital, it's even worse. An MRI that is $138 in expensive Switzerland and $250 in Mexico is a whopping $1,145 in the United States. My late father's hip surgery bill in South Carolina was $45,740. Sure, our Medicare tax dollars and his supplementary insurance paid most of that, but in Malaysia it'll be less than half that. In Mexico or Ecuador, it's half again. In India even less. Heart surgery that can literally bankrupt someone in the U.S. will cost less than a used car from the 10 years ago in most of the cheap places to live.

For those Americans who are poor or self-employed, medical care is a huge chunk of the monthly budget, even if there's seldom a need to make use of the insurance. Before the Affordable Care Act got pushed through, many small business owners and freelancers couldn't get insurance at any price because of pre-existing condition exclusions. Within a year of that law going into effect, the number of Americans without insurance dropped from 18 percent to 12 percent, but that still means 12 out of every 100 citizens have no coverage at all, usually because it's a choice between that, rent, or food. While the number of mothers who die during childbirth went down 3.1 percent across the developed world since 1990, it actually went *up* in the USA by 1.7 percent.

For the countries covered in this book, healthy people often don't even carry any kind of insurance. Medical costs are so reasonable that paying out of pocket is not an issue. Even if they're in an accident and end up in the hospital, they can probably cover the cost with a Visa card that has a $5,000 credit limit. In many countries, residents are automatically covered under the national universal health scheme or they can get on it by just submitting the proper paperwork. If they do want private health insurance, it will cost a small fraction of what you would pay in richer countries and then you can use the best medical facilities available—with no waiting time.

If you're coming from a country that already has a national healthcare system, like the UK or Canada, your costs won't drop as much in this department. You can skip the wait now though because you can easily afford to open your wallet and pay for whatever you want or need from the medical establishment—including the dentist's office.

Lower Transportation Costs

For every expatriate I've talked to who owns a car, there are another two who don't. Few countries are as geared to motorists as the U.S., Canada, and Australia. In most of the cheapest, most desirable places to live in the world, a car is a status symbol more than a necessity. Cities and towns are more walkable, public transportation is cheap and frequent, and almost nobody thinks it's acceptable to put up with hour-long commutes to get to work.

For many of the countries profiled in this book, you can get a luxury bus ticket for less than it would cost you for just tolls and gas to get where you're going a few hours away. If you take a taxi or Uber every day like I did when my daughter had to get to a private school across town, you'll spend less than you would on a monthly car payment.

If you do need a car, you will probably not find one as cheap as you can find in the USA, where margins and the number of middlemen are both compressed. There's often not much of a used car market because everyone passes an old car onto a relative who then runs it until it can't run anymore. Fuel costs may be higher or lower, but maintenance costs will certainly be lower, from an oil change to an engine repair. The American Automobile Association reported that a person driving 15,000 miles a year in the USA spends an average of $760 a month on all car-related expenses, or $967 a month if they own a sport utility vehicle. In much of the world, that could get you a private chauffeur at your beck and call instead, all expenses included. Or better yet, a nice vacation on a regular basis with the savings.

In some countries profiled in this book you can import your vehicle duty free as part of the residency permit perks, so if you're set on keeping a vehicle, look into that option. In Europe you can just drive it there if you're coming from another EU country, but to go from Canada or the USA to Latin America you'll likely have to send it on a cargo ship.

Chapter 3:
Why Move to Another Country?

A vast majority of my friends and relatives thought I was absolutely bonkers for wanting to leave my home country, much less to cut ties and make another nation my base.

Many people who leave the USA, Canada, or England to live elsewhere say the biggest resistance to overcome is not internal, but external. There are a lot of doubters, haters, and envious people who have a myriad of reasons to tell you this is a dumb idea. These reasons can range from rah-rah nationalism to envy of your freedom to the kind of fear that makes their stomach clench up in knots. We all have an innate fear of the unknown that served us well in caveman times. For many, this instinct is impossible to ever overcome without an effort to do so. They may not be happy with their life, but they're comfortable, so they can't imagine rocking the boat and dealing with change.

While some may not be able to vocalize it, your decision represents a threat to everything they hold dear. If you think the grass is greener on the other side, well, what if it *is*? What does it mean for this place they're still stuck in, which is looking worse than it used to look, with fewer good job prospects? This place where their costs keep rising but their incomes don't?

For those willing to research, prepare, and then take the leap, however, the post-transition time often turns out to be easier than they expected. Of course, this is not true for everyone, so do read the Chapter after this on why *not* to move abroad. Some people clearly aren't cut out for this and it's better to find that out before selling the house and investing the proceeds in a foreign land.

Naturally, I wouldn't have moved abroad multiple times and written this book if I didn't think the positives outweighed the negatives, so let's look at what you gain by moving to a cheaper country.

The Ability to Hold onto More of Your Money
The number one reason cited by most expatriates who move abroad by choice is financial savings. (Number two is climate, third is politics.) Simply put, they spend less on monthly living expenses than they would on a comparable life at home. This doesn't mean it's always an apples to apples comparison of course. There are things you take for granted in Europe or the USA that you can't take for granted in many developing countries. Usually those are offset though by something you can get in your adopted

country that's better, cheaper, or more satisfying than you had before. It's all a trade-off, but usually one where the odds are greatly in favor of the cheaper place.

Many find they can become nomadic, living wherever they want in the world, for what would be a poverty existence in the country they grew up in. One of my blog readers Dean commented on one of my posts like this: "I've lived in Airbnb apartments for 19 months now in Latin America with my $1000-a-month retirement income. That has been easy to do in a whole lot of countries."

Even without taking an economics class, it's pretty easy to understand why a country like Honduras or Cambodia is cheaper than Canada. The per capita gross domestic product figure is around $5,600 per person annually for Honduras according to the IMF, around $5,000 for Cambodia. For comparison, it's around $67,000 for the USA and $52,000 for Canada. There are inherent problems with GDP statistics and exchange rate fluctuations can warp the figures, but as a rough yardstick they show you the average citizen in the first two countries is several times poorer than in the other two. They're also far poorer than other English-speaking countries like the UK, Ireland, Australia, and New Zealand.

If an average salary for an office worker in Peru is $7,500 per year, then you're not going to find many Peruvian houses going for $2,300 per month—what I paid in downtown Tampa, Florida to rent a three-bedroom condo. You're not going to find hair stylists charging $50, housekeepers charging $150, or restaurant meals going for $75 each. The local taxis have to be priced at a level local people can afford or there won't be any taxis. The bus fares have to be affordable to low-wage workers or there won't be anyone on the buses.

The local income level roughly impacts a wide range of costs, some direct, some trickle-down. Taxes, home costs, construction materials, food costs, and the price of a custom piece of furniture are all directly or indirectly impacted by two things: the cost of labor and the cost of real estate. Picture a ladder with lots of rungs. Let say you have Cambodia and Nepal at the bottom, then Vietnam, Thailand, Malaysia, Korea, and up it goes through Asia to Japan. You can walk up that ladder via the capital cities: a street food meal in Phnom Penh is under $2, one with similar ingredients in Tokyo is $10-$15. A one-bedroom apartment in the former? For $300 it'll be decent. In Tokyo, good luck getting an even smaller one for $2,000.

You can visualize this same ladder within a country as well. The differences won't be that stark, but imagine noting the costs for Dubuque, Iowa, then Omaha, then Portland, then Atlanta, then San Francisco, and finally New York City. Getting transferred from Dubuque to New York City for a job better come with a corresponding tripling of salary just to stay reasonably even. But when friends in an old job of mine got transferred from New York to Nashville with no cut in pay, they felt like sudden millionaires. Keep this in mind when moving abroad as well. It's easier to cut your expenses in half making a lateral city-to-city move or city to rural than to go from a tiny town to Panama City or Lisbon.

Many expatriates say they feel downright rich when they settle into living in Mexico, Panama, Hungary, or Thailand. Often, they have cut their expenses substantially, but are able to do a lot more with their money. Or they keep their spending level the same as home and go from feeling like they're barely getting by to feeling like they've got more money than they need. All that was required was a change of address.

"In Medellin, Colombia I am living the life of a rich man," says American early retiree Steve McPeek, "while if I were still living in Dallas, I would have to get a second job just to pay the bills. My goal is to never work again, have no boss, and have the freedom to do what I want. I can easily do that in Medellin."

Money is nearly always at the top of the list for what's stressing people out at one time or another. Being short on money can take a toll on relationships, on health, and on success levels of a career or business. It can impact your children's education, how your aging parents are cared for, or whether your golden years are spent seeing the world or being stuck at home in front of a TV.

Doubling the amount of money you earn is really hard though, especially in the short term. And in a country with a progressive tax structure, the more you earn the less you keep. But what if you could just cut your expenses in half, without giving up any of your normal expenditures? What impact would that have on how much you have left to save, invest, or spend on what's important? By picking the right place to move to, this is not a difficult feat to achieve.

More House for Your Money

Whether you're renting or buying, if you spend anything close to what you were spending in your home country in one of the destinations profiled here, you'll end up with a far superior living space. Often you can spend half what you did before and still get an upgrade. For what I paid for a 3-bedroom apartment in downtown Tampa, I could rent a sprawling mansion with a private swimming pool in the interior of Mexico. Instead, when we rented, we paid one-third the amount and still got more space.

You probably already know it's crazy expensive to buy a house or condo in coastal California or a city like San Francisco, Vancouver, New York, or London. It's not just those outliers that are expensive though. *Outside* magazine published the median price of a home in many U.S. mountain towns in 2020 and here are a few examples: Durango, Colorado: $368,590. Stowe, Vermont: $427,500. Park City, Utah: $716,654. Ketchum, Idaho: $945,000. Jackson, Wyoming: $1,025,000.

Now, what will it cost you to buy a house in an equally desirable mountain town in one of these cheaper countries? In Bariloche and further south in Argentina, you can find something with a lake and mountain view for less than $200,000. In the ski town of Bansko, Bulgaria you can get a modern two-bedroom condo with a view for under $80,000. For beachfront property, there are dozens of places in the Americas and Asia where you could purchase a place for a quarter of what it would cost in your country of birth.

Naturally, this ratio applies to the rental world too, so there's no need to buy something and tie up your money to start getting a better house or apartment for far less money. Take your time and enjoy the upgrade.

For Better Weather

The "ideal climate" is not the same for everyone, otherwise we wouldn't be spread across the globe like we are. Where people go on vacation, however, tells you that many people like to be in a warm and sunny place near an ocean. If you ask people to pick their ideal retirement spot, more are going to pick a hot place than a cold one.

If that's you, there are plenty of cheap destinations to choose from that are hot. Some of them have great beaches too. You've got swaths of Mexico, Central America, and some of South America on one side of the world, most of Southeast Asia and southern India on the other. Or you can be a real pioneer and move to a beach in Africa.

If you hate bugs and would prefer an "eternal spring" climate, it's easy to find one of those too. You can move somewhere that the daytime temperatures are always between 60 and 90, all year long. Your utility bills will be next to nothing and one or two light jackets could be all the outerwear you need to bring.

If you want to keep experiencing all four seasons, there are options in this book for that too. There are European destinations featured that go from snow to hot summers, or you could move to the bottom of South America and feel like you are in Switzerland or British Columbia.

Whatever the ideal climate is that's going to make you happy, you can find it in a much cheaper place than you are living now.

To Improve Your Health
The medical care reason comes up more from Americans than it does for those with more logical healthcare systems, like, oh, every other developed country in the world. Unless you're old enough to be on Medicare in the USA and you have good supplementary insurance, almost anywhere you go is going to have a cheaper and better healthcare system for those of average means than what you are used to experiencing.

You will pay less, get far better service, and have no inexplicable surprise bills arriving in the mail months after your treatment. In most of the world, the medical system is designed to deliver a service that will make people better for a cost that everyone understands. Or no cost to the patient at all.

Despite what you may hear on Fox News, the U.S. does not have the best healthcare system in the world—not even close by any objective measures. What it *does* have is the best-paid doctors, the best testing equipment, and the latest drugs. Doctors in the United States are more likely than any other profession to be in the top one percent of earners. According to *Bloomberg News*, the actual cost of a caesarean birth is $606 in Canada, but $3,676 in the U.S. Medical device companies average a profit margin of between 16 and 20 percent; so, getting an MRI and a prescription in the U.S. can cost four times what it will in France. We're talking rich country to rich country comparisons here. Imagine the drop when you then get medical care in a place where the average annual income is a quarter of what it is where you live now.

We have a dysfunctional healthcare system that benefits private corporations more than the patients and there's so much profit built in that it is easily the most expensive care in the world—with results that are average at best. Then when a disaster hits, as it did during the COVID-19 pandemic, the flaws of this for-profit system literally end up killing people.

Plus, there's the flaw that insurance is tied to employment, in an environment where more than 25% of people now (and growing) are self-employed or working for a company that doesn't provide insurance. For those who are self-employed or not covered by a really solid employee plan, the insurance costs can easily eat up 20 percent of your income. The Affordable Care Act put a Band-Aid on the problem in some states, but it was still just baby steps toward curing an ailing system. We have huge swaths of the population that don't have access to regular preventive care and check-ups. Tens of millions have no insurance at all. The United States is the only developed country with no mandated time off or medical care for mothers having a baby.

For the countries featured in this book, you can probably have a long list of pre-existing health problems upon arrival, pay everything in cash out of pocket, and still spend less than you did just on insurance and co-pays the year before. It's not uncommon for some procedures to literally be one-tenth of prices in the United States, from x-rays to doctor visits to a dental cleaning and check-up.

Other expats, especially older ones, decide to get some kind of international catastrophic care insurance to cover major accidents or sudden cancer treatment, but pay for little things as they come up. In some countries you can opt into the national healthcare system, with varying degrees of how good that care is, only paying if they elect to go to a private hospital. Or you can get insurance that covers private hospitals and any doctor in that country. Most digital nomad types who don't spend long in one place will either just wing it, treat their credit card as an insurance policy, or get some kind of travel insurance that covers them in case of accident for a whole year.

Even for those coming from a country with a national healthcare system, the care you get abroad will often be better than what you're used to at home, with no queue to wait in for elective procedures.

You'll get in to see a doctor more quickly, that doctor may make house calls or hand out his or her cell phone number, and if you need an operation you won't go on a months-long waiting list. You won't dread the bill you get, and you won't have to hire a third-party service to decipher it.

Because healthcare costs are so much lower, you can afford to take better care of yourself and go get things checked out whenever you need it. If you decide to get screenings, an MRI, an eye exam, or a full dermatology scan, you can probably do it the next day and it won't cost you the equivalent of a month's rent. When you get sick, you can afford to go to the doctor. If you need your teeth cleaned and a crown put on, you won't delay getting it taken care of because of the cost. If you need surgery, the price will be three or four digits, not the price of a new Mercedes.

Great care from western-trained doctors in state-of-the-art medical facilities is the norm in some countries, which is why they have become medical tourism hubs. If you're getting up in years and this is a high priority, you'll be in good shape if you're in or near a city in Malaysia, Mexico, Panama, Ecuador, Thailand, or India. For others, it may be great in the capital, but hit and miss elsewhere. In a country like Cambodia or Nepal, people often end up flying to another country for something serious. I've covered this in more detail in the individual country Chapters.

Many expats will tell you they are far healthier than they were in the place they left. Even Canadian snowbirds who hold onto their home health insurance say they feel better knowing they can just call the doctor and get treated immediately (often with a $40 or less house call), as opposed to waiting for weeks to get an appointment or paying out the nose for private care. There's no reason to put off a trip to the dentist for a cleaning and check-up when it's only going to cost you $30. You don't have to fret over whether to take a certain asthma drug or not when it's $20 a month instead of $200. Caring for your pet becomes a minimal budget item instead of something that can wreck your finances.

There are many other factors contributing to better health though, often brought on by changes in climate, in habits, and in diet. It's no secret that the USA is the inventor of and chief marketer of junk food and soda, that the making of unhealthy processed food is almost an art form there. Other countries have adopted the practices like we were handing out crack and the whole world is getting fatter. Still, when you move to a less developed country, you often do find it easier to eat less crap.

In Asia, the street food is healthier and "fast food" is still good-for-you food. In Europe there's a greater emphasis on slowing down and savoring, of conversation instead of a quick face-stuffing. In Latin America, food is communal and works with nutritional building blocks like rice, corn, beans, potatoes, and squash. Sure, you can buy processed food in every convenience store, but the average "meal of the day" you get for $4 at a typical, basic restaurant is going to be well-balanced and much healthier than a McDonald's combo.

If you move to a place where most people walk or use public transportation, you'll probably get more unstructured exercise. I lost 10 pounds in a few months all three times I moved back to Guanajuato, Mexico, in great part because our house is on a hillside, on a pedestrian-only street with 30 steps to climb. Half the foreigners in my town don't have a car. The only reason they would need one is to drive to Costco or Walmart in another city to stock up on what they can't find locally.

If you're not spending all your time working, commuting, or watching TV, you can pursue outdoor activities as well. Walk, run, go for a hike, surf, swim, or ride a bike. Your stress level gets deflated from multiple angles.

To Experience Another Culture
If you only move abroad to save money, you are probably not going to be happy. This book uses your reduced living expenses as its main theme, but with no sense of adventure or a desire to get to know another culture, you may become one of those bitter expats that keeps complaining about everything that's wrong in her adopted country.

Let's start with an assumption though: your normal life is probably kind of boring. Every week you do the same things, see the same people, watch the same shows on the same screens, and then repeat the cycle. Your brain is probably crying out, "Feed me! Give me some stimulation!"

Some people are content to ignore that little voice and stick to a routine. They like routines. They'll keep repeating them until they die and be perfectly fine with that. If they need some variation, they'll take the kids to Disney World and buy a bigger TV. Or a new SUV with better built-in TVs.

Then there are the restless people, the curious people, the ones who want to see something surprising, different, and amazing. They crave a change of scenery and some variety in their passing years. If you've thought enough about picking up and moving that you picked up this book, I'm guessing you're one of those.

When you move to another country, your brain shifts gears and everything starts moving faster, with more stimulation. Each day is a little different. The sights, smells, and sounds are all new. Different food, different names, often a whole different language. The thought of all that terrifies the hell out of some people, but for the curious ones, it's like an adrenaline injection. Suddenly the switch goes from "blah" to "bodacious," from black and white to saturated color. And you're not just getting a quick fix of this: you're *living* it! Your dinner table conversations start out with phrases like, "I saw something really interesting today..." or "I discovered this great little street food stall..."

To Improve Your Career Prospects
A lot of people are afraid to make the leap because they're afraid they won't be able to get a good job or even make a living. There are plenty of well-meaning friends, relatives, and (bad) mentors who will reinforce this fear for you.

The thing is, they're usually dead wrong. Seek out the right kind of advisers—people who have done what you're looking to do—and you'll find they have a much more optimistic view. Most will tell you they had an easier time getting the kind of job they wanted abroad and even had a leg up if they returned. After all, their resume/C.V. stood out from the hundred others that all looked similar. By moving abroad and doing something different, you've shown initiative, an ability to adapt, and the means to think creatively. In today's *real* job market, those traits are far more desirable than the ability to do what you're told for years and not make any waves. Some recruiters say they actively look for people who have studied or worked abroad because those people are proven problem solvers who don't give up easily. They have learned to negotiate and to adapt to new challenges. If they've become fluent in a second language, even more doors open up.

When writing the first edition of this book, I interviewed a young man named Michael Gans, an American on his third post-MBA job who was finally feeling financially stable. He was living and working in India, at a much higher level in his company than he could have even applied for in the USA. "I am a huge advocate for going abroad," he said. "I feel that it builds your personal character and your view of the world. It advances your career and gives you a better perspective on life." He eventually moved back to the USA but at a level that would have taken him 10 more years to get to if he had stayed put.

For others, the move abroad puts their life in perspective and convinces them the regular rat race wheel they've been told is a normal life is not for them. So, they find a way to combine their passion with a market need and they become successful freelancers in a certain niche, or they start their own business with a newfound confidence. They can toss out the resume altogether because they're making their own future on their own terms.

Many people I interviewed for both editions said they wanted to find a way to avoid returning to their own country, so they found freelance gigs or set up companies that would enable them to keep working from the road. Some of them are now pulling in more money than their friends back home in "the real world" who stayed on the tried and true career path.

To Get Off the Treadmill

You hear a frequent lament from people living in developed countries that they feel like they're on a treadmill, that they're not making progress. They say they have lost control of their schedule and feel like all they do is work. Some spend years doing this and don't realize how bad it has gotten until they take a long vacation or get laid off and are forced to relax. They're working non-stop, their buzzing smartphone essentially putting them on call at all hours, and if they're a parent they've got all the over-scheduled school and sport activities in the mix as well.

Cathy Brown, a mother of three, has this to say about her move to Argentina, where she's now been living for a decade: "I didn't want to have to work two jobs just to get by and have a crappy apartment to come home to. I can freelance here as a writer and make it, spending a lot of quality time with my family."

Expatriates in other countries are busy too, but it's a very different kind of busy. "Our schedule is fuller than it was when we lived up north," said Tim Rumsey of Mazatlan, Mexico when I interviewed him and his wife Nancy for an article. "But it's a social schedule now. We've got tee times, happy hours, dinner parties, and theater shows. They're things we *want* to do instead of have to do."

In most of the world, a workaholic is not something to be admired. Family and social groups take priority over slaving away at the office and you work to live, not the other way around. The idea of a junior lawyer or stockbroker working 80-hour weeks just plain does not exist in most countries and nobody there wants it to exist. For many people who move abroad, this change in outlook feels like a big weight being lifted off their shoulders. Whether they get an international job posting or are working on their own as a virtual "solopreneur," the rejiggering of priorities in life brought on by the new environment is invigorating. Their work is a focus, but no longer *the* focus of their life.

Before you make a big move though, you have to do some soul-searching. You have to affirmatively answer the question, "Are you really ready for this?"

Chapter 4:
Are You Cut Out for This Life?

There are plenty of reasons why you should *not* move abroad. There are certain people who are cut out for this kind of move and others who are definitely not. If you want the benefits without being able to bear the compromises, you're going to be a very unhappy resident of wherever you're going. In expat circles these people who moved and shouldn't have are often referred to as bitter "economic refugees."

Naturally, if you purchased this book, I'm assuming you are seriously thinking of moving to another country. I don't want to be the one to push you over that line, however, and have you cursing my name two months after arrival if you aren't mentally ready for this kind of change. Moving to a whole new country means new customs, new bureaucracy, new standards of living, and maybe a new language, which can be way too much for many to handle.

Some people are stuck in a comfort zone and they like it there. Sure, they may be broke, and have no real chance of their future getting better, but it's a discomfort they know rather than the risk of one they don't. Most people will dream and say, "Wouldn't it be nice to move to..." but they will never do it. They just don't have the initiative and they're way too scared. It will always be a fantasy for them.

This Chapter could be a whole book on its own, but one valid criticism of the likes of *International Living* and *Live and Invest Overseas* is that they're very heavy on the cheerleading about moving abroad and very light on addressing the problems many people encounter. The negatives are presented in passing if at all. You can understand why: they are large organizations with a staff to support and they have courses, workshops, and e-books to promote. Like glossy travel magazines that never met a hotel or cruise ship they didn't like, these companies will either say something nice or say nothing at all. They don't want to dissuade their potential customers from plunking down their money. The overhead is too high.

Surf any expat message board for areas you're considering, however, and you'll find plenty of disenchanted expatriates with real beefs. Some people who have moved get downright depressed. Some try it out, then go home in a year or two because they miss the comfort zone. They miss their old community and are having too much trouble adapting.

What do you give up when you move abroad? Some conveniences, of course, and proximity to relatives and long-time friends. You also give up some intangible things you didn't even realize were important to you.

Many people don't realize how attached they are to certain aspects of home until they move away from it. Before you make that clean break, it's best to go live somewhere else for a while to see how strong your feelings of homesickness are. You can dip your feet in instead of diving in headfirst and staying there. Here are just a few things people end up missing that maybe they hadn't thought much about in advance.

- The greenness, the mountains, the changing seasons, or the colors of changing leaves.
- Their lush garden full of plants they know and recognize.
- Their church, their community, their local clubs, their golf buddies, their college friends.
- Their extended families they may not see so often.
- Their favorite grocery store, their local bar, their regular restaurant.
- Their 278 channels of TV in English.
- Their lightning fast fiber-to-the-home internet service.
- The ability to buy 24 types of mustard and 48 kinds of beer in their local supermarket.
- The ability to walk into a hardware store and explain exactly what they need without pantomime.

You'll find plenty of people living abroad who never should have moved in the first place. Every location has its problems—including wherever you're moving from—but some people are going to be unhappy no matter where they moved to because it's not home. It's not what they're used to, so it's inferior. They spend their days bitching and moaning about what doesn't work right and why things are screwed up.

The place has its problems, sure, but the real problem is *them*. They moved to save money and forgot that saving money cannot be the be all and end all of a relocation. As David Morrill from Cuenca Real Estate told me, "If you are just coming to stretch your savings and don't appreciate the culture or the people, you probably won't be happy. Some spend a lot of time and money learning that lesson the hard way."

In my experience, the people who have the hardest time adjusting after a move like this have several of the following characteristics:

- They love convenience in all its forms.
- They are super-patriotic and think their home country is the "best in the world" at everything.
- They didn't travel much internationally before they made the big move and didn't do a proper trial run.
- They are dreadfully worried about safety in the big scary world out there. (Often related to the point above.)
- They have lived in one place most of their lives and are very connected to that community.
- They like things to be neat, orderly, logical, and well-kept. (As in a suburban gated community with lots of rules.)
- They are impatient and can't stand waiting around for things to get done.
- They like to be in control of every situation at all times.
- They expect to be able to pay extra to make extra demands— like having people work on a Sunday.
- They don't want to exert the time and effort required to learn even the basics of a new language.
- They have trouble taking things as they come and expect everything to work in a logical manner.

One or two of these issues can easily be overcome and we all struggle with moving pains to some extent. Only a tiny percentage of people are naturally blessed at learning a new language as an adult and all of us get frustrated with bureaucracy at one time or another. We all get annoyed when rules and customs seem ridiculous to the point of being comical.

The people who are cut out for living abroad cope and move on, however, just as emigrants have for a couple thousand years. Others never manage and they drive themselves (and everyone around them) crazy. If you're one of them, do everyone a favor and retire in small-town USA or UK. Live frugally there instead of moving to Ecuador or Bulgaria just because it's cheap.

What Will Be Different?
When you move from a developed country to one that's further back on the development compendium, you can expect to compromise on some things you formerly took for granted. That's why in each country Chapter in this book I have a "downsides" section. Here are a few that are going to be more common than not.

- You may not be able to flush toilet paper and you may have to use a squat toilet sometimes.
- People will probably be late a lot and appointment times are just a rough estimate.
- The electricity may go out sometimes.
- You might not be able to drink the tap water.
- Regulations will be lax or unenforced, from food preparation to road safety.
- The police may be understaffed, underpaid, ineffective, corrupt, or all of the above.
- There will be a higher tolerance for garbage, graffiti, and poor aesthetics.
- Private interests of the well-connected will often be more important than the public good.
- The judicial system may be overtaxed, underfunded, under the thumb of the ruling party, or corrupt.
- Zoning laws for building may be lax or unenforced.
- The noise level will probably be much higher than you are used to and complaining about it will just make you look like a crank.
- People will often tell you they don't have change when you buy something, even when it's a trifling amount.

You may encounter more corruption, but don't assume the gulf is vast. Your own country's form of corruption is just what you're familiar with. A report by the European Commission estimated that corruption in the EU costs member states $160 billion per year. You don't have to read the U.S. news much to see that big business has a stranglehold on politicians of both parties there and special interest groups can easily get congressional representatives to write laws two-thirds of the electorate opposes (just look at the lack of gun control.) In recent years, the U.S. Supreme Court has swayed even more to the side of big business, even granting companies the same rights as citizens.

Can You Take a Punch?
Did you or your kids ever play with one of those inflatable punching toys with a weight on the bottom, usually a clown with a squeaking nose? You would punch it in the nose, and it would fall to the floor, then rise back up straight to be punched again. Unless you busted a hole in it, the thing would keep popping back up for more.

You need to be that clown.

Especially in the early days, when you're learning the ropes and going through residency paperwork for a long-term stay, you'll feel punched a lot. You will make mistakes. You will overpay often. You will be asked for surprise paperwork nobody mentioned before and of course it will need to be stamped, notarized, or paid for in another office or on another day. Everything you attempt to do seems to take twice as many days as it should, including a simple home repair or buying ingredients for a meal. Most of these developments will make no logical sense. "There's got to be a better way," you'll keep saying to yourself.

Yeah, there is a better way, but inertia and tradition are hard things to break, so the better way is not coming anytime soon. Deal with it.

Some people have a real problem becoming that clown, even when it means a big payoff at the end. Competitive, type-A personalities used to instant gratification take the punches as a personal affront and they want to fight back. They get angry, they yell, they ask to speak to the boss—and they expect to have that conversation in English, of course.

In the end, they either change their behavior and win or they get deflated and give up. Often, they go home eventually, cursing the country, the people, and their big mistake. "I don't know how people keep living there," they'll say to their friends back home, exasperated.

"It's easy," I would answer, "They're just better at bouncing back."

Living in another country, among people who have different traditions, beliefs, and ways of doing things requires one major attribute: adaptation. It's evolution in the modern age. I'm not going to quote Charles Darwin here as his prose is much too verbose for this book, but here's a paraphrasing of one of his best-known theories: "It's not the strongest or most intelligent that survive, but those who can best adapt to a changing environment."

You may need to learn another language to get things done and become immersed in the culture. If nothing else, the basics for just buying things and getting a taxi will take you beyond helpless. Gord MacKay moved to Nicaragua from Canada with his wife and was thrown into learning Spanish in a hurry. "When I moved here, I ordered a beer because that's the only thing I could say. They asked me

'bottle or can?' and I was stumped. I will chat with my neighbors now, all Nicas. I can have a conversation, but after an hour I have to come back and take a nap because it wears me out. I'm totally comfortable at the market but taking a car in to get repaired is a different story."

This is an evolution that everyone has to make at some point in a country where English is not widespread, but at first it can feel like an overwhelming task. Stick with it though and the gradual payoff is worth it. If nothing else, learning a second language has mental health benefits for your aging brain that needs the exercise.

Here are a few really cheap and easy tests to carry out in your spare time before taking the plunge. Read *The Castle* by Franz Kafka. Watch the movie *Brazil* by Terry Gilliam. Read blog posts and message board laments on what people went through in their quest to get a residency visa in a country that makes it difficult. If you laughed or were entertained and viewed these stories as comments on the human condition and government absurdity, congratulations. You are ready.

If they made your blood boil, gave you nightmares, and caused your fists to clinch until your fingernails made marks on your palms, you may want to rethink this whole idea of moving to a new country. Or bank a lot more cash so you can go live in Switzerland.

The best test is going to cost you more money, but it will be a lot of fun: take your destination for a real test drive. Let's head to the next Chapter to talk about that.

Chapter 5:
The Importance of a Trial Run

In Mexico, they call it "the margarita effect." In Spain "the sangria effect." In Thailand I would call it "the hot young babe who says she loves you effect." They all refer to someone visiting a place for a week on vacation/holiday, thinking it's heaven on Earth, and deciding then and there it's time to pack their bags and move.

You see this fantasy play out often in popular culture too, whether it's a bad movie with Ben Stiller moving to Los Cabos or the dopey formula on *House Hunters International* where they make it look like it's a good thing to swoop in and plunk down $300,000 on a house based on one weekend of looking around. (Spoiler alert—they had decided on a place before the shooting ever started. It's an acting role.)

Many people do buy a house abroad on impulse and do just fine. A rising market will soon erase any overpaying and if the block-by-block neighborhood situation is not too variable, it's harder to make a big mistake. Sometimes a house just feels right and so does the neighborhood, so the buyer gets lucky and is thrilled.

For each case like this though, there are probably three or four times as many where a hasty decision was a bad move. Even if you're just renting, finding yourself next to a house where people party all night until dawn and have four barking dogs will wear you down fast. Or in countries where zoning laws are lax, you may suddenly find yourself next to a dry cleaner, an auto repair shop, a music club, or worse. If you're renting though, it's a short-term problem. You can just leave when your lease is up. If you've bought the place, you're stuck.

The even bigger problem though is when the whole location is a bad fit. Often what looks great on vacation turns out to be much uglier when you are in a real neighborhood with monthly bills instead of on a $500 a day all-inclusive vacation budget. Or it was great fun hanging out on the beach in a lounge chair for a week, but then after two months of that you get bored out of your skull. Playing golf every day might sound great when you rarely get time to do it. Like anything though, it can get old fast when that's all you're getting up for day after day. That "charming colonial city full of local color" may not seem as charming when you realize there's no good grocery store and there's nothing to do besides eat, drink, and stroll.

Other times, I've heard of people buying a house in a hurry without asking many questions, in a place like the Dominican

Republic for instance. Then after moving in they find out that nearly every house in the area gets broken into on a regular basis if there aren't four levels of security and someone watching the place 24/7. Now they have to try to unload the house to another equally naive foreigner willing to overpay.

The solution to all these scenarios is simple: try the place out first. At the least, do a true scouting trip. The best remedy though is lengthy trial run. It's the equivalent of renting a car for two weeks instead of taking a 15-minute test drive through a dealership.

If you can go on a scouting trip during the worst part of the year weather-wise, that's especially great. If not, ask locals what is like in the worst months. Many people visit Mérida or Puerto Escondido in Mexico during the month of January and think it's heavenly. Then they come back in super-hot May and ask, "How did I end up in the mouth of Hell?" People visit Cuenca, Ecuador in the dry season and think the weather's perfect. Then the overcast rainy season hits and they say, "If I wanted this weather, I would have moved to Portland." People go to some tropical beach destination in the dry season and it's just as postcard-perfect as they imagined. They come back during "green season" and get stuck in the house for a week, putting buckets out to catch the leaks in the roof from the deluge.

If you know these seasonal issues going in, you'll be ready for them with no surprises. Or you can make plans to leave during the worst weather period. That becomes the time of year when you go traveling or visit relatives back home.

Travel, then Move

Ideally, you have traveled enough to know which kinds of places are right for you and which are not. (See the next Chapter on choosing a destination.)

It's hard to really know if a place is going to be right for you without doing two things: inner soul searching and exterior evaluation. The first is a matter of truly knowing yourself, while the latter is a matter of truly knowing a place.

In general, it's easier to strike a place off your list than it is to decide if it's perfect. I like Ecuador a lot and I could probably be happy living there if I had to do it. It wasn't until my third trip though when I finally set foot in Cuenca, a place that I've read 50 articles about and thought would probably be at the top of my list there. It just goes to prove though that you can't rely solely on how a place looks on paper. For me, Cuenca is a great place to visit or even spend a month, but I wouldn't want to live there permanently. After a few days there I found it doesn't meet some of my key criteria and it wasn't a good match. For many who live there though, it's just the right place and they would probably feel more negatives about where I call home. The smart ones knew that before making the move because they gave the place a trial run.

The people who seem happiest where they've settled are those who have traveled enough to figure out what their key criteria are, what kind of place gets them excited. Most of them traveled internationally whenever they had the time and money, not when they turned 65. I've met expatriates who carried out their research in a very methodical way: one actually rented places in five different locations in Mexico before he settled in Guanajuato where I live. Others have done it subconsciously over decades, asking, "Could I live here?" each time they land in a new place. Some set out for a trip through a dozen countries, looking for the perfect spot.

However, you do it, once you have a place narrowed down, go do a trial run and see if this destination is really a place you can call home. Find a way to rent an apartment and stay for at least a few weeks, preferably longer. If you want to do it on a tight budget, house sit for someone through an organization like TrustedHouseSitters.com.

Another option is to do a home exchange, either through a formal exchange membership program like HomeExchange.com or informally through Craigslist, word of mouth, or message boards.

Whichever method you choose, the goal is to live in a real neighborhood, not in a business hotel or smack in the middle of the tourist district. You want to feel what it's like to live there, not be a short-term tourist. Shop at local markets. Explore different neighborhoods by foot or bicycle. Eat at cheap places serving typical local food. Check the prices of things you love to consume and experience regularly. Take some language classes. Ask other expats what they struggle with.

Here are some ideas on what to do to get a real feel for the area:

Run every possible errand you would in the future. Go to the hardware store and buy something, even if it's just an electrical adapter or screwdriver. Get meat from the butcher shop, bread from a bakery, shoes from a shoe store. Pick up local liquor or juice where your neighbors do.

1) Find a festival. Follow the noise and go see what's going on. See how the local celebrations work.

2) Try local services. Get your shoes shined or fixed, your pants hemmed, your clothes cleaned, your hair cut.
3) Take local language classes and ask lots of why and how questions of the teachers. They'll be able to explain the accumulated mysteries in English.
4) Rent a bike or scooter. You can see a lot on foot but doing a little exploring will get you outside the bubble. If the safety worries you, take random buses to random places during daylight hours to assess the real situation.
5) Go to a local gym. What classes do they offer? What kind of shape are the machines in? Can you live with what's around? If not, you'll need to find other exercise alternatives you'd use instead.
6) Go to church or poke your head in for a wedding. Even if you're not religious, this experience offers great insight into the local culture.
7) Go to a sports event. Ditto #7. (When it comes to football/soccer, church and team seem to be on an equal level, and in both cases the locals' enthusiasm can be both baffling and eye opening...)
8) Linger in public spaces. In countries that aren't car-centric, people spend much of their time outdoors, walking, socializing, and just hanging out. Join them and observe.

When you're done, did you love or hate this experience? Is there one factor really bugging you that could be a deal breaker? Or are the negatives manageable?

Within 24 hours of my first visit to Guanajuato during a travel writing assignment, I told my wife that "I've found the place we should move to." She thought I was nuts to be that sure that fast, but the next summer we rented an apartment for a month and did all the things we needed to do to be confident about it. In addition to the steps outlined earlier, my wife also went around and checked out potential schools for our elementary age daughter. We found a school we could live with, so the city eventually became our home.

Sure, there were some negatives. We found a scorpion in our apartment a few times. The dog barks echoing off the narrow canyon we were in got annoying, especially combined with early morning church bells a few buildings over. Seeing people indiscriminately tossing their garbage on the ground was disappointing. Putting toilet paper in a trashcan instead of flushing it was hard to get used to. But we could deal with all those negatives. The positives were much greater, and the place ticked off most of our requirement boxes when it came to climate, walkability, culture, and quality of life. A year later we made the move. A year after that, we bought a house. By then we knew what we were getting into and what was a good value.

The key thing to remember during your trial run is that you need to get a glimpse into expatriate life, not tourist life. That's why it's key to rent an apartment where lots of people live rather than staying in a hotel zone. Eat where you'd be eating on a monthly living budget, not on an inflated tourist budget. (Sure, go out for a nice meal now and then, but don't eat at the most expensive places every night). Drink what the locals drink regularly, not Starbucks lattes in the morning and gin & tonics at night. Shop at the local grocery stores and markets, not the Costco 45 minutes away. Try activities and performances where people who look like you are in the minority, not the majority.

After all of that, as you're coming to the end, evaluate the pros and cons and think about how this place makes you feel emotionally. If the pros outweigh the cons and the place still pulls you in, mission accomplished. If the negatives are too great and are gnawing at you after a month, they're *really* going to gnaw at you after a year or two. Still, mission accomplished. Better to come up short after a month of fun away from home than to make a full-blown move and then be miserable. Learn from the experience and find a more suitable spot. It may be just one town over, or it may be another country at a different latitude or altitude. After this valuable experience though, you'll be better equipped to figure that out.

Get a Feel for Local Prices
Toward the end of this trial run, if you think this might be a good place to live, take one last important step: find out what the real value of real estate is. I'd strongly advise renting first, so be bold and ask other people what they're paying or find the local classified ads (they'll often still be printed, not online) and sit down with a dictionary.

If you intend to buy something, it's even more important to get a real sense of the market. If you don't, you'll likely end up overpaying because you'll be comparing prices to where you came from. If that's somewhere like California, Vancouver, or the Gold Coast of Australia, your sense of worth will be especially warped. As Antigua, Guatemala resident Rich Polanco says, you need to take off the "dollar glasses" and start thinking in local currency terms. "Get a sense for what things cost in your new surroundings and then you'll be able to make better buying decisions."

Now let's narrow down the places you could possibly live.

Chapter 6:
Choosing Your Destination: Head, Wallet, and Heart

There are three main criteria most pros and cons about a destination fall into. There are head factors, wallet factors, and heart factors.

The head items are factual "must-have" factors you can easily substantiate from the comfort of your sofa with a laptop or tablet in hand. This book will help with that, plus it will help even more with the wallet items: costs for basic living expenses and setting up residency. I'll help you home in on the places where you can really live well for half price.

The heart factor though is very difficult to work out remotely. Sure, you can collect e-books, watch Travel Channel shows, check out YouTube videos, and join Facebook groups or message boards for that destination. Really though, none of those things will fully prepare you for how that place will make you *feel*. This is why I often brush people off when they leave a blog comment or e-mail asking where they should move, like I'm some kind of psychic. The only person who can really answer that is the person who is asking—after they've done some traveling.

Let's look at each factor on its own.

Head Factors

If a place doesn't meet your main criteria for an ideal place to live, you're probably not going to be happy living there. As a travel writer who visits 6 to 12 different countries in a year, I often ask myself when visiting a new place, "Could I live here?"

Usually the answer is no for some very specific factual reasons— my head reasons. It's too cold, too hot, too cloudy/rainy, too isolated, too overrun with gringos, too ugly, too unfriendly to pedestrians, there's not much to do after a few days, and so on. For other people, there may be no such thing as "too hot" or "too overrun with gringos," They may think a steamy tropical place where they can speak English every day with their fellow countrymen and women is *perfecto*.

If you have health issues though, this may be the first place to start in narrowing down your choices. If you are allergic to mold, you may want to seek out a dry climate. If you have limited mobility, you don't want to live in a city built on the side of a mountain. If you're someone who just doesn't want to die young, you're probably not going to want to live in Beijing or Delhi, where pollution levels are frequently 20 times the levels considered healthy and you can't see more than two blocks away because of the smog. If you're a retiree, you probably also don't want to be in some remote location that's a day's drive from the nearest decent hospital. In almost any area where you find lots of foreigners in your age bracket, there will be at least one good medical facility in town and many other larger ones you can get to in a couple hours or less.

What's on your checklist? Think about climate, culture, food, air connectivity, land connectivity, and apartment/house options. What's a deal breaker?

Wallet Factors

While you may be dreaming of retiring on the Amalfi Coast of Italy, on the beach in the Virgin Islands, or in a nice slope side chalet in Switzerland, your bank account might not agree with those plans. You need to find a way to combine your checklist of ideal factors with places you can actually afford.

If you picture yourself in a lakeside cottage looking up at jagged snow-capped mountains, you don't have to spend $100,000 a year in Switzerland. You can move south of Bariloche in Argentina or to a village in Bulgaria and live for one-fifth that amount instead. If you want to be on a warm-water beach with hot weather, there are 100 choices in Latin America and Southeast Asia that are a fraction of the cost of a Caribbean Island residence.

For most of the places profiled in this book, a pair of retirees living off two social security checks or an equivalent pension can get by just fine. For a middling $1,500 for one person, $2,500 for two, you'll be living on far more than the average middle-class local. In some countries, that may be double or triple what's considered a good local salary. If you've got more than that coming in, you can be choosier about where to go and can upgrade your living standards.

Keep in mind though that there are major variations within a country, especially a big country. The more expatriates and wealthy locals there are in an area, the higher the prices will probably be: witness San Miguel de Allende in Mexico, Antigua in Guatemala, or Punta del Este in Uruguay. The more of a tourist destination it is, the higher prices will be, witness Los Cabos, the Algarve, or Phuket.

Also, just because you can live on $1,500 a month doesn't mean the government thinks that's enough wealth to grant you permanent residency. In Nicaragua, a retiree only has to show monthly income of $600 a month, but in Mexico you have to show nearly $2,000 a month for you and another $650 for your spouse. There are ways around this sometimes if you can show significant savings or finagle a work permit but do keep these restrictions in mind before making big plans to go beyond a tourist visa.

Heart Factors

The authors of *Freakonomics* and *Think Like a Freak* do a regular podcast on NPR and in one episode they answered a listener's question about how an economist would pick the perfect place to live. Stephen Leavitt said some of his most important factors—what economists would call "amenities"—were access to golf courses, fast food drive-throughs, and houses with big yards. He didn't care much about museums and cultural activities, but he could never live in a place without easy access to a golf course. In other words, he was meant to live in the suburbs, and specifically an American-style suburb.

Steve Dubner lives in New York City and said his most important factors were the density of ideas, people, and creativity—and the resulting spillover effect. Without being in a big city where people interact a lot, he wouldn't get any of that. "I could never live in a place without a good diner," he added.

In the end, they decided that choosing a place to live was only an economic decision when it came to finding a place with the right amenities: childless couples don't care about schools, but for parents it may be #1. Otherwise, it's a decision you make with your heart.

The thing is, your heart may be very set in its ways. For example, are you liberal or conservative?

This may seem like a stupid question to ask in a book about moving abroad, but it turns out that will probably have a big impact on the kind of place you choose and the kind of house or apartment you will want. A study by the Pew Research Center asked Americans whether they would prefer to live in a community with smaller houses close together and everything within walking distance, or a community where larger houses are spaced far apart, and you drive several miles to restaurants and schools. Liberals chose the first option by 77 percent; conservatives chose the second option by 75 percent. "Conservatives would rather live in large houses in small towns and rural areas—ideally among people of the same religious faith—while liberals opt for smaller houses and walkable communities in cities, preferably with a mix of different races and ethnicities," the study concluded. Three-quarters of liberals want to be near museums and galleries, while this only matters to one quarter of conservatives. Looking at this, it's no wonder that people who agree with each other naturally clump together.

You do often see this preference play out abroad, with some gravitating to city centers and historic towns where you don't even need a car, others gravitating to towns that are replicas of American suburbs, with gated communities and garages.

Most "heart" factors aren't this predictable though and they can vary a lot even between couples who are on the same page in most other attitudes and ideals. A place may feel "just perfect" to one of them, while feeling like "a total shithole" to the other. As you can imagine, this can be the beginning of the end if they ignore these differences and try to plow forward.

For all these factors, it's worth taking some quiet time with no distractions to talk them through, maybe even writing down the answers mind-map style. When I've asked people what they love about a place, there's often a mix of head and heart in the answers and the heart ones can end up being really esoteric. Some cite a specific yoga teacher, a local hike they love, or the kind of pottery they use in their kitchen. One told me she left the first place she lived because "the coffee really sucks there. I was annoyed every day."

For couples, talk out loud when you're traveling about why a place would be a good place to live and why it wouldn't. The time to argue about what's important is before you move, not after.

Chapter 7:
What's Cheaper and What's Not When You Move Abroad

How do you feel about super-cheap mangoes and super-expensive deodorant?

People who have not traveled much or lived in different places often have one very wrong assumption about prices. They think if they move somewhere that's less expensive, *everything* will be less expensive. Eventually they get a rude awakening when they start shopping for something like peanut butter, electronics, good sneakers, or name brand fashion items.

Soon I'll get into some universal truths about pricing, but it's hard to say you'll automatically save money on x, y, and z if you move from one place to another. Even if your home country has a median income of $50,000 and the one you're moving to has a median income of $20,000, you can't assume everything is going to be 60 percent less. We're in a global economy now, after all, so many items have a "global price" that has nothing to do with local conditions or exchange rates. Except for places where fuel is subsidized or heavily taxed, the price of oil is the price of oil. The variables come from taxes, subsidies, or in the case of taxis, labor costs.

Gasoline is one example of a commodity sold around the world for a fairly standard price but can vary at the consumer level due to taxes and the cost of importing it. Other commodities include grains, cooking oil, rubber, coffee, gold, and copper. If the country you're traveling in or visiting produces one of those things, the price might be less for a kilo of flour or a set of tires for a car. If not, the price will only be lower because sales would be zero otherwise. And when it comes to tires or copper gas lines, there aren't a lot of good alternatives. So, people suck it up and pay.

Many expatriates are surprised to learn, however, that some items cost far more in a developing country where many people are living hand to mouth than they do in the "first world" country they came from. Cars frequently cost 30-40 percent more than they do in the USA, despite people the lower average salaries. This is even true in countries that are major producers, such as Mexico. It makes no sense and I have yet to find someone who can explain the huge mark-ups in a satisfactory way. It's just the way it is.

Another cost that varies dramatically from place to place is alcohol. I have photos from a grocery store in Quito, Ecuador where six-packs of imported beer brands like Stella Artois and

Negra Modela are $13. No, I didn't say Copenhagen, I said Quito. When I tell people what it costs to order a glass of wine in Cuenca or order a cocktail in Quito it's like a robot that's going to start smoking from the head because, "This does not compute." The sole reason anything alcoholic that's imported is expensive in Ecuador is because the previous president wanted it to be expensive. Taxes were more than doubled after he took office and he would have been thrilled if nobody took another drink. His predecessor kept the policy in place. You see the same situation in many countries around the world. There are Islamic ones like Turkey, Indonesia, and Malaysia where the ruling party would be happier to ban the stuff altogether. Then there are "sin tax" ones like Thailand. More than half the price of that beer you pop open there is taxes.

Governments are frequently more pragmatic and are not on a moral crusade when it comes to taxes. More often the goal is to favor local industries, something that makes a lot of sense for getting votes and staying in office. So, it's common that local booze will be cheap, while anything imported carries a higher tax. Food produced within the country is subsidized or at least not penalized, while imports from abroad incur tariffs. "Living in India, you practically have to take out a bank loan to buy a block of cheddar cheese," says Mariellen Ward.

My country of birth heavily taxes imported sugar (thus the crappy high fructose corn syrup shoved into anything sweet) and heavily subsidizes domestic crops—especially corn. Corporate welfare is often a much larger percentage of the budget than the kind benefitting poor individuals. Handing out favors to big donors gets you reelected, whether you're in Buenos Aires or Birmingham.

Giving credit where credit is due though, the United States does have the most efficient distribution system the world has ever seen. Walmart may inspire derision and scorn, but that company has done more to cut waste out of packaging and shipping costs than probably the rest of the world's retailers added together. They have the clout to make big changes happen and they know how to use it. Companies sell directly to them, Target, Best Buy, and others without the entrenched layers of middlemen you find elsewhere. On top of that, the U.S. has the most advanced e-commerce delivery system of any large country on the globe. So, nobody has the ability to charge premium prices unless they are truly delivering some kind of additional premium service.

One previous advantage is under threat though as I write this: the trade relationship with China, the world's cheap goods factory.

Every once in a while, there's some saber-rattling and some tariffs are tacked onto a particular product line, but in the past that has been rare. Anything made in China—which means most electronics, tools, toys, and clothing these days—is cheaper in countries with a low-tariff relationship with China. Without that, anything produced there is going to cost more where you live.

In general, shop for expensive imported stuff at home (especially electronics and brand name goods). Shop for what is made locally abroad.

There are a few universal ways to play this game that will put the odds in your favor. You may have to tweak the strategy a bit here and there after arrival, but this is a good general game plan.

- Eat what's local and in season.
- Reap the benefits of lower local labor costs
- Hire local craftspeople to make exactly what you want instead of buying factory made items.
- Buy medicines locally (usually), but buy expensive cosmetics in your home country

To lay this out in a more concrete way from my life, we've gotten lots of custom things made by local craftsmen for our house. I'm talking a whole dining room set, bookcases, a desk, tables, wardrobes, a bed, and nightstand lamps. We've got cool mirrors, glasses, and pottery we've bought in Mexico. But whenever I go back to the states, I return with lots of cosmetics, sheets, clothing, and gadgets. The TV we bought locally because it's big. The phones and speakers, elsewhere. You'll know soon after arrival how to proceed in your case.

In conclusion, most things you spend money on day in and out are going to go down in price when you move to a cheaper country. Assume some are going to inspire sticker shock though and be prepared.

Chapter 8:
Family Life and Bringing Pets Abroad

I know from sales of the first edition that the majority of people who are going to pick up a book like this are singles or couples. It's much easier to take off and start a new life somewhere else when you're not thinking about schools, childcare, and supporting a family.

There are a sizable number of families who do move abroad while the kids are still in school though. Besides the obvious situation of one parent getting a job transfer to another country, many move abroad to have a calmer, more fulfilling life at a lower cost. There are big advantages to escaping the rat race and lowering the bar on how much you have to earn each month just to pay the bills. Without so much financial pressure, it's easier to spend quality time together.

Families can move to any country profiled in this book and have good school options, but in many cases, they're limited on where they can live within that country. In general, the international schools are located in urban areas or at least in areas where there are a lot of foreigners. If you're dreaming of moving to a small village in Romania or Argentina, you're probably going to need to home school or have them learn remotely. Or you'll have to take what you can get from the local school system—in the local language.

My daughter was enrolled in private schools in Mexico for three years, but they were in Spanish only. We wanted that for her because becoming fluent in a second language was at least as important to us as what she actually learned in classes. We know her future career options will be brighter in almost any field if she's bilingual. Some kids really struggle with this though and you can't assume yours will be a whiz at picking up a new language. Plus, Spanish is quite useful later in life. Thai or Vietnamese? Not so much.

There are many advantages to moving abroad as a family, but some clear disadvantages too. It's important to be aware of these up front.

Pros
- Cheaper cost of living overall
- Lower healthcare costs
- More time together
- Less competition in the classroom

- A more family friendly culture
- Fewer cliques, less social pressure
- Less focus on standardized tests (usually)

Cons
- Different school rules and requirements
- Communication struggles
- Effort required to keep up with home academic standards
- Learning a new language is not automatic
- Healthcare adjustments and communication issues with pediatricians
- Less time with relatives (maybe)

The way schools run, and the parents' level of involvement are bound to be very different than what you're used to. Seek out others already living where you're planning to go and get their advice. Pick up a few books on moving abroad with a family.

You also don't have to look very hard to find blogs written by parents who have moved abroad. There's probably at least one for wherever you're thinking of possibly moving. Poke around on search engines with the right keywords to find them as they're in a constant state of appearing and disappearing with the writers' moves. I can give you lots of advice for where I live, but not much for other areas: your best sources are families who are already there. You will also find useful info on local message boards or international ones such as Internations and ExpatExchange.com.

After you've done some research, you may learn that home schooling is going to make a lot more sense for the area where you really want to live. This also gives you the advantage of being able to move on to somewhere else in the middle of the school year if you want. It's much easier in the digital age to set up a good home school program, provided you have the right temperament as a parent to pull it off.

"For us, the home schooling always made the most sense," says Chuck Holton, who lives in Panama with his wife and five children. "It was a good fit for our lifestyle when moving around and we could take them with us when we went traveling. You can also customize the curriculum for each child, which makes so much more sense than doing the same thing for every kid, no matter what their particular needs or strengths."

I'll touch on this aspect of moving abroad with a family in more detail in the last section of this book.

Moving Abroad with Pets

Pets are sometimes tougher to bring along than children. I'm putting them in this Chapter because some people think of their pets as family and can't imagine moving without them.

This is going to be a short section though because the rules vary quite a bit from country to country. In some cases, you just need to have the proper paperwork showing that your pet is rabies-free and has had a recent health check-up. In other cases, your precious will have to go into quarantine for months before being allowed to join you—especially for islands. Any book on moving to a specific country is going to cover this in detail, or you can poke around on the internet and find the specific rules through a government website.

My American friends Ryan and Ang of JetsLikeTaxis.com have lived for stretches in Germany, Spain, Austria, Montenegro, and Mexico. For each of them their little dog Louis has come along for the ride. Wherever they live next, he'll be making his home there too.

Moving abroad with a pet is a bit more difficult than moving without one, but it can be done. For Americans heading to Mexico or Central America in their own vehicle, it's just a matter of having all the paperwork in order and tossing Fido in the back seat. It's a similar story for Brits heading elsewhere in Europe (though this could change post-Brexit). If you're flying though, there are a few more considerations involved in the actual flight and airport immigration steps.

For wherever you are going, you'll need to check into the local laws about bringing in a pet. Some require a pile of paperwork and time in quarantine. The more exotic the pet, the more difficult it can be. Taking your python or lemur abroad is not so simple. Or with a tropical bird, getting it there might be easy, but bringing it back may be next to impossible because of your home country's import restrictions.

You will likely need to buy the proper regulation-sized crate to fly with your pet and in many cases pay extra airline fees. In a few countries the regulations may be so onerous that you'll want help from a professional pet relocation service. You can find lots of great information on the website of the International Pet and Animal Transportation Association.

Keep in mind too that landlords everywhere are wary of having animals in the home they own. Everyone has a very high opinion of their own pet, but reality is that there's statistically a much higher risk of damage from tenants with pets than ones without.

So, you'll probably have to hunt much harder for a place to live, temporarily or permanently, and you may find pet-welcoming hotels to be difficult to find where you're going. Put some extra time into planning for this.

Also do some digging to find out what veterinary care is like, how easy it is to get the kind of food you want to buy for your pet, and how easy it's going to be to go get exercise if you have a dog. These may become major factors for your "head" list: the items you can list on a piece of paper as your requirements.

Chapter 9:
Making a Living and Getting a Visa

To live abroad, you'll need some kind of visa or permit to stay in a foreign country. You'll also need to have some money coming in to qualify for anything beyond a tourist visa.

If you are just going to bop around the world on tourist visas as a digital nomad, staying as long as you can and then heading somewhere else, you won't have many restrictions if you're from a developed country. The Japanese actually have it the best as this book comes out, with access to 191 countries without applying for a visa in advance. Only 1-3 countries behind are Singapore, Germany, South Korea, Finland, Denmark, Italy, Luxembourg, Spain, France, and Sweden. All of those can get into at least 186 countries for the asking. Citizens of the UK and USA can get into 184 (when there's not a botched pandemic response), while those from Australia and Canada can get into 183.

If you need a reason to thank your lucky stars that you were born in a rich country, consider the disparity there is for those at the bottom, the ones with the most limited mobility. People from Nepal are only allowed into 38 nations without applying and getting prior permission. For Pakistanis it's 32. There's hope for mobility though: people from the UAE used to have access to less than 100 countries in the '00s, but now they can get into 171. The country of Georgia gained access to 50 more nations in the past decade.

When you want to stay longer than a few months, however, that's when things get tricky. Only a few countries will let you stick around for more than two or three months as a tourist.

What you're going to live on and what kind of visa you will be eligible for go hand in hand. In nearly any country in the world, their main concern when evaluating your status is whether you are able to support yourself. In Country A that may be a low bar of $600 a month coming in each month or the equivalent of that times 12 sitting in a bank account. For other countries it may be several thousand dollars a month—plus more for each dependent.

If you can't meet this income or assets threshold, you will likely be hopping around on tourist visas, never being able to stay longer than three to six months at a time. If you do earn enough already though, you won't likely meet much resistance from the authorities. As Mark Ehrman says in the book Getting Out, "Unlike your parents, countries don't really mind if you sit around all day doing nothing, as long as you spend money and don't become a burden on the system."

When I surveyed readers of my Cheap Living Abroad newsletter on what was holding them back from moving to a cheaper country, how to earn a living was at the top of the list, with around a third of them ticking off that check box.

The funny thing is, there were another third who didn't check that box and would probably put it at the very bottom of their list. That's because they have a location independent job or business they can operate from anywhere. Whether they're in Los Angeles or London or Lisbon makes no material difference in their income. They can live almost anywhere and not miss a beat.

This is the ideal situation for a whole lot of reasons. The main one is that you have true arbitrage: you're earning money in a wealthy country and spending it in one without the accompanying high expenses. You need less to live on and if you have a really good month, it's easier to put away some savings. You can show embassy officials that you can easily support yourself while being a net positive contributor to their economy. You're not taking much from them, but you're giving a lot. Most countries like to open their doors to people like this.

There can be downsides to this arrangement of course. You need to be in a place with a good internet connection and if your business requires a lot of bandwidth-heavy applications like real-time stock trading programs, video chats, or constant uploads of large files, you'll simply have to strike some destinations off your list completely—for now. This list is getting smaller all the time though. Every year the average internet speeds around the world keep going up and it's hard to find a major city anywhere now that doesn't have some kind of fiber-to-the-home, high-speed cable, or very fast mobile speeds. There are still a lot of really desirable places to live though where the pipes just aren't fat enough to support that kind of data flow.

If you need to talk or meet online with clients, you will likely need to work a very non-conventional workday to be available during their regular work hours if you don't base yourself in a similar time zone. If you're in the Americas somewhere and your clients are too, no big deal. But I've heard of many freelancers or business owners who had a lot of sales calls in their mix that ended up having to move out of Southeast Asia. The difficulty of being on the exact opposite schedule of the people paying for their services was hurting revenue and relationships. Those who forge on often end up becoming night owls: their client wants to talk at 2:00 p.m., so they're on the phone at 3:00 a.m. where they live.

In the digital age we're in now, however, most jobs require more e-mail and file sharing than meetings or phone calls. One person I interviewed for this book said she blocks out two days every month for calls. The rest of the time she never talks to anyone. It's just not necessary. I've hired more than a dozen people to do one-off jobs for me, from book cover design to WordPress installations. I have only talked to one of them on the phone and that's because we were getting bogged down in too many e-mails and wanted to hash out the punch list all at once.

What kinds of jobs do these digital nomads or location independent business owners do? It's a wider range than you probably think. In this book you'll hear from business consultants and a t-shirt company owner, travel writers and a CPA, software coders and web marketing specialists. Here's a list of what people I've run across are doing as they make a living abroad.

Virtual Jobs - Very Portable
Transcriptionist
Systems Analyst
Web Designer
Programmer/Code Writer
App developer
Online Teacher
Professional Blogger
Freelance Writer
Author
Ghostwriter
Technical Writer
Web Editor
Online team leader
Translator
Online Entrepreneur selling products
Online Entrepreneur selling services/info
Software as a Service Developer
Graphic Artist
Illustrator
Voice talent
SEO Consultant
Online marketer/consultant
Stock or Forex trader
Wealth manager

Tax adviser
Sales rep (when few face-to face meetings are required)

It's far easier now than it was even five years ago to both look for virtual employees or to be one. You could start out with no clients and gain them through services such as Upwork. There are services advertising remote jobs only, like DynamiteJobs.com and HireMyMom.com. An easier route is to strike out on your own while you're still in your home country, then keep working for those same clients as you change physical locations. If you're good enough at what you do and keep meeting or exceeding expectations, you'll probably build up more clients through referrals and actually increase your income.

Keep in mind that the 2020 COVID-19 pandemic changed the whole attitude about remote work, probably permanently. Many companies finally realized that everyone didn't need to gather in one building to get things done. Some actually saw productivity go up without so many useless meetings happening and without people stuck in traffic getting to those buildings.

Shannon O'Donnell is known in the travel world for her popular blog *A* Little Adrift and has a story that has become rather typical now. Her "real job" is an online marketing consultant for multinational brands, helping businesses strategically build targeted, relevant traffic from search engines. "While I was still living in the USA, before traveling, I asked my biggest client, 'If I keep up the same standard of work, you won't fire me, right?'" She kept that client and a decade later she has built up many more. "Now I'm at the point where I have more business than I can handle," she says. "I've never pitched, I don't even have a website — it's all from referrals."

Many International Jobs Are Not Virtual

Parachute into any place with hundreds or thousands of expatriates and you'll probably find a hundred ways people are making a living abroad. For many it's some kind of hands-on but skilled job that requires their physical presence. They play in the local symphony or teach at the international school. They work for Oracle, GM, Marriott, or Unilever as a manager. Or most commonly, they teach English, sell real estate, or run a restaurant. Some options may be obvious through the skill set you already have. For creative entrepreneurial minds, the options may seem so unlimited that you have to reign in your idea fountain and focus.

If you're a nurse, engineer, doctor, financial analyst, or a specialist in a specific technology or software that's used worldwide, you'll probably have very little trouble finding a job in your field and getting a work permit. Most countries are welcoming to those with professional skills that will transfer.

Experienced teachers can often make the leap by teaching for their own state department, for a certified international school, or by doing a short stint on a Fulbright program. For English as a second language (ESL) teacher, some jobs come through formalized programs aimed at recent college graduates, while others are filled by a network of international recruiters and online ads for teachers.

Think beyond the obvious though and dig around. When I was teaching English in a suburb of Seoul, the other foreigners in my town who were not teachers were some fish-out-of-water contractors and carpenters from the Pacific Northwest. They were building American-style wood framed houses for wealthy Koreans. I've met tennis instructors, dive masters, fishing charter leaders, archaeologists, helicopter mechanics, and fashion designers plying their craft in a cheaper location—while still making a good living.

Here are a few occupations where the right degree or certification can be your ticket to portability.

Portable Credentialed Jobs
Import/Export Manager
Hotel Manager
Financial Industry Analyst/Manager
Personal Trainer
Dive Instructor/Trainer
Corporate Trainer
Business Team Leader
Doctor
Nurse
Dentist
Massage Therapist
Yoga Instructor
Acupuncturist
Chiropractor
Pilates Instructor
Ski Instructor
Classical Musician
Architect
Interior Designer
Fashion Designer
Film/Video Technician

Certified ESL (English as a Second Language) Instructor
School Teacher
College Professor
Engineer
Chef
Scientist

With these occupations you can generally make a good enough living abroad to enjoy a similar or better lifestyle than you had before—even if you take a sizable salary cut. Many find that their quality of life betterment makes up for a lot as well: the doctor who can spend twice as much time with patients instead of on paperwork, for example, or the teacher who gets to actually teach her students something lasting instead of just "teaching to the test." In some cases, the leap abroad takes the person from being a small fish in a big lake to a big fish in a small pond. There's less competition and less stress.

There are also plenty of jobs out there that don't require any special certification or experience. Just be advised that the closer you come to skills the locals already have, the less money you can potentially make. You'll also have a much harder time getting a work visa or business visa.

For the unskilled labor jobs, if you're not bringing any special experience to the table, you're competing with locals willing to work for far less than you. Here's a good rule of thumb: if people from *that* country are coming to *your* country to do this job for more money, trying to go the opposite direction for the same job is just stupid. Mexico and Bulgaria don't need fruit pickers or hotel maids. Nicaragua and Vietnam don't need coffee bean pickers. Colombia and India don't need people who can operate a sewing machine. There can be exceptions now and then. Nobody really needs your basic bartending skills—unless it's an expat pub and they want a native English speaker. Or if you have five years of experience working in a high-end cocktail bar and the Ritz-Carlton is hiring, then you're a better match than any local could be.

For the sake of opening your mind to the possibilities, here are some no-certification (some would say no qualifications) jobs many expats are doing across the globe right now. One note on real estate agents: many are experienced and skilled. It's just that in more countries than not, neither certification nor skill is required to peddle houses for sale. The barriers to entry are low or don't' exist. Keep that in mind if you're a buyer.

Portable Non-credentialed Jobs
Organic Farm Helper
Real Estate Agent
Property Manager for Rental Homes
Musician
Bartender
Waiter
Cook
Hotel Worker
Sales Rep
Public Relations Rep
Business Consultant
Business Owner
Airline Worker
NGO/Aid Worker
Actor
Low-end ESL Teacher
Tour Leader/Organizer
Fishing Charter Leader
Construction Worker
Au Pair/Nanny
Yacht mate
Cargo ship worker
Cruise ship worker

For all of these jobs, you can't really generalize about what you can find in advance and what you can find in person after arrival. There's some correlation though between how specific the skill set is and how often the positions are advertised online. If you're a petroleum engineer or financial analyst, you can likely find ample positions to apply for without leaving your comfy desk chair. Some positions are advertised in industry-specific trade magazines or websites, which you'll probably be able to find easily if you're already in that industry.

At the other end, if you're trying to find one-on-one work for clients (personal trainer, massage therapist, etc.) you will likely need to get your feet on the ground and start hustling. That's not as hard as it sounds though since at least at first, most of your clients will probably be other expatriates. Word of mouth and getting your name out there on the local message boards may be enough to get your business moving in a hurry. My wife's a part-time personal trainer and although there are probably only a few hundred expats in my Mexican city, she could probably make it a full-time job if she wanted to.

There are some social and visa dynamics that come into play as you move through these kinds of jobs. For a virtual, digital nomad gig, you don't need a work visa. If it helps you stay for longer periods, then get one or see if there's something for online workers, but governments are generally happy to have you spend money in their country without taking any of it from them. You can come in on a tourist visa, work away on your laptop, and keep taking cash out of the ATM. Usually you don't even need a local bank account. Some countries are starting to think more progressively with visas meant for online business owners, recognizing that more and more jobs are international and border-agnostic.

For jobs requiring certain credentials or education, you may have to go through the right channels and apply for a work visa...eventually. As we speak though there are plenty of ESL teachers at private language schools, dive instructors giving scuba lessons, and bartenders mixing up classic cocktails in boutique hotels on a tourist visa. That's riskier for both the employer and the employee though. If you're not in a country with very liberal labor laws, or one that turns a blind eye, sooner or later you'll probably want to go legit. There's usually more security in this arrangement too: you've got someone vouching for you with the local authorities, someone who knows how to work within the system. If you're legal, you're also less likely to get cheated out of your pay.

Think Creatively

If you don't have a professional skill that easily transfers, I *strongly* advise you to find a job you can do remotely. Or make your own. That may be a freelance job, a structured job that allows you to telecommute, or a business you can run online. There are some very good reasons this works much better than the alternatives:

1) You earn first world currency and spend it in a cheaper country.
2) You can show proof of income to immigration without needing to work locally.
3) You can set your own hours and probably work fewer of them.
4) You can hit the ground running instead of taking months to ramp up local earnings.
5) You have zero dependence on the whims and pay rates of the local market.

If you have no earthly idea how you get from your current position to one that works like this, first start thinking of what skills and experience you already have that wouldn't require much of a pivot. Who is willing to pay for those skills? Also consider ways to turn your expertise into some kind of online platform that would attract a community and enable you to sell products or advertising. It seems like there is an infinite number of e-books, websites, and podcasts out there providing advice on this subject. You'll find some that I'm comfortable recommending in the resources section. Most will give you one key piece of advice I agree with: find paying customers and the rest will take care of itself over time. Don't procrastinate by spending months on a website, a logo, business cards, or detailed projection spreadsheets. Just get moving and test the waters.

There's one way you can get a virtual job tomorrow that can potentially pay you a nice salary: become a sales rep. These days many sales jobs are done entirely by e-mail and phone, so unless you're on the other side of the world, you can keep prospecting and selling in your home country just as you would from where you're living now. If you're willing to work on straight commission and you're a hustler, you can barge into nearly any industry and be hired in no time. Sure, you don't get paid until you deliver, but if it's a product or service that aligns with your interests and the quality is good, you should be able to get ramped up before too long.

There are also all kinds of online money-making opportunities out there if you just have a little bit to invest in testing and tweaking. Read the book *The $100 Start-up* for some inspiration. A free online resource is SideHustleNation.com. There's a forum site called where members pay $99 a month to talk about how they're making a living with affiliate marketing sales. Basically, that's driving people to purchase a product online and then getting paid a commission. They do it through blogs, through newsletters, through social media, and ads. People spend x amount on search ads or Facebook ads, for example, then get y amount in commissions. As long as y is a good bit more than x, it's a profitable campaign. Do this enough times in the right way and you can be making more money than you would have as a cubicle jockey using your college degree.

One good shortcut is to lay out a little capital to buy an existing online business or blog and take it over. You can find opportunities on Flippa.com, Empire Flippers, Latona's, and other sites geared to online entrepreneurs. Sure, you have to make an investment up front, but then your cash flow positive immediately and it often will take less than a year to recoup your investment if you improve the traffic or the earnings. Try finding a deal like that on Wall Street or your local real estate office!

Between when the first version of this book was released and the second, we saw two huge virtual money-making opportunities explode and then plateau: Bitcoin mining/trading and selling custom products through Amazon that you never touch yourself. (The latter is referred to as "Amazon FBA" for "fulfillment by Amazon.") By the time you read this there may be a dozen more ways to make money online that I haven't touched on or that didn't even exist when I wrote this. There will be people living somewhere exotic just killing it because they got in early, pulling in serious bucks while working wherever they want in the world.

The key to any of these though is actually doing it. You could find enough online courses and e-books to buy that would keep you reading and dreaming for a year. The people who really make an online business work are the ones who get out there and take action. You learn by doing and tweak as you go.

Types of Visas
Some countries have only three or four visa types, while others have a whole laundry list. You'll probably need to dig deeper after reading the specific destination Chapters before making a move, but here are the general categories. I'm lumping all the following together as "visas," though in reality the ones that let you stay a year or more are probably going to be called a "residency permit." For those you'll have something extra in your passport and probably some kind of local identity card. All of them will have rules about how long you can stay, whether you can leave and re-enter the country, and what you can and can't do while you're a guest there.

Tourist Visa - If you're from one of the advanced countries of the world, you can often just show up at the airport counter and get 30 to 90 days with a *thwap* of the passport stamp. For others, such as India or Vietnam, you need to apply in advance. Sometimes you have a choice in advance too of how long you can stay: pay more to get more. In general, you are not allowed to work in a local capacity on a tourist visa. (Earning money from abroad is fine.)

Student Visa - If you're enrolled in a formal study program, this is one of the easiest long-term visas to get. Some expatriates have found a way to get one by taking language classes or enrolling in a graduate program at a local university.

Work Visa - You usually need to have a job secured in advance and the employer takes care of much of the paperwork. If you have a real job with a written contract, these are typically easy to get with the employer's help. If you secure the job after arrival, you'll often need to go back home to apply for a work visa or at least leave the country to come back with a fresh start and a new residency status.

Freelance Visa/Residency Permit - For some countries, if you can show regular income as a freelancer or self-employed person who is a sole proprietor, this is the visa to get. Demonstrate the means to support yourself and follow the right steps to get permission to stick around for a year and you can probably renew to do it again.

Retiree Visa/Residency Permit - Show sufficient pension income, social security income, or a fat bank account and most countries are happy to have you. Some will even roll out a big red carpet of enticements. Age is surprisingly not a factor across the board to get a "retirement" visa. In some cases, you can be one at any age, in others 45, 50, or 55 years.

Spousal Visa - Marry a local and you'll be on the fast track to residency. Not right away of course—you'll have to be together long enough to prove you're a real couple—but you'll seldom get kicked out of the country if you've found true love and gotten hitched.

Specialist Visa - Various categories have special visas for limited use. These include professors, artists, journalists, and aid/NGO workers. In many cases though these are one year or less and may be difficult to renew.

Permanent Residency - For most of the countries in this book, if you've renewed your temporary residency for years on end and have been a good boy or girl, you can be granted permanent residency. For very lenient countries (like Ecuador) it can happen much sooner. For some (like India and Nepal), never.

What You'll Need to Present
Documents required by the country you're interested in moving to vary greatly. Usually they are posted on the official government website, but only sometimes will that information be in English. Frequently it won't be current either, so you can be sure you'll get hit up for something that's not on there. Surf the local expat

forums and Facebook groups for the real deal and assume that if you hire an attorney, he or she will be able to fill you in. If you have the money to pay someone, they can save you days or weeks of headaches. They can also get you past the language hurdle.

You'll be asked for things you haven't thought about for years and may have trouble locating, like your marriage certificate or birth certificate. To make things more difficult, you may have to produce an "apostille" version that has the equivalent of an internationally recognized notary seal or accompanying document. Getting this done from halfway across the world can be difficult to say the least.

Speaking of notary seals, you'll probably need some of those too, on things like bank statements or investment account balances. If you go teach English in Japan or Korea, you may need to show your actual university diploma, so dig it out of the frame. If you're getting a work permit, you may need to show professional certifications and you'll almost surely need some kind of employment contract or offer letter.

In general, it's better to over-prepare than to have to return to the office four times. Especially if you're applying for residency as a "solopreneur" or freelancer, the more documentation the better. Bring copies of any bank or investment statements, real estate holdings, professional memberships, and anything else that can show what you do isn't just a hobby. You want to show beyond a doubt that you're not going to need to lean on the state for support. Cover up the 'tats and wear a nice clean shirt too for good measure.

It may turn out you brought a lot of things you didn't need. When Jim Lynch applied for his residency permit in Nicaragua, the immigration person skimmed through his documents without seeming to really look at them, then asked Jim if he had a car. When Jim replied yes, the man asked him what kind of car it was. "A Nissan Pathfinder" he replied. Apparently, that was a sufficient display of wealth because that was the end of the interview and Jim walked out a legal resident.

A Back Door to Europe
In some European countries, you can be granted citizenship or at least a second passport if you can show a clear bloodline to that country in the past. For Ireland, Greece, Iceland, and Croatia, for instance, if you are a child or even a grandchild of a naturalized citizen of that country, you can apply to become one yourself. For Germany, if you're descended from someone who lost citizenship

in the past or was forced out of the country during the Nazi period, you can apply to become a German citizen.

Even if you have no desire to live in any of the countries where you are eligible, the peculiarities of the European Union make it worth doing there. That's because once you have citizenship and a passport from any EU country, you're good to go in any of the 26 others. So, if you planned it out and went through all the right steps, your Irish passport could be your ticket to a cheap life in Portugal, the Czech Republic, Hungary, Romania, or Slovakia.

If you're a UK passport holder facing an uncertain future after your country separated from the EU, getting a passport from another European country could get you back to the options you used to have.

In each of the countries profiled in detail in this book, there's a section on visas. Don't take my word as gospel though and remember that I'm not an immigration attorney. Not even close. So, consult local sources who know far more and double-check that their advice is current. In some countries the rules seldom change, but in one like Thailand the rules seem to change multiple times per year.

Chapter 10:
Where Should I Move To?

Just picking a spot on the globe that's cheap is easy. Picking one where you'll actually want to live for an extended period is much more difficult. After all, the very cheapest cities on the planet by cost alone are not exactly paradise. Karachi (Pakistan), Harare (Zimbabwe), La Paz (Bolivia), Ashkhabad (Turkmenistan), Calcutta (India), and Tegucigalpa (Honduras) are the kinds of places that are at the bottom of the cost list on Mercer's annual cost of living report for those living abroad. But I wouldn't recommend any of them to someone who has a choice in the matter. These are places people move to because of a corporate transfer, not because it ticked off most of the boxes on their wish list for an ideal place to call home.

I want to guide you to a place that is a bargain but is a pleasant and stimulating place to settle down in as well, maybe even a place where you would raise a family.

In this book you'll find lots of possibilities. Some may have the kind of climate you want and the right-sized community. Others will be a good fit in terms of your personal interests, the time it takes to get back to see relatives, or the level of English proficiency you think you need. Others may not fit any of your requirements and you can ignore them.

Unfortunately, finding the right place to live is almost as complex as finding the right mate. You can't just list a few requirements on a page, find the one that checks the right boxes, and be done. That doesn't work on dating site and it doesn't work for choosing your perfect destination. What you can do though is narrow it down by looking at the important factors and at least writing off the ones that aren't in the ballpark.

In the following Chapters, I'm going to tell you stories, introduce some people living in these places, and give you a sense of the pros and cons of each destination. I'm not going to give you pages of statistics though on leading export products, the current state of abortion laws, or the national debt. You also won't get the kind of super in-depth details on a specific country you will get by buying a book just on that country that is hundreds of pages long. This book is an idea generator and a way for you to think through your future, cheaper life. When you settle on a place, you'll be ready for a second round of research that's more specific to that one location.

Since this is a book on cutting your expenses in half and ending up with a better life, I'm going to give you a feel for the countries where you can easily live for half what you're spending now and give you a sense of how much it should cost you if you're not going to live like a rock star. You'll see real prices for real things you'd spend money on, like rent, utilities, a taxi ride, and a beer in a bar. I'll talk about the things that are a great bargain there and things you might want to bring with you or pick up on trips back to your original home.

Keep in mind though that all this information can never be more than a combination of facts and anecdotes. To know if a place is really right for you, there's no substitute for going there. Jeff Johnston, who moved from Canada to South America, says that after all his research, he went to Ecuador looking for "a reason not to move there." When he didn't find a good one, he packed his bags and made it his home. He has lived in Cuenca, in Cotacachi, and at the beach.

Susan Korthase and her husband landed in Portugal for the first stop on their country-hopping trip and then didn't hop any more. They had found their place. Susan had already traveled a lot and lived other places though, so she had a good sense of what kind of place they wanted. When I first wandered the streets of Guanajuato, Mexico and decided I'd love to live there, it wasn't exactly my first time out of the country. I had lived in Turkey and South Korea teaching English and had traveled through countries on five continents. I'd also been to expat enclaves like Playa del Carmen, San Miguel de Allende, and Puerto Vallarta in Mexico and knew they were not for me (or my wife).

For some people, it's like trying on a dozen pairs of shoes before finding the one that's just right. I've met some expatriates who traveled to 10 or 15 locations before settling on the one where they live now. Others distilled their 20 or 30 years of travels into a wish list they knew would make them happy. After an either/or trial run between two top contenders, they made a decision.

Others figure out that they made the wrong decision and end up moving again. Sometimes this happens after a change in the local environment, a change in their health, or just a "falling out of love" change of heart. A move abroad does have similarities with dating and a long-term relationship in that way, but if you rent instead of buying it is more like shacking up than getting married. You can move on without suffering as many consequences.

The worst thing that you can do is watch *House Hunters International* on TV and think that reality shows are actually real.

Smart people don't fly into a country for the first time, look at three houses over a weekend, and buy one instantly. If you want to see how the show really works, read articles from people who have appeared on the show. For starters, the place they "picked" is always a place where they are already living. The whole agonizing choice set up, complete with arguments, is just for show. Sometimes the "real estate agent" is really an English-speaking friend who doesn't really sell real estate. Shows like that are filmed as entertainment, so treat them as such. (They're worth watching to see the prices though: list prices are actually based on reality.)

Also, don't assume it's a good idea to sign up for an expensive seminar on location in a country you've never been to and buy something there from one of the partner real estate agents or developers invited to talk. Besides this arrangement being ripe for conflicts of interest, it's never a good idea to be under time pressure when making a big, life-changing investment. If you want my opinion, don't buy anything at all until you've lived somewhere for a while and truly know the local market—including what the locals are paying. Sure, there are exceptions, like people who have a close friend or relative in the area who knows the scene well, or savvy real estate investors who already own 50 properties and this is just one more for the portfolio. But for the average person who is pouring a significant amount of their net worth into a purchase, it's better to take your time before getting hitched.

Some people will surely quibble with my overly simplistic directive to just change addresses and instantly cut your expenses in half. So, one qualifier: I am talking apples to apples when making this "half price" comparison. So, if you live in New York City or London now, you can move to any big city in the countries profiled in this book and live for half price. Heck, you can probably even move to the most popular tourist area and still cut your expenses in half. If you're moving from Nowheresville, Oklahoma or some obscure town in the Outback of Australia though, you're probably already living pretty cheaply when it comes to housing. So, you can't move to Kuala Lumpur or Puerto Vallarta from there and say, "No fair—you said my expenses would be cut in half and they're not!" If you go from one of the cheapest areas of your own country to one of the most expensive in another, your prices will still be lower, but you may not save such a fortune. The half price living refers to a mid-sized city to a mid-sized city, one resort area to another, or one big metropolis to another big metropolis. A lateral move.

Even so, if you go from rural Oklahoma or the Australian outback to any location in the countries profiled here, you will save a lot of money and you'll be able to live a life you couldn't have lived making a similar move at home. In other words, if you move from an inexpensive town in your own country to a beach resort town in Mexico, Nicaragua, or Thailand, your costs are going to go down—not up like they would if you moved to more desirable city in the country you're living in now. Keep this in mind if you're anywhere close to retirement age and are looking at making the typical move to a sunnier, warmer climate. Move to Florida and you may go broke. Move to San Juan del Sur in Nicaragua and you'll be living large.

Now that we've gotten that out of the way, you can read the country Chapters that follow in their entirety or skip over the countries you have no interest in whatsoever. Last time I put them in roughly the order of popularity, but then people who didn't finish the book said I concentrated too much on popular Mexico—they didn't get any further. As a result, this time I'm going in alphabetical order. Keep an open mind as you're going through: maybe a place you hadn't thought of will tick off more of your requirement boxes than the ones you're more familiar with. Many times I've visited a town or city I knew next to nothing about and said to myself, "Living here would be pretty nice!"

If you don't see a cheap destination that was high on your list, check the "Also worth considering" section at the end. Usually because of visa hurdles or a small expat population to get info from, I've covered some in less detail.

If you find all this to be a tantalizing appetizer that fills you with questions you want answered, see the specific resources at the end of each section and at the end of the book. Beyond that, if you're not part of our Cheap Living Abroad community already, sign up there to connect with like-minded individuals and me on a regular basis, with more in-depth information on an ongoing basis. See the Packages section of CheapLivingAbroad.com.

Chapter 11:
Albania

Pros: same climate as southern Italy, lots of beaches, one-year tourist visa for Americans, relatively easy residency, good food and coffee, welcoming people, low crime and harassment.

Cons: under-developed by European standards, baffling inter-city bus system, communist architecture, limited air connections, low English proficiency outside cities.

Most people probably can't find Albania on a map, but this formerly reclusive communist country is in an enviable spot on the globe. It's on the Adriatic Sea, north of Greece and south of Croatia. If you had a reasonably seaworthy sailboat you could easily get to the boot of Italy from the coast of Albania. (Or there's a frequent ferry you could hop on instead.) So there's a southern European climate, lots of great beaches, and—here's the important part—costs that are a quarter of what they would be in Italy.

I spent some time there a few years back and have plans to return for longer. I was impressed by the hospitality of the people, the chilled-out capital of Tirana, and the gorgeous countryside. This is a country that boasts a long coastline of beaches, serious mountains, and lakes, but with prices that are some of the cheapest in Europe.

There are some strange juxtapositions of culture, architecture, and food here. Albania was occupied by various countries over the years, including the Greeks, the Romans, the Venetians, a few centuries under the Ottomans, then the Italians for a while. It became one of the strangest communist dictatorships in the world after WWII, eventually isolated even from Russia. It built the world's largest collection of bunkers (one for every 11 people) and handed out guns to all citizens to prepare for the inevitable invasion that never came.

The country only shed that leader and his constant surveillance in the 1980s and the transition to a market economy has naturally been a rough one. Albania finally appears to be hitting its stride, however, with low inflation and a rising quality of life. The younger generation is learning English fast, in the cities and in beach towns at least, and there's now a sense of optimism about the future. Unemployment is lower than in many other Balkan countries and the economy is varied enough to provide a wide range of jobs.

The average monthly salary here is under $500 in the capital though, lower in less populated areas, so if you land here only pulling in $1,200 a month from retirement or a fledgling online business, you can still live quite well by local standards. It would be relatively easy to get by for $800 as a single or $1,400 as a couple, with a bit more putting you in the high middle class. Rent prices here may just be the cheapest in Europe—about 40% lower in Tirana than Budapest just to compare another capital city in this book.

Most expats live in the capital, which is a relatively mellow capital since the population is less than half a million. Only one other city has more than 100,000 people. Other places foreigners settle include Pogradec on Lake Ohrid, Shkodra on a lake near Montenegro, in the UNESCO World Heritage town of Berat, or just part of the year in one of the beach towns. Albania has a long coastline, so most expats will at least take frequent vacations to the seaside in the summer, while some rent a getaway house for the whole summer. By the time you get to the bottom of the country around Sarande you're parallel with Corfu Island of Greece, the country's neighbor to the south.

Because of the varied geography, the climate can vary quite a bit here. The warmest parts by the ocean can get hot and sweaty in the summer, while the Albanian Alps in the north stay below freezing in the winter at the higher elevations. In between these two extremes though, the Mediterranean climate is similar to southern Italy's. There's a winter, but it's not a brutal one.

Housing Costs
James Leithart, who documents his experiences in the My Albanian Life section of his YouTube channel, admits he got a great deal, but he pays a mere $90 per month for his one-bedroom apartment in the lakeside city of Pogradec. Even in Tirana though, you can find a similar sized place for under $200 and get a nice three-bedroom place for $650 in the city center.

Blogger Anita Hendrieka avoided the two most popular months in Saranda and twice rented an apartment for $180 per month. Once it was a studio, but the second time it was a two-bedroom, two-bath place a five-minute walk from the beach.

You'll get the best deal with feet on the ground and time to look around, but I pulled up a few rental sites just to see what I could find online in English. There were dozens of attractive furnished apartments in the range of $300 to $800. One I would move into tomorrow: two bedrooms, two baths, two balconies, 1,300 square feet, and a 10th-floor view for $540 per month in the heart of Tirana.

Searching year-long rentals on Airbnb, I only found three (very nice) apartments for more than $700 per month and most were below $500. There were fewer available in Pogradec, but they ranged from $350 for a small one-bedroom apartment to $755 for a two-bedroom one with a large balcony and a lake view. All of these are furnished and include utilities.

Canadian expat Terry worked in the mining industry in the region before falling in love with an Albanian woman who managed the hotel where he was staying. He and Eva bought their 2-bedroom, 2-bath penthouse in a new building where they were able to customize a lot of the finishes and appliances. They ended up spending around $120,000 on the unit itself and another $25,000 on the finishing out. This is for a spacious place with an outdoor terrace bigger than most European apartments. "We used to rent a two-bedroom duplex with an office on top," Terry says, "in the most expensive, most prestigious neighborhood in Tirana. We paid 1,100 euros per month. If we had just rented an average place in an average neighborhood, it would be 1/3 of that probably, but I had company money paying, so I didn't have to worry about the budget." Now he's retirement age and wanted a place they could call their own.

There are plenty of bargains to be found if you want to follow in their footsteps and buy something. You can own property free and clear in Albania as long as it's not agricultural land. In doing a cursory search, I found condos in several regions of Albania for sale below €50,000—even in beach towns—and plenty of houses from €60,000 to €100,000. For new condos, you can expect to pay between €400 per square meter to €1,400 per square meter for an ocean view. For an apartment of 100 square meters (1,076 square feet), that equates to a wide range of €40,000 to €140,000. While that top price of $167,000 in dollars wouldn't get you a dark basement studio on the coast of California or the Cinque Terre of Italy, in Albania that will get you a luxury penthouse with all modern appliances and a panoramic ocean view. If you can get financing, mortgage interest rates are not onerous—generally just a couple points above the rate in the USA.

If you move into a smaller town or village, you could probably buy a place for what you spent on your last car. You might need to pick up some Albanian though if there aren't many tourists or young locals around.

Food & Drink

Albania, bordering Macedonia and Greece, was ruled by the Ottomans, and is a ferry ride away from Italy, so those signposts will give you a good idea of what to expect from the cuisine. You can expect lots of kebabs, cheesy pastries, and pizza, as well as plenty of stews and great bread. Although the Muslim religion claims the largest share of the population, this is officially a secular country and in the last census, 70 percent of the population refused to check a box for the type of religion they belonged to. So, you can easily get a beer or wine with your meal anywhere.

The relatively long growing season and altitude variations contribute to a wide variety of fruits, vegetables, and herbs at terrific prices. Most of them make it into the local dishes, along with seafood from the coast and meat from the interior. James gives this rundown from his weekly shopping trips, where he generally spends less than $4 for a bag of fruit and vegetables for the week:

Kilo (2.2 pounds) of potatoes - 35¢
Kilo of apples - 90¢
Kilo of peaches - 80¢
Kilo of red peppers - $1.40
Kilo of green peppers - 40¢
Kilo of rice - $1.20
Liter of milk- $1.40
Large loaf of fresh bread - 85¢

I saw similar prices in the markets on the edge of Tirana where I was staying, including watermelons for 25¢ per kilo and cured olives for $2.40 per kilo.

If you indulge in the national pastime of drinking little cups of coffee in a cafe several times a day, that's not going to set you back much. An espresso is typically less than 50 cents and it's only slightly more for an Americano or cappuccino.

When I had a meal of kofta meatballs, dill yogurt dip, salad, and bread in Tirana, it came out to $2.40 per person including a nice wheat beer. When I would order a sandwich at a local kebab place, it was never more than $1.75.

When I had dinner with Terry and Eva at a lakeside restaurant it was around 15 euros for three: fish, vegetables, rice, and three half-liter beers. "This is probably the biggest line item in our budget," Terry said, "but that's because we eat out a lot, several nights a week, drinking good wine."

Albanian wine dates back thousands of years, so there's no trouble finding that here, at good prices. Again, the climate is similar to that of Italy and Greece, so it's a good place for growing grapes. Expect to pay as little as $3 for something decent, or $6 to $10 for something good to serve with dinner.

"We don't go wanting for much when it comes to food," Terry says. "The supermarkets are well-stocked, and prices are good. A lot grows in this region plus there are enough imports to get what you're missing if you're willing to pay for it."

Just be advised that your restaurant choices will be thin once you get beyond the larger cities and beach resort areas. "There just aren't a whole lot of ethnic restaurants though, especially Asian," adds Terry. "Albanians meet in cafes, but don't eat out all that much when they're not on vacation. So, there's not a lot of variety."

Transportation
If you live in Albania full-time and have a car, that part is going to cost you. Automobiles are more expensive here than they are in many other European countries, plus gas prices are quite high considering what salaries are like. You can easily spend $24,000 on a basic compact manual sedan. Gasoline is around $6 per gallon, though at least you won't get hit with tolls on the roads. Because of the high car prices though, it's tough to find a rental car for less than €45 per day. A hotel or agency can usually hook you up with a driver for less than that.

Public transportation is a bargain, though figuring it out isn't easy. The bus system is rather chaotic throughout Albania, with vans and minibuses that don't gather in any large central station. As one travel website put it, "Tirana remains the last major city in the known universe without a bus or train station." Even traveling between the two biggest cities takes some sleuthing around and you may be shuttled from one van onto another midway. You'll have to travel pretty far to pay more than 10 euros though for inter-city rides. You can get a bus from Pogradec to Tirana for around $4.50, for a ride of several hours. Tirana to the southern beach resort area of Sarana is around $12.

Taxis are metered and a bit over two euros to start, then a euro or more for each kilometer, making them rather expensive by local standards. Unfortunately, you can't turn to Uber either to get a better value—the country has managed to keep them out so far. The fare goes up during the night and if you're going really far, they might just quote you a price. You will probably pay more than $20 to get to or from the airport.

Local city buses are 35¢ to 65¢ if you can figure out the route.

In the lake regions, there are ferries to other towns. On Lake Scutari in the north, there's an international ferry to Macedonia.

As mentioned earlier, you can get to Italy by ferry. Six companies collectively run routes from four Italian ferry ports: Trieste, Ancona, Bari, and Brindisi. They arrive in Durres, Vlora and Saranda. The most common route is between Bari and Durres, which costs from $45 for a low season deck seat to $85 for an outside cabin with bathroom. For most of them, you'll probably want to go overnight and splurge for a cabin: the shortest route is 7.5 hours, while the longest is 27 hours.

Healthcare

Albania guarantees healthcare as a basic human right in its constitution and ensures that every citizen is covered. This system is funded by taxes and payroll deductions though, in a country that's far from rich. After a decade of transition that followed the fall of communism, the country began upgrading facilities, equipment, and training. They are still playing catch-up in many ways though and some studies have rated their public health facilities dead last in Europe. The under-funded system is still tough on the poor too: there are still many services—such as medicines and lab tests—that citizens need to pay out of pocket.

While small-town clinics and hospitals can handle basic needs for as little as $12, most expats head to Tirana to take care of anything serious. There you can find modern hospitals, well-trained doctors, and the latest equipment if you choose the best private facilities.

Expect to pay less than $50 to see a doctor or get a dental cleaning and check-up. If you find the care in the capital lacking, there are plenty of cheap flights to other locations in Europe, where you can roll into the waiting room a few hours later.

Other Costs

Utility costs in Albania are relatively stable except for electricity, which can double if you're running electric heaters in the winter or air-conditioning in the summer. James pays at least $23 a month for electricity for his one-bedroom place but the year-round average in Tirana is around $85. His apartment came with a wood stove though, so if he buys enough wood to use that for the winter, it's around $140 for enough to last the whole season.

He pays $16 a month for water, $15 for decent internet in the home, and $12 a month for a phone plan with ample calls and 2GB of data. Internet speeds can vary quite a bit, from mobile-only in some villages to high-speed fiber in more dense areas, with 60 megabytes per second for around $22. Where it's good, it's really good: the average speeds are well above the world averages for both fixed-line and mobile internet. The speed testing site Ookla rates Albania 20th in the world for mobile data speed.

A haircut starts at $2 in a village barbershop, but for $5 you can go to a nice salon. If you want someone to clean your apartment regularly or be a nanny, that won't cost you much here. Figure on $3 to $5 an hour depending on experience and regularity.

If you have kids, this is one of the cheapest places in the world to send them to an international school in English. Costs are around $325 per month for primary school, which is just a shade more than what we spent at a Spanish-language private school in Mexico.

Going out for some entertainment won't cost you much here. A movie ticket averages $5 and many cultural performances and concerts are less than $10 a ticket.

When you head out to the beach, succumb to the easy button and rent a chair and umbrella ($2.50 to $5 per person for the day). Eventually someone will come by and get you what you need for food and drink.

Visas in Albania
If you're American, you can give Albania quite a long trial run to try it out: you get to stay a year before you have to leave. (Why Americans? It's a payback for getting Kosovo their own country in the Dayton Peace Accords to end the Bosnian war. Kosovo is full of ethnic Albanians.) Once that year is up though, you need to leave for three months before returning again unless you've applied for residency.

For around 85 other nationalities, Albania is much like the rest of Europe. You can only stay for three months at a time and then have to leave for at least three months unless you apply for a Type D visa online that's good for 180 days instead. This is the best path if you intend to apply for permanent residency if you're not American and you want to rent instead of own.

There are several types of temporary residency permits depending on how long you intend to stay. The longest can be renewed every year or two for a period of up to five years and then you are eligible to get permanent residency instead, which does not require renewal. The visa itself will cost around $100, but you'll likely spend several times that on obtaining documents, translations, and some expert help pushing it through. Allow far more time than needed.

You can get on the fast track to residency though by taking one step: buying real estate. There's no minimum purchase amount like you see in a lot of countries. Since you can find a condo relatively easily for less than $30,000 in most of the country, you can gain residency quickly and stick around legally for cheap.

Downsides

There's no denying that Albania is one of the least-developed countries in Europe. The population is still trying to shake off a half-century of strict government control and fully join the modern world. While the economy is relatively stable and growing, infrastructure spending is limited by the size of the tax base. The quality of healthcare is substandard outside Tirana, so this is not a great location for someone with a long list of medical problems and 14 prescriptions to fill each month.

English proficiency is growing fast in Tirana and the coastal beach areas, but still lags quite a bit in areas where most people have never left the country. Since the language is unique to this one country, nobody arrives knowing more than a few words.

Zoning laws are lacking or badly enforced in many areas and buildings seldom go beyond basic and functional. While there's some interesting historic architecture here and there, especially in the UNESCO World Heritage city of Berat, the coastal towns are more apt to be rows of chock-a-block concrete ugliness.

In theory you can drink the tap water throughout the country, but it's heavily chlorinated and some visitors end up experiencing stomach problems. A Brita type filter pitcher might be enough to clear this up.

Most people who move here manage to get past all this though thanks to good food, good people, and a safe environment.

For More Information

James Leithart's YouTube channel (youtube.com/jamesleithart)
TheBalkanista.com
AnitaHendrieka.com
Plus see expat boards on Facebook for Tirana or the whole country

Chapter 12:
Argentina

Pros: vibrant capital, European attitudes, great wine, good food, good beer, beautiful scenery, fashion, arts, culture, easy visas, gay-friendly, sensible drug laws, fast internet, mostly free healthcare, good infrastructure.

Cons: frequent financial crises, fragile banking system, wacky politics, petty crime, long distances, long way from other continents, expensive flights, very late dinner/nightlife hours

Cathy Brown was looking to escape the boring, predictable life of a mother in suburban Michigan and wanted to find somewhere that was exotic but safe, cheaper but with decent infrastructure and education. Her kids were 4, 6, and 8 at the time and she wanted their view of the world to be broader. She wanted their life and their options to be more flexible. "So, I bought one-way tickets to Buenos Aires," she says. "I figured that if we were going to learn a second language, Spanish would be the most helpful. I had been to Peru before and liked the Latin culture, the warmth and hospitality. People actually smile and hug constantly. Argentina seemed like a good choice and if it didn't work out, we could always move on."

She quickly decided that Buenos Aires was too big and too congested, so the family went to Mendoza. "That still didn't feel like the right place," Cathy said, "and everybody who knew me well kept mentioning this town of El Bolson in Patagonia, saying that's where we should go. They were right."

She and two of her three kids, now more than a decade older, are settled in El Bolson, an "artistic, hippy mountain town" that's a center for hiking and is the microbrew valley of Argentina. "Living here is about as laid-back as it gets," she says. "There's gorgeous scenery, with mountains on all sides, and a really welcoming community. People get together on weekends to do projects. It's very safe: you see old ladies out hitchhiking to get to town and back. We do a lot of bartering in this area, which keeps the costs down. You can have a really nice family life here for $1,000 a month. It's a huge part of the reason I live here."

Cathy fully admits she could not live on even twice this amount in the capital though. Also, if she were further south in Patagonia where transportation costs of goods are higher (and there's a shorter growing season), it would be more expensive. Then again, in Buenos Aires it's easier to find or create a real job, as opposed to where she is, which really requires having a virtual job paying the bills.

Keep in mind though that $1,000 a month is higher than the average Argentine salary and high inflation can hit food prices hard, especially for workers whose wages don't rise at the same rate. Most expatriates have it much easier since they're cashing in dollars instead of working in pesos. With this country being a financial basket case most of the time, earning in a stable foreign currency is especially useful.

Many a traveler has landed in Buenos Aires and within less than 24 hours started to ponder the question, "Could I find a way to live here?" Some don't just ponder it; they actually make the move.

Author and book coach Helen Wilkie echoes the feeling that many have with her story of what happened after her first visit to Argentina. "I came again that same year and realized a couple of weeks would not be enough. So, I came for three months, then six months, then six months again, and finally I realized this is where I want to be. So, I moved here last November. I couldn't be happier."

Ron MacDonald, a private chef and the guy behind Palermo Craft Beer Tour, moved to Argentina with his family more than four years ago. He and his wife stayed on after they left for university. "After 30+ years in Colorado, we were really tired of dealing with the winters, icy roads, and cold. The culture is what sold us on Argentina, and Buenos Aires in particular. We live in the Palermo neighborhood now, but have also lived in the Congreso, Monserrat, and San Telmo neighborhoods. We spent some time in Cordoba (more like Colorado) and have considered moving there as well because it is beautiful and is also cheaper than the capital city. Mendoza is another option."

There's no shortage of iconic images you can associate with this country: tango dancers, gauchos, soccer champs, the Mendoza vineyards with the Andes Mountains behind them, and the glorious peaks of southern Patagonia. There's a lot of diversity in these landscapes. Up north you have a dramatic desert on one side and Iguazu Falls on the other. There are seasides, cities and farms in the middle, down to glaciers and freezing cold in the jumping off point to Antarctica.

I could hear birds singing outside the window when I interviewed Leigh Shulman, a mother who moved with her husband and child from Brooklyn to Argentina. Eventually they ended up on the outskirts of the northern city of Salta. "We lived in Panama for a while and didn't like it so much," she says. "We went to Costa Rica and actually had a job offer from a friend who ran an organization, but we had planned a trip down here anyway after we arrived, we wanted to stay. We were originally looking at Montevideo in Uruguay. We stayed in Buenos Aires for a while, but some friends were moving to Salta and we ended up following them. We liked it so much here that we eventually bought a big house and stayed."

The distances here are vast though, so getting around the country or returning from your remote home somewhere to see relatives in the country you left is no easy task. Driving distance from Buenos Aires to El Bolson is more than 1,000 miles (1,695 kilometers). Buenos Aires to Salta is almost as far in the opposite direction. Internal fights can be expensive and require a stop in Buenos Aires when going between cities, though thankfully a few budget airlines have popped up the past few years to provide some competition.

You can take a bus, and it may be quite nice, but on many routes, you'll be on that bus for 24 hours or more. It can be worth it to upgrade to a flight to save a day or more. Round-trip flights to the U.S. or Canada from Buenos Aires are rarely less than $1,200 and to most cities in Europe they're even higher. It pays to be a travel hacker banking frequent flyer miles you can cash in.

Once you get settled in though, prices can be very reasonable, especially if you have a way of bringing in lots of U.S. dollars or euros in cash. That's because there are two exchange rates in Argentina's fragile economy: the official rate and the "blue rate" you can get on the street from moneychangers. This disappeared for a while under the previous president who had a degree in economics, but then a populist got back in and is propping up the currency for the sake of appearances and foreign debt payments. The unofficial rate can be 20 to 50 percent better than the official one. (As this book went to press, the official rate was 75 Argentine pesos to the dollar, the real rate was 140.)

Getting to your money electronically is almost like a weekly hobby here though: many banks limit ATM withdrawals to around $150, so you end up hopping from one bank to another or using a service like Xoom to take out larger amounts of pesos. Hold onto your home country PayPal account because the banks here are too unstable to work with that service locally; the best bet is to get a debit card you can use to pull money from in Argentina using your original country account. It's not unheard of to get counterfeit money either. Leigh has even gotten a bogus bill from her bank teller!

The good news is, they're not real big on rules in Argentina and that includes visa rules. The tourism-killing retaliatory visa fee policy went away after the first edition of this book came out, so it won't cost you anything to enter the country now if you're American or Canadian. Check the current rules if you're coming from elsewhere. Many expats renew their tourist visa indefinitely, leaving the country every three months for a short hop to Chile or Uruguay. If you overstay your visa, there's a fine that is less than $60 unless you've overstayed for more than four years.

There are also no nanny rules about drugs either, especially marijuana, which is essentially a non-issue for personal use. (Neighboring Uruguay is even more lax, with legal dispensaries.) This is also one of the friendliest countries south of Mexico for gay couples or singles.

As I write this, the cost of living in Argentina is cheap again thanks to yet another financial crisis and government debt defaults. Since locals are earning in a depreciating currency, that brings down a lot of costs for those earning in a stronger currency abroad. Bolson, Patagonia resident Cathy Brown says she can get a 1.5-hour massage "at a fancy holistic place" in her town for $15. Haircuts, shoeshines, and cleaning services are all a bargain compared to home.

Housing Costs
Keith Lang of the Nomad Flag blog traveled to Argentina to learn Spanish on his way back to Europe from New Zealand. He ended up moving there, staying five years. Now he's a digital nomad on the road, but he returns to Argentina a few months at a time to live. "Inflation is rampant, and landlords even set the rates at two levels, increasing the price every 6 months, instead of every year (even though contracts are yearly)," he says. "In 2006-2010 it was one of the cheapest places in the world. After that prices increased a lot. But since the recent financial problems started, it's a value destination again. However, this could change at any moment. For a lot of singles, $1,000 a month will be enough for expenses and rent (long-term) in Buenos Aires. Cities like Mendoza and Salta are cheaper than Buenos Aires."

Ron MacDonald says he pays $650 a month for their family apartment. That's for a two-bedroom place with a nice terrace with a BBQ area and includes W-Fi, cable, and electricity. "Gas, electricity, and water are ridiculously cheap in this country," he adds.

Will Aquino, a DJ and event producer who came from Atlanta more than a decade ago, says he generally spends between US$1,000 and $,1500 a month in Buenos Aires depending on the time of year. "My rent, utilities (gas, electric, house supplies, building expenses, housekeeper) and phone bill run me around $700 per month. This is for an unfurnished 3-bedroom/3-bath place in front of a plaza with a church in Palermo." At times though, that is probably a few hundred dollars under market value.

Cathy Brown lives in Patagonia, but when her daughter was old enough to head off to college, she moved to Los Angeles...then came back after a year when she realized how expensive it was in comparison. "She has a great group of friends in Buenos Aires and instead of paying $2,300 for a shared place in downtown LA, she is paying $400 for a private apartment in Belgrano, BA."

"Life in Buenos Aires is definitely much less expensive than in Toronto," says Helen, "even though I live in one of the most expensive barrios in the city: Recoleta. Argentina is definitely a bargain for those living on dollars—even Canadian dollars! For locals earning pesos, sadly, not so much."

She says her monthly spending budget is $2,500, "and on that I live very well. My larger-than-Toronto apartment costs $1,300, but many of my friends live much more cheaply. I just happen to like living in a badass apartment in a posh area and am willing to pay for it! On that budget I eat out a lot, take tango lessons and travel when I want to."

The prices drop when you settle in a smaller city or town. While most apartments are between $600 to $1,200 in the most desirable neighborhoods of the capital city, that will get you something large, furnished, and modern in the mid-sized cities of Salta, Mendoza, Cordoba, or Rosario. Where Cathy lives in rural Patagonia, $350 a month gets you a full house with some land. She says you can find a one-bedroom apartment in her area for less than $200 per month, "a bit more in Bariloche."

Lining something up ahead of time is quite difficult though; only a few agencies list prices online for long-term rentals. The best plan is to rent a short-term apartment or stay in an apart hotel at first so you can take your time looking around. Get recommendations from others (both locals and expatriates) on which agencies are trustworthy and look at plenty of apartments to assess what's a good value. The other option is just to search Airbnb and put in a period of three or six months to see what comes up. More landlords are willing to rent for longer when tourism is down, and this eliminates a lot of the legal hassles. Ron explains it this way:

"If you aren't local, don't even think about renting long term unless you can rent from a fellow expat. Most Argentines require a property guarantee from a local. That means that a local property owner puts up their owned property to pay your rent if you don't. Usually that has to be a family member. The laws in Argentina are very protective of renters, and this is the reason. If a deadbeat moves into your apartment, it can take years to get them out if they don't pay the rent. So, property owners are very careful of who they rent to, and if you can't get that guarantee from a local, you probably won't get a long-term rental. That being said, there are a few companies that specialize in renting to expats, but you are going to pay more than a local."

If you're going to buy a house or condo here, figure on paying the whole amount in cash, in dollars. People literally bring bags of money to a closing. In theory you can get a mortgage, but with interest rates running at 20% at times, you probably don't want to. You can't find the bargains here you could 15 or 20 years ago since Argentines view real estate as one of the few reliable places to put their cash and there have also been buyers from Brazil coming in too. If the financial system completely collapses again though like it did in the early 2000s, who knows?

Land can be surprisingly expensive in many areas, but construction costs are not. "You can hire a skilled workman for $40 to $50 a day," says Cathy.

Food & Drink

Most expats will tell you this is where the real bargains are—assuming you like red meat and wine that is. You have to bow to local norms to eat like a local here: a coffee and a couple medialuna pastries is the typical breakfast, around $2 in a Buenos Aires cafe. A big lunch is supposed to get you through most of the day, then it's not uncommon for a 10:00 dinner to be "too early" for the locals.

If you like a good steak dinner accompanied by a nice bottle of wine, you'll be in heaven here. They take their grilled meats very seriously in this country and it's considered a God-given right to sip wine with every meal. Prices are quite reasonable on both, to the point where a group of people can go out and eat to their heart's content for $10-$20 a person in places that aren't overly fancy. The things Argentines do well they do very well: barbecued meat, wine, coffee, ice cream, and pastries. Some would add Italian food to that mix, though it can be hit-and-miss.

Ron MacDonald says eating out can cost as much as it would in the USA for cuisines outside of the local sphere. At the high end though, fine dining is a relatively good value. "We went to eat at one of the top 50 places in South America (Don Julio) and paid about US$120 for a lot of food, but it would have easily cost us $200 - 300 in the USA for what we ate."

"A meal at a restaurant in Salta ranges," says Leah, "but going to one of the best restaurants in town and getting appetizers, main dishes, dessert, and wine would be under $50 for two people. "Empanadas are around $7 a dozen."

Ron supplied these prices for groceries from a recent shopping trip the day we talked:

One onion: 20¢
One tomato: 25¢
One head of leaf lettuce: 40 cents
Two 1-liter beers: $2.25 (total for two)
One bottle of pretty good red wine: $3 (most expensive wines range between $8 - 10 dollars)
One 750 ml bottle of local whiskey: $3
Chicken: $1.50 for 2.2 pounds of chicken.
One artichoke: 90¢
One pound of potatoes: 25¢

Will says he spends more than most because of eating out most of the time. "I generally spend $300-$400 a month on food, which is a good bit more than the average person that cooks at home I'd imagine."

When I was in Buenos Aires last year, I saw coffee and two pastries for $2 all over the place, draft beers for less than $2 a pint, and set multi-course lunches for $6-$9 in nice neighborhoods.

This is a farming nation, so it's easy to find local meat, fruit, and vegetables at good prices. The closer to the source you are, the less they'll cost. "I'm a real foodie, but I still probably only spend $60 a week for food and wine for the three of us," Cathy says. "I get most of our food from neighbors who grow it. The flour is from locally ground wheat and we can get honey, milk, vegetables, and meat from neighbors who produce it. I can get really high-quality microbrews for $2-$3 a liter. I typically spend $4.50 or so for a decent bottle of wine, or around $10 for a bottle of *great* wine from a *vinoteca*."

Transportation

"Public transportation is a bargain, and you can take a bus from anywhere to anywhere else in Buenos Aires," says Helen. A bus or metro ride is 35 - 50 cents and a monthly pass is less than $14.

A taxi ride of a couple kilometers will cost $2 - $5 in Buenos Aires, less in smaller cities.

"One of the low-key best things about living in BA is that it's very flat, making it very walkable/bikeable," says Will. "Add to that a practically non-stop public transportation system with buses that can get you pretty much anywhere in the city and it's easy. The alternatives are basically taxis and Uber or Easytaxi." The "taxi mafia" has been fighting these services hard and you actually have to sit in the front seat if you go alone to avoid problems. "I would say I spend an average of $20 a month on public transportation, which accounts for the overwhelming majority of my non-walked trips. Then "I have Uber hooked up to PayPal and with current dollar to peso rates, the average trip to another neighborhood runs you $2-$5. I spend at most $50 a month on Uber during the winter. It's very cheap in general.

"If you are thinking about coming long term, and you want to explore the country on your own, consider importing your car," says Ron. "If you do it within six months there are no import taxes. Cars are very expensive here, and parking is a big expense, but worth it if you want to drive around the country."

Domestic flight prices have gone down since the last edition of this book thanks to more budget airline competition. Cathy says her frequent Bariloche to Buenos Aires trip costs between $60 and $100 one way. (Which avoids a 24-hour bus ride). As I was writing this though, LATAM pulled out of the market during the pandemic and it sounded like a permanent move.

Healthcare

Get ready to see a dramatic drop in your healthcare costs when you move to Argentina, from emergency care to elective care to medicine. Some expats who move to Argentina from the USA often see their healthcare costs drop by more than $10,000 per year.

Lisa Besserman, who has moved away since I was first doing interviews, had an ankle injury that required going to the emergency room, getting x-rays, and seeing a doctor. It cost her the equivalent of $60 at a private hospital. Getting adjusted at a chiropractor will cost $25-$30.

Cathy Brown's son was kicked by a horse and suffered several broken bones. He was in the hospital for days. Although they had just arrived in the country on tourist visas, when it was time to go there was no bill to pay. It was completely free, no questions asked. Whether you're a citizen, tourist, or legal resident, healthcare in public hospitals is gratis.

"I spent 9 days in a hospital earlier this year with pneumonia," says Helen. "It was the public hospital system, and I paid not a single peso."

Dental work comes with a cost but is still a fraction of the cost of the U.S., Canada, or Europe. A cleaning may be $25, getting a cavity filled is $50 tops.

"To give you an example of the difference in drug costs," Lisa adds, "birth control pills used to cost $30 to $50 a month in the U.S. even with insurance. Here the same package is $5-$8 without insurance, just walking in and buying them."

If you do purchase health insurance in Argentina, that won't set you back too much. A full-blown family plan that makes use of the best private hospitals and clinics will run about $300 per month. "If you pay $60 more you can get plastic surgery done once a year," Leah adds with a laugh. If you do want to have a nip and tuck—very popular here—you will find some of the best rates in the world, performed by doctors with plenty of daily experience.

Other Costs

Subsidies on fuel have been rolled back a bit in recent years, but Argentina still has some of the lowest monthly utility costs in Latin America. It's not uncommon to receive an electric bill for less than $20 per month in the capital, maybe $35 in the hottest months with air conditioners running. The average utilities total across Argentina is $65 per month including water, gas, power, garbage collection, and fast internet.

Cathy Brown pays even less in her small town. Her water is free and comes from a well, while cooking gas is $7 for a tank that will last a couple months.

Leah and her family live in a large house they own in Salta, but still only pay around $20-$30 per month in electricity if air conditioning is not running. The biggest cost is their internet/cable bundle since they went for the highest possible package, but she says, "Our monthly expenses aren't much more on the whole than they were in 2014."

Cable and internet together can be anywhere from $15-$80 per month depending on the package and speed, but the average internet bill for 60 mbps speed is under $30. Fast broadband is available in any non-remote area and mobile speeds are generally good.

Private school costs for the kids range from $120 to $350 per month, with only a few elite international ones in Buenos Aires charging more than that.

One of the ongoing time sucks in Argentina that can also have real costs is getting to your money earned outside of Argentina. The country is an economic mess and the population keeps electing leaders who make it worse. "They just officially defaulted on their debt for the 9th time in their history," says Buenos Aires resident Wade Fitzpatrick. "The Peso was already eroding fast and Argentines started paying a serious premium to get a hold of dollars to preserve their wealth." The government kept trying to hold the rate down for debt payback, but it's hard to fight market forces.

As a result, this is the only country in this book that has a black market for foreign currency. This "blue rate" is not exactly a back-alley affair though: you can get that rate from Western Union and sometimes services like Xoom, as compared to the official government rate that has no relation to reality.

Visas
When it comes to visas, most foreigners in Argentina assume they're going to have to leave the country every three months. With Uruguay and Chile on their doorstep though, that's not really a big deal. People who have come to work for an international company tend to get a work visa, but many others just leave four times a year—indefinitely. If something happens and they overstay their visa, it's not the end of the world. "Argentina is one of the laxest countries for visas," Cathy says. "I don't want to do anything wrong because I've got kids, but I've heard from a lot of people that if you overstay your visa, you just have to pay small fine, whether you overstayed a day or three years. They sign off and you're on your way." Officially as I write this, the fine for overstaying your visa ranges from 4,500 if you overstayed less than two years to 15,000 pesos if you overstayed more than four years. At the time of publication that was $60 to $200.

If she's not leaving for her travel writing job and the kids haven't gone back to the USA, they make a quick crossing into Chile. "If we really wanted to, we could do it on foot," she says. "We rent a car, cross the border, and can be back in the afternoon."

If you're only going to stay six months at a time, you may be able to renew your tourist visa locally without leaving the country.

That's generally only going to work once though, so it's best for people not planning to spend the whole year here.

Getting a business visa requires a letter from an employer, a specified time period, and the employer's acceptance of financial responsibility for the traveler. For obvious reasons, the employer really has to want you to make this happen. If you get one though, multiple-entry business visas are valid for four years.

There are various long-term residence permits valid from one to three years, but you'll probably need to hire a lawyer and be prepared for a long slog. The Argentines love bureaucracy and paperwork and you'll need to navigate a dizzying array of papers and people. The financial requirement is not daunting though: proof of income of anywhere from $900 to $2,000 a month (depending on the current exchange rate) that you can transfer into an Argentine bank. For those of retirement age, it's even lower.

Once you do manage to secure a one-year residency visa and have renewed it twice, you can then apply for permanent legal residency. You are then allowed to work legally. If you spend the majority of your time in the country, you can apply for citizenship. All of this will likely require the help of an attorney though, which can run close to $2,000 to set up and more again the next year to renew.

In a country like this, there are ways around the rules. If you buy property under a corporation you have formed, you could offer yourself a job and get a business visa. Invest enough money in the local economy, and you could get on the fast track. If you spend enough time in the country asking questions, and you have some capital, you can certainly find other options for speeding things along.

Downsides

In many ways Argentina sounds like paradise, but of course like anywhere there are problems. The economy could collapse again at any moment and nobody has much faith in the government to get anything done. People are used to fending for themselves and finding ways to get around the system. (Check out the Oscar-winning movie *The Secret in Their Eyes* to see the country's typical bureaucrats in full public service glory.) Leah had to give up on the first internet company they contacted after weeks of calls and waiting for someone to show up. Promises are often not kept, customer service can be non-existent, and times to show up to do work are treated as just suggestions.

"Banking has always been a major headache in Argentina," says Keith. "Nobody trusts the banks (and why would they?). I used local bank accounts and when possible, services like Xoom to transfer money. But I ran a business in the country, so all of my income was generated there."

Many ATMs have a low limit on the maximum you can withdraw, which creates a lot of stress if you need to get to your cash. "Currently ATM's are maxed at a withdrawal of about 150 dollars, and the fee is $10," says Keith. "Add home fees charged by your own bank and that can be substantial. We do use our debit card when we can and that lowers the percentage fee significantly. Otherwise, we travel to the USA fairly often and always bring back cash which we can change at good rates. I wish it were easier, but for now, it isn't ideal."

Helen says it's even worse for Canadians than for Americans. "My business is still based in Canada, as are my bank accounts. I get money by using a debit card and withdrawing from my Canadian bank accounts in pesos. But the charges are outrageous! I pay the equivalent of C$15 every time I take out money. Most of us use our credit cards as much as possible to avoid this."

"I do not have an Argentine bank account so I either use cash or an international credit card," says Canadian Danielle Thompson, who runs FreelanceTravelNetwork.com. "I use World Remit to handle money transfers. I try to mainly use cash in Buenos Aires."

Will says it's good to have lots of options for getting to your money. "I currently have an Argentine account in pesos, my U.S. account in dollars and my PayPal account in dollars attached to my US accounts. PayPal has been my saving grace for the last 11 years, as it's easy to send money to/from friends with US accounts. I have a WhatsApp group of friends here that is dedicated to USD/AR$ money transfers because someone is always looking to exchange dollars for pesos and vice versa." As you can see, it makes sense to spend some time on message boards and time talking with long-time foreign residents to figure out how to keep the cash flowing without losing your shirt in the process.

"Despite new laws requiring all vendors to accept credit and debit cards, you still will find places where their machine is 'broken' or your card 'doesn't work' so it's not really possible to rely solely on cards," says Will. At the time we talked, because of a problem with the current Argentine law, Uber couldn't officially pay its drivers so the only money that drivers could get paid in was cash. "This means that when a driver sees you're paying with a card they often cancel on you."

Everyone complains that electronics in Argentina are both out of date and overpriced. To the point where people only buy them in Argentina if it's an emergency.

"Small appliances, particularly electronics, are very expensive here," says Helen. "In the expat community, I find that when anyone is going to the US or Canada or the UK, they pretty much expect their friends to bring stuff back for them. We will order an iPhone on Amazon, then have it delivered to a friend who will bring it back here. Also, I paint in acrylics as a hobby, and the supplies are very expensive compared to in Canada."

Cathy saves up her electronics purchases for when she returns to the U.S., saying the prices in Argentina "are exorbitant and make zero sense."

Will also says to remember that Argentine Castellano Spanish is distinct to the region. He says to get the book *Che Boludo* to brush up on all the Argentine slang. "Do some homework before coming because no matter how good you think your Spanish is you will struggle to understand the Porteños." (People of the port city of Buenos Aires).

"Go with an open mind and lots of patience," Keith advises. "Argentina is one of the most bureaucratic countries in the world. Learn to love eating late and staying up late. Make sure you can access funds outside of Argentina before you go, for emergencies and for survival. Knowledge of Spanish is essential for getting a job but be warned that work permits are very difficult to obtain."

Some expats with family in other places can feel like they're a long way from loved ones, which they are. Getting back to the northern hemisphere can take a whole day or night at best, longer with connections, on an expensive ticket.

Expatriates here say the effort will be rewarded. "Most locals are friendly and open, and we have made good friends with many locals," says Ron. "In general, Argentines are curious about outsiders and sincerely interested in our thoughts and opinions. I want to emphasize this because I think Argentines have a reputation of being hard to connect with, but I have found the opposite to be true."

If you're able to exchange dollars for pesos at anywhere close to the street rate, the cost of living in Buenos Aires will likely be half or less what you would spend in a big city in the USA, Canada, and Europe. Even you're coming from a smaller town, you can still get by for half if moving somewhere other than the capital in Argentina. If you're sharing a place, it's even easier. For a couple or family, $1,500 a month will put you above the middle-class average and if you're pulling in a few grand a month, you can live an upper-crust life here.

For More Information
Wander-Argentina.com
BAExpats.org
TheBubble.com
PickUpTheFork.com
SolSalute.com
Search Facebook groups for Argentina and individual cities

Chapter 13:
Bulgaria

Pros: cheapest housing in Europe, fast internet in cities, stable currency, fresh food, good beer, cheap alcohol, well-preserved nature, skiing, outdoor activities, relatively easy residency.

Cons: government corruption, oligarch power, aging population, very few local jobs, poor shopping, inconsistent healthcare.

"I know who made the yogurt you are eating and who made the cheese. I've been to the farm where we got the eggs and know the guy who raised the pigs for the pork you ate last night. The rose petals in that jam are from our own farm."

In much of the world, this declaration I got from the owner of a guesthouse in Bulgaria would seem boastful, the product of serious effort to establish credibility amongst the organic food police crowd. If true, it would require years of relationship building with the right farmers who could ensure a steady supply.

In Bulgaria, this kind of boast is followed with a shrug. "We buy from our neighbors because it's good for the village. And we like to know where our food is coming from."

I didn't expect to eat and drink so well in Bulgaria and I start salivating again when I think back on my meals there. When you get your bill at the end though, it's always a pleasant surprise. There's plenty to lament about the current state of Bulgaria: government corruption, a net population loss because of job seekers heading elsewhere, and not nearly enough jobs to go around for those who are left. Don't come here expecting to land a local job unless you can connect with a multinational in Sofia or get hired as an ESL teacher.

The country has managed to do three things quite well though: preserve its heritage, preserve its green space, and produce great food. Some 30 percent of the country is protected forest land. This is the kind of figure you expect to hear for some eco-poster-child country like Costa Rica or New Zealand, not for a former Iron Curtain nation in Europe. As I hiked all three mountain ranges there, I was continually surprised by the rolling waves of green on mountains that show no sign of deforestation. I was also surprised by the purity of the springs, the lack of garbage, and the clear connection between the people and the land. With fewer than eight million people in a country that stretches from Serbia across the tops of Greece and Turkey to the Black Sea, there's plenty of wide-open space.

Cruising the highways now, despite the grape trellises and garden plots gracing almost every house, the Soviet era is still a dominant feature of the landscape. Ladas, smoke-belching motorcycles, and even an occasional Trabant are parked in the towns. Abandoned factories with busted windows are a regular roadside fixture. It was three days into my trip before I saw a smokestack that actually smoked. In the old days, things were different. "We grew a lot of things here and could produce a lot," said my driver Marin, who once kept the export books at a steel factory. "The Russians weren't very picky, so they bought it all. Whatever we could make and package, we had a market for it. So, you can imagine why some people think those were the good old days."

Marin told me this as we ate at the only dining spot in one town we passed through. It was called the Central Cooperative Restaurant and it had survived since the fall of Communism. We paid 10 euros for three after feasting on our multi-course meals and beers. After I expressed what a bargain this was, I found out that the minimum wage in Bulgaria is about the lowest in all of Europe. As I write this in 2020, the minimum wage is less than €300 per month and the average wage throughout the country is around €500 per month. So, if you move here with a monthly pension or income of $1,200 a month, you'll be living an upper middle-class life along with elite computer programmers and VP-level executives.

What you spend in Bulgaria largely depends on how frugal you're willing to be and how much you want to venture outside the country. "I was making about $32,000 a year teaching at the American College of Sofia," says American Carolyn Emigh. On that salary she lived well and spent vacations touring around other parts of Europe. "I did spend my first year in Sofia on a Fulbright where I made only $1,000 a month though and had to pay rent from this," she adds. "This was significantly more difficult to do given how much travel I wanted to do. But if you were willing to stay in country most of the year and live simply one could pretty easily get by in Sofia on this amount of money—most Bulgarians do—but you wouldn't have a lot of Western comforts."

Joanna Newman lived in multiple locations in England before moving to a small village in northern Bulgaria. She lives in a house she and her husband bought outright for less than what most people spend on a new compact car. "When in the UK we would spend a £1,500 per month on rent, food, and bills," she says. "But here I live on less than £200 per month." In US dollars, she cut her expenses from $2,500 to $335. And she's still in Europe.

She had plenty of time to give it a trial run and prepare for what to expect before moving. "My husband had a heart attack and this led us to move out here for a quieter life," she explains, "but we had to wait for redundancy in his job, which we knew was coming at some point and we did not want to lose out on the money which would enable us to get settled. This took three years, so in the meantime we came out a couple of times a year to soak up the atmosphere and do a bit of renovation on the house we chose to live in."

She's not alone. An article on the BBC website about Brits moving abroad to inexpensive countries pegged the number of them in Bulgaria at 18,000. There are an estimated 60,000 to 70,000 foreigners here overall.

This is primarily a rural country with small towns and villages. The second-largest city after Sofia has fewer than half a million people and it drops off fast after that. You'll find the most expatriates in the capital of Sofia as it's the largest city, the business hub, and the place you're most likely to find people who can speak English. Others settle on the Black Sea coast though, where a steady stream of tourists means a higher English (and German) proficiency.

Another popular spot for foreigners to settle is Bansko, which is one of the two biggest ski resort areas in the country but also has a historic city center and plenty of hiking opportunities in the summer. Others move to the second city of Plovdiv, which is a bit cheaper than Sofia but still has plenty of restaurant choices and nightlife.

If I were moving there though I'd probably head to Veliko Turnovo up north. It's the kind of place that, in a more popular country, would be jammed with tour buses and hundreds of bored waitresses would know how to say, "Anything else?" If a luxury hotel opened, *Travel + Leisure* would soon be calling it the next "hot destination." That's because it's a beautiful town with lots of historic character and houses clinging to a hillside overlooking a river and a stone fort. There's a university to ensure lots of life and culture, and there's plenty to see and do in the countryside. It was the seat of power during Bulgaria's heyday in the 1300s, when the king's territory extended to three seas.

Bulgaria has done a major about-face from the Soviet era in one respect: it's quite open to foreign investment and business formation. Because of this, many find that coming here with a bit of money and some patience presents a lot of opportunities for entrepreneurs. Taxes are some of the lowest in the EU and there are relatively few bureaucratic hassles compared to many other countries on the continent.

While Bulgaria is part of the European Union, it has not met the requirements to use the euro as its currency. Instead you'll be withdrawing Bulgaria lev, plural leva, which generally trades at a rate of 1.6 to 1.7 to the dollar, roughly 2 leva to the euro.

Housing Costs

Joanna Newman wasn't even considering a move to Bulgaria until she saw a house for sale online that was too crazy cheap to believe. "I had a shop on eBay and while I was working one day a house for sale in Bulgaria popped up, it was a silly price and it piqued my interest. I showed my husband and we watched it to see what would happen," she explained.

"After this we checked out other eBay sales then looked elsewhere on the internet and did a lot of research. We decided to take a trip out to see the country, meet the people, and look at houses." After falling in love with the first place, they ended up buying three properties for investment. "We found our dream home after looking at many houses over a couple of days. It was the third house we said we wanted. Had we seen it first we would only have bought this one. As soon as the gate was opened it was just love at first sight."

What did she spend on this nice country home in Vinograd, northern Bulgaria? A whopping 8,000 pounds sterling, which was around $13,500 at the time. "In the UK it would cost hundreds of thousands of pounds!"

If you've got money to invest, real estate prices here are among the best values I've seen anywhere in the world. You can find a wide range of village houses and city condos listed at less than €20,000. In the top ski destination of Bansko, larger condos with a view go for what works out to $60 a square foot. That's $48,000/€35,000 for a 2BR newly constructed condo of 800 square feet. Really nice places in prime areas in Sofia seldom top €100,000 in the real estate office windows. This is one of the few places in Europe where you can get a condo with a sea view (on the Black Sea coast) for less than €70,000.

Technically foreigners can't own land, but there's an easy way around this by setting up a local corporation and buying through that. No local has to have a partnership or ownership stake. You can buy a condo as an individual very easily.

Rental prices are a good value in the capital, a screaming bargain in smaller towns. In some of the villages it seems like every second or third house is empty because the owners are off working in another European country with better job prospects. So, it's a renter's market and if you have feet on the ground you should be able to find a furnished rental house for one-fifth or less what you would pay where you live now. If you ask how much a place is in one of the villages, they might ask, "Well, what can you pay?"

A decent two-bedroom apartment near the Sofia city center would cost at least €300," says Todor Bozhinov of Kashkaval Tourist, a European travel site.

Outside of the center of Sofia the rent decreases by around 50€ per month for the same space and if you venture further out the accommodation is even cheaper. It's still possible to find a one-bedroom apartment under €200 on the edge of the city and you can get a house for that amount in some villages. To buy a place in Sofia averages under 100€ per square foot unless it's a luxury development in a prime neighborhood for executives.

While most working expats settle in the Bulgarian capital of Sofia, many bargain hunters head elsewhere. They go to the second city of Plovdiv, where rents drop by 1/4 to 1/3, the ski area of Bansko, or into smaller towns that are downright cheap.

Sarah Carter and her husband own a 400 square-foot studio in Bansko that they bought "at the top of the market unfortunately" in the late 2000s for €40,000, but it's right by the ski gondola and the complex has an indoor pool, sauna, whirlpool, outdoor pool, garden, and security. "If you're willing to buy in an older building or a little further of a walk," she says, "You could easily buy a studio condo for less than €20,000 right now." I found listings of larger one-bedroom places for €20,000 to €30,000 doing a quick search online, two-bedroom places for not much more.

Sarah only pays about €900 a year for condo fees, property tax, maintenance, and someone to check in on the place now and then when they're out of the country.

Food & Drink

There's nothing wimpy about Bulgarian cuisine. Restaurant portions are so huge that most salads could easily serve two or three. Every time I ordered a glass of house wine, it was filled to the brim. A shot of *rakia* must be lifted carefully in order to avoid spilling any. If something on the menu says it's for two to share, assume those two will be bringing leftovers home unless they're really starving.

This is not filler food piled high and cheap, however. Outside of winter, plates are loaded up with fresh vegetables that are in season, all picked when they were ripe. The meat is from free-range animals because they can't imagine eating it if done another way. Of course, the beef is grass-fed and of course the bacon is really smoked in a smokehouse, not flavored by some nasty chemicals. Often when you eat in Bulgarian villages, the distances from the source are measured in walking distance, not highway markers. I'm not buying the premise that dairy is bad for you after seeing the muscle-bound men and curvy women of Bulgaria: every salad is covered with shredded cheese, usually with chunks of cheese in it as well, and a meal without yogurt is like, well, breakfast without cheese. They don't do this just to fill up; they do it because it's locally made and yummy.

Situated between Greece, Turkey, and Romania, Bulgaria has had a lot of different influences on its cuisine. A lot of it will seem vaguely familiar, while in some ethnic Turkish areas you'll feel like you're back in Anatolia.

"If you're coming to live in Bulgaria make sure you pack some bigger jeans because for really reasonable prices, you'll get a lot of food," says Maria Stoynova, a bilingual Bulgarian who runs the TravellingBuzz.com blog. "Eating out is very affordable. Bulgarians love having 'banichka' (a feta cheese pastry) and 'boza' (a thick malt drink) for breakfast, which costs no more than one euro for both. Restaurants, taverns and pubs are not only a local's favorite place for socializing but are also very easy on the pocket. A nice three-course meal in an inexpensive restaurant will cost you around 8-12 euros with drinks, so you can be wined and dined for very little money."

Sarah agrees and says they generally spend around 12 euros for two at a nice local restaurant in Bansko "so we go out to eat every other day I'd say."

"Most of the restaurants in Sofia offer lunch menus," says local Bilyana Petrova. "You can get only a main dish from the menu or have a 3-course lunch. For a 3-course lunch, expect to pay around €5 - 8 (under 10 bucks).

Nearly everyone makes their own wine. If you need to buy some, you can fill up a jug in the market for a couple dollars. A good bottle will frequently be $3 - $8 in a store. In restaurants, it's common to pay $4 - $8 for a typical table wine bottle, $8 - $15 for the best. "We buy a lot of Bulgarian wine and it's quite good," says Sarah. "A liter of table wine in a restaurant will typically be about $5 if it's not a touristy place. About the most we pay for a good bottle in a store is 25 leva, around 12 euros."

The delicious beer here is one of the best values on the planet, flavorful and varied but bargain priced. It's usually cheaper than ordering soda. Figure on 50 - 80 cents a liter in stores, $1 - $2.50 in a bar/restaurant for a half-liter bottle depending on decor. Liquor in a bar is as little as 75 cents for a shot of *rakia* (firewater distilled from grapes or plums), but generally $1-$2. Local vodka is as little as $2 a bottle for something drinkable in cocktails, imports are $3 - $9.

Non-alcoholic drinks like herbal tea and mineral water are the cheapest at 40 - 80 cents, coffee is often $1 or so or $1.50 for a nice cappuccino.

You can get good street food in Sofia for 50 cents to $2 that will fill you up. Typical menu prices for locals' restaurants are as follows: soups/salads $1.50 - $3, mains $2 - $6, desserts 50 cents to $1.50.

Fruit and vegetables are abundant, and bargain priced in season, though in winter most families switch to what's been preserved and pickled: not much is imported from warmer climates like it is in wealthier countries. You'll generally pay $1.40 a kilo or less for peppers, cabbage, potatoes, greens, grapes, plums, peaches, and turnips. Some items, like strawberries and fancy mushrooms, will be a dollar or two more. Dairy products are consumed with gusto here and are a great deal. Yogurt is around $1 a liter, milk $1.50, cheese is $4 - $6 a kilo fresh, $8 - $10 aged.

"Weekly groceries for me hover around 20 euros," says Todor.

"One of the great things about living in Bansko is the freshness of the food," says Sarah, "Fresh produce is abundant and cheap, and the sun-ripened tomatoes here taste better than any tomato I've ever had anywhere."

Transportation Costs
Once you figure out how to get to where you're going here, transportation is cheap. With the local wages being quite low, many public transportation options are subsidized to keep them affordable to locals. Local buses, metro lines, and streetcars are around 75 cents in the capital and can be less in smaller towns. Public transportation passes from three days to a month can bring down the cost even more if you're moving around a lot. Taxi fares range from 40 to 70 cents per kilometer.

The longest train route is the Sofia/Varna trip, which is $25 round trip in 2nd class. Sofia to Plovdiv is under $10 one way. First class is around 40 percent more on all routes. You can easily reach Romania or Turkey by train.

Inter-city buses are priced roughly the same as the train, at $3 to $15 one-way, but they are faster on some routes.

Bike rentals in Sofia are $1.50–$4 an hour, or you can work out a daily rate. If you're going to stay a while though, you can pick up a new or used one at a good price and in the warmer months you'll have plenty of company on two wheels.

Cars and fuel are both priced at typical European levels here, which make them expensive by local standards. It can be worth it to have a vehicle here though if you're not in one of the cities. You can easily do without, but having a car gives you the freedom to explore and you can drive to other EU countries easily. Rental prices are relatively standard, but parking is cheap: generally, one euro or less per hour.

If you buy or bring a car, there's a quarterly or annual fee with plate recognition that covers all the highway tolls in the country. It's around 50 euros for the year.

Healthcare
Joanna says she has had excellent healthcare and the cost is unbelievable. "My doctor is great and only charges 2 leva a visit and sometimes won't charge at all for a follow-up. I have been referred to a neurologist and was seen the next day. I was diagnosed, given treatment, and had a follow up appointment all for 14 leva (7 euros) & a big apology!"

Residents from the UK love the local system because there is almost never a wait. While they may have had to schedule appointments weeks or months ahead in their home country, here you can just show up and see a doctor most of the time, or at most you may have to wait until the next business day. A doctor's appointment seldom costs more than $25, even with x-rays or lab tests.

Medicine is not as cheap as the doctor visits though, especially name brand ones that require a prescription. Also, since hospitals tend to specialize, it can mean long journeys to get to the right one for regular treatments if you're not in the capital.

Sofia is a popular place for Europeans to come for dental treatment because of good care at a drastically lower cost. Crowns and implants are commonly one-third what they cost in Western Europe. Fillings and check-ups are one-quarter or less.

Permanent residents can tap into the national healthcare system, though with costs so cheap to pay out of pocket, most just use it as an emergency backup. In general, the doctors in Bulgaria are well-trained and in the cities the hospitals are good. This is a country with limited resources for the national healthcare system though, so you may not find the breadth of new equipment you would in a developed country. There is also a shortage of nurses since many experienced ones find they can earn far more in other European countries, so they move.

Other Costs

To give you a rough idea on utilities, here's what Joanna spends in her house. "My electric is 50 leva per month ($33), water 5 leva ($3.30). Home phone with plenty of free minutes to call England is 16 leva per month ($11), internet 25 leva a month ($17), the mobile phone runs from 10 to 15 leva a month ($6.70-$10)."

For Sarah, their condo fee includes internet and water, so they just pay about €40 per month for electricity, which they use for heating or A/C, the washing machine, and cooking.

Todor says utility costs don't vary much from year to year in Sofia. "Under €50 for electric, heating, and water is pretty normal, though in winter it could be a bit more." he says." Home internet service is €10 - €15 per month and Bulgaria surprisingly has some of the fastest internet speeds in Europe in the population centers.

You can also get a maid to clean your place regularly for €4 - €8 per hour. A guy will spend €7 - €8 for a haircut in a nice business neighborhood in Sofia, less in a working-class one or in a small town.

A local SIM card and data for a mobile phone won't cost you much, around $6 for 2GB of data for a pay-as-you-go plan and about the same for a new card to get started.

It won't cost you much to go sightseeing here. Only the Rila Monastery gets busloads of foreign tourists and that's free (like all churches and monasteries here) unless you want to visit the museum or tower. I visited stunning caverns, amazing citadels, and a great ethnographic village, all for 4 lev each, (less than $3).

Most museums and attractions are in the $1.50–$4 range for adults, half that for kids and students. The national park hiking trails are free and there are inexpensive mountain huts and hostels to stay in along the way. Skiing prices will make you think you took a time machine back to the 1980s. The most expensive walk-up one-day lift ticket in the country is under $40 and that's for a place where you can catch a gondola right in the center of town that takes you to the summit. Some slopes are half that amount. Full rental equipment packages are most commonly 10 euros a day ($12) for a basic package, a few euros more for an upgrade to demo level equipment.

"It's great to catch up and take our time indulging in doing things like going to the cinema, which only costs around 3 to 5 euros," says Maria. "If you're feeling like doing something a little fancier a ticket to the theater can be found for 5 to 10 euros."

Sarah says one of the great benefits of living in Bulgaria is how cheap it is to explore the country as a traveler. "We take a lot of trips around and generally spend $20-$25 per night for a comfortable hotel with a private bath where someone speaks English."

Visas
As in the other Schengen countries, those from outside the EU can visit Bulgaria for 90 days, but then you must leave the whole region for that long before starting the clock ticking again. So, if you want to stick around longer, you need to apply for a "type D" long-term visa at a Bulgarian consulate or embassy in your own country, come in on that, and then apply for a long-term residence permit after arrival in Bulgaria. You'll have 90 days to work that out and get approved, though if you've got all the right paperwork it should take a week or so. That's good for a year until you have to go in and renew it, but you must spend six months and a day in the country. (This would seem impossible to check if you've traveled within the EU of course.)

You can apply as an employee, freelance professional, or pensioner. Since employment is hard to find in this country, a work permit is mainly limited to English teachers, ski instructors, specialized tour guides, and those working for international corporations where English proficiency is essential. For the other two, proof of sufficient income to support yourself is the main criteria. If you have a clean record and can demonstrate you'll be bringing money into the local economy, you should get approval.

Sarah says it's quite easy to get a resident permit, as long as you have the patience to put up with a day of bureaucracy. "You are supposed to open a local bank account, but you don't have to show a high income or have a lot of money in the bank to show them."

After five years as a long-term resident, you can apply for permanent residency. After five years of that and fluency in Bulgarian, you can apply to be a citizen.

If you've got half a million dollars lying around, you can also buy your way to permanent residency by investing it in Bulgaria.

If you're looking for a place to lower your taxes (if you're not American), some parts of Bulgaria offer a flat 10% income tax. "So, you're starting to see a lot of digital nomads and retirees moving here to save on taxes," says Sarah.

Downsides

Bulgaria is cheap for a reason: it's one of the poorest countries in Europe when you look at per capita GDP, average wages, or middle-class wealth. The bloated communist system employed everyone, but now that everyone is on their own, the country is still struggling to attract enough industry to keep its population occupied and the entrepreneurial spirit has been slow to catch on with locals. There's an upside there for foreigners with good business skills, but of course you'll have to prepare plenty of paperwork in a foreign language, which will require a local English-speaking attorney and some patience.

"Everything takes much longer than you would expect," says Sarah. "Trying to sort things out in a short period of time is probably not going to happen."

Much of the infrastructure in Bulgaria dates back to the Soviet era and hasn't had much attention since, with the exception of surprisingly fast internet for those who have it. (Broadband is widespread in the larger cities.) The admission into the EU in 2007 has had some positive impact, but it has also resulted in a lot of fake improvements just for show. There are recycling bins all over the place, for example, but all the locals say the separated items just get dumped in with the regular garbage. Internet and fast cellular data penetration here remain low in some parts of the countryside.

There is frequent petty crime in the larger cities, including pickpockets, plus there is a significant organized crime element that you don't want to get on the wrong side of. The police force isn't known for being highly effective.

The Bulgarian language is an especially tough one to crack and they don't use a Roman alphabet. It's Cyrillic, like Russian. But it's not quite the same as Russian, so you'll need a good phrase book or app and some language lessons just to navigate the road signs or bus schedules.

"Learning Bulgarian is really hard, especially when you are older," says Joanna. "Mine is rubbish. I can say basic Bulgarian and talk pidgin fashion, but I have friends who took lessons and are coming along great. It is a really difficult language for me and many others to grasp that many words mean the same thing and the way you say them is very important." She gets by with the basics and pantomime and has both Bulgarian and Russian friends, "but I do wish I could speak better and have better conversations with them."

Thankfully, the English proficiency gets better all the time, especially with the younger crowd. "There's a massive difference between when we first came here 13 years ago and what it's like now," says Sarah. "Back then it was often a struggle to find someone who spoke English. So, a lot of Brits set up businesses and did quite well. Now you see local Bulgarians running businesses catering to foreigners because their English is good."

The population can still seem quite old in the rural areas: all the youngsters have left to find work in another country or at least the capital of Sofia. Some are starting to come back and start businesses, but not as many as there are leaving each year.

Shopping for clothes and durable goods leaves a lot to be desired. "Bring all the electrics, tools, and furniture you can with you as the quality here is really bad and costs a lot," says Joanna.

Also don't expect all Bulgarians to welcome you with open arms. T.W. Anderson lived in Sofia for several years before moving to Mexico. "In Bulgaria, the older people flat out hate Americans. We were the enemy in the communist days and some of them haven't forgotten it."

For More Information:
Kashkaval-Tourist.com
TravellingBuzz.com
Justlanded.com/english/Bulgaria/Bulgaria-Guide
Owlovertheworld.com/category/bulgaria/

Chapter 14:
Cambodia

Pros: ultra-low prices, easy visas, good food, relatively good internet, beach getaways, attractive neighboring countries, cheap booze.

Cons: second-tier healthcare, limited school options, limited property purchase abilities, tropical heat and mosquitoes, low literacy rate, poverty.

When I visited Cambodia with my family, we got two adjoining hotel rooms for $44 a night total, including a huge breakfast. It was air conditioned, had maid service, and they baked my wife a cake when they found out it was her birthday. We hired a tuk-tuk driver for the entire day for $14. Often our family of three would completely chow down on multiple courses in Siem Reap, I'd have a few beers, and my daughter would get a fruit shake. The bill would come, and it would be $11 or $12—in tourist places. We got a massage almost every day, including an hour-long four-hand one (two masseuses) for $10.

We were tourists, fresh off the bus, not knowing where to get the best deals. If we lived there, we would have paid less. At every price range level, Cambodia is a terrific bargain.

Picture a 2-bedroom apartment with a pool for $400 per month, a $5 massage for an hour whenever you want, a full-time nanny or housekeeper for $120 a month, meals out for $2, taxis for a dollar or two.

How much different would your life be if your expenses were in this range? What would it feel like if you were in the top 5 percent in household income just by earning a household income of $2,000 per month?

In most respects, Cambodia is the cheapest place to live in Southeast Asia. It's also one of the easiest to get set up in as a legal resident. It's not quite as simple as when I put out the first edition of this book, when you could get a year-long business visa by paying a guy at a motorcycle shop to take care of it for you, but it's still far easier (and cheaper) than Thailand.

Justin Garnett lived in the capital for years and stayed on because he liked the ease of renewing and using his business visa. "When you have that it's very easy to rent a space and open a bar, a restaurant, or a service business. As long as you don't do anything stupid, it's no problem."

Cambodia is not for everyone, of course. It's a hot tropical country with the bugs and diseases that implies. Most people fly to Thailand for serious medical care. The Khmer Rouge killed off two million people, including everyone who seemed intelligent or part of the "urban elite."

The country is trying hard to make up for lost time though, with minimal regulations, low taxes, and a mostly welcome climate for foreigners. Infrastructure spending has gone into overdrive this century and this is clearly an economy on the rise. Many young people speak English well and the U.S. dollar is the de facto currency for most transactions. The only time you even see the local currency in the main population centers is in the fruit and vegetable market.

About the only things that are going to seem expensive here are imported items, and even among those there are some happy surprises. Sin taxes are very low, so if you're a smoker or a drinker you won't pay a premium. Many Chinese items—like cheap cell phones—come in without extra duty. It's just when you're buying items the locals don't use or can't afford that you'll really see sticker shock.

When I asked Phnom Penh resident Humphrey, who grew up in New Zealand and has lived in England and Australia, what he spends on a regular basis, he stressed that he was living large and wasn't very careful with his money. "I earn about $2,000 a month and I spend about $1,500," he said. "Even in the nicest bars, it's still 50-75 cents for a small beer. Liquor here is cheaper than at duty free in an airport. If you spend more than $4 on a meal it is a fancy place."

The country attracts a fair number of "sexpats," though, like Thailand. "There are plenty of dirty old men on a pension down at the beaches especially," he adds, "and I know a few that easily get by on $1,200 a month. They live well on that amount."

Justin is a family man, so his story was very different before he eventually moved everyone to his home country of Australia recently. He had his family and a few relatives of his local wife in the compound, spending around $750 on rent, utilities, and maintenance for a 4-bedroom house "with a huge garden." He estimates that he probably spent $3,000 a month total, including education for the kids. "I lived a good life on this amount. I would pull up to the house and let the kids run inside. I always knew there's someone to take care of them. We never paid a babysitter."

In terms of where to live, this is not a huge country and the foreign population drops off rapidly after the first few choices.

Phnom Penh is the most popular choice for its wide range of apartments, nightlife, and restaurants. Siem Reap is a tourist town because of Angkor Wat, but it's also home to a fair number of expatriates, many of them lured by the boomtown atmosphere and the chance to build a business in a hurry. Cambodia's third-largest city, Battambang, has a fair number of expatriates amongst its population of 165,000, especially French ones.

The rest of the foreign population is mainly near the beaches. There's a coast to the south of the country, anchored by Sihanoukville, with multiple beach towns down the coast from there, with national parks and uninhabited islands breaking them up. This area has been through massive changes in the past decade though, probably more than any other city in this book. According to the travel trade publication Skift and confirmed by several former residents, after China invested a billion dollars in the city, tens of thousands of Chinese moved in and completely changed the character of the place. More than 100 casinos opened to cater to them and there was a rapid rise in shoddy construction projects. Rent prices went up with the rapid population increase and tour companies like Intrepid starting skipping it, citing increased garbage and reports of safety problems.

Then came the bust. The government started closing casinos and then COVID-19 hit, sending many Chinese back home. By then, most of the other foreigners had moved on to more desirable areas like Kampot. You can find a few island paradise spots offshore, but most of the land on those is protected and there are very few long-term rental options besides hotels.

Richard Sterling is a professor and author who has lived quite a while in Southeast Asia. "I came to Cambodia in 2014 by invitation of Pannasastra University, in the capital city of Phnom Penh, to teach journalism. Prior to that I had been living in Ho Chi Minh City since 2008 doing similar work, as well as writing a monthly column for *Asia Life Magazine*, which is published there. Rapid, uncontrolled development drove me out of Phnom Penh just as it had in Saigon. In 2017 I fled to the provincial town of Battambang in the far west of Cambodia, near the Thai border. Here it's like Lake Woebegone, Minnesota. A quiet little town where nothing ever happens. And nothing should happen. All is well as it is. I went to work at the local campus of Pannasastra U and here I still am."

"If I don't get crazy, my total cost of living is about $1,000 a month," Richard says. "I do have a friend, though, an American woman, whose regular monthly budget is $500 per month. She does live skinny, but she wants for nothing necessary, and she does put away a little something every month."

For the right kind of people, Cambodia is still a land of golden opportunity. Do your homework and give the place a trial run before making a move. If your funds are limited, however, this is probably the best bargain in Asia outside the Indian subcontinent.

Housing Costs

As with anywhere you'd want to live, it pays to take your time finding a place to stay to get the best deal in Cambodia. Patience will be rewarded. If you look online though, the prices are still quite reasonable even for those in a hurry.

In Phnom Penh, the most expensive places are right by the river and you can pay as much as you do now if you want. That's where a lot of the corporate expatriates and local business tycoons live. Prices go down quickly as you count the blocks back from there. It is common to spend $250-$400 for a modern one-bedroom condo in an elevator building and $400-$750 for one that has several bedrooms and lots of facilities like a gym and pool. You can spend far more in a luxury building and far less if you're willing to live in a "Khmer style" local place on the outskirts with a very basic kitchen and no air conditioning. Doubling or tripling up with others will get you more value for your money since you can get more space and split the costs.

For those willing to spend time pounding the pavement though, there are plenty of deals. Surf the local message boards and you can find people living in three- or four-bedroom houses in the capital for $400 or less, one-bedroom places under $200. "We only pay $400 per month in rent (including utilities) plus $50-$80/month for electricity," says Jen Joslin, half of the couple behind the TwoCanTravel.com blog. "Our rent includes housekeepers who come twice a week. Previously we lived in a 3-bedroom Cambodian style apartment for $350 per month on the west side of the Russian Market. There we paid $75-100 for utilities (trash collection, internet, water, electricity) and $40 a month for a housekeeper who came twice per week."

In Siem Reap, prices are far lower. If you spend $600 there, you're likely going to have a swanky villa with a pool, all utilities included. When I interviewed a hotel general manager living there when working on the first edition, he said he didn't know a single expat paying more than $500. Past that level, you're looking at a luxury multi-bedroom apartment or a whole house for rent. Many people work with a local real estate agent to save time and get around the language barrier. The owner pays their commission, not the renter.

Matt Gibson, who runs the digital marketing agency Upthink says $300 to $400 will get you a nice furnished expat one-bedroom place in a complex with a pool in Siem Reap. "If it doesn't have to be so fancy, you're looking at $150 to $200." If you spend $30 per night on a hotel room while you're looking it'll come with air-con, maid service, a great breakfast, TV, fridge, and maybe even a pool.

Go to a smaller town with fewer tourists and it drops again from there. "I've had a few residences in Cambodia. The cheapest was a studio apartment here in Battambang at $100 per month," says Richard. "The most expensive was a 4-bedroom, 5-bath house in a gated community with 24-hour security in Phnom Penh. That was $500 per month. Currently, in my 1-bedroom, fully furnished apartment, my rent is $140 per month and utilities run $10 - $30 depending on how much I use the AC.

Unfurnished places are generally less if you're coming for the long haul and will buy furniture. (You can get handcrafted wood items for very reasonable prices).

You can spend more of course if you budget is higher, and you want to live it up for less than you ever could in your home country. Some apartments come with a full amenities package of high-speed internet, security, elevator, parking, a rooftop pool, a gym, and western appliances for $500 to $1,000 per month. The latter being a three-bedroom luxury penthouse that a few playboys could share and only owe $333 each for rent.

In some of the beach areas, prices are still very reasonable for those who want to be near the water. Online you can find 1BR furnished apartments with A/C units and Wi-Fi included for as little as $200 per month, or large two- to four-bedroom houses for $400-$700. The most expensive long-term rental I could find online outside of the capital city was $1,500 a month. That was for a 7-bedroom/7-bath furnished mansion with a 2-car garage.

Buying in Cambodia is a bit tricky. Per the letter of the law, you can't buy land without partnering up with a local. There are a few ways around this though, like by establishing a local corporation with a Cambodian. This way when you "buy" a piece of property you really get a 99-year lease for the land it sits on via the partner. Since most people aren't going to live that long, it can work for a lifetime and you can still sell it or pass it on. But this requires a good bit of faith and a good attorney.

You can marry a local and then you can buy what you want as long as he/she is on the title with you. If you end up splitting up and leaving the country though, your spouse gets the house.

In general, you're better off buying a condo above the ground floor. That's straightforward and easy. Transaction costs are relatively low: negligible as a buyer, 7–8 percent as a seller, including the real estate agent's commission.

Purchase prices are all over the map so it's hard to generalize about what it's going to cost you just by looking at what's listed online. Since you should rent for a good while before buying anyway, take your time to find the right place in the right neighborhood.

In the capital, prices are very dependent on location. A condo in a prime spot with a river view in Phnom Penh could cost you more than $200,000. If you poke around is less prestigious neighborhoods though, you'll find nice modern condos under $100,000 and ones that can be renovated to suit for under $50,000. It's relatively easy to find a one-bedroom or studio in better shape for that price.

Get out of the main population centers though and prices take a nosedive. Justin rented a house for his extended family for $750 a month in the capital, but he also had a getaway place in the countryside that he owns. "I bought a block of land with a 3-bedroom house that needed some improvements," he says. "All told I spent $21,000 with an acre of land. If you buy land somewhere, you can build a home here for 10 grand."

Beach property here is still a relative bargain in some areas compared to the rest of Southeast Asia, though again you can't buy it outright as a foreigner. You need a corporation or a partner for a land lease arrangement.

Food & Drink
Matt moved to Siem Reap from Thailand and says one of the best upsides has been how good the food is in the former French colony. "There's surprisingly good food for surprisingly good prices. Even at the nicest places you're looking at a max of $10 for a main dish. The place I recommend the most does French Creole cuisine and they make their own rum, which you can get a sampling flight of before dinner for five bucks. That's the high end."

Ironically enough, most of the people frequenting the most expensive restaurants in the capital are staffers at charity organizations or other NGOs. If you splurge where they dine all the time, a meal for two will be $35 – $60 going all out with a bottle of wine.

"Here in Battambang, dining out can cost as little as $1 if I eat on the street," says Richard. "At the swankiest joint in town, having New Zealand Lamb or Australian beefsteak, about $25, depending on the wine I choose. On average, I pay about $5 for a dinner (without drinks)."

As long as you eat what's grown in the region and don't need a daily fix of imported items, this is a place where you could potentially eat out three meals a day and spend less than $6 if you go where the locals go. Step up to a nicer restaurant with waiters and you can still get a meal for a few bucks. If you spend $5-$8 on a meal it'll be in a pretty nice restaurant frequented by foreigners and probably include a beer or fresh fruit juice.

A can of beer in the store will be 50 to 75 cents. A draft beer will run 50 cents to $1.50 depending on whether it's happy hour (which in some places is 24 hours). A bottled beer will be 75 cents to $2. A soda or good coffee runs 50 cents to $1.50 in a restaurant or nice cafe. A fruit shake will be about the same. Cocktails here are some of the cheapest in the world, even with name brand vodka or bourbon, at $1–$4.

If you buy regional food ingredients in the market, you can stock your kitchen well for $20. For that amount you could get a week's worth of rice, vegetables, fruit, baguettes, and some meat or fish. "The local markets around probably about 60% of what the supermarkets cost you," says Matt.

Transportation
If you don't plan on having a car, transportation is not going to be a big part of your budget. Tuk-tuk prices in Siem Reap are actually lower now than they were 10 years ago, and you can rent one for the entire day for $10 - $15. "I feel kind of guilty about how cheap it is actually,' says Matt. "I always give them extra because if I use the Grab app or Passapp it will usually be around 75 cents for a ride into the center of town in a tuk-tuk, sometimes 50. There's a major oversupply of drivers."

In Phnom Penh, a taxi ride will run $1 to $4. If there's a meter, $1 per 2 kms, but often you have to negotiate. Ride sharing apps are less hassle sometimes.

Bus prices can vary a good bit on popular routes and you generally get what you pay for in terms of room, comfort, and the company's safety record. Here are some sample prices for getting around:

Siem Reap to Phnom Penh by bus: $8 – $17 (working A/C and Wi-Fi).
Bus from Phnom Penh to the beaches: $6 – $15
Taxi from Phnom Penh to the beaches: $40 – $60 (up to 4 people)
Bus from Phnom Penh to Saigon, Vietnam: $7 – $14
Bus from Siem Reap to Bangkok: $22 to $30
Bus to Thai border from Siem Reap: $9 ($10 - $17 from the capital)

Foreigners technically aren't supposed to be able to drive a motorbike in Siem Reap, so if you rent one ($6-$8 a day) you might have to pay a "fine" of a dollar or two if you get pulled over. You can rent a bicycle for a couple dollars though. In the rest of Cambodia, you're fine on your own motorbike and can buy one for under $1,000 or rent from someone by the month.

You'll pay more to get to and from airports of course. You could end up paying $20 from the airport to your hotel, though getting back will cost half that.

Several budget airlines serve the county, so you can usually save some time and fly to other cities in the region for $50 to $200 one-way.

Healthcare
Every expat I've every interviewed about Cambodia suggests that money in the pocket for a flight to Bangkok or Singapore is the best healthcare plan. While there are some good hospitals in the capital city, the care is rudimentary in most of the other locations. In theory there's a public healthcare system, but you generally want to avoid the public facilities for anything beyond a minor injury. Here's how Brett Dvoretz of the WanderGoGo blog described one private clinic in Sihanoukville:

At the newly opened Eriko Clinic, you have the option of either a Ukrainian doctor, with limited English abilities who prescribes drugs at random without asking any questions about other medications you might be on or giving any instructions on how best to take the meds he is prescribing. Your other option is a Chinese doctor with no English abilities whatsoever. When I saw him with an ear infection, he wanted to prescribe me serious antiviral drugs that would generally be given to people suffering from HIV or other severe life-threatening viruses.

He added, "At least in the capital you have the option of a few hospitals that actually have English-speaking specialty doctors, sanitary room conditions, and some of the technology needed to diagnose and treat semi-major medical problems."

The good news is, you won't pay much to visit the doctor. Prices at the best private facilities will be $15 to $40 per visit, even for a specialist.

Dental care is a different story for some reason, with far more internationally trained dentists at work and an emerging medical tourism trend for care here. Expect to pay $15 to $40 for a cleaning and check-up, less than $100 for a crown or root canal.

You can buy nearly any drug you would want or need over the counter here, but as with many countries where a lot of Chinese people are running shady scams, you need to be careful about what you're actually getting. Stick with the larger chains that are regulated and avoid the corner store with half-stocked shelves.

Other Costs
Utility costs can be all over the map and are impacted a lot by how much air conditioning you use. Some rental units include utilities, but most of them don't. Cambodia does not subsidize fuel costs, so although this is a cheap country, energy is purchased at world market rates. So, electricity costs will depend greatly on how heavily you are running air conditioning. Most locals of normal means go without, but when I visited in July because of school schedules for my daughter, the mercury was passing 100F degrees (38C) on a regular basis. The cost for electricity was 20 cents per kilowatt hour as I wrote this, which equates to $80 to $200 a month for many expatriates. Yes, it could be possible to have a power bill that's almost as high as your monthly rent.

The rest of your utilities will be cheap though. Water is $5 a month, tops. Garbage pick-up varies from $1 to $20 per month depending on the size of the house or business. The cable TV bill will be around $10-$20, internet $10-$35 depending on speed and location.

Domestic help will be even less. "I know the Siem Reap hotels are paying full-time housekeepers around $140 a month, so you can extrapolate from that what it would be to hire someone part-time for domestic work," says Matt. There's no national minimum wage across all sectors, but for garment factory workers it was $190 per month in 2020—higher than most jobs because of international pressure on big brands manufacturing here.

The local cell phone market is very competitive, so most expats get a SIM card for $5 or less and spend $25 per month at most on calls and data.

You can easily get a massage for $5 for an hour, or a four-hand one (two masseuses) for $10–$15. A manicure or pedicure runs $3–$5. Laundry service is $1–$2 per kilo.

Taking local tours of any kind will be a minimal expense. If you want to tour remote villages or kayak on a lake with a guide, often $10 to $15 will set you up with pick-up service from where you're staying.

Clothes are cheap if you can wear local sizes, but you might want to go custom if not. "I recently bought a pair of counterfeit Nike shoes for $6," says Richard. "Otherwise, all my clothes are made to order by a local tailor. She charges me $10 per garment (plus the cost of material, a small amount)."

Visas

Coming in on a tourist visa only gives you permission to stay for 30 days, though it can be extended once (and only once) for another 30 days for $45. Anyone intending to stay for longer should get a longer-term visa. You used to be able to get a business visa just for the asking, but that got scaled back a couple years back and now you have to apply for it.

Matt got a six-month visa that allows you to work if you want. He just has to leave the country and return every six months to renew it. "I think I paid around $250 all-in for it including agent fees," he says.

With that visa, you don't have to worry about sneaking around if you want to tend bar or take scuba divers out for PADI certifications. "This is one of the few countries in the world where you can just roll up and work," says Humphrey. "It's not like Thailand."

"From my arrival in Cambodia till earlier this year I was on a work/business visa," says Richard. I spent $305 per year plus a work permit at $100 per year. Just before COVID-19 struck I had decided to take some time off. I switched to a retirement visa (very easy to do) at the same price, but with no need for the $100 work permit."

You can buy your way in too, by investing enough money in the country that you're granted citizenship.

A foreigner may be granted honorary Cambodian citizenship if he or she donates a significant sum of money to the Royal Government of Cambodia for the purposes of benefiting the people of Cambodia. Foreigners who have made a special impact or rendered exceptional help to the Kingdom may also be granted this honor in recognition of their expertise or altruism.

Does "significant sum" sound vague to you? In practice, it is. Some have bought citizenship for as little as $50,000. Others have paid more than $250,000.

Downsides
Cambodia is very poor, more than a little corrupt, and doesn't have a ton of money to spend on infrastructure. Some people are drawn to this lack of regulation and (almost) anything goes approach to building codes, driving, and starting a business. For others though, the lack of basic services and the deplorable condition of some roads is too much to deal with after a while. It has gotten a lot better though as tourism has increased and the government has gotten more stable, so if the trend continues, infrastructure should keep improving little by little.

You can't drink the tap water, food-handling methods may not be up to your satisfaction, and customer service may not be super-quick or efficient. The power grid is overtaxed in parts of the country, so there can be outages that last for hours or a day. Most people have backup generators. For serious medical issues, most foreigners fly to Bangkok.

This is a tropical country, with all the creepy crawlies that implies. The less urban your location, the more you can expect to see mosquitoes, spiders, and other insects. Large rats and snakes aren't uncommon either.

There are serious problems with environmental degradation, human trafficking, corrupt NGOs who use children as donation pawns, and other frequently encountered third-world problems. There's a fair bit of crime in the capital, including bag-snatching. How well you can deal with all this without screaming will determine how happy you'll be living in this libertarian paradise.

Also, you don't move to Cambodia without being ready to roast sometimes. "Honestly, the only drawback I really complain about is the heat," says Matt, who grew up in Canada. "It's *extremely* hot here for about half the year, then just tolerably hot the rest of the year. I have a nice bike I like to take out for a ride, but if I'm not back by 8:00 a.m. it's just unbearable."

For More Information
Khmer440.com/chat_forum
Movetocambodia.com plus e-book of the same name
Cambodia sections of TransitionsAbroad.com and ExpatExchange.com
Plus see expat boards on Facebook

Chapter 15:
Colombia

Pros: great climate in Medellin, beaches, adventure activities, scenery, nightlife, culture, long tourist visa, easy residency, air connections, strong economy.

Cons: medium street crime, two rainy seasons, chilly capital, long surface connections between cities, so-so cuisine, expensive real estate in some areas.

I know what you're probably thinking, but today's Colombia is a far cry from the one that hosted Carlos Escobar's cocaine kingdom. As an article in the *Telegraph* said, "At the peak of Escobar's reign, in 1991, the murder rate was 381 per 100,000 people. Simply stepping outside your front door was an enormous risk—children were not allowed to play outside, and when relatives left home for work in the morning you never knew if they would return that evening."

Now the murder rate is a tiny fraction of what it once was. The nation's economy is often growing at a clip of 5 percent or more and many international companies are basing their Latin American operations here. Thanks to a long and steady decline in the Colombian peso though, the big cities of Colombia are now cheaper than those of Mexico or Panama, especially when it comes to rents. Traveling around the country is cheaper than it was 15 years ago. The quality of life is generally good too.

Peter Lombard runs incentive travel and team retreats company Globe Guides. He is rather typical in the sense that he moved to Colombia for a slower pace of life and a lower cost of living combined. He lives in Bucaramanga now and has no intention of leaving. "My lifestyle here involves more walking, more community, more actual relationships (not just virtual ones). I like the fact that food is made fresh, that people make the time to enjoy what they have (even if it may be deemed minimal by American standards), and that work isn't the overwhelming priority."

Steve McPeek, who is retired, lives in Medellin and absolutely loves it. "I live in an Airbnb and pay about $325 a month for rent (including utilities), $400 for food and the rest for entertainment. I eat all lunch and dinners out unless I feel like cooking. I can usually live on $1,000 to $1,100 a month unless I decide to indulge. I walk every day and along with better food, I have already lost 10 pounds. Other than the pollution and rainy season, I have no complaints. I am a pensioner and I can bank more than 2/3 of my money each month, which I use for travel. I plan to stay here unless a disaster happens which would force me to leave." He sees few downsides though, so he doubts that is going to happen, partly because "The weather in Medellin is the best I have ever experienced."

Colombia is at the top of South America, with the Darian Gap jungle between it and Panama. After decades of dealing with paramilitary separatists, drug cartels, and one of the world's highest murder rates, it is now like a whole different country. Crime is now lower than in many neighboring nations and tourism is growing at a healthy clip. Expatriates who live here rave about the agreeable climate in Medellin, the culture and nightlife in Bogota, and the walled city grandeur of beachside city Cartagena. Santa Marta has even nicer beaches, on the Caribbean, while others who have moved here choose to live in a small interior town or city with lower prices and fewer tourists.

This is a country of varied climates, from sea level to high Andean peaks. It's one of the world's largest coffee producers, but also grows a staggering number of fruits and vegetables at different altitudes. Ask people what they like about Medellin and the weather usually comes first in this placed nicknamed the "City of Eternal Spring." There are two rainy seasons though, which can range from mild to ongoing deluges from year to year. GoBackpacking.com editor David Lee spent a lot of years in Medellin and says if expats complain about something, that's usually it. Bogota is higher and colder. It has the big city attributes on the plus side (museums, great restaurants, the arts), but also more of the normal big capital city problems and in addition to the worse weather.

Traveling around the country is not as cheap as somewhere like Bolivia or Ecuador, but prices are reasonable, and comfort can be higher. Domestic tourism is actually most of the tourism here, so prices are geared to locals nearly everywhere. There are lots of little rustic hotels dotted around the countryside, many priced below $35 a night with breakfast. A zipline trip I did in the coffee region was $20—less than I paid in Guatemala many years earlier. A tandem paragliding trip outside of Medellin is $32.

Avianca, one of the major airline players in the Americas, is based in Colombia, so assuming they survive the travel lockdown that was happening worldwide as this book went to press, you can expect frequent air connections in normal times. Several international airlines fly here, including Copa, American, and budget carrier Spirit.

You get a three-month visa upon arrival as a tourist and you can extend that to six months without leaving the country. That's the limit in one calendar year but getting residency here is relatively straightforward and there are multiple visa types for different situations.

Americans who move to Colombia generally spend half or less than they did in their home country, while going out more and eating more meals in restaurants. "I try to limit myself to less than $1,200 per month, as a 'rule' but can sometimes go over if I have to have some dental work done or whatever," says Ryan Shauers. He runs the Desk to Dirtbag blog and writes a lot about life in his adopted country. He has lived in Medellin for several years and included in his budget is "$100-150 or so for traveling to nearby pueblos."

Jason Bennett, who leads marketing for Colombia-based hospitality and real estate investment company LifeAfar, owns his own condo. He says, "My expenses range from $750 - $1,000 with household expenses (utilities, property tax, insurance), groceries, dining out, and transportation. I would expect another $100 - $200 once I am eligible for the healthcare system."

Business owner Matt Seager has lived in several spots in Colombia, mostly in the Coffee Triangle region and on the Caribbean coast. "I have generally spent in the range of $1,700 - $2,500 per month," he says. "This covered everything from rent, food and entertainment, some local activities and excursions, and money for partying. One consideration is the strength of the Colombia peso to USD, which is more favorable to Americans today than it was a few years ago. Costs have actually gone down. The coffee region is a great value as it has several university cities like Manizales, Pereira, and Armenia. The Caribbean coast also has good pricing in Santa Marta, Palomino, and Minca, which is a great value in the Sierra Nevada mountains."

He says an income that would have you struggling to pay the bills in the USA lets you live it up in Colombia. "For $2,500, you can live like a king in the sense that you can have your own apartment in a decent area, and be able to basically do whatever you want in terms of activities, eating out, etc."

Be advised though that the country's main tourism draw, Cartagena, is significantly hotter and significantly more expensive than living elsewhere, especially if you compare it to interior locations. You're competing with wealthy Colombians and

Venezuelans who have long seen a condo or home here as a solid second home investment. Most of the tourists who come here are on a short jaunt vacation budget, spending freely.

Housing Costs
Rental prices are attractive throughout Colombia, but Cartagena is in its own world. Rental prices in the historic walled city and at the beaches are geared to short-term vacation renters and this is a favored spot for wealthy investors. "Real estate prices here are on par with those in Miami," says Paul Juan of CartagenaRealty.com. You may not be able to live here for half what you were spending at home unless you're coming from a high-priced city like New York, London, or San Francisco. Santa Marta, four hours away, is a better beach deal.

One of the interesting facts about living in Colombia that you discover when apartment hunting is that the system is very socialist or progressive depending on your point of view. Apartment rental prices in Medellin and other big cities closely align to their zone because taxes and utility costs also vary by zone. So, a "Zone 6" house will have the highest rates and a "Zone 1" place will be in a slum—but with super-cheap subsidized utilities. Most foreigners who are getting corporate housing paid for by an international corporation end up in a 6, while most independent workers on their own dime find a compromise in 4 or 5.

Jason Bennett says that if he didn't own a place already in the best part of Medellin, he would probably have to pay $1,200 to $1,500 in rent for a similarly furnished place in a new building with 1,000 square feet and great views. This is the tippity top of the market though and usually if someone is paying that much on their own, they've got a partner or at least one roommate.

Ryan is paying around $400 a month for rent and utilities combined in his Medellin apartment. "The cost for a house or apartment is an incredible value, at least for someone who was originally from Seattle and then lived in Washington D.C. Back in college I was paying $500 a month for a tiny studio apartment in Seattle. Then in D.C. there were 'English basements' which were going for $1,200 a month. Here in Medellin I can pay $315 a month for a spacious three-bedroom, two-bath apartment with a balcony, in a great neighborhood that is walkable to everything."

"My last apartment in the north of Bogota ran $690 per month including HOA fees (called *administración*)," says former resident Jeff Jung. "Renters should find out both parts of the cost when looking for an apartment. You could find something old but decent for as low as $400 and spend up to $1,000 per month for rent only. I'm quoting unfurnished prices, so a furnished place might start closer to $500. Gas and electricity will run about $15 and $50, respectively, per month. Cable and internet can run closer to US pricing at $50-80 per month. A common money-saving tactic of Bogotanos is to live with others so you can get a larger, nicer place with all common housing costs shared."

"In a university city like Manizales, a small studio apartment can be found for around $300 per month" says Matt. "Furnished apartments are not as common but can be found in the $350-$500 range. If a person is willing to share an apartment with another person this will lower the monthly expense. For short-term stays, a single private room can be found in a hostel, pension, or family-owned hotel for $15-25 per night. Rooms can be rented for weeks or months at a time in these establishments for even less if you ask. I usually pay around $300-$400 a month for a decent sized private room with private bathroom in a small hotel in Manizales, with internet and cable TV included."

"My monthly expenses, aside from travel, are roughly $1,000 a month," says Peter. "This includes a lovely 3-bedroom apartment in a secured high-rise in Bucaramanga, food, transportation, utilities, and even someone to come in and clean on a weekly basis. I do run my American companies from here, so I spend a bit more on Telcom than average, but even high-speed internet and unlimited calling together cost me less than $100."

Sasha Savinov and his partner Rachel were digital nomads for many years before staying put in Medellin and teaching English online a few hours a day. (They blog about their experiences at GratefulGypsies.com). "We pay $740 a month for our large furnished apartment in Medellin, including all utilities," Sasha says. "It was actually an Airbnb place we had rented for a week and then we negotiated a long-term rental with the owner after we decided we liked it enough to stay in it long-term. You can easily find something for a similar price if you spend some time on the Facebook groups here."

It's easy to find a good-sized house for under $50,000 in the smaller towns and cities of Colombia. That's especially true if you don't mind buying something older: the resale market for existing homes moves slowly here so you can get a great deal from someone who has been trying to sell the place for years. Just take your time to look around for the right deal. If small-town Colombia appeals to you, unfurnished rental houses can be found for as low as $100 per month and $400 can get you something with a lot of indoor and outdoor lounging space.

If you really want to keep your expenses down for a while and immerse yourself in Spanish at the same time, you can find a homestay arrangement with a family quite easily where you get your own room in a private house and your meals are included. This arrangement runs from $300 to $500 and gets your two main expenses covered for cheap. You'll give up a few things though, like privacy and diet choices, plus you had better check the internet speed when evaluating places if that's important to you.

Food & Drink

Columbian food generally isn't anything to write home about, with ingredients prepared simply, without much spice or enhancement. It's satisfying and filling though, with the usual Latin American staples, plenty of seafood near the coasts, and *arepas*.

A decent "meal of the day" lunch will run you about $5 throughout Colombia. You can certainly pay less at places where local workers eat or spend a few dollars more and get much better quality. That'll generally get you a soup, a main meat dish with a side or two, dessert, and a fresh juice or something else to drink.

"Breakfast is a small and cheap meal, but lunch presents an opportunity for a great value at local restaurants," adds Matt. "Lunch specials are often generously portioned and priced. For example, a large chicken cutlet served with salad, rice, fries, and a drink can be purchased for $3-$4 in a local restaurant in Pereira or Manizales. The same meal with fish replacing the chicken cutlet can be found in Santa Marta for roughly the same price."

"Dining out is an incredible value," Jason says. "I usually spend around $5 for lunch and for dinner it is very hard to spend more than $20 including a couple drinks."

Dinner options ranged from cobbled together street food for a couple dollars up to high-end restaurants at a 5-star hotel that will cost nearly as much as you would spend in Europe. In general, the food is not worth raving about, as there's limited variety in what's traditional fare and you have to be in a city to go beyond that. You can get plenty of fresh ingredients for cooking yourself though and prices average out to half or less what you'd pay in a developed country.

Everyone I've spoken to who has lived in Colombia says they eat better and feel healthier after moving there. "Fruit is the way to go—incredibly varied, delicious, and cheap throughout the country," says Matt. The list of vegetables you can get for a dollar a kilo or less is a long one: potatoes, tomatoes, onions, peppers, and greens for a start.

"We generally spend about $60 a week on groceries," says Sasha, "plus it's not expensive to go out in Medellin unless you're ordering cocktails. There are lots of happy hours and a beer will often be $1.50 to $2 in a bar. Aguardiente is the cheapest buzz for the buck, at a few dollars for a box of it, but all that sugar can lead to a rough hangover."

"You can get a big cup of chopped-up mango or papaya for less than a dollar," adds Jason.

Getting a great cup of coffee is harder than it should be in Colombia since most of the best beans are exported. There are a variety of quality coffee shops in tourist areas and expat zones though and the fallback choice if all else fails is the Juan Valdez chain. You can usually expect to pay about half what you would in the U.S. or Europe for a quality cup of Joe, far less for the little cups served everywhere, even on the street, for a quick pick-me-up.

You can drink alcohol on the street in Colombia, which makes walking around the walled city of Cartagena at sunset a lot more fun. Dave says going out to clubs and having a blast is not going to set you back very much in Medellin compared to a place like London, Las Vegas, or New York City. In a nightclub the usual routine is for the group to get bottle service. You pay $30 or so for a 750ml bottle of rum or less for aguardiente (the favored anise flavored local spirit) and you get ice and mixers. "Colombians go out in groups," he says, "so if there are five of you that's $6 a person. Very few places have a cover charge. If they do it's generally a couple dollars and at the most, maybe the equivalent of $12 at the very fanciest place."

This is one of those countries where you can still find dollar beers in a bar or restaurant when you order the domestic ones. "The cost of restaurants and nightlife in Medellin is pretty crazy," says Ryan. "You can go to an awesome local brewery and get five craft beers for about $8, which is sometimes what *one* beer costs back in the United States."

You can find a whole lot of different street food (*empanada, arepa con queso*, boiled/salted potatoes) for a dollar or less when you want to refuel for cheap. For a dollar you can also get a 600ml bottle of water, a local mass-market beer in a store, couple little *tinto* coffees on the street, a glass of fresh juice from a stall, or a kilo of seasonal fruit or vegetables.

Healthcare
Expatriates in general praise Colombia's healthcare system, which is simple, transparent, and has well-trained doctors in the cities. Care is quick and prices are displayed on signs, with rates that can start as low as $15 for a consultation with a doctor. To see a specialist is around $30 and an emergency care consultation from a doctor in a hospital is $50.

In Colombia you just take a number and wait your turn or for a specialist, make an appointment and probably be in the next day. Forget reams of paperwork and medical history you have to fill out in the USA before seeing the doctor. Here they'll only ask you what's relevant for the condition you're having, and the red tape is almost non-existent.

You'll seldom pay many extra fees beyond medicines and the tab for lab work is usually under $10. Just to give you an idea for comparison's sake, a full colonoscopy will be less than $100 and a mammogram less than $40. Sasha spent $55 to see an English-speaking doctor at a private hospital, including the cost for a batch of medicine.

If you have a family or are older and want to be safe, you can buy a local comprehensive health insurance plan for $250-$400 per month that will also cover you for 30-90 days outside the country. For Colombia only policies for a single person, figure on $150 per month or less. Steve pays around $100 per month for a health and dental plan that covers him within Colombia. Many get by with a travel insurance policy if they're healthy and don't know how long they'll be staying.

This is not really a "dental tourism" destination like Mexico or Costa Rica, but costs here are well less than half what you're probably spending now. A crown will be $250 to $450, a filling $35. Veneers that could costs you $2,000+ in the USA or UK will be more like $400 or $500 here.

Transportation
City buses are around 60 to 75 cents one way in most of the country. A one-way ticket on the nicest "TransMilenio" rapid bus line in Bogota will run you about 85 cents. The Medellin metro, bus, and cable car system ranges from about 65 cents to $1.30. A monthly pass is less than $30.

Taxi fare will seldom top $10 unless you're crossing a whole city or coming in from an airport. In Medellin the flag drop is $1.25 and then it's 40 cents per km. Prices don't vary from company to company and drivers here aren't usually inclined to take you for a ride to pump up the fare. "We generally pay $3 to $4 to get across Medellin to another neighborhood," says Sasha. Oddly though, taxis don't use a meter in Barranquilla, Cartagena, or Santa Marta, so you have to work out the fare before taking off. You might want to try a ride sharing service in those places to eliminate the hassle. Uber has been an on-and-off drama but should be available when you arrive—with a few local loophole arrangements to keep it legal. DiDi and Beat are alternative ride-sharing apps available in Colombian cities.

In smaller cities like Bucaramanga, taxi rates are low. "I pay somewhere in the area of $10-15 a week in Uber/taxi charges, with the average ride being somewhere between $1.20 - $1.90," says Peter.

Intercity buses are comfortable and have bathrooms: you generally won't have to deal with a "chicken bus" unless you're way off the beaten path. They start at around $7 for a three-hour trip and can cost as much as $50 for long overnight routes, so sometimes it's worth it to fly instead. The two most expensive air routes in the country are Bogota to Cartagena and Bogota to San Andres, but there are frequent specials if you book ahead. You can sometimes find internal flight fares as low as $45 and often the longest routes are going for around $100.

"Intercity long distance buses often cost me about $50 per ticket round trip," says Ryan, "but you can also get a ticket on a budget airline like Viva Air for about the same price if you book in advance and have some flexibility with your dates. "That will save you many hours on those winding mountain roads."

"They don't do straight roads here so it's hard to sleep and slow going, but it is cheap if that's your priority," says Peter.

Don't take the prices you pull up on Skyscanner or Kayak at face value, however, when you're checking domestic flight fares from abroad. "Domestic flights purchased from within Colombia are significantly cheaper than when purchased from outside the country," says Matt.

Colombia is the home base of Avianca, one of the two largest airlines in Latin America. Plus, it has several cities on the route map of Spirit Air, one of the bare-bones budget airlines in the USA. You can also connect to Copa via their hub in Panama City. So, this is a relatively inexpensive country to base yourself in if you plan on traveling outside the country a lot or visiting relatives on a regular basis. You won't be isolated here.

Cars are heavily taxed in Colombia and it's hard to find even the most bare-bones model for less than $15,000. So, if you try to buy a used car on the cheap, it will likely have high mileage, manual transmission, and no air conditioning. Gasoline is slightly more expensive than in the USA, but lower than Europe.

Other Costs

It won't cost you a lot to feel cultured in Colombia. Many museums are free on Sundays and when they aren't the cost is negligible. The Gold Museum in Bogota, for instance, is less than $2. Cultural events are often free, especially if affiliated with a university, and if not, you can usually get tickets for $10 or less. When I scoured ticket prices for Bogota and Medellin as I was writing this, I only found a few concerts priced higher than this, at $12.50 for the very best tickets. Admission to a national park will never top $9.

A cell phone with data will run around $10-$25 per month for the average person. "My pre-paid cell phone plan is another steal," says Jason. "2GB of data is about $10 per month. Same with my gym membership, just $20." Sasha says his gym membership in Medellin is a bit over $30 but includes lots of classes. A yoga class at a dedicated studio will be around $7 and a monthly unlimited membership will be under $50.

As mentioned in the housing section, Colombian neighborhoods are graded by income level. So not only does your neighborhood say volumes about how wealthy you are, it can also impact your utility costs. Those in strata 6 pay a much higher rate per kilowatt hour for electricity than those in strata 3, so you don't necessarily want to be in the same neighborhood as the captains of industry unless you have more money than you know what to do with. (Supposedly those in the poorest sections don't have it easy though: their rates may be lower, but the meter works on a pre-paid card system.) Renting in strata 4 or 5 can mean not just lower rent, but lower utility costs too. If you're not in strata 6 and you're a single or couple, you can expect to pay between $40 and $100 a month for everything, sometimes more with a very fast internet connection.

A lot of clothing is made in Colombia and if you stick to what's typically sold domestically, prices can be quite reasonable, though quality is hit and miss. Aspirational brands like Levis, Nike, and Adidas will cost more than you'd pay where you came from though.

Ditto for electronics, which you should bring with you or buy in duty-free Panama when possible.

Prescription medicines are drastically cheaper in Colombia and most non-narcotic items can be purchased over the counter without a prescription. That's if you can find it: I spent two hours hoofing it around Cartagena trying to find a specific allergy medicine for my wife and came up empty. The selection is better in larger cities.

Most people who can afford to have a housekeeper clean their house or apartment twice a week spend $120 to $250 a month depending on where they live. Sasha says the going rate in his apartment complex is $15 a week for a cleaning that takes about three hours.

Sasha adds that group Spanish classes in Medellin are a good deal, at around $140 for 20 hours in the classroom. There are often promo deals going on that can bring it down more and sometimes it's not much of a premium to upgrade to private lessons.

Visas
Is too much choice a bad thing? There are a head-spinning 17 options for a visa in Colombia, so some people throw up their hands and let a lawyer sort it out. The good news is, with that many options you can almost surely find one that will fit your situation. With plenty of patience and an ability to read forms in Spanish, you can manage it yourself in time. Otherwise, part with a bit of cash and let someone else sort it out.

Most of the residency permits cost $150 to $350, not counting what you may lay out for preparation or translations. In general, Colombia gets high marks for its visa application process. It's a lot of work, as always, but what's required is generally transparent and not subject to change every time you visit the office. With these many options though, laws do change regularly and there was an overhaul in late 2017. Make sure any article you read on the subject is more recent than that. The first level of straight temporary residency visa is good for six or twelve months, then you can apply for a longer period.

Steve is on a pensioner visa and says it wasn't all that daunting for someone who speaks Spanish, but he got some help to speed things up. "Initially I tried to apply on my own, but later changed my mind and hired a company to apply for me. The fee I paid was $450 for everything. My visa is good for 3 years and when it does expire, I have the option of extending it or leaving."

When you first arrive, a tourist visa will probably be fine. You get three months in Colombia upon entering the country as a tourist. To extend that another three months you can either leave the country and return or go apply for an extension for about $40. But you can only stay six months of a calendar year this way, so you have to get out after that and not return for half a year. "If you time this right though," says Sasha, "you could come in June or July, stay six months, then return in January when it's a new year."

Dave obtained a business visa by showing a steady stream of income and what he was working on. It's good for 19 months. He says some digital nomads and freelancers opt for an "independent activities visa" which is more ambiguous.

Those who have found local love can apply for a "civil partnership visa." If you're married to a local or are just declaring them as a civil partner, you can get a one-year visa that can then be extended to three years. After that, you can get permanent residency. For a work visa, you need to apply in your home country or Colombia, pay a non-refundable $50, and submit a slew of paperwork. This includes your work contract, a copy of your degree, a translation of that, and on and on. Once approved—which may take a few office visits to tie up loose ends—you then finish up with the rest of the payments.

If you're retired, the income requirement for a M-11 pensioner visa has actually gone down quite a bit since I put out the first edition of this book. That's because it's based on three times the Colombian minimum wage, which in dollar terms is a lot lower because of exchange rate erosion. Now you only need to show income of $710 or so per month—far less than the average American social security amount. That visa is good for a year and can be renewed indefinitely, but you can't be out of the country for more than six months at a time to keep the renewals going. So, it's not a good option for digital nomads.

You can buy your way in more quickly to get a "resident investor" visa, but that requires a real estate investment of at least $165,000. Still, for many people selling a property in the USA before they move abroad, this is a low hurdle. What you get for that amount, even in Cartagena, can be attractive. Outside the big cities, it will get you more space than you need. That residency can then lead to citizenship after five years, with a relatively valuable passport. You only have to spend one day in the country every six months.

A business owner visa cannot be for a sole proprietorship: you must be planning to hire local employees.

After you have been in the country for five years on temporary residency visas, you can apply for a "qualified resident visa" or a "permanent resident visa" that doesn't require regular renewals.

If you can read Spanish, see the link at the end to get the official word on all these and more from the Colombian government.

Downsides

Colombia has come a long way since its cocaine cartels made it the most dangerous country in the world for a while, but it's still not a fairytale land of peace and joy. The Medellin homicide rate has dropped dramatically, but it's still 25 per 100,000 people annually. That's lower than New Orleans and Guatemala City, but higher than a whole lot of other cities in the Americas. As usual though, most of this is turf war gang-on-gang violence. One out of every six murders is from a single bad neighborhood. Cali has gotten a bit less dangerous the past few years, but it still has the highest murder rate in the country, usually around 50 per 100,000 residents.

Some say the official stratification of the population by level of wealth holds down mobility and the poor are likely to stay poor for life. While wages at the bottom are low ($400 a month including benefits), many local business owners complain the quality of work is low too and getting rid of someone costs more than paying them. Still, the middle class here is a much larger percentage of the population than in many other countries profiled in this book.

Many who move here are less than thrilled with the food in Colombia, so their budget creeps up as they start frequenting more international restaurants to get some variety. While there are gourmet level restaurants in the cities, in much of the country real foodies are going to be disappointed.

Punctuality is not a prized trait here, even by Latin America's lax standards. Expect to wait around a lot for everything from business appointments to appliance deliveries.

Some foreign women admit having a tougher time than usual here finding someone to date. The competition is probably stiffer here than anywhere else in the Americas—at least in the opinion of most men I've talked to who live here or have traveled here. (There's a real reason all the people quoted in this Chapter are men—they vastly outnumber the foreign women.) You'll have a little easier time if you're a natural blond with blue eyes because you'll be exotic.

Overall, those who have moved to Colombia find plenty to be happy abou. Peter says the dramatically lower cost of living and slower pace he was seeking out have done wonders for his overall well-being. "My new life in Colombia allows me to life comfortably, pay down debt, and save towards a house, without having to work the hours I used to work. I'm more involved in my community, youth groups, church, and a healthy social life than I ever was in the states."

For More information
MedellinLiving.com
MedellinGuru.com
ColombiaVisas.com
Cancilleria.gov.co
Expat Exchange Colombia forum
See Facebook groups for individual cities

Chapter 16:
Ecuador

Pros: dollar economy, drinkable water in some areas, choice of climates, bountiful food, beaches & mountains, low fuel costs, mild inflation, ever-improving infrastructure, good retirement incentives, easy residency, low costs for nearly everything.

Cons: very little press freedom, autocratic government, extremely high alcohol costs, difficult to start a business.

When Bill Bushnell decided to move to Cuenca, the reasoning was very simple, "I looked at where my finances were and where they were going to be. I didn't want to be living in a double-wide trailer in the southern swamps somewhere, so I moved somewhere I could live really well on the same amount instead."

He and Leita Hulmes do live very well indeed. They own a luxury condo with a view of the mountains and the cathedral lights in the distance, with a terrace space of 1,000 square feet going around two sides of their building, plus a walk–in closet bigger than most bedrooms. There is even a maid's quarters with a separate entrance. Nearly everything inside was crafted by local artisans, including the custom stone fountain and the made–to–order living room set: two loveseats, four chairs, and two tables made from heavy hardwood, plus ten pillows thrown in without asking—delivered for under $2,000. They were so happy with the work that they got custom wood desks, file cabinets, and bookcases.

What they spent total is more than a double-wide trailer in Tennessee, yes, but far less than the average condo where they came from.

For Keith and Tina Paul, a trip to Guatemala from their home in California opened their eyes to how cheaply expats were living abroad. That sparked a lot of research and soul-searching and they eventually settled on Ecuador. "Three weeks after we put that country at the top of our list, we were on a plane to Cuenca, a place that seemed to meet all our criteria," Tina says.

"We were 54 years old at that time," says Keith, "After we realized how little money it took to live there, I gave my notice at work as soon as I got back and six months later we retired early and moved to Cuenca. We both had very stressful jobs before, so this was something we really strongly wanted to do." (They now run a popular blog called RetireEarlyAndTravel.com.) In between they took a trip down to line up a place to live and found a newly built apartment about a 10-minute walk from the center for $735, including all condo fees. "It's bigger than what we had in California," says Tina, "and there we were paying $3,600 a month in rent outside Pasadena."

The number of foreigners in Cuenca has swelled past 5,000 by most estimates, which is still less than one percent of the population, but that compares to fewer than 500 of them when Holly and Brian Walker arrived from Saskatchewan. "There is a Gringolandia area here, but I'm on the opposite side of the city, immersed in the local neighborhood," she says. "I'm shocked at how many foreigners I see now when I visit the center."

Holly has seen a dark side of this influx, with some "economic refugees" being bitter that they couldn't afford to live well on what they have in their country of birth. "Some don't even bother trying to learn Spanish and fit in. They get mad when they can't communicate in a store or restaurant in English."

Besides the low costs, Cuenca has become so popular because of the climate. While Ecuador's very name means "equator," its third largest city sits at an elevation of more than 8,000 feet (2,500 meters), so it has one of those cool spring climates with no mosquitoes that so many retirees crave. The daytime highs are around 70F most of the year, the lows around 50F. Pack a rain jacket and a windbreaker and you're set. (You will need the rain jacket a fair bit though: if you want year–round sun there are better choices.) Holly likes to take advantage of the great hiking opportunities nearby, especially in gorgeous Las Cajas national park.

After Cuenca, the most popular spots for expatriates are Quito, Vilcabamba, Cotacachi (near Otavalo), and beach towns on the coast. Vilcabamba, in a valley where many locals claim to be more than 100 years old, the elevation is around 5,000 feet. Temperatures average between 65F and 81F all year long and it gets more sun than Cuenca.

Can you name one beach in Ecuador? Most people can't, but there are some nice ones on this Pacific coast near the equator, with strikingly low prices compared to other coastal resort cities. Plus, thanks to ever-improving road systems, you can now get to them much faster from Quito (a few hours) or Manta (less than an hour). Because of Pacific current patterns, however, they're not popular all year because the water gets too cold for swimming outside the hottest months.

What does it cost to live in Ecuador? There's no easy way to answer this because it depends a lot on how you live. Some people have told me they live on a budget of $1,000 a month for a family, not counting travel, and live what they consider a pretty good life in Cuenca. There are other people in the city who pay twice that much for one person, living in a lavish apartment, driving a car, and eating at nice restaurants for dinner several times a week. Even at that level though, they're living a far better life than they could for twice as much in the USA, Canada, England, or Australia.

Holly and Brian moved to Cuenca from Canada after spending a lot of time in the country because of Brian's job as a helicopter mechanic. "It didn't really matter where we lived because his job was international," Holly explains. "He was six weeks on, six weeks off in various locations. But we really liked Cuenca after visiting a few times. Eventually we went back and sold our house and most of what we had except 13 suitcases between the 4 of us." Their son was older, but their daughter had just turned 16 when they moved down in 2008. She took classes online through the Canadian school system, while also going to a local Ecuadoran school and quickly becoming fluent in Spanish. Her daughter eventually went back to Canada and to a boarding school to finish and graduate. "The local schools have gotten a lot better since then," she adds. "In Quito there are also several international schools with high standards."

The government has put a lot of money and effort into improving Ecuador's schools the past decade and has roped in some American tech companies to help out with getting laptops into a lot of them. So, if you have children of school age to consider, get the current lowdown from expat families living in the country before assuming you won't be able to find a decent school for the kids. You should probably assume they will be learning in Spanish though, unless you're in Quito or Guayaquil.

Otherwise, family life is pretty easy here. You can find a big house or apartment to rent without much effort, feeding a family is cheap, and you can get domestic help for a few dollars an hour.

Ecuador is especially popular with retirees because of all the perks they receive. More on that in the visas section.

Housing Costs
Ecuador is not the rock-bottom buying bargain it was a decade or two ago for real estate. That's partly from more foreigners arriving, but more from an improving economy and the return of lots of Ecuadorans who made a pile of money abroad. It's still a great value to rent or buy here though, with prices half or less

(sometimes a *lot* less) than what they would be in a comparable city or town in the USA or Canada.

John Potts moved to Quito from London after traveling around South America and now runs the Happy Gringo tour company (HappyGringo.com). "I spend approximately $1,000 per month to live comfortably," he says. "This does not include rent as I bought an apartment, but it includes all other living costs: food, transport, bills and eating out at decent restaurants once or twice each week. In the UK I guess I was spending more like $3,500 per month many years ago, including rent. I would say that my standard of living is considerably higher in Quito though."

He bought an apartment in 2012 so he doesn't have rent or a mortgage to worry about. He paid $140,000, for 140 sq. meters (more than 1,500 square feet) with a terrace and incredible views in a luxury part of the city.

Susan Schenk, author of *Expats in Cuenca, Ecuador: The Magic & The Madness* lived in California for 23 years before moving to Ecuador at age 54. "I knew I could not live in the USA on my pension–not if I wanted to have a roof, or food, or a car! In San Diego I was spending $4,000 to $5,000 a month," she says. "It was impossible to save as much as I do here on $1,400 a month." She bought a penthouse condo for a small fraction of what a comparable one would cost where she came from and since she owns it outright, her housing cost is just the HOA fee of $170 per month, plus $80 in utilities.

"It would rent for $900 due to the size and view and location," she estimates. "But most of my friends rent smaller places and pay around $300 to $600 a month."

Keith and Tina Paul pay $735 for their large apartment that was newly built when they moved in. They say theirs is a premium place to rent because of the condition and location and estimate that you could easily find something for half that a little further out. "Our water bill is about $9 a month and electricity is about $45," Keith says. "The internet is also $45 a month but it's faster than what I got in the U.S., at 60 mbps fiber optic. We pay about $50 a month for the two cell phone plans."

As in many places, the best deals are found when you take your time looking for your ideal place. I've heard tales of handy people renting a huge house for $300 a month, but with the agreement that they would slowly fix up a few things that needed work.

Holly Walker and her husband rent a three-bedroom home for $550. "That felt quite expensive at the time when we first moved in," she says. "But it's a beautiful house, with some personality to it."

Rental prices in Quito can run from $350 for a one-bedroom apartment in the historic center to $2,000 for a luxury three-bedroom place in the best neighborhoods where foreign company workers live. The average take-home salary in Ecuador is around $500 and in Quito it's only about $100 more, so it's hard for landlords to charge four-figure rents unless they are catering to the local elite or the foreign business community.

In Vilcabamba you can find a place to flop while you're looking around for $100 to $200 a month. For a real apartment or house with some size, figure on $300 to $800. Cotacachi is even cheaper, with most apartments and homes in the range of $150 to $650 per month.

Purchase prices in Ecuador can be too cheap to believe in the countryside, with many homes for sale at less than $50,000. Prices have gotten rather standardized in urban areas where condos are more prevalent. Most Cuenca houses fall in the range of $60 to $100 per square foot if in good condition. Condos usually cost more because they're better equipped. You can get a new luxury condominium in a secure building with 24-hour security and parking for roughly $90 to $130 per square foot, finished to your specifications if it's a new build or often sold furnished if not. Expect to pay less for a more modest one. In Quito, condos can actually be less than this due to more abundant competition, as in $75 to $150 per square foot instead, varying a lot by how prestigious the neighborhood is and what kind of amenities the building has.

Quito is a city where you still see apartments (or even whole houses) for sale for less than $50,000 and decent places to rent for $350 to $800. Last time I was in Quito, I met a couple from Florida who owned an apartment right in the historic center. They didn't live there all year, but they came down regularly. They bought it "on a lark" they explained because it seemed too good of a deal to pass up. It was around $30,000, so they figured there wasn't much downside to that deal. They put about $20,000 into it over four years with renovations, appliances, and furniture. Now they have a very comfortable place in a prime area, about two blocks from the Plaza Grande.

In and around Vilcabamba, you can still find building lots for $4 to $10 per square foot (under $100 per square meter). Most houses—even the largest ones—are listed for less than $200,000.

This is one of the best countries in the world to build your dream home on the ocean or find a nice condo with a view for a good price. Most of the buyers of beach lots and condominiums on this coast are Ecuadorans, not foreigners, which has kept a lid on prices. You can still find a big beachfront building lot for less than $50,000 or a condo in a great area, facing the Pacific Ocean, for well under $100,000.

Property taxes are quite low throughout Ecuador. Most people pay less than $100 per year and to top $200 you'd have to have a huge mansion. If you're more than 65 years old, your rate is halved.

If you're going to buy something, it's better to rent for a while and really get a feel for the different areas. "I always advise my clients who are considering moving to Cuenca to rent first for short term for one year, to make sure this is the right place for them. This way they are familiar with the different neighborhoods and they will make a better choice buying real estate," says Maribel Crespo, a local agent. Some make a hasty *House Hunters International* kind of move and then end up leaving a year or two later, put off by a couple months of rain, the city exhaust fumes, or the hurdles in getting past a basic vocabulary in Spanish.

"When buying, always look around you and assume that what you see is what you get," says David Morrill, who has sold a lot of property in Cuenca over a period of more than a decade and a half. "Don't think that things will improve to be more like you want them."

One of the false sells of moving abroad articles, David adds, is that a certain city or a big house with a maid will make you happy. "If you are just coming to stretch your savings and don't appreciate the culture or the people, you probably won't be happy. Some spend a lot of time and money learning that lesson the hard way."

"I try to always remember I'm a guest here in this country," said Leita Hulmes when I visited, as she looked out her window at some chickens pecking at the ground in the yard of the house next door. "There's a lot to appreciate if you don't focus on the negatives and learning the language helps a lot too. My comfort level increased a lot after I knew what was going on around me."

Healthcare

Getting sick in Ecuador is not going to kill your bank account. Modern facilities and well-trained doctors are available at costs that are a fraction of what they would be in developed countries. Going to see a specialist will likely cost you less than $50 and here a couple nights in the hospital will cost you less than a couple nights at a luxury hotel. Health insurance costs are a good indication of the differences: a policy for a 60-year-old male that would be more than $1,000 a month in the USA will be around $80 in Ecuador. The majority of expatriates don't even bother with insurance. They know that whatever comes up, they can easily foot the bill with their savings.

"We just self-insure here," says Keith Paul. "A doctor's visit is going to cost you $25 to $50 and the follow-up visits are included. I've heard of people being in the hospital for days and the bill is less than $1,500."

There are close to 20 hospitals and outpatient medical facilities in Cuenca, most staffed by at least a few doctors who speak English well. Anyone 60 and over has access to the public healthcare system at a discount, with no co–pays, no pre–existing conditions denials, and a monthly premium under $100. Private care is a terrific bargain compared to what most U.S. citizens pay, with many doctors giving out their cell phone number and making house calls.

Ghostwriter Lynne Klippel once paid $2,500 for two days in the hospital with surgery after breaking her leg hiking. Otherwise though, her medical costs have been minimal. "My physical therapy appointments after surgery were $20 each. Dental check-ups and cleanings are $30, office visits for physicians are usually $30 - $45."

Options are even better in Quito, where first-class medical facilities treat government officials, business tycoons, and a large population of international business executives and their families. It's a similar story in business-oriented Guayaquil.

John Potts pays $3,000 per year to Cigna for an international healthcare policy, saying, "This is important for me because I travel a lot. Last year I broke my wrist and had an operation with two nights in a private hospital room all for $7,000. This was with one of the best surgeons in the country, in a top hospital, and was covered on my insurance. Otherwise, local healthcare is very cheap in Quito: doctor appointments costs $40-50 with a US-trained doctor, and medicines rarely set me back more than $20."

In the smaller towns there won't be as many choices, but you can't beat the prices: an office visit to a doctor may be less than your co-pay was before you moved. If you have to come back to the doctor for a follow-up, there's usually no additional charge. When a local newspaper listed top-range prices to see a doctor in Ecuador, no specialist was more than $100 and the top price was for a highly rated neurologist at the best hospital in the country.

Prices to get dental work done are generally 15-25 percent of what they would cost in the USA or Canada, and for serious procedures it can be more like 10 percent. Stories abound of travelers getting an estimate of $20,000 at home and having the work done in Ecuador for $2,000 to $3,000. The actual dentist will do more of the work too, spending time with you to get it right instead of shuttling between six patients in adjoining rooms. Back surgery that would typically cost six figures in the U.S. will be $10,000 in Quito.

The same savings show up in most drugs too, which you can usually buy at a pharmacist with no prescription. Retirees that were spending a few hundred dollars a month on medications in the USA often find their monthly bill in Ecuador reduced to less than $40. "The insulin our dog is on is over ten times higher in the USA for the exact same product," Keith says. "A friend of ours uses a drug where the co-pays are $850 a year in the USA. He bought a year's worth of meds here in Cuenca for $78 cash."

Legal residents can tap into the public healthcare system in Ecuador. Some foreigners join this as a back-up plan, paying the $70 or so a month in case of catastrophe, but visiting the doctor of their choice for routine care. A private health insurance policy issued in Ecuador will run $90 to $120 a month for most people.

Food & Drink

Imported goods are expensive in Ecuador. Anything alcoholic besides local beer and (bad) rum is insanely expensive—as in more than double what you probably pay now in Canada or England because of taxes that are more than 100 percent. The past president was reportedly a tea-totaler and wanted everyone else to be too unless they were rich enough to help fill the government coffers. His successor has kept the same tax scheme in place. When I was in a Quito supermarket, I saw Stella Artois and Negra Modela beers for $15 a six-pack. A bottle of Bacardi white rum was $40. If you're flying to Ecuador through other airports, you will definitely want you to bring as many bottles in from duty free as you can.

Otherwise, prices for most things you consume are a bargain. You can go to the market and buy a big sack of fruit and vegetables for $10. Your haul will be a great variety too. With so many elevations here and volcanic soil, they can grow most anything, from bananas, sugar cane, and mangoes on the tropical coast to coffee, apples, and berries in the highlands. It's quite common to see fruit and vegetables selling for 50 cents a kilo. Plus, they grow coffee beans and cocoa beans for good chocolate.

Traditional food in Ecuador is not the healthiest stuff in the world: think lots of fried things with corn in them and thick stews and soups with cheese. It's pretty tasty though and if you're not on a diet (or are doing a lot of hiking), you can eat a set meal with several courses for three dollars or buy street food for a dollar or less. If you're cooking yourself, you can feast on food that's very fresh and bargain priced, including good meat and cheese. "I can get 100% organic produce, grass-fed beef, truly free-range chicken, with bright orange egg yolks...for $200 - $300 a month total!" says Susan.

You can spend a lot more of course if you are buying imported food and you go out to higher-end restaurants on a regular basis. If you don't order wine, high-end restaurants are a bargain. Outside of the trendy parts of Quito and the five-star hotels, it's hard to spend more than $25 each on a white tablecloth meal with good service. I was actually taking pictures of menu prices and posting them on social media last time I was there to show people what an unbelievable value some restaurants are.

"For my birthday we went to the most expensive restaurant in Cuenca," Tina says, "and the main courses ranged in price from $14 to $28. That's a five-star experience kind of place though. Normally we're paying $6-12 for dinner, half that for lunch."

"An *almuerzo* set lunch is juice, soup, main dish with some rice or beans, and dessert," Keith adds." On average that's going to cost you $2.50 per person. It can be as low as $1.25 and a rather fancy one will be $5."

Some foreigners readily admit they spend a third or even half of their budget on food and drink, however, counting dining out. This is partly because it can be less expensive to eat out than to cook at home, but also because beer and wine add so much to the tab even if you're cooking. This is a budget line item that can vary drastically from person to person or couple to couple in Ecuador. It can be quite low if you eat and drink what's local and dine in simple restaurants. If you crave imported food and alcohol, however, and go to restaurants filled with foreigners, your budget may triple.

Transportation Costs
Unless fuel subsidies suddenly disappear, taxis in Ecuador are some of the cheapest in the world, with most rides in the cities coming in between $2 and $6. A local bus ride is 25 cents, a long-distance bus ride topping out at around $1 an hour of travel. Gasoline is frequently $2 a gallon or less, while diesel is even

cheaper. This is not going to last forever though if the government ever manages to dial back the subsidies.

The official tourism people like to talk about their new roads with the promise you can "eat breakfast in the Andes and have dinner in the Amazon." And that's if you don't fly. When I went from the capital to a remote cloud forest one time I visited, it took less than three hours. When you do need to fly, it won't cost you much. Even if you walk up to the airport counter the day of departure, a flight from Cuenca to Quito is under $80 one-way. Those on a retirement visa get discounted rates too, even when flying internationally.

Cars are imported and generally cost more than they would in the USA, but in line with what they cost in Europe. Financing is available if you have local roots and a bank account, but interest rates are high. Toll roads are not common. Many expatriates do without a car, especially if they live in the center of a city, but those further out often end up getting one for shopping and excursions.

After a huge investment, there's now a train line from Guayaquil to Quito again. This is more of a tourism route than a transit one to go the whole way, but one that has been poorly marketed and offers poor choices for accommodation during the stop-offs. You can get from Quito to quite a few nearby places by train though.

Domestic air connections are good, with two airlines competing on most routes. Apart from the Galapagos, one-way fares are usually less than $100. For now, there are no direct international flights to Cuenca, however, even from neighboring countries. You must go through Quito or Guayaquil.

Other Costs
One of the main reasons Ecuador converted to a US dollar-based economy in the year 2000 was to tame inflation. It has worked, bigtime. "We don't even know what inflation looks like anymore," said one hotel owner to me. "The only things that go up are imports and whatever the government decides to raise taxes on."

As mentioned before, the government has repeatedly tried to wean its citizens off fuel subsidies, but massive protests break out and they have to cancel the plans. Until those go away though, propane costs remain artificially low. Much of the electricity is generated by hydroelectric power, so that is relatively inexpensive as well.

Most expatriates report paying less than $100 a month for all utilities combined, including super-fast fiber optic internet. Water bills average $5 to $10 per month and you can drink the tap water in Cuenca. Electricity runs between $25 and $60 per month. Propane is $3-5 for a canister that will last a month or two.

A men's haircut is easy to find for $3-$4, a massage can be lined up for $15 or less. Many women go for a regular manicure for $8 and a facial for $20-$25. A local SIM card for your phone is $4 with some data, and roses are 25 cents each. Museums cost $1-$3.50 to enter. Many cultural performances are free and those that aren't seldom cost more than $10 for a ticket.

"Somehow, I live on $800 a month (average) and save the rest of my pension of $1,400," says Susan Schenck. She supplements that for travel money by doing workshops and classes on book marketing, raw food, and health/weight loss.

Visas in Ecuador
You can visit Ecuador for 90 days on a tourist visa and in theory it's possible to extend that a few more months after arrival. Becoming a legal resident seems to get a bit easier each year and you can cut the hassle down considerably by paying $400-$1,000 to a lawyer. Qualifying is straightforward, especially if you're buying property, you have a graduate degree, and/or are of retirement age.

Keith and Tina Paul came in on "professional visas" which are available to anyone with a degree from an accredited university. They applied on an advance trip and picked it up upon arrival later. You can also get an "investor visa" by putting $25,000 into a bank CD or spending at least $40,000 on property. "We didn't bring in savings to get the visa," Keith adds, "but we did end up buying a bank CD because the interest rate was 10% and it's in U.S. dollars!"

Once you're in, if you're 65 or older you get a dazzling array of discounts on travel and entertainment, including 50% off all national and international airfare, 50% off all cultural and recreational events, and 50% off some utility charges. Foreign retirees pay lower taxes all around, though you have to keep records and apply for a refund on sales taxes.

There are restrictions on the residency visa. For the first two years you need to spend all but 90 days of each year in Ecuador or you can lose your status. After that, you can't leave the country and stay out for more than 18 consecutive months. So don't move to Ecuador and apply for residency if you're really planning on being nomadic most of the year.

It's much quicker here to transfer to permanent status, however. You can apply for that less than two years after getting temporary residency. Once you gain permanent residency, it does not need to be renewed.

The easiest option if you're old enough is to get a retirement visa. You only have to show a mere $400 a month in verified income plus $100 for each dependent. Even someone on partial social security payments only can clear that bar. A Cuenca real estate agent I spoke to guessed that "Probably 98 percent of the people who apply get it."

There's also a *rentista* visa with the same low-income threshold as the retirement visa. You just have to demonstrate a steady flow of income over a period of two years and if you've got bank statements showing ample savings, even better.

As in many countries, you'll have to show documents such as a background check, a marriage certificate, and a birth certificate, all bearing apostille stamps. Line it all up before you leave your home country.

Downsides

Ecuador is more stable now than in has been in earlier decades, but some think that the stability has come at a high price. The opposition press was crushed in the 2010s and during Rafael Correo's presidency, the country was rated the second worst in the Americas for press freedom, right behind Cuba. Former president Correo is in exile in Belgium and probably won't be able to return after being convicted in absentia for taking bribes. The court found him and 19 other defendants guilty of accepting $7.5 million in payouts from private firms in exchange for state contracts. The country also got in the habit of not paying its debts. As the BBC said, "Correa's rule was characterized by large-scale social welfare spending and infrastructure projects, as well as defaulting on foreign loans and tensions with the US."

His hand-picked successor, Lenin Moreno, has been in office since 2017 and things have changed slightly for the better, with Ecuador rising above Bolivia, Venezuela, Colombia, and Nicaragua now in terms of press freedom. Still not stellar, but the government no longer dictates everything that's printed or airs on TV.

Things move more slowly than you might be used to in Ecuador, whether that's the bureaucracy in government offices or the speed at which any work on your house gets done. It's better to get used to it and go with the flow rather than trying to fight it. "Visit first and see if you like it," says Susan. "If you are a type A and have to have everything perfect, either learn to relax or don't move here."

Virtually everyone complains about the Ecuadorans' driving habits. Holly says, "You take your life into your hands every time you get behind the wheel. They are incredibly aggressive drivers. I used to stop for pedestrians when driving, but then people would just drive around me, which was even more dangerous."

Pedestrians have very few legal rights and seem to be viewed as a pesky annoyance by most drivers. The absolute best time to be in Quito is on Sunday, when many of the streets in the historic center are closed to traffic. People complain about the bus fumes a lot too, though the tram service in Cuenca has helped a little on some streets.

"Get used to less competitive customer service," says Susan. "Here, for Ecuadorians, it's not about money, but leisure time with family. So, don't expect things to be as competitive as they are in the USA, consumer capital of the world."

There can be petty crime worries and people are used to having an extra layer of security in the way of window bars and extra locks. It pays to be vigilant when walking around at night and flashing expensive jewelry or a Rolex is not a good idea.

Last, the country has a habit of talking up their jungle wildlife in the Amazon Basin, but then putting oil interests first every time. After telling the world that they wouldn't put off drilling in the pristine Yasuni National Park unless the international community gave them $3.6 billion to save it, the president canceled a national referendum on the measure and moved ahead with oil drilling in what the tourism brochures call "one of the most biologically diverse areas in the world."

Overall though, most expats are happy they moved to Ecuador, especially when they look at how much they are spending. Lynne Kippel was "working herself to death" in St. Louis before she got laid off from her job. "I cashed out my 401K to purchase land and build a home high in the mountains about an hour away from Cuenca. My ghostwriting and publishing support me well here. I love being debt-free for the first time in my adult life. I've got a great life here: a beautiful home, kind neighbors, access to a wonderful community of other expats and Ecuadorians, and the ability to work from home with clients in the US, Canada, and Europe. I love to travel and am able to afford trips to the US and other locations each year. I pay $120 per month for a handyman/gardener who comes one day each week. My property taxes are $12 annually.

An open mind is essential and the willingness to adjust is essential," she adds. "If you don't compare everything to the way it was 'back home' it is easy to adjust to living in Ecuador."

For More Information:
GringosAbroad.com
CuencaHighLife.com
Expats in Cuenca: The Magic and the Madness book
Relocating to Ecuador book
International Living—they seem to cover this country almost every month.
Facebook groups for the country and specific cities.

Chapter 17:
Georgia

Pros: terrific wine, good food, cheap beer, hiking, skiing, mild four seasons, one-year tourist visa, low crime, drinkable tap water, very limited bureaucracy.

Cons: limited air connections from the capital, city air pollution, difficult language, dangerous roads, limited LGBTQ options.

"We got talked into coming here the first time by another nomadic couple, then ended up getting pulled back for good" says Tom Williams, who runs a podcast (The Dish), a blog (FoodFunTravel.com), and a local wine tour company. "We kept hearing that it was the birthplace of wine, that there's fantastic food, great cheese and bread, and it's a bargain. So, we had to see for ourselves." They went for six weeks in 2016, then lived in Mexico for a while and traveled a bit, but the place kept coming up in their conversations. After a second visit and then an attempt to get a residency visa in Europe that didn't work out, they returned to Georgia and are very happy there. He and his wife Megsy actually got married in the country and have committed to a local business.

"The two factors that were keeping us from moving here were scarce flight connections and dealing with winter," he explains. Between that first visit and now, however, RyanAir has entered Georgia and Wizz Air has added more than 20 flight connections to Georgia from Europe. "So, we decided if we could handle a winter then we would stay," Tom adds. "The winter wasn't so bad really, so we've made this our home."

When Jon Sterling moved to Tbilisi, it was to investigate real estate investment opportunities for him and his company's clients. "In a few of these former Soviet states, there are some great opportunities for appreciation," he says. "If you have the stomach for it and a long enough timeline, there are some attractive investment values available as Georgia continues its steady gains."

He hasn't bought there yet though because, "I have a personal rule that I need to experience all four seasons in a place first." Instead he pays a few hundred bucks a month for rent in a good part of Tbilisi.

He loves the hospitality of the Georgian people, personified in their saying, "Guests are a gift from God." Jon says, "That makes this a very friendly and safe-feeling place to be, where you feel welcome by everyone. I have female friends who walk home alone at night and aren't worried that something bad will happen. It's a nice feeling to have in a big capital city of a million people."

Sitting underneath Russia at the far eastern end of Turkey and the Black Sea, most cartographers would say Georgia is in Asia. Most Georgians consider themselves Europeans, however, and the country has more in common with Bulgaria and Ukraine than it does with Anatolia or the Middle East countries to the south of neighboring Armenia. So, most descriptions hedge their bets and say it's in "the Caucasus region of Eurasia."

Known outside the country as Georgia, the local name for it is Sakartvelo. Although it occupies a sizable area, there are fewer than four million people living in the country, so it's not hard to find some open space to get away from crowds.

While Tbilisi can feel cosmopolitan and bustling, this is still the capital of a developing economy, one where the average local wage is less than $400 per month, under $500 per household. So, if you're pulling in more than $1,200 per month from a pension or online business, you'll be living large in Georgia. Tbilisi has an equivalent population to Seattle but is in a different world in terms of living costs. According to Numbeo, "You would need around 1,714$ (5,298 GEL) in Tbilisi to maintain the same standard of life that you can have with 6,300$ in Seattle, WA (assuming you rent in both cities)." Yes, if you move to Georgia's capital from Seattle, you can expect your spending power to quadruple.

Most expats choose to live in the capital, where it's easiest to get by in English and get a variety of food, but the much smaller second city of Kutaisi has less pollution and better flight connections. Living in the countryside here may sound idyllic, but unless you speak Georgian or Russian, it will be near impossible to communicate with anyone over 30—and most of the young people have moved to the capital or another country for work.

If you're an entrepreneurial type, this is one of the easiest countries in the world to get set up in business. "I had to do very little paperwork to set up a tour company and be able to sell wine," says Tom. "It's easy to start a company and open a bank account, plus only income earned in the country itself is taxed here."

Georgia was so off-the-radar when I put out the first edition of this book that I just briefly mentioned it as another place to consider. Since then, at least 20 people I know, or follow have moved there, at least for a few months. Since Georgia already offers a year-long tourist visa and now is experimenting with a location independent worker visa as well, it's likely to see an expat boom in the coming years. It's been ranked as one of the least expensive places in the world to live in by Mercer, Expatistan, and Numbeo, so if what you read here sounds good, beat the coming rush and stake your claim.

Housing Costs

All the expats living in Georgia talk about what a great value the living expenses are, especially when it comes to housing. "With a budget of $500 per month," says Jon, "You can get a nice furnished apartment in a good part of the city center. Maybe add another $50 or $60 for utilities, including fast Wi-Fi." He paid more than $400 per month for his apartment until the COVID-19 crisis closed the borders. "After that, all the Airbnb places flooded the market," he says, "So when I started looking around for a better deal, my landlord dropped my rent to $300 to get me to stay."

Tom had a similar experience. "You can get a decent one-bedroom furnished apartment near the center for about $350 in normal times. Our first place was $400 for a bit larger place, but the air conditioning was in the living room, not the bedroom, which is an oddity here." When the coronavirus pummeled tourism and more inventory came on the market, they upgraded to a $500 apartment to get two bedrooms, close to 1,000 square feet, and balconies with views on two sides. "It would have been $800 in 2019 though," he cautions. "That's a more normal rate for something this nice."

Keith Lang of NomadFlag.com lived in Georgia for a while when roaming around as a digital nomad and paid $450 per month straight off of Airbnb for a furnished one-bedroom apartment that was in a good spot for walking to places to eat and drink in Tbilisi. "For long-term, you can rent a brand-new, furnished, one or two-bedroom apartment in somewhere like Vake or another trendy spot for $400-500 per month," he says. "It's one of the cheapest rates in Europe."

Richelle Gamlan, who taught English in China and runs the Adventures Around Asia blog, says she loves the affordable cost of living in the capital. "The rent for our beautiful modern one-bedroom apartment in the popular neighborhood of Vake is $500 per month. Because our apartment was sometimes listed on Airbnb, we barely had to buy anything. Dishware, linens, towels, etc. were all provided by our landlord, and the place was already nicely decorated. I only ended up buying a few cooking implements, a $20 desk, a bigger trash bin, and a few other things to make the place feel more like home. We also have a big balcony with an incredible view of the mountains!"

You can spend more than $1,000 per month in Tbilisi if you want, but that's likely to be a huge three- or four-bedroom apartment in a new building with lots of high-end appliances and parking included. I couldn't even find anything listed for more than $1,400 at the agency sites (and that price was a huge house with garage and yard).

Ask around or see Facebook expat groups though to find a reputable local real estate agent. Many of them will waste your time with bait-and-switch ads, so find a trustworthy agent through those who have already gone through the experience.

As for buying in Georgia, it's probably best done for a place you're going to live in—at least at first—rather than as a speculative investment. "You could buy one apartment here and maybe the most you can get for rent is $400 per month, so you'd have to buy a lot of them to start clearing a sizable amount," Jon says. "I would go for quality, buying in a good building in one of the best neighborhoods so you could potentially rent to executives or diplomats." You can see some of his listings at ExpatHomes.io.

Foreigners are allowed to buy property anywhere in Georgia with no restrictions except for agricultural land. If you spend enough, you can buy your way into residency. More on that in the visas section.

Food & Drink
If you like to drink wine with a good meal on a regular basis, you'll probably be in heaven in Georgia.

"If I spend $30 for a night out in Tbilisi, that would be a good dinner in a nice place with lots of drinks—an expensive evening," says Jon. "What's that get you in the U.S.? Two drinks or glasses of wine?"

One of the big advantages of living in Georgia is access to great wine, with hundreds of grape varieties and as many methods and blends. Some are officially recognized in this cradle of wine: 20 varieties that are unique to the country have their own origin of appellation status. Even if you buy one of the more expensive options in a store or a restaurant, it won't cost you close to what you're probably used to where you are now.

Tom says you can get someone's homemade hooch for a dollar a liter and since you don't need a license to sell wine from your house or store, almost every family sells their surplus. Regular table wine will cost a few dollars a bottle or you can get decent table wine in bulk for $5 a liter or less. "A good premium wine starts at around $10 a bottle in a store," he adds, "and I've almost never paid $20. That would be the very top of the line."

If you prefer beer, you won't pay much for that either. A half-liter domestic beer may only cost you a buck in a local bar. On par with Bulgaria and the countryside of the Czech Republic. A craft beer scene is starting to spread in the capital and upgrading to something more interesting will cost $1.50 to $3, maybe $4 for something imported from Germany. A good cup of coffee will be less than $2 in a coffee shop.

They don't do much street food in Georgia, but there are a lot of deli-type places where you can grab things to go. A simple locals' restaurant tab will often come in between $2 and $5 for a set lunch with a few courses. "It's not unusual for us to go out and order a big dinner with multiple courses, breads, salad, and a liter of wine for $10 each," says Tom. "The wine part of that is usually $4 or so." He says if they go to a nicer place it might rise to $15 each. At the high end, "You can get a romantic six-course dinner with a private chef and unlimited wine from the pairings for $75 each. That's about the most you could spend here."

When you're stocking up your kitchen to cook for yourself, you might need someone to help you carry things home if you're buying more than $30 worth of groceries. In-season fruit and vegetables are normally 50 cents to $1.50 per kilo and there's a wide variety of them grown here. Eggs and milk are inexpensive, and meat is often $3 - $5 per kilo. Good Georgian bread, which is a staple of every meal, is three loaves for a dollar. In the winter though, many produce items need to be imported and prices go up. Many imported items will cost more than they do in their country of origin.

"Chris and I love getting 1 *lari shoti* bread (about 30 cents USD), dipping it in fresh sunflower oil or pairing it with a few slices of homemade mountain cheese as we enjoy the view from our balcony," says Rachel. "Every month we spend around $500 on food. This is a combination of cooking, eating out and delivery, along with drinking wine at local restaurants. Thankfully, things like bread, cheese, wine, pasta, vegetables, and seasonal fruit are all very affordable. If we splurge it's usually on sushi or Korean— something you need to pay a bit extra for if you want it to be good."

Transportation
It won't cost you much to get around in Georgia, whether that's from place-to-place or within the city. There are only two metro

lines in the capital, but you can't complain about the price: 17 cents for any metro or bus ride of an hour and a half or less. A monthly pass is around $11.

"Taxis are probably the cheapest anywhere I've ever been," says Keith. "I used the Bolt app exclusively and paid on my credit card. Every transaction was just a dollar or two. You can get anywhere in the city for less than $5." Even coming in from the airport will cost a fraction of what it does in most countries: around $10 on Bolt.

Richelle lives in a neighborhood with no metro station, so she always walks or takes Bolt rides. Still, "Per month we probably spend less than $20 on transport to get around town," she says.

If you want to get around by bike, there's a local pay-as-you-go public bike system in the coastal city of Batami called Batumvelo. After you buy the card, use of the bikes is only 66 cents for an hour. Biking around traffic-choked Tbilisi is a lot more hazardous, however.

Gasoline prices are low by European standards, so you won't spend much to get around in a rental car. If you want to save six to eight hours of driving or bus time though, you can fly within Georgia on Vanilla Sky for $35 to $80.

You can actually travel around Georgia by train as well, then venturing beyond to Armenia or Azerbaijan. As one example on fares, going from Tbilisi to Batumi on the coast is around $10 for a second-class ticket and $17 to go first class. An overnight sleeper to Yeravan, Armenia comes in less than $50 in first class.

A bus is even less, going 6.5 hours from Tbilisi to Batumi for $8 in air-conditioned comfort. Heading to Kutaisi, where there are more budget flight options, will only be around $7 on a bus of four hours. "Those Kutaisi buses are timed to coincide with flight arrivals too," Tom says. "You can take one right from their airport to the capital." There are also direct shuttles to ski resorts from the airport.

Healthcare
Healthcare is generally good in the cities of Georgia and there are many quality hospitals in the capital with the latest equipment. There are actually more doctors per capita in this country than the majority of countries in Europe, some 27,000 overall. There's a national healthcare system for citizens that's fairly decentralized and modern, with private companies providing reimbursed services.

Most foreigners just pay out of pocket since costs are so reasonable. A doctor or dentist visit will run $15 - $30 and you'll pay less than $40 to get a cavity filled.

If you don't have some kind of expat health insurance already, a policy to cover you in Georgia will probably come in between $300 and $500 for the whole year. Some expats say this just serves to slow things down and cause more paperwork though—that you're better off self-insuring unless you're worried about getting hurt in a car wreck that will put you in the hospital for weeks.

Other Costs

Jon says his biggest budget line items have been going out: dinner, drinks, and other social activities. "Food and wine are a great value here, so it's not that I'm spending a lot on them, but they're the only significant expense besides $35 a month for a gym membership." He also budgets some money for local travel around the region but says you can get a really nice hotel room for $75 or $100 at the high end, a lot less for something simpler."

Tom says their electricity bill has never topped $30, even with the air conditioning running a good bit in the summer. "Utilities are minimal all around here. Our worst gas bill in winter when the heat was going was around $35, the water has averaged $5." He says the typical internet only package for 20 mbps via fiber is only $10, but if you pay more you can get up to 100 mbps and adding TV is only around $10 more.

"Our utilities are very cheap here," says Richelle. "My husband and I have been paying about $30-$40 total per month to cover our internet, electricity, water, garbage collection, and cable. However, it will be a bit more now that it's summer and we have the aircon going 24-7."

There are three healthy mobile phone networks competing with each other, so prices are good for staying connected. You can get a monthly plan with 5 – 10 gb of data and a reasonable amount of phone call minutes for $8 to $11. Some packages include some international calls as well. Or you can just purchase a SIM card for a few bucks and top it off when you need more data. High-speed internet in your apartment, if it's not included, will seldom top $20 per month.

A men's haircut or a movie ticket will cost around $5.

If you have a child you need to enroll in school, your choices are free ones where everything is in Georgian or private ones where classes are in English, French, or German depending on the affiliation. The website Moving to Tbilisi says the average cost of private primary school is $3,000 per year. Expect to pay more for a private high school.

Four ski resorts are open in the winter in Georgia, from December to April if the snow cooperates. The biggest one has 11 lifts and a day ticket price that's easy on the wallet: less than $20. At the three smaller resorts, it's more like $14.

Visas for Georgia

When it comes to visas, this is one of the best—if not *the* best—country for digital nomads and location independent workers. Citizens of more than 90 countries can stay for a year with just a tourist visa secured on arrival. The country has even taken it a step further, issuing residency visas to foreigners who can show steady income from their online business or remote freelancing.

If that weren't enough, you're even allowed to work on a tourist visa. Wages are low unless you're doing something really specialized, but you're not going to get kicked out of the country if you decide you want to tend bar, teach English, or sign up as a ski instructor for foreign tourists.

Renewing your tourist visa for another year is no big deal. "A lot of people just drive two hours to Armenia, then come back in the same day with a new visa," Tom says. Or you can use this as an excuse to hop a budget flight to Europe, of course.

Georgia is also a country where you can fast-track residency by purchasing real estate. Here's what international investor Andrew Henderson from NomadCapitalist.com has to say on the subject:

Georgia's investment minimum has also nearly tripled over the past two years from just $35,000 to $100,000. That amount will get you a one-year residence permit. A permanent residence requires an investment of $300,000.

While I personally think that this is a bit high, you can get quite a lot for your money considering how cheap real estate is in the country, and you can also get a sizable return on your investment.

Downsides

"The only time I'm fearing for my life here is when I'm on the roads," says Jon. "There's no real enforcement of traffic rules and people drive like maniacs. You also have to pay attention when crossing the street and look out for aggressive drivers." Georgia ranks among the most dangerous countries in the world when it comes to traffic accidents.

Air quality in the capital can be bad in the summer when smog gets trapped in the valley. It's not China or India level, but still noticeable. It doesn't help the lungs that cigarette smoking is still widespread here as well.

In some neighborhoods the water can cut out occasionally when the system gets overwhelmed, which can be a big problem since the water comes direct, not via roof tanks. Tom says the government is pouring resources into infrastructure though and promising to get this resolved.

Expats report a wide variance in internet speeds, from 10 mbps to 100, so it's hard to generalize what you'll end up with if it comes with the apartment. In general, the expat areas with new buildings are more likely to have fiber-to-the-home than some older areas. Cafes and even co-working spaces are not consistent in their speeds, so it's good to have an app on your phone (like Speedtest by Okla) to check it. When you do find a co-working space with fast speeds, it can seem expensive to join when you consider local rent prices—more than $120 at some spots for a monthly pass.

Oddly, this is one of the toughest countries in this book to get in and out of, so it's not ideal for an international business traveler expecting easy flights to the rest of the world. Tbilisi is underserved as a capital city. Most of its flights leave in the wee hours of the morning and require a long stopover in Ukraine or Turkey to connect to other locations. Russia cut off all flights in 2019 after a diplomatic tiff. Supposedly a Turkish company actually owns the Tbilisi airport and has used its muscle to keep out most competitors to Turkish Air apart from the national carrier. So, there are better connections from Kutaisi, mostly because WizzAir and Ryanair both fly into there from destinations in Europe. This creates the odd situation where people take a bus from the capital city to a much smaller city for flights out.

Keith says to be ready to go old school with your telephone to get any information from businesses or offices in the country. "You can expect over 50% of your emails to bounce. Unfortunately, email as a way of communicating appears to be an afterthought, even for government departments." Most websites aren't maintained and even a company's Facebook page will usually be out of date or incorrect. "If you check out the Facebook page of a local business, you might find some stuff in Georgian written six months ago. And the opening hours will be a mere guideline," he adds.

You get a real summer here in July and August where temperatures can break 35C or 95F on a regular basis for a month or two, then a real winter in January and February where temperatures can drop below freezing. Some expats decide to make one or both of the most extreme months their travel periods. The winters in Tbilisi are not extreme though, often with no snow, and they're warmer than in Sofia or Bucharest.

Overall, Georgia is one of the best values in the world. The site *Expatistan* says Tbilisi is cheaper than 97% of the cities in the world, where an "average" single expat can live for under $850 per month and a family of four can easily get by on $1,700 per month.

For More information
MovingToTbilisi.com
ExpatHub.ge
GeorgiaStartsHere.com
MyHome.ge (apartment listings)
Search "expats Tbilisi" on Facebook for groups

Chapter 18:
Guatemala

Pros: gorgeous scenery, variety of locations, colonial and Maya history, close to USA, cheap real estate/rent, colorful indigenous population, all-ages expatriate community.

Cons: gigh crime rate, corrupt/ineffective police, poor infrastructure, unattractive capital city, ownership limits on waterfront property.

A beautiful lake surrounded by conical mountains, the greatest Mayan city of them all in a thick jungle, a Spanish colonial city amidst hills and coffee farms, and cheap prices on nearly everything—what's not to like? Guatemala sounds like paradise!

Well...Guatemala is a perpetually troubled country whose stark divisions between rich and poor have sometimes gone from simmering to erupting. No government seems to be able to get a handle on its myriad problems. The most visible one since the civil war ended in 1996 has been crime. With Guatemala being a natural conduit between the cocaine-producing countries of South America and the lucrative market up north, it's hard to keep people who would normally make $2 a day from turning to a life of crime that pays 10 or 20 times that amount. To put things in perspective, the way our right-wing politicians want to repel poor Mexicans from the U.S. border, Mexico's right-wing politicians want to do the same with "those poor Guatemalans." The Mexicans are rich in comparison. Guatemala City is where most of the gunshots are ringing though and few foreigners live there unless they're working for a foreign organization and got transferred there.

Despite the problems though, tens of thousands of foreigners come here on vacation or to take Spanish lessons and then end up returning for good. Luke Armstrong was backpacking north from Chile when he stopped in Antigua, planning to volunteer for two weeks. He ended up signing on for a year after the director quit right after he arrived. "The executive director and founder somehow thought offering me the position was a good idea, even though I was only 22 at the time. I ended up managing a staff of 50 employees and 500 annual volunteers. The project provided education and health resources for people to break out of poverty and had a program to rescue victims of human trafficking, so it was eye-opening, but also came with a feeling of accomplishment."

To give an idea of what you can get by on in Guatemala though, Luke was earning the local equivalent of $250 a month as one of the staffers, and eventually as director he got them all bumped up to a living wage of $400 a month. "That's enough to live on and go out a bit," he says. "On $600 to $700 a month you can live reasonably well in Antigua. For $1,500 a month you could live like a king—unless you have expensive tastes." He says there are loads of single retirees living in gringo communities on the outskirts of Antigua and are getting by fine on just social security payments—often around $1,200 per month.

Richard Polanco runs a useful blog about living in Guatemala (OKAntigua.com) that's filled with resource links, advice, and sample prices. He moved to the United States when he was nine and didn't have any real plans to move abroad. Then he met the love of his life from Guatemala. He visited the country with her several times and after getting frustrated with the interminable wait to get his wife's visa sorted out in his home country, he gave up and moved to hers.

"I don't have any regrets about moving here and I really wish we had done it sooner," he says. "We have a much better life here and it's a really inexpensive place to live."

Any expatriate you talk to in Guatemala will have a crime story for you, though most will say being smart and aware of your surroundings goes a long way. "Antigua is not unsafe if you play is smart," Luke says. "Always carry at least 100 quetzales: you never want to have nothing to hand over to a mugger in a hurry. I carry a broken phone just in case; be prepared to give away something and be done with it. Reporting it won't do much good: the police are really inept. Calling them is like calling another set of bandits."

"I was more worried when I first got here," says Rich. "The worst thing that has happened to me was having a bike stolen. I feel fine going out, but the issue is kind of always in the back of your head." He notes that the main adjustment is getting used to the idea that everyone is integrated and living together. "In the USA you can live in the suburbs and you're always in your car, so you don't have to interact with people that aren't like you. In Guatemala you can be in a really nice condo and have poor people right outside. It's very hard to put yourself in a bubble. If you're from NYC or Miami—or are at least well-traveled—it probably won't bother you as much, but if you're coming from a suburban town where nobody walks anywhere, it can be an adjustment."

The largest concentrations of expatriates in Guatemala is in the lovely colonial city of **Antigua**, which is not too huge or overwhelming and can be navigated by foot and taxis quite easily. It's also the place to go if your Spanish skills are negligible as there are plenty of local English speakers and a lot of bars and restaurants owned by foreigners. The real estate and rental markets are well established, and you can find plenty of your own kind to lean on for advice.

The next most popular area is **Lake Atitlan**, which is more isolated but offers stunning views of the water and mountains and even lower prices on a place to rent. Here you can get a million-dollar lakeside view for a few hundred dollars a month. The main town is Panajachel and that's where the most action is, but there are several smaller towns around the lake with lower prices.

Quetzaltenango—better known as Xela—and Rio Dulce are other areas where foreigners tend to congregate. The former is the county's second-largest city, with a population of 225,000. It attracts adventure lovers and those looking to get involved in helping the local community. It gets plenty warm most days, with highs ranging from 78 to 86°F, but can get quite cold at night, with lows throughout the year ranging from 36 to 48°F.

Rio Dulce is a hot and tropical river port that leads to the Caribbean. It attracts people who live on their boat, those involved in shady business deals, renegades, and outcasts.

Guatemalan beaches are underwhelming and don't attract many foreigners who want to put down roots there. Head north or south to another country for palm trees and hammocks by a gorgeous white-sand beach.

Housing Costs

Guatemala is a cheap place to rent an apartment or house if you're willing to make some concessions, even in popular Antigua. Go further out and prices drop even more. As usual though, you'll find far better deals on the ground after arrival. Rich says inexpensive housing is one of the best reasons to move to Guatemala—as long as you do it right. "The biggest mistake I see is people trying to set up a place to live in advance and have everything settled in two days. They end up paying twice as much. They should have just chilled out in a cheap hotel for a week or two and looked around. "A lot of business is done by word of mouth even in Antigua. Many landlords don't even know how to use a computer, much less how to post an ad on Craigslist Guatemala.

When he first moved down his family rented a big house in a gated community with a pool just outside of town for $500 a month. It seemed like a great deal, but only about a quarter of the houses were occupied full time and it was hard to feel any sense of community. They then moved five minutes away to a smaller house in a less ritzy neighborhood, but they enjoy it a lot more and pay less than $200 per month.

Luke lives right in the center of Antigua, a block from the central park. "I have three rooms off the main room, a kitchen, and a courtyard, and I pay about $220 a month for rent," he says. "When I lived here before I paid less for a larger house with more bedrooms a bit further out. If you're alone, you can rent a bedroom from a family and pay $300 a month with all meals included. Rents have gone up in Antigua the past five years though, so it's hard to find an apartment for less than $300 now that's anywhere near the center."

If you're looking for a nice place on par with what you'd rent in the USA though, with 24-hour security and lots of space for a family, you need a hefty budget to compete with retirees and snowbirds in Antigua. "The average 3- or 4-bedroom house in a gated community, with nice appliances and bathrooms, can go from $800 to $2,000 per month," says Marina.

Prices in lesser-known areas like Xela and Lake Atitlan go for significantly less because in those you're not competing with so many retirees, snowbirds, and domestic renters from the capital looking for a getaway place. You can find a furnished two-bedroom apartment in Xela for $700 per month or less whether renting for a few months to a year, utilities included. One-bedroom places abound at the $300 to $400 level. Even looking at year-long rentals on Airbnb, I could only find one priced about $1,200 per month and that was a 5-bedroom house with a roof deck.

Many nomadic types who settle down on Lake Atitlan for a while end up paying $600 or less for a house with a lake and mountains view. Nick and Dareice of GoatsOnTheRoad.com got a place for two months that they loved, a 2-minute boat ride or a 20-minute walk away from the village of Santa Cruz. They paid $550 per month, which included all utilities and a twice-weekly cleaning service. They just paid for drinking water and cooking gas.

When I pulled up long-term rentals while researching the new edition of this book, 80% of the rentals listed were in a price range of $325 to $900. This is online though, in English. You can do much better if you rent a short-term place first and then start asking around, as little as $200 per month for something basic. Different villages around the lake have very different vibes and views anyway, so you're better off getting a feel for the area before making a long-term commitment. "We looked at quite a few rentals before deciding on our casita," says Nick. "If you're comfortable with just showing up and walking around to find an apartment, that is totally possible. You can find 'for rent' signs on the actual homes that are available, or you will find numerous ads and listings in cafes, bars, hostels and tour agencies."

Buying something requires some capital and some time to look around. Maybe some legal maneuvering too: foreigners cannot buy waterfront land direct. You must form a corporation or partner up with a local. Otherwise you're in what's really a long-term land trust lease. This is the case on the coast in Mexico too, so it's something many foreign investors are used to, but what's different here is "waterfront" also refers to lakes and rivers. That pulls a lot of prime real estate out of consideration if you're looking for something to keep in the family for generations. If you're going to sell in a decade or two anyway, it's immaterial.

Also, be advised that while you can find a house and a couple acres of land for the price of a BMW in the countryside, in Antigua prices are high because of a limited amount of inventory in the center, high interest from wealthy Guatemalans, and restrictions on new construction. A house that will cost you $400,000 in Antigua could easily be half that anywhere else in the country. Since labor costs are low, building your dream house could be an even better route if you have the time and patience.

Food & Drink
Eating out in Guatemala is not going to set you back much if you go where the locals go. You can sit down and get lunch for as little as $1.50 and if you double that you'll likely get several courses and something to drink.

If you step up to a nicer restaurant, $5 or so will get you the kind of meal local business owners and office workers will be eating. Naturally, the tourist restaurants can be several times that, but they'll have a wider variety of options. The local splurge is usually a big *parilla* place where you order lots of grilled meats and starchy vegetables for everyone to share.

If you drive to the big city every week just so you can shop at Walmart, or even at the biggest local supermarket, you're going to spend a lot more money on food and the produce will be of worse quality. If you shop in the *mercado* instead the food is very cheap. Rich outlined his regular expenses in one of his blog posts and here were a few examples from the market:

Two pounds of tomatoes - 80¢
Head of broccoli - 25¢
Head of lettuce - 40¢
One eggplant - 40¢

Cilantro bunch - 15¢
Kilo of onions (2.2 pounds) - 85¢
Kilo of strawberries - $1
Kilo of blackberries - 90¢
Pound of chicken cut up - $1.15

As in many developing countries though, you buy what's in season to maximize your budget and maybe do without when it's not the right time: no constant supply of blueberries from Chile here. When things are in season though, supply and demand forces kick in. "I paid a visit to the Mercado and discovered limes were back in season," said Rich. "Sellers couldn't give them away fast enough. Limes that we had just bought last week for 1.25Q each could now be had at five for 1Q." (That equates to almost 40 for $1).

Many expats report that the fruit and vegetables are of better quality than they're used to, but at one-fifth the price. Since they don't have to travel very far, they tend to be picked just a day or two before they're sold.

The odd place out on cheap food is Lake Atitlan. The area is somewhat isolated anyway, and super-hilly, plus you've got the issue of some villages being easier to reach by boat than vehicle. So, while seasonal fruit, vegetables, eggs, and chicken will be "normal" prices there, you'll probably pay 25-50% more here for processed food and some kinds of meat. When Nick and Dariece were living there, they noted costs of $2.50 to $3.50 for coffee, olive oil, cheese, bread, and butter. Easily transported dry items like pasta, rice, and regular cooking oil were less than a buck. They paid 50 cents or less per pound for most local fruit and vegetables, including avocados.

Transportation

In Guatemala there's a vast range of transportation prices depending on how much you value comfort. To give you an example, a taxi from Antigua to the airport in Guatemala City costs around $25. The direct shuttle van is around $10. If you pack yourself into the local bus that stops every 100 meters, it's a dollar.

There are very few bus lines offering "luxury" bus trips outside the most popular routes. The local buses are cheap but are merely converted school buses on their second life—often after living out their usefulness hauling U.S. school children. Combined with some rough mountain roads, it can be trying. But at least they're cheap. Most of the time you'll want to make use of the shuttle vans plying the popular tourist routes. Antigua to Lake Atitlan for example is $8 there, $12 coming back.

Taxis are (in theory anyway) metered in Guatemala City, with official fares $1.50 upon entry and $2 for each kilometer. In other locations you have to work out the fare before taking off. You should be able to get around almost anywhere outside the capital for $4 or less. On Lake Atitlan you get around on public boats that drop passengers off at various villages. These run $1.40 to $3 in local currency depending on distance, though if you're carrying a lot of bags you may get charged more.

There are only a few internal flight options. The most frequently used one is Guatemala City to Tikal (Flores), which is generally around $160 one-way. International flight prices from here often defy logic: a trip to nearby El Salvador or Chiapas can be more than one to Chicago. Thankfully, there are good, relatively inexpensive buses running to neighboring countries for when it's time for a visa run or a cheap vacation. Antigua to Copán should cost you around $16.

Healthcare

As in a lot of Central American countries, the medical care quality drops off rapidly once you get beyond the capital city and the most popular vacation city. There are seven large hospitals in the capital that have good equipment and some English-speaking doctors, but pickings are slim elsewhere. In Antigua you have some good doctors who cater to the foreign population and there are clinics to take care of the basics, but most people make the short trip to Guatemala City for something serious like surgery.

There are actually some assisted living centers for the aged around Antigua, obviously pegged at a much lower rate than those in the USA or Canada. You can also find agencies providing home healthcare personnel.

In smaller cities and towns, however, the only local option may be a poorly funded government clinic or public hospital, so if you're moving somewhere remote it can pay to have some kind of evacuation insurance. If you're in a place with an airport, keep some cash aside for an emergency flight to Panama City, Mexico City, or home if your insurance covers it.

Most medicines can be bought at a pharmacy without a prescription and most of what you'll need is available. The price depends a lot on whether it's a name brand or not and if so, it may not be any cheaper here. You won't know until you start pricing things out in person, with a calculator for the exchange rate.

Visas
Most citizens of developed countries get a three-month tourist visa upon arrival in Guatemala. Technically you have to leave the country for at least three days to renew it, which isn't such a big deal the first time or two if you want a vacation in Mexico or Belize, but if you are ready to endure a day of bureaucracy in Guatemala City you can extend it for another three months without leaving. You can only do this once, however.

A trip to the Central American Alliance countries doesn't count for these purposes, so you can't go to Honduras or El Salvador unless you fly and go through airport customs. The easiest overland option is a trip up to Chiapas in Mexico. To do any kind of paid work in the country though, you need a work visa, which requires a contract, a few documents translated into Spanish and officially stamped, and a clean police record.

Not so bad, right? But here's the word from the U.S. Consulate for Guatemala on what you need to prepare for:

> *Applicants should be aware that while the following requirements appear straightforward, applicants for residency often report that unexplained delays in the issuance process makes obtaining a resident visa very difficult. Delays of one, two and even four years are common. During such delays, an applicant's residency status may be uncertain, requiring regular departure from and re-entry into Guatemala in order to re-establish temporary status.*

For a residency visa that doesn't involve work, you need to show a documented income of $1,000 a month, plus $200 for each dependent. This is a country though where you can double-check and triple-check everything you're supposed to get done in the USA before arrival, then find out at local immigration that it all has to be done over because...who knows? It's probably best to assume you're going to have to return to your home country get more documents with one certain notary stamp approved by one certain department of your government in order to proceed. Build it into your plans if you want to retire here.

There are some countries where you should hire a well-connected local immigration lawyer to speed up the process and save you a few trips to the immigration office. This is one of them.

Other Costs

If you ask expats what their utility costs are in this country, the answer can be anywhere from $50 to $300. Electricity costs per kilowatt hour are actually higher than in many parts of the United States, so if you're running air conditioning a lot the costs can rise fast. Much of Guatemala is at a high enough altitude that you don't need this much though, especially around Lake Atitlan.

Marina had years of utility costs to look at and says her costs are minimal most of the time for their family house. "Electricity ranges from $30 to $100 a month, water is $5 per month, gas is $13 for a 25-pound canister that lasts a couple months."

High-speed internet averages $30 - $40 a month (sometimes including TV as well), though some people get by with a USB stick and use wireless. Speeds are generally good in the cities but can be slow in the countryside.

Having a full-time maid (five days a week) averages around $250 a month. Naturally, if you just have someone come in a couple days a week it will be significantly less, as in $3 - $4 per hour. Automobile prices in Guatemala are on par with those in the United States and gasoline prices are a bit higher. "Electronics prices are about 40% higher though," says Luke. "You definitely want to wait until you leave before you buy those."

Most families who settle in Guatemala end up sending their offspring to private school, which can range from $300 per month to $500. "I pay $5,000 per year per child," says Marina in Antigua. "This includes everything. Part of the reason we are still in Guatemala is this amazing school, which I love."

Downsides

Expatriates here do all have to have their crime radar up more than those in Panama or Nicaragua, but most of what anyone deals with is petty crime. The most common manifestation of that is people getting robbed at night walking home alone.

"There's a high tax on imported goods in Guatemala so clothing and shoes are actually far cheaper in the USA than they are here, of better quality," says Rich. "Cheap clothing here is truly cheap— it'll fall apart in two days." He agrees that electronics and appliances are also far more expensive.

This is a tough country in which to run an online business unless you're willing to pay for redundancy. Outside a city, you need a DSL land line, a USB wireless stick from a cell phone company, and maybe a second USB stick for when both those fail. Or a regular chair at the local internet café—they still exist here. It's hard to get high-speed cable or fiber connections in many places in Guatemala, so it can be tough to run webinars, upload long videos, or do intensive stock trading if you're not in one of the cities.

When I asked Luke and Rich what expats usually complain about, both mentioned government bureaucracy and the inconsistent rules. "You go in one day and they say you need color photos with your application. You go in the next day with those and a different person says, 'you were supposed to bring black and white photos,'" says Luke. A lot of patience is required. *"Guatever"* is the common sigh.

For More Information:
OKAntigua.com
Expat Exchange Guatemala
AtitlanLiving.com
Atitlan.com
Expats Living in Guatemala Facebook group

Chapter 19:
Honduras

Pros: coastal reefs, beaches, adventure activities, good roads, easy air access, very low prices in the interior.

Cons: high crime rate, election fraud, weak institutions, weak environmental protection, pollution.

Julie and her husband hadn't really planned to live in Honduras. They were backpacking around Central America when she got pregnant and "There was just something about Honduras that drew us in." While working for a hostel they met the owner of a local mine at a trade show and he ended up offering Julie's husband a job. They lived in the nearest town for three years, enjoying a laid-back life and putting money away since many of their expenses were covered.

"We really wanted to get to the beach though, so we moved to Roatan Island and my husband worked as a construction manager. We lived on $42,000 a year, which included sending my son to a great private bilingual school, $700 a month to rent a three-bedroom, two-bath house near the beach, and $20 a day for a nanny/housekeeper. It didn't compare to what our life in Dallas would be like on that kind of salary. We'd be poor."

Honduras offers a wealth of geographic beauty, including some stunning island beaches that are postcard perfect. The Bay Islands offer some of the best scuba diving in the world, with the planet's second longest reef right off the shore. Prices to take advantage of it, however, are quite low by international standards.

Adventurous travelers can also find plenty of hiking, white-water rafting, and sea kayaking options. The country also boasts the impressive Mayan ruins at Copán, as well as some dense jungles full of wildlife, especially birds.

There's just one catch: thanks to drug runners having their way with a coast and river system that's hard to defend, this is now the most dangerous country in the Americas in terms of stats. It probably doesn't help that guns are "limited to only five firearms per person." The stats look worse on paper than they are is in practice for most expatriates though. Most of the violence is of the gang-on-gang variety and despite nearly a decade and a half of this violence, very few foreigners have been affected. It is a valid deterrent for many though, so this Chapter is shorter than some others. If you're an inexperienced traveler who gets spooked easily, you're probably wise to steer clear of Honduras for now. If not, at least avoid the two main cities and be very wary about touring the Miskito Coast. It's a jungle out there in more ways than one.

The homicide numbers and the size of the drug shipments have both dropped somewhat since the first edition of this book, partly due to some outside funding and training. Eventually the situation may turn around like it did in Colombia but keep an eye on the news before making grand plans to invest your life savings in property. Meanwhile, by any means necessary, avoid the capital city of Tegucigalpa as well as San Pedro Sula except for essential business unless you get a job posting and a housing allowance. There's no "must-see" anything in those cities anyway and drug gangs are a serious problem. The larger the town/city, the more precautions you should take, especially after dark. This is especially not a good country for single women to stroll around late at night, swinging their purse.

Honduras, the original "banana republic," is a poor country, right behind Haiti and Nicaragua. This is the second-largest country in Central America, but much of it is undeveloped or set aside as barely managed nature reserves. This means that there are plenty of bargains, but the most developed tourist and foreigner-friendly living facilities are in a rather narrow range of locations—namely Copán, Tela, La Ceiba, Trujillo, and the Bay Islands—with the islands putting forth a far more luxurious face than the interior. Even if you stick to these spots, you'll find Honduras to be a great value. Venture further afield with a good command of Spanish and you'll find idyllic colonial towns with prices too cheap to believe.

The West End of Roatan Island has the biggest concentration of foreigners in Honduras. Apart from La Ceiba, it's probably the only place you could have an expat party where more than a few dozen people show up. It's the most expensive area in the country, but this is a relative term. Compared to Ambergris Caye in Belize it's still a good value and compared to better-known Caribbean islands or the Caribbean coast of Mexico, it's a screaming bargain. Also, unlike in Ambergris, the beaches here are really stunning: you don't have to go below the water to enjoy the beauty, plus the reef is very close to the shore, so it's good for snorkelers as well. With a whole range of troubles hitting Honduras over the past decade—from a coup to fishy elections to drug violence—property prices in some prime spots are lower than they were in 2010. The downside of that, of course, is you can't assume your purchase will appreciate in the near future.

Be advised that we're almost talking about two countries here when it comes to the cost of living. As Canadian diving instructor Rika said on her blog when she lived there, "Roatan is not mainland Honduras. Honduras is a dirt-cheap, third-world Central American country. Roatan is a touristy island. Touristy + island = expensive."

Outside of the Bay Islands, prices for almost anything you would spend money on are low and have stayed low since I put out the first edition of *The World's Cheapest Destinations* book back in 2003. The exchange rate of the local lempira currency is pegged to the U.S. dollar at a rate of 20 to 1. To give you an idea of what travelers are paying, the most expensive hotel in some towns is $40 a night and it's hard to pay more than $250 a night anywhere, even on the most popular beach in Roatan. You can drink piña coladas 'til you're legless and you'll be out $10 or $15.

You don't have to live on the Bay Islands to have a beach life. Trujillo, La Ceiba, and other mainland coastal cities are much more Caribbean, with lots of seafood, great music, and all-night dancing. Prices are lower across the board in those areas because items can arrive by truck instead of boat.

If I were moving to Honduras, I'd head to the west, near the Guatemalan border. The town of Copán Ruinas, near the great archeological site, is one of the nicest towns you could ever chill out in. Nearby Santa Rosa de Copán is a center for growing coffee and making cigars. It can get cooler away from the coasts because of altitude, with Julie saying it would get down to 50 at night where they lived in the mountains and much of the year the house was wide open to the breeze. Most parts of the country where foreigners live are tropical and hot, however. Do some climate research before you go: temperatures and rainfall can vary drastically according to location, time of year, and altitude.

It's surprisingly easy to get to Honduras, partly because there's a lot of export business here. Air connections are good to three international airports. Honduras is only a two-hour flight from Houston or Miami and direct flights to Roatan are usually available from those airports as well as some months from Atlanta and New York. The highway infrastructure on main routes is good too, thanks to a few rounds of international aid after bad hurricanes hit.

Housing Costs
In most of Honduras, you can just show up and start looking around to find an inexpensive place to live. Long-term rentals are

available in a lot of interior areas for $100 to $350 a month for a one-bedroom place. At the top of that range, you can probably get a monthly rate on a hotel room while you find something more permanent. On the islands you will pay three times as much though, especially if you want an ocean view.

Trying to find something ahead of time is tough, especially on Roatan or Utila, since much of what you'll encounter online is vacation rentals for people coming to dive for a week or two. A lot of local owners with long-term rentals available don't have internet access or the foggiest idea of how to post something online. The good news is, once you find them, there's a good chance they'll speak some English.

You'll pay a premium on Roatan because there are so many foreigners and on Utila because it's so small. If you can find a two-bedroom place for $600 near the water, it's a good deal. Julie paid $700 a month for a three-bedroom, two-bath house with an ocean view. Some people pay $400 or $500 a month for a small apartment in the busiest tourist area. If it's low season though and you only need something for a few months, you could score a bargain from a snowbird who just doesn't want to leave their place empty.

It's a whole different story in the interior. "We have a friend on the mainland who rented a house near where we worked and he paid $125 a month for a place with two bedrooms and two baths," says Julie.

You can own property outright here if you are a legal resident and there's a lot to choose from on the islands and on the mainland. Prices have flatlined or declined in many spots in the last decade as the U.S. housing crisis, a coup, and rising crime really put a dent in demand. The COVID-19 lockdown will probably end up dealing another long-term blow. It's a buyer's market if you're convinced, you're here for the long term, or can buy a good property that will break even at least with rentals.

You have to exercise a lot of caution when buying, however, and it's not wise to skimp on legal costs. The U.S. embassy in Honduras has a specific page about land disputes in the country and advises people to take special care with title searches and attorney vetting. If you tread carefully though, you can find a beachfront lot for as little as $50,000 in some areas and a building lot away from the coast for under $10,000. In the range of $50,000 to $150,000 you'll find plenty of houses for sale in desirable areas on the mainland. On Roatan and Utila the prices are much higher, though the soft market means it can pay off to be patient and look beyond the online listings in English.

Food & Drink
As in the rest of Central America, you don't move here because the food is fantastic. Expect the staples of tortillas, beans, rice, eggs, and potatoes, with plenty of seafood anywhere near the coast (including lobster dishes for under $10). A fish soup with coconut milk is a standard dish, as is a similar concoction with vegetables served over rice. The yucca vegetable finds its way into a lot of dishes here, and there are Honduran versions of burritos.

You'll also find plenty of burgers, pizza, and kebabs. There are fast food options for the homesick in the cities and plenty of international choices in tourist spots. Vegetarians won't have much of a problem in the tourist centers, especially on the islands. The influx of expatriates in the Bay Islands has given birth to a huge variety of international cuisines there, with good bread and dessert to boot. You'll pay more to eat out on Roatan Island, but you'll get much higher quality as well.

The problem with the Bay Islands is that they're, well, islands. Whether you're talking about the Bahamas, Hawaii, or the Azores, it just plain costs more to get supplies to islands by boat or plane. "My trips to the grocery store cost as much as or more than my trips when I lived in Washington, DC. And let's just all agree that DC is not exactly a cheap place to live," says Amanda Walkins, a dive instructor who lived on Roatan. "Average grocery store trip? I'd estimate $100. That's for two of us, and we spend about that once a week."

"Food seems expensive, but then we return to the USA and it's even more expensive there," says Julie. "Staples from the mainland are a decent price, but it's the import items the foreigners want that really drive up the total."

Breakfast out is usually a tortillas/eggs/beans concoction, with some fruit here and there, often for less than $2. Other meals range from a dollar for a quick burger or burrito to $6 for a three- or four-course meal or pizza at a local eatery. A set meal in a basic local joint is often just $2 or $3. It's hard to even find a main dish in most interior towns priced higher than $12.50, even if you're at the restaurant of the best hotel in town. On the touristy Bay Islands the restaurants are serving those on a vacation budget, so it's very easy to spend $20 a person on dinner.

A beer in a restaurant or bar will average a dollar or two depending on how fancy the place is, with the price dropping below a buck during the numerous happy hours. Salva Vida is the most popular, but some others similar lagers pop up here and there. Rum is a good alternative for those on a budget, and fruity cocktails are commonly $2-$4 or so on the coast.

Transportation
There is an extensive bus system and it's easy to find a connection from one point to another. Finding a comfortable one can be another story, however. You can sometimes find an "executive" bus that costs double the normal fare. Since this only amounts to, say, $2.50 instead of $1.25, it's well worth it. In general, the regular buses run about 80 cents to $1.50 an hour. There's one main road in Roatan that connects all the beach towns and the buses plying the island cost $1-$3 depending on distance and time of day.

On Roatan, you have to haggle over a taxi rate and it'll cost you at least a few dollars, more if heading to another town. A city taxi ride will rarely top $5 in the rest of the country (usually not metered) and local city buses are usually less than 30 cents.

You need a vehicle to get around in many parts of the country, as the only other choice is a packed and slow local bus. Some decide to get a scooter and fill up the tank for $5 a week. Fuel costs are quite high on the islands since gasoline has to come by ship tanker, which impacts taxi costs or your own vehicle.

Internal flights are quite inexpensive ($30 to $100) and can be a reasonable splurge to avoid a long bus trip or ferry ride.

The boat trip out to the Bay Islands is $16 to $20 and a flight may be $50 or $60. Island hopping boats run regular trips or you can hitch a ride with someone making a supply run.

You can easily cross to Honduras from Guatemala by land, with Copán being a short hop from the border. A nice bus or van shuttle from Copán to Antigua, Guatemala runs $12 to $20. There are also land crossings to Nicaragua and El Salvador, as well as boat and land connections to Belize.

When Debbie Besserman and her husband moved back to Texas from Roatan for family reasons, they found a unique way to do it for a good price. "Moving away from Roatan, I realized that we could hop on a cruise ship bound for Galveston for less than a plane ticket and we were able to bring as much luggage as we wanted!" They did this on Norwegian and say you could probably use this method for getting there too if you weren't in a big hurry.

Healthcare

This is not a medical tourism destination like Panama or Costa Rica. "Adequate" best describes what you get here. The issue is further complicated by the fact that most people try to avoid the two largest cities whenever possible, but that's where the best medical facilities are. Roatan has much better medical care than the rest of the country when it comes to private clinics and doctors though, thanks to all the tourists and expats. For conditions that are not life-threatening, you can probably get it done there.

Plan on making use of the best private doctors and hospitals regardless, as this is not a place where you want to be under the national health care system. Doctors sometimes go on strike because they hadn't been paid for months and their salaries haven't been adjusted for inflation. The virus crisis put even more attention on the lack of medicine, supplies, and equipment for patients.

So, as you can imagine, private doctors are happy to see foreigners who walk in with ample funds to pay the bills and you can see one for $20 or less in many areas. In areas where foreigners congregate, you can find English-speaking doctors who studied abroad, and they will be able to take care of most of what ails you. For serious conditions or surgeries, however, you'll need to travel to Tegucigalpa or San Pedro Sula, where your costs will probably not be more than $60 a day for a hospital bed and care.

For serious surgery or treatments that can be planned in advance, some foreigners choose to fly to Panama City, or Mexico City for care. It's probably best to keep some money (or a credit card) aside for this purpose as you can be much more confident about the medical care, you'll receive in Panama especially and you're more likely to find English-speaking doctors.

Other Costs
"The kicker here for costs is electricity," says Julie. "Our bill was frequently $150 a month, just running the air conditioning at night in our son's room. But five months a year we ran it in our room too and we've had electric bills as high as $400." A wind farm went online in 2015 and brought costs down about 20%, but homeowners who can afford the investment often install a whole-home solar system that also serves as a back-up when the grid goes down. Ask any expat on Roatan what's overpriced and the services of Roatan Electric Company will be at the top of the list.

Most people use a pre-paid cell phone plan and spend anywhere from $10-$40 per month depending on how much data is involved. Internet is usually on a pre-paid system too instead of a monthly subscription, whether it's wired or through a mobile USB stick. So, if you use lots of bandwidth you may have to keep feeding the meter. Figure on $25-$75 per month on the islands, at the low end of that on the mainland. Cable/satellite TV can be anywhere from $30 to $100 a month depending on the number of channels, but bootleg DVDs are $2-$3 each.

If you've always wanted to get your scuba diving license, you can do it on Roatan or Utila islands for around $300 for a five-day open water PADI course. Sometimes there are attractive package deals with lodging included. If you're already certified, it will be $20 to $25 per dive, with volume discounts available.

"The one thing that's really cheap here is labor," Julie says. "We had a maid on the mainland that we paid $10 a day and were told we were overpaying. She also took care of our son. On Roatan we paid $20 a day for a combination nanny and housekeeper." Others report having a full-time housekeeper for anywhere from $150 to $300 per month. Expatriates praise the cost of car repairs, a gardener, or a handyman to be a great value and fixing up or adding onto a house here will cost very little in terms of labor costs.

You can get your laundry done by a service for a couple dollars a kilo if you don't want to wait for things to dry in the high humidity. When you need to relax, lots of places offer a one-hour massage for $10 to $15 on the mainland, but triple that on the islands.

To give you an idea of how inexpensive living costs are, here's what you can buy for $1 or less on the mainland: simple breakfast, a burger, a beer, a hand-rolled cigar, two or three cups of coffee, three sliced pineapples or huge mangoes, a fruit shake, two coconuts with a straw, a kilo of oranges, a small wood carving, admission to some museums, or more bananas than you can carry a long distance.

Visas
Most developed country nationalities can get a one-month tourist stamp on arrival and can extend a one-month one twice for a maximum of three months. Or you can request a three-month visa upon arrival and hope they'll grant it. Hop to another country for a few days, return, and you can start over. You have to choose that country carefully though from among the neighbors. The other four in the Central American Alliance don't count: Guatemala, El Salvador, Nicaragua, and Costa Rica. Belize and Panama are not part of that alliance so they're better bets for a visa run. Plus, immigration doesn't have to grant you three months when you

come back and can choose to only give you one if you're a regular visa run hopper.

The long-term visa options here aren't complicated. You either get a residency permit for a "rentista," pensioner, or investor, or you get a work permit if you're employed by a Honduran company. There's no age requirement and not a whole lot of paperwork: a passport, proof of income, and a recent clean police report are the key items. But documents need to be in Spanish and need to be authenticated through apostilles in your home country and you're supposed to hire an attorney to submit all the right forms. For the work permit, you'll need the usual documents proving you have a job and that the employer needs your skills. Or you can buy a local company that's profitable and hire yourself as an employee, with a bit of help from a lawyer.

A pensioner needs to show an income of $1,500 a month, a "rentista" $2,500 a month (the highest in the Americas), and an investor needs to put at least $50,000 into a local business. This country is not very welcoming to the self-employed, however. Many have experienced problems trying to get a residency permit based on variable monthly income generated by their business, even if it's rental property earning $10,000 per month or an online business throwing off tons of cash. It's far easier with a pension and/or social security. We're still waiting for Honduras to join the digital century.

There are no additional charges for dependents, though you will have to pay an extra fee for them, and you may need a birth certificate or marriage license as proof. Fees for residency permits are $300 per year for the principle person, $200 for each dependent.

Residency visas have to be renewed annually in one of the mainland immigration offices, though you may be able to have a lawyer do it without you making regular trips. This can all be arranged after arrival and you'll get better info locally than you will online. After five years, you can become a permanent resident.

Downsides
Stats don't tell the whole story, but San Pedro Sula held the dubious title of being the murder capital of the world for several years running, hitting 187 murders per 100,000 people. The capital city has never been far behind. The drug gang violence in those two cities badly skews the overall rate.

In the areas where lots of expatriates congregate, robbery is more of a concern. Most people who are in remote areas or who leave their houses unattended for months pay a local watchman to keep an eye on things. You can probably find a house-sitting opportunity in this country quite easily to do a trial run.

Blackouts and brownouts are frequent due to an overtaxed electrical grid in some areas, so many homes have a back-up generator. It's also wise to have some kind of combo surge protector/battery pack for expensive electronics.

On this health side, there is some risk of malaria and dengue fever in some areas and sanitation is poor.

There are very few good schooling options for families outside of international schools in the two largest cities, and the two largest cities are not very conducive to family life otherwise. You can find options in Roatan though. Track down parents who already live here and ask lots of questions.

The government of Honduras is far from stable and every time there's an election there are loud cries of vote rigging and obstruction. Protests can get ugly and the most common tactic is to block roads to get attention.

For More Information
Roatan Online (Roatan.online/roatan-expats)
Roatan Net (RoatanNet.com)
Also search Honduras on Expat.com, InternationalLiving.com, and Facebook

Chapter 19:
Hungary

Pros: european lifestyle and architecture, great wine, good food, inexpensive public transportation, easy access to other parts of Europe, culture and the arts, bike-friendly, clean.

Cons: difficult one-country language, cold winters, weak institutions, racism, anti-Semitism, far right one-party political system, dour (but improving) service.

Imagine visiting your local wine bar and ordering three different varieties from assorted regions, being served by someone who can explain the climate where the grapes were grown and what awards that vintner has won. The chalkboard list behind the bar has over 100 wines by the glass to choose from and there's something for every taste. The interior is elegant, and the location is perfect, right across from a busy pedestrian plaza fronting the city's huge historic cathedral. It's the kind of place you could linger for hours, but how much is it going to cost you when the bill comes?

$8.50 with a tip.

That's what I spent at the best wine bar in Budapest. For three glasses that took my taste buds on a terrific ride, from three distinct wine regions of Hungary.

I bring that up first because it's emblematic of the appeal of Hungary. Not super cheap in every way, but a good value in most ways. Budapest is thronged with tourists that are firmly in the middle of the pack budget-wise. After all, the Hungarians consider themselves "Central Europe" and they are right next to expensive Austria. They're on the Danube, with docking river cruise ships a defining feature of the waterfront. So, this may be a value destination, especially outside the capital, but not the place you go just to find the very cheapest food and lodging.

Gary Lukatch was grossing around $5,000 per month in New Mexico working in the financial industry, after having lived in a lot of other states before that. "When I moved to Budapest and began teaching English, my monthly net earnings after one year were around $600 per month, increasing to around $1,500 per month after, say, five years," he says. "In short, I took a *huge* pay cut, but was 1000% happier."

After teaching English in Budapest for eight years, he retired and is living a much better life than he could elsewhere on what he has to spend. "The cost of monthly house payments or rental, plus car costs alone, would be more than my monthly income, which is around $2,100 net," he explains. "Here in Budapest, my monthly flat rental, plus utilities, averages around $400, right in the middle of town." He says public transportation is excellent, so he doesn't need a car. "I eat out several times a week and I still have enough money to travel wherever and whenever I want; I have now been to more than 60 countries."

Australians Karen and Neil came to Budapest because her husband got a job offer in his industry and they thought it would be a great adventure. They had already lived in Poland and the Czech Republic though, so they didn't have to make a huge adjustment going to Hungary. "Hungary was been the cheapest of the three," Karen says. They watched the city get easier and easier as the years went by, partly through them adjusting but also because the level of English fluency locally got steadily better.

They have since moved back to Australia, but they loved how everyone is outside and mingling in Hungary, even in the dead of winter. Instead of being couch potatoes, Hungarians will gather in a coffee shop, in a bar, in a park. "I love that there are so many outdoor festivals," she adds. "And Christmas is not all about presents. People aren't spending all their time shopping. Instead they're making homemade food and mulled wine to share, spending extra time with their families and friends. It's not a stressful time but is very relaxed. People are singing carols, walking in the snow, enjoying each other's company."

Hungary joined the EU in 2004, but the country still uses the forint, which is a volatile currency. Prices in this book are based on 290 to the dollar, but I've seen it as low as 210 and as high as 320 in the past decade. Check the current rate before cursing my name because prices have changed.

Just be advised that integrating into the community here by learning the local language is a much tougher proposition than it is in countries where Spanish, French, or Portuguese is spoken. One press release on Hungary's government website started with this:

A mezőgazdasági termelés biztonsága magában foglalja az élelmiszer-termelésre alkalmas környezet hosszú távú fenntartását is, az agrárkörnyezet védelmét, különösen termőföldjeink megőrzését, a talajvédelmet és a fenntartható, integrált növényvédelmet, növényegészségügyet – fogalmazott köszöntőjében Kardeván Endre, a Siófokon megtartott Növényvédelmi Bizottság ülésén.

I have no idea if they're talking about the price of wheat, provincial elections, or the decline of morals among today's youth.

As has happened from Vietnam to Peru to Turkey though, anyone who wants to make a buck from tourists or to move up the ladder of business is learning English. Plus, many young Hungarians go work abroad and come back with another language or two. Hungary has gotten a huge influx of tourists the past decade because of the booming river cruise business, so if you go where they are, you will probably find someone who speaks at least a bit of your language. The further you get into the rural areas though, the less that's true. There are only 10 million people in this country, so you get into the countryside pretty quickly.

Few expats live in the rural areas though unless they're in the wine industry. Most choose to live in Budapest, around Lake Balaton, or in one of the smaller cities like Eger or Pecs.

Hungary got hit hard in the European economic crisis last decade like many other nations on the continent, but it recovered faster. This has become a strange country since then though, with more young people staying put and more economic opportunities, but under one-party rule that is increasingly authoritarian, racist, and hostile to immigrants. The EU has threatened punitive action several times due to a lack of democracy and a muzzled media.

Housing Costs
The residents of Hungary give their rent costs in hundreds, not thousands, and you won't find many local single people or couples paying more than $600 a month, even in the capital. When you get into smaller towns, you can get a large house for that. When I was last in Budapest, I asked several locals I talked to what they were paying per month for an apartment and the answers came in between $150 and $300. In the southern wine region, there were houses with a nice garden going for the same. I met an expat from New Zealand working for a winery by Lake Balaton. He was paying $210 a month for his two-bedroom apartment with a lake-view balcony.

The site Numbeo.com shows higher prices than it did five years ago, but they still only rank Budapest the 332nd most expensive city in the world out of 546 cities tracked, with rents on par with Mexico City and lower than most of Europe. This will vary greatly by location, of course, but on average you can expect to pay between $350 and $1,200 for an apartment in Budapest if you go looking now, much less in smaller towns and cities. Even just pulling up Airbnb, most of the monthly rates are in that range for one or two bedrooms.

Canadian Sarah Hughes and American Nathan Sado of LiveDreamDiscover.com spent four months in Budapest as digital nomads and found the cost of living quite reasonable. "Our 2-bedroom, 1-bathroom furnished apartment in the popular and vibrant District VII was $700 per month (€600) including utilities" says Sarah. "It was rather basic, but spacious and bright. This is the mid-range price for this area if you're renting for a minimum of three months. If you're willing to be a bit further away from the center of the city but still within easy access to everything you should be able to find a similar place for about $550 per month."

Gary got in years ago and pays a shade under $300 for his apartment in District 5, one of the most desirable and central areas of the city. (If you've come to Hungary as a tourist, you've been there to see the sites.)

Jennifer Walker, a long-time Budapest resident who used to write for my Perceptive Travel Blog, laid out her housing costs for me. "I pay around €400 a month for a 2-bedroom apartment. A friend of mine in a studio in the center pays around €290 before utilities. Common costs in an apartment will usually run €32 – €96, which can sometimes include water, repairs, cleaning of the apartment block etc. Then heating can be €30 - €80, electricity around €16." (The euro is generally equal to US$1.10 to $1.20.)

"In my case, in the winter I pay around €545 for rent + common costs + bills," she adds. "In the summer that goes down to €480 as I am not paying heating."

Mitko Karshovski, who runs the That Remote Life podcast has lived in many places around the world and sees Budapest as a good "middle of the pack" city that offers a good life without high expenses. He paid the equivalent of $409 per month for a one-bedroom apartment in a good area of Budapest. After rent, he estimates that a couple could easily get by on another $580 of expenses, coming in around $1,200 a month for two with no medical bills or travels. "In my experience this is a pretty average amount of money to spend on things like groceries, going out to dinner and drinks, and all the other good stuff that you look forward to doing on a day-to-day basis."

You will pay a premium for a modern apartment with lots of amenities though. Cory Varga and his partner ended up spending more than they expected. "We find the market to be incredibly competitive. We are peculiar and have a lot of requirements, but we also find that good flats go fast. Competition is fierce, especially during term time when university students are also looking to rent houses. The good news is that you don't have to pay for a real estate agent, the owner does. We pay €800 for our 2-bedroom flat in District 6, right behind the Opera House. (2 minutes from the UNESCO Andrassy Avenue.)"

Katie and Geoff Matthews of Wandertooth.com moved to Hungary from Canada. "Most expats look for housing in Budapest's city center, with the 5th, 6th, 7th, and 13th districts being the most popular. We live in the 7th district in a completely renovated, 2-bedroom flat (roughly 730 square feet) with high ceilings, wood floors, and an exposed brick wall. We pay €730 per month in rent, plus a building common cost of roughly €50 and utilities. Our housing costs total roughly €805 to €850 per month. It's certainly possible to find housing that's much cheaper than this. Rooms in shared, modern flats can be found for less than €250 per month and studios in the city center run around €320 to €420 per month from what we've seen."

Prices drop dramatically though once you get outside of the big city. In Eger, for example, you'd pay less than €250 for a 1-bedroom place right in the center, or an average of €465 for a 3-bedroom one.

If you decide to buy something eventually, which you can do freely as a foreigner, prices here are still less than half what you'd pay in Vienna. For years after the financial crisis it was a buyer's market for a very bad reason: a lot of Hungarians took out loans to buy property in the pre-EU days and did it in Swiss Francs because that was a stable currency. Then they owed far more than what the property was worth because of the Swiss Franc's rise. More foreign buyers have come into the marketplace since then though and the Hungarian economy was doing well before the pandemic hit, so there are fewer deals on purchases in the capital.

You can get financing to buy property, but it usually requires a significant down payment of 30 percent or more. Interest rates are better than in most countries profiled in this book though, a few points higher than the U.S. rate instead of quadruple.

Food & Drink
The cost of living in Budapest depends a lot on how much you eat out—and where. You can normally have a fine cloth-napkin dinner with a glass of wine for €12. If you eat at more humble places, a soup will be a euro or two and main dishes range from €2.50 to €8.

"We typically spend between €16 and €24 on a meal out for two people in a restaurant, including a few beers or glasses of wine," says Katie. "If you're just going out for a drink, a half-liter of Czech Pilsner costs about €2, although local beer is cheaper. A glass of house wine is about the same, but you'll pay more in a wine bar. Most restaurants offer set-meal lunch specials that are much cheaper than ordering the same meal at dinner, so if you're on a budget and like to eat out, do so at lunchtime. Expect to pay around €4 for a 2- to 3-course set lunch."

"We cooked at home a lot and our food costs averaged $450 per month for 3 meals a day," says Sarah. "In the shops you can buy a decent bottle of wine for $3 and a standard big beer for $1 or less. As with any city there are some higher-priced restaurants, especially in the touristy areas, but dining out doesn't have to be expensive. If you eat with the locals you can get a decent meal for $5 and even in the trendier spots, a really good meal can be as little as $10. Craft beer and fancy cocktails can be a bit pricy in the bars but if you're fine with local wine and beer you'll be paying about $2 for a glass of wine and $1.50 for a beer."

When you shop in the market, prices are at the low end for Europe. You can get rolls for 10-25 cents each or a huge baguette for a dollar or less. Get 100 grams (around one-fifth of a pound) of good cheese for a dollar, 100 grams of good local sausage for $2, and a jar of pickled veggies for another dollar or so.

For a buck or less, you can generally buy 100 grams of many items in the market: raisins, peanuts, sunflower seeds, banana chips, or dried apricots, for example. Or you can get a kilo of seasonal fruit or peppers, cabbage, potatoes, radishes, or carrots. I saw a big bunch of white asparagus for about a dollar when I was there. How much do you pay for that in your local Whole Foods?

"We probably spent $80-$100 a week on groceries, not including wine," says Karen. "In Australia we could spend $300 or $400 a week easily."

Hungarian wine should be known around the world, but the Soviet occupation days seriously hurt its reputation and the recovery will be a long one. For now it's still one of the best quality-to-price values in the world. In many countries profiled in this book, expats complain about the difficulty of getting decent wine for a decent price, so if that's a big priority, put Hungary on your list. You can find a decent table wine bottle in a store for $2, something quite good for $4 to $8. If you spend over $10 you might end up with something from a "winemaker of the year" who has adorned local magazine covers.

If you're out with rowdy friends doing shots, you might end up downing the local brandy. "Palinka/brandy varies depending on where you drink and the quality," Jennifer says. "A low-quality one in a cheap bar in the suburbs is probably around a euro or two but can be five euros for quality in nicer places."

This once being part of the Austro-Hungarian Empire, you can get a killer coffee and pastry here just as you can in Vienna—but for literally 1/4 the price. After you do a double take at your low bill in a wine bar, finish with a coffee (€1.50 or so) and dessert for another nice surprise.

Transportation
Getting around Hungary is relatively cheap by bus or train when you want to get out of town. Figure on 9 to 12 euros for a domestic trip of two hours, or €25 to go as far as you can possibly go within Hungary. Seniors and young children travel free. The longest ride on the suburban railway out of Budapest (30 kms) is around €2.20. Rental cars are quite expensive though, so save that for the road trips that are worth it.

Budapest has a metro and while it's no real bargain on a ride-by-ride basis (around €.90 to €1.30), a monthly pass that also works for the trams and buses is a good value at less than €30. If you're of retirement age, you might squeak by for free. "Technically senior citizens who are Hungarians or EU citizens can ride for free, not Americans or Canadians, but they never ask me where I'm from," Gary says. He has lived in Hungary since 1999 without a car and done fine with public transportation. See more on the Budapest public transportation options at bkk.hu.

Apart from the ride from the airport, taxis in Hungary are a bargain, especially outside the capital. In general, you can get around the center of Budapest in a cab for €2.50 to €7, less in smaller cities. It's around €2 to start in Budapest and under a euro for each kilometer, so it's hard to spend a lot unless it's a long haul. Like much of Europe, this country is set up well for those on a bicycle and some expatriates use a bike as their main means of transport. In Budapest there are lots of dedicated bike lanes and in the countryside there's not nearly such an abundance of cars as you see in the capital.

Some expatriates keep a car here, but they use it mainly for shopping, commuting to an office job, or short jaunts. With gasoline costs about double what they are in the USA, it's cheaper to take the train or bus for long distances. Car purchase prices are in line or slightly higher than other European countries, making them more expensive than ones in the USA or Canada. You don't want to get behind the wheel here with even one drink in your system. Any alcohol at all (rumors abound that cough medicine is too much) can get you a drunk driving conviction.

Frequent promotions on the train system and Eurolines bus make international travel from here a bargain. Regiojet train service launched a new bargain-priced offering in 2020 to compete with budget airlines and it's as low as €16 between Prague and Budapest and starts at €9 from Budapest to Prague, which includes reserved seating and Wi-Fi. If you plan ahead you can also find bargain tickets to beach locations of Greece, Bulgaria, or Croatia for around €50. Sometimes budget flights are even less if you pack light.

Healthcare
In this country, the medical care is good, and the dental care is great. With the rise of cross-border medical treatment happening in many places in the world, Hungary has jumped on the trend with both feet. Many Europeans come here to have dental work done or to receive good medical care at a discount. I was actually having some dental problems while in this part of the world at one point and started asking around for prices to get a new crown. I ended up not getting it done because of timing, but prices I was quoted ranged from $250 to $350 all-in. (In the United States or Canada, this can easily top $1,000.)

Getting a cleaning and check-up at the dentist is around $30, getting a set of x-rays about that much again. You'll often pay $50 or less for a filling. You can find rates listed online for teeth whitening, implants, or a root canal, with rates generally a third to a half of the UK prices.

Hungary has a public health care system, which you can tap into if you're a legal resident or have a work permit, but the public hospitals tend to be understaffed and underfunded. It's usually worth it to pay out of pocket and have more options. It's comforting to know, however, that even as a tourist, you are automatically covered for first aid and emergency treatment in the public system.

The one time Gary had to have serious medical work done, the total bill was about one-tenth the price of what it would have been in the USA. For serious care, it's best to make the trip to Budapest if you live elsewhere. In the provinces, the doctors are often not as well-trained and the hospitals not as well-equipped.

If you become a legal resident, proof of health insurance is required. It's usually cheaper and more comprehensive to get an international policy covering Hungary than it is to buy a program within the country.

If you need a lot of meds, this is a good place to be a resident. Drugs are subsidized, so your rate for an asthma inhaler or blood pressure pills will be a tiny fraction of what you probably pay now.

Other Costs

As noted in the housing section, if you pay your own utilities, they can change a lot according to the season. Gary's utilities vary widely, from $30 to $200 a month. "My place is not the best insulated in town, so I pay more in the winter for heat. In the summer, it's very low." Utility costs are significantly lower in the south of the country, where the winters are sunnier and milder.

Internet is $15 to $30 depending on speed and if you want a great connection, you can usually get it in the cities, reaching 100 mbps or more now. The lowest average speed in a Hungarian city keeps climbing and a 2020 study rated Hungary as having the 15th fastest internet speeds in the world. Mobile speeds are fast 4G unless you're in a dead spot, so this is a great country for remote workers and digital nomads.

Katie and Geoff use pre-paid SIM cards and pay about 6 euros per month for 1.5 GB—enough for the basics when out and about. Their home internet is 19 euros for high speed. Geoff also pays the equivalent of 60 euros per month for 40 hours of access at co-working space.

The land of Liszt and Bartok has an abundance of cultural performances going on at all times, from high-brow opera in the capital to an annual festival of wine songs in the south each year. Performances that aren't free are very cheap by European standards. "The theater is amazing in Budapest," says Karen. "The cost of going to a ballet or opera can nearly bankrupt you in Australia. Here it's for everyone. Tickets usually start at $5. If you buy really great seats on a weekend for a popular show it might cost you all of $25."

While average salaries have gone up since I put out the first edition of this book, they still average only 600 to 800 euros per month throughout the country—under $1,000. So, you can get your apartment cleaned for what would be minimum wage where you live now and private primary school averages $600 per month.

Visas

Hungary is part of the Schengen Agreement covering much of the European Union, which means you can't just stick around here on a tourist visa. You get three months upon entering the zone, but after that you have to leave the whole Schengen area for three months before returning. No problem if you're only coming for the summer. Terrible if you want to settle down for longer.

To get residency without being tied to a specific employer, you generally have to show you're doing work a local can't do, like teaching English, or you have to show that you're self-supported by income from abroad. You can see a sample of costs and documents needed for Americans at this embassy site, which also warns you that requirements may change at any time: washington.mfa.gov.hu/eng.

A work visa is good for a year and renewable. Expect to endure a lot of bureaucracy and if you don't have a college diploma, it's going to be even tougher. You will have to apply in your own country and will then have 30 days after entering Hungary to get the local paperwork sorted out.

Cory came from within Europe and the couple can therefore stay as long as they want. "Nowadays, the Hungarian government is trying to make it easier for digital nomads and foreign investors to come to the country," he says. "However, Hungary is still a bureaucratic hell, where people have to run from one office to the other and get their papers notarized. We believe this will become much easier in the coming years."

"We are both Canadian," says Katie, "so we had to apply for a visa. As we work for ourselves and run our own business, we applied for an 'other' visa, which allows us to live in Hungary, but not to work beyond running our own business. We arrived in Hungary as visitors and then hired a lawyer to complete the visa application process for us. To get the visa, we had to provide financial statements proving we earn enough money to support ourselves (there is no set amount the government states is sufficient, although our lawyer suggested $2,500 per month would be fine). We also had to write a letter of motivation explaining why we wanted to live in Hungary, demonstrate we had health insurance, and provide financial statements for our business. We had a clear plan and business reason for being in Hungary and were told by our lawyer that a general reason, such as 'Budapest is beautiful' or 'I want to learn more about Hungarian culture' would not suffice.

You can also look at getting a student visa to study Hungarian. "We've also heard of a visa that allows you residence if you invest €10,000 in a Hungarian business," says Katie, "although we don't know anyone who has done this."

Most people who want to stick around either get a work permit connected to a specific job and company, or a residence permit that's not tied to one employer. "Americans can only get residency for two years," says Gary, "then they have to renew." He was looking into permanent residency though, which you can apply for after being in the country for three years. This costs money for a lawyer and requires a lot of additional paperwork. Most of the items need to be translated into Hungarian as well, plus you have to show proof of health insurance or buy into the Hungarian health care plan.

Do you have Hungarian blood? If so, you could be on the fast track to residency. If you have ancestral roots in the country, you can get real citizenship without giving up your original one, making you one of those enviable people with two passports. You have to speak Hungarian, but you can take intensive language courses while you're living there and collecting paperwork. This is a back door into the EU, which would give you the ability to live elsewhere too if you decide to try out another place.

Downsides
The political winds have been blowing strongly to the right under the current authoritarian Hungarian ruler who keeps consolidating more power. Overt racism, anti-Semitism, and discrimination against minorities and same-sex couples are all rearing their ugly heads on a regular basis. In 2020 the government outlawed gender-neutral names and forbid anyone from legally changing from a masculine to feminine one (or vice-versa) later, an attempt to further marginalize transgender people. Press raids, the shutdown of an esteemed university, and defiance of EU rulings on immigration are regular points of contention. As in Russia and Turkey, there is no longer a functioning opposition as the current regime has effectively shut them out. If you are a news junkie who is leaving your own country to escape fascist politics and a breakdown of human rights, Hungary is not your destination.

This is Central Europe, next to Austria, so you get four distinct seasons here. This is not a retirement destination you move to in order to escape the cold and gray unless you leave here every winter when the birds do and go south. It can be bleak and cold for a few months. (There are some ski hills though at least!)

While many people speak English in Budapest, fluency drops off rapidly in smaller towns and cities. Seek out other expats our tour around the country (it's not all that big) to gauge this for yourself and see how much trouble you will have. Hungarian is a tough language to pick up with just a couple weeks of language classes.

The customer service gets a little better each year as Hungarians who worked abroad return here, but in general it ranges from adequate to terrible. Older Hungarians are often described as "glum" or "unfriendly" and Gary says, "Generally speaking, the work ethic is not particularly alive and well in Hungary."

For More Information:
Budapest Business Journal (BBJ.hu)
DailyNewsHungary.com
XpatLoop.com
ExpatsHungary.com
Seek out embassy sites and Facebook groups for more

Chapter 20:
India

Pros: world's largest train system, robust domestic flight industry, low labor costs, landscape variety, climate variety, interesting food, abundant local produce, unique culture.

Cons: creaky infrastructure, heavy pollution in cities, layers of bureaucracy, endemic corruption, poor sanitation, repressive caste system, petty crime, above-average sexual assault instances, constant badgering, and more "cons" in the other sense of the word than anywhere.

Mariellen Ward, a writer who founded the BreatheDreamGo.com blog and runs tour services in India, kept going back and forth for years between Toronto and India. After getting tired of a divided life and having her feet in two different places, she decided in 2018 to make her move, "That's it, I'm going," I declared. "I gave up my apartment of 11 years in Canada with no idea where I was going to settle down. After a month of looking around in Delhi, I ended up renting a place in Rishikesh."

Anna Phipps, travel writer and blogger at Global-gallivanting.com, settled on Goa after trying a lot of other places on for size. "I was having a quarter-life crisis and decided to quit my job and travel to somewhere as different from the UK as I could get—that was India! That first trip was really challenging but I also fell in love and nowhere else has captivated me so much. After another year of traveling around Southeast Asia and Australia I decided I wanted to take a break and settle down a bit somewhere interesting. I missed the excitement of India and Goa kept calling me, so I decided to head back and rent a house here. The longer I'm in Goa the more people I meet and the harder it is to leave."

India is a place where many people have decided to shed their baggage—physical, mental, or spiritual—and start anew with a fresh outlook. There's a long history here, dating back before the Beatles and *The Razor's Edge*, of people coming to find enlightenment or at least do some soul-searching. What they expect and what they find are usually quite different though. This is not a country where anything is simple or easy. Almost everything is cheap in monetary terms, but extremely taxing in emotional terms. Outside the biggest cities, you can live in India for less money than almost anywhere else in the world. It takes a certain kind of person to do that, however, without wanting to scream or strangle someone on a daily basis after dealing with the non-stop annoyances.

Let's cut to the chase and say that India is about the wackiest place you can choose to live. The less you are able to spend, the wackier it's going to get. This is a country in the midst of massive changes, with its economy sprinting forward quickly, then pulling back just as quickly by a crumbling infrastructure and a government that can't get out of its own way. If the country's economy were a train, it would be a third class one lurching through the countryside, occasionally picking up speed before having to clear cows and make small station stops.

There's an incredible amount of technical talent and education in place, but a maddening bureaucracy and stubborn inertia that together seem to stifle any real momentum.

Then there are the Indian people themselves: the hustlers, the cheats, the liars, the beggars, the gropers, and the scammers that seem to be around every corner, waiting to pounce on the next foreign face that drifts by. Ask anyone who has spent a month or more in the country for some stories about maddening experiences and they will regale you with entertaining tales for hours on end. Liz Scully eventually moved back to the United States to give India a rest for a while because it was wearing her out. "I began to lose my sense of humor. The corruption, bribery, and being fleeced all the time didn't amuse me anymore. I need to live in the west for a while, so I'll appreciate it again when I go back."

So why move here? Well, for starters India is one of the world's greatest bargains. You get more for your money here than nearly any other spot on the globe you can point to. Liz says most people could pretty easily get by for $1,000 a month. "For $1,500 you're living an amazing life." This is one of many countries I've highlighted in this book that's cheaper now than when I featured it in the first edition, thanks to a currency value decline. In most of 2011, a U.S. dollar would get you around 43 Indian rupees. As I was finishing up this book in 2020, you could get 75 rupees. By the time you read this it may be 80.

Young American Michael Gans was longing for a more interesting life when he moved to India, but another big motivator was his lack of disposable income while living in London and San Francisco after he got his MBA. "The price for a basket of goods in Delhi is minuscule in comparison to the last two places I lived. For example, my one-bedroom apartment in San Francisco Bay was $1,340 per month. In Delhi, my one-bedroom apartment of comparable quality was $247 a month. A five-mile cab ride in San

Francisco would be about $25, while the same distance cab ride in Delhi would be about $2 at the most."

People will tell you India can be expensive though—especially expatriate executives—because there are really two sides to India. There's the side the tourism bureau likes to emphasize, of $1,200 a night hotels, luxury train trips, and spectacular restaurants. This coincides with surveys listing Mumbai as one of the most expensive cities in the world for expatriate business executives—if they want to live the same kind of life as they had at home, with the same kind of apartment and appliances.

If you're not trying to live the life of the top two percent though, it's a different story. There are backpacker types living in Goa, Kerala, and the Himalayan regions up north for less than $500 a month. Total! Spend $600 or more a month outside of the largest cities and you will be living better than a middle class local. You'll probably have more space than their whole family too when you come home.

Margot Bigg, author of Moon Handbook's *Living Abroad in India* book, outlines some of the places popular with foreigners who move here. "Goa is a hotspot for artisans from around the world, and there's a large community of self-made expats there. The southern state of Kerala attracts fewer foreigners, although it's arguably more pleasant. Pondicherry is also popular, especially with the French. The hills of Himachal Pradesh and Uttarakhand are also nice, and Dharmsala in particular attracts foreign visitors interested in studying Tibetan Buddhism (as it's the home of the Dalai Lama and the Tibetan Government in Exile)."

Janet Hasam had a high-paying job for a British organization when she first moved to India, but then lived with her Indian husband in Hyderabad, after a fairy tale wedding at the Taj Mahal. Her husband is a university professor and they're better off than many, but while living there they only spent around $250 a month for the two of them. "We lived in a family compound, so our living expenses were limited to paying utilities and food," she says. "That helped a lot. Still, we could buy a huge batch of groceries for the equivalent of four British pounds and that would go a very long way. We had a regular maid and a cook." Their biggest expense was electricity, at about $80 a month in the hot climate, and "cosmetics seem far more expensive there than in England," she says.

India is a big country with vast distances, so you'll find other expatriates scattered all over the place. The ones working for a big company tend to be in Delhi, Mumbai, Bangalore, Hyderabad, or Chennai. These are not the most pleasant places to live though, with an abundance of noise and pollution. Foreigners who live in India by choice and have money coming from elsewhere tend to gravitate to quieter, less hectic places. You can find them on southern beaches, northern mountains, and many places in between. The personalities of Shimla and Hampi are as different as separate countries would be; so much of where you would go depends on what feels like a good fit. Kerala is progressive, tropical, and has a lot of vegetarians. Gujarat state is more conservative, drier, religious, and has a lot more meat on the menu. Rishikesh is "the yoga capital of the world," cool at night, and full of restaurants catering to health nuts. Dharamsala is Buddhist, wet, and full of Tibetan food.

"Goa has a magical and unique culture," says Anna. "It's India's smallest, most laid-back and westernized state and you can still see, feel and taste the influences from nearly 500 years of Portuguese rule and the hippie past. That creates an intoxicating and captivating blend of East and West. There's really nowhere else in the world like it." India's version of beach paradise comes with a reasonable price tag too. "When I first lived in Goa in 2014-15, I was living on about $425 a month (when sharing with one other person). Nowadays it's more like $700 per month because prices have gone up and also because I like more comfort and Western food. I consider myself on a mid-range budget. You could probably scrape by on $500 a month but wouldn't have so much fun. Each year things get fancier in Goa so you could also spend a lot more, especially if you were to book your accommodation online or on Airbnb, especially for a short time in peak season."

Some areas are easy to get to, others are popular in part for their isolation. (India attracts a fair share of renegades, runaways, and outcasts.) To give you an idea of how this can play out, the popular mountain town of Manali is 193 miles (310 kms) from the closest real city and getting to Delhi requires a long overnight bus ride or flight. Other towns in the Himalayan region can only be reached on foot. If you want to be close to civilization, a mid-sized city with an airport or first-class train connection might be a better bet. "Spend some time traveling around the country before you decide where to live," says Philippa Kaye, founder of Indian Experiences, a travel consulting company. "I started traveling around India 22 years ago and there are still places I have on my list to get to that I haven't visited yet."

Typical local wages reveal quite a bit about how little it requires to just get by here. "When I ran our charity organization in Chennai, I used to pay workers between 6,000 and 10,000 rupees a month," Janet says. "That worked out to around $100 to $170. One of them, his mom worked in a hospital and she only earned 4,000 a month ($67)."

If you can navigate the legalities, there are a lot of opportunities here to open a business that fills a hole in the market. The establishments run by foreigners who've settled here often do a brisk business in the absence of serious competition. With very little investment, it's possible to own a profitable restaurant or bar. This becomes much easier to pull off if you have an Indian spouse or at least a local partner to deal with the hurdles: both above the table and under it.

One thing's for sure: life won't be boring after your move. "Old friends at home can't wait to hear what I've been up to the past week," Janet says. "My life is so interesting compared to what it was like in England. Life is so different all the time and I never know what a new day will bring."

Housing Costs
You can rent a penthouse with a waterfront view in Mumbai for as much as you would pay in Hong Kong or London. Delhi and Bangalore are no bargains either. "I looked at a lot of apartments in South Delhi but was getting really despondent after a while," says Mariellen. "I saw so many dumps that were a worse value than I could get in Toronto. I couldn't believe it."

Philippa has lived a total of 13 years in India. She has lived in Jaipur, Delhi, and in a wildlife reserve. "When I first came to Delhi a company was paying for my apartment, then later I had to go out and find my own. What I discovered was that most corporate expats were living in these gated expat complexes where the rents were ridiculously inflated and overpriced," she explains. "I met women in those complexes who almost never left home because they thought it was too dangerous to travel. I didn't want to live like that in a foreign country. I fortunately had lots of Indian friends to turn to and both apartments I rented in Delhi were $800 or so per month then. That's three bedrooms, lots of space, in a high-end area."

She says Jaipur was significantly cheaper, around $200 for a small three-room house with two bathrooms and a kitchen. "You can easily find a place in Jaipur to rent long-term for less than $300 a month."

In most of the country, rents drop dramatically once you get outside the big cities and can sometimes be too cheap to believe. Spend some time on message boards like IndiaMike.com and you'll find people paying $100 a month for their half of a two-bedroom apartment in Goa or $60 for a one-bedroom with a kitchen and mountain-view balcony in Manali. Others hike into the Parvati Valley with a backpack on and decide not to pick it up again until five months later because they've found a whole house to rent for under $100 a month, loads of cheap restaurants, and—it must be said—lots of bargain-priced, locally grown hash to smoke.

After the disappointments in Delhi, Mariellen moved on to the yoga center of Rishikesh in the foothills of the Himalayas and found a furnished apartment in a secure gated community with its own electricity system for $350 per month. She calls it "a really posh place" of 1,200 square feet with two bedrooms, two bathrooms, two balconies, and a roof deck. "Someone referred me to this place before I even got here and about a week later, I moved in. I didn't realize this residential area existed apart from the tourist zone and I really like it here. The manager told me it was 'very expensive' when I said I liked it, so I was worried. Then he told me the price and I was thrilled."

It's not going to cost you much to stay in a guesthouse while you look around for an apartment. Many people check into a cheap hotel and find that'll do just fine. This is a country where you can still find rooms for as little as $2 a night in some areas and for $5 a night there's a good selection.

There are lots of regional quirks though, especially in cities where demand is high from workers making a decent salary. In Bangalore, for instance, you need to put down a deposit for six months' rent. Liz Scully lived in Kerala before Bangalore and says, "It was much cheaper there and I didn't have to put down as much."

She notes though that in India, you often get what you pay for, with more expensive places having screens on the windows, plus a better bathroom with a western toilet. "In India," she adds, "it's hard to find a place without loads of bathrooms and bedrooms: houses and apartments are set up for extended families. Most have at least 3 bedrooms, often a maid's quarters too. Sometimes you can find two-bedroom places, but more common is three bedrooms, three baths."

Liz paid 47,000 rupees per month for her last Bangalore apartment "It had three bedrooms, four bathrooms, in a complex with a swimming pool, squash court, gym, 24-hour security, and parking. My expat colleagues thought I was paying a tiny amount, my Indian friends thought I was paying an outrageous amount."

She says you're almost sure to get some nasty surprises though, or downright cheating. "I had to pay a fee to move out. When I asked what that fee was for, they told me, 'Because the committee that runs the homeowners' association has to make money somehow.'" Plus there's that hefty deposit she had to pay up front, which the owners often use as an interest-free loan. "A ditch digger in Bangalore makes 200 rupees a day—around $3. So, giving a landlord the equivalent of almost $6,000 up front is just nuts."

Anna says you can get a decent apartment or house to rent in Goa for $200 - $300 per month, but you shouldn't expect soft mattresses and comfy couches. "Houses are quite basically furnished so if you want to live a comfortable lifestyle by Western standards then you'll need to invest quite a bit in furnishing and appliances."

Food & Drink
India is one of the world's greatest bargains when it comes to food, whether buying it at the market, eating at a simple restaurant, or going for a fine dining meal. "I'm from Canada," says Mariellen, "where we have a short growing season and we're used to fruits and vegetables being expensive. Here they are so cheap in comparison that I almost feel like they're free. A lot of Indians struggle when the price of onions goes up, of course, but compared to what I used to spend in Toronto it seems like next to nothing. I'll fill up a massive bag with juicy tropical fruit like papayas, watermelons, mangoes, and pineapple and the price ends up being 200 rupees—less than $3. The biggest food shopping bill I ever had was around $100," she adds, "but that was stocking up during the early days of the pandemic, where I got a taxi and went from store to store getting enough to last for weeks. Normally I spend $15 - $20 per week on groceries if I'm not buying imported items."

This is a country where you can still stuff yourself for a dollar at a basic place to eat. In a *thali* restaurant where you'll get heaps of different curries with rice or chapati bread, you can ask for seconds if you're not satisfied. If you step up to a nicer version with more atmosphere, it may be $3 or $4 but you'll also get better quality items. Just don't expect the huge variety you see on Indian restaurant menus at home when you eat out here. Those restaurants abroad usually cover the whole country, while in reality there are regional differences according to tradition, religion, and what's easiest to grow in the area. In some spots the food is really spicy, in others it's more likely to use milder spices and coconut. Naturally on the coast there's more seafood and in the northern mountain regions more lentils and potatoes.

"There's only one really fancy restaurant where I live in Rishikesh but even there you'd really struggle to spend more than $10 on a meal. Usually a nice one in a normal restaurant will be half that." No alcohol is served in her sacred city though, so add a few bucks if you're somewhere that will bring you a beer or glass of wine.

You can spend a fortune in a 5-star hotel in Mumbai or Delhi of course, if you want. "One of my favorite contrasts when in Delhi was when three of us went out to a typical *dhaba* local eatery and had three thalis, something to drink, and dessert and the tab for three came to £1.50. Then I went out with some posh friends who will only eat in the nicest places. We shared a starter and a bottle of wine with our meal and it was £100 each!"

She adds that, "In most of India, it gets a lot more expensive when you start drinking alcohol." Drinking anything considered intoxicating is a mixed bag in India. In some whole states alcohol is not available at all except at a high premium from a smuggler. Or it can be as little as $1.30 for a large half-liter beer in a simple place in Goa. The cheapest hooch is Indian-made whiskey, some brands better than others, while wine—all imported—will cost more than what you would pay at home. As often happens in these places where sin taxes are high or drinking is banned altogether, drugs are plentiful and cheap.

"I spend about $140 a month on groceries and eat out at least once a day," says Anna. "You can eat in a simple Indian restaurant in Goa for about $1.25 or you could eat Western food in a fancier tourist restaurant for about $7."

In general terms, the areas with more Muslims will have a lot of meat—though when you see the open-air butcher shops in the 95-degree heat (35 Celsius), you'll probably decide to be very careful about where you partake. In the south of India, it's almost completely vegetarian, as it will be in sacred cities like Pushkar and Varanasi.

In general though, unless you're really on a super-tight budget, you will eat very well in India and your taste buds will seldom be bored. Just understand that if you want food that tastes like what you're used to from the home country, you'll have to seek it out (often in an international chain hotel) or make it yourself. Even the McDonald's menu is going to look very foreign, with mutton burgers and spicy veggie burgers.

Transportation

Getting around is quite cheap in India, once you figure out what's what and get a sense of real prices. The 14,000-kilometer train network tops all kinds of lists, from being the largest employer in the world (1.6 million people) to having the most continuously running routes. Almost 14 million people travel on the train every day.

An overnight second-class sleeper can be as little as $3, and the 17-hour trip from Delhi to Jaisalmer is around $6 for a bed. Air-conditioned first-class is roughly 2-1/2 times the price of second class, but you get what you pay for and you'll be far less annoyed, especially on journeys that can last all night and half the day. Your belongings will be more secure too. All train prices are set according to the number of kilometers. You can go 2,000 kilometers (1,240 miles) on an air-conditioned sleeper train for less than $50, including bedding. On the one-day A/C express trains ($13 from Bangalore to Chennai, for example) and on all Rajdhani Express trains, multiple meals are thrown in as well.

Buses can be dusty, crowded hulks crammed with people and a pig or two on the roof or can be a "luxury" bus that at least has assigned seats. Prices are comparable to the train (in 2nd non-A/C class), but the buses are more direct for some routes. As a rule of thumb, a cheap bus is a dollar for 2-3 hours, while a private express bus costs 70 to 90 cents per hour traveled and it's unlikely you'll want to stay on board for more than 12 hours. Long distance night buses have "sleeper" options as well (usually for a 25 percent extra, but avoid those buses whenever possible as they are not the safest option. When the number of passengers plus the age of the bus is over 100, you have discovered the real rural India. And it's a good time to get off.

Apart from a cruise down the backwaters in Kerala, there aren't many opportunities to get around on a boat. Internal flight prices have come down in recent years with more competition. A flight can shave days off a long trip. Delhi to Mumbai (Bombay) can take at least 24 hours on the train, so $65 to $120 for a flight can be money well spent. Budget airlines can get as low as $40 one way.

"There are something like two hundred thousand bicycle rickshaw and auto-rickshaw drivers in Delhi," says Michael. "You can't go outside for five minutes without seeing a few of them. When I lived in San Francisco, it was a minimum of $20 to take a cab, whether you were going 100 yards or two miles. Here you would a buck fifty to go five miles in an auto-rickshaw."

"Uber and Ola have changed our lives," says Philippa. "They have standardized prices and made things so much easier. Normally, every morning I had to start over with the bargaining just to get them to use the meter and it was exhausting. I would still end up paying a 'white face tax.' Now I use one of the app services and it's a dollar or two for a ride of 30-40 minutes in Delhi."

In most of the major cities the cabs and auto-rickshaws have a meter, but you'll have to fight to get them to use it. Elsewhere you'll need to bargain like crazy up front. Ask a local first what a reasonable fare should be. There are usually enough drivers hanging around that you can end up at a reasonable price by haggling. Prepaid taxi and auto rickshaw booths are available at major railways stations and airports with government-approved fixed rates.

Only a foreigner with a death wish would try to own and drive a car here. India has one of the highest road accident rates in the world and five minutes on those roads will show you why. You can hire a driver ($20 - $60 per day) and agree ahead of time on what is included in the price. Then kick back and let him navigate around the sleeping cows and loaded-down auto rickshaws. Mariellen had furniture and belongings in Delhi that were too much to fit in a regular car, so she hired a driver with a SUV to bring it all from the capital up to Rishikesh. It was around $100 for a trip of five hours.

If you're living here and need a car regularly, there are car services that can have a regular driver on call or if you have to commute each weekday, you can get a monthly rate. "For a lot of people who have corporate jobs, a driver is the biggest expense. If you found someone direct you could trust, it could be as little as $300 a month for just the labor, before fuel costs. But if you go through a firm, which is the best way to keep from getting fleeced, it'll be at least $600 a month," says Janet.

If you do want to explore on your own and you're not in a huge city, a motorbike is cheaper and probably safer. You can dodge the potholes and cows more easily. This is the transport method of choice for most foreigners in Goa. "I spend about $80 per month on scooter hire and petrol," says Anna. "Local buses are cheap (30 cents from Anjuna Beach to Mapusa city) but taxis go from expensive to *very* expensive if you don't have a local contact or good haggling skills. A reasonable price from the airport to Anjuna, for example, is $20."

City infrastructure in India has typically lagged far behind growth, but Delhi has done a commendable job with its city rail projects. There's a high-speed rail line to the airport and the fast-expanding, air-conditioned subway is the 12th-largest in the world, with 285 stations and 389 kms (242 miles) of track so far. It runs until 11:30 at night and the fare is 14 cents to 84 cents depending on distance, with discounts for using a fare card and riding in off-peak hours.

Healthcare
Pharmaceuticals cost a small fraction of what they do in the USA and for most things you don't even need a prescription.

India is a major medical tourism destination, with the best hospitals having western-trained doctors and great facilities. Patients will fly from a high-priced country like the USA to India for major surgery, getting a knee replacement or a heart operation for one-fifth or less. From check-ups to shots to lab work, you can expect to pay a fraction of the rates in your home country, with little to no waiting. Complete hip surgery here can be well under $10,000: one-fifth of the U.S. cost and with one-tenth the waiting time in the UK or Canada. Want to get a facelift to get rid of some of those sags and wrinkles? Your bill will probably be $1,250 instead of the $10,000+ it would cost in New York or California.

Naturally, all the doctors speak English in India. Even though they may know another dialect, English is the language of government, education, business, and medicine. It may take a while to get used to the accent, but you won't have any trouble communicating your symptoms.

"The health care is quite good in the cities," says Philippa, "and the prices to pay out of pocket are quite cheap. I got a set of three MRIs for around $120 and once when I had to spend a stint in intensive care in the best private hospital it worked out to around $60 a day. A full set of blood tests to check for just about everything was $30."

This assumes you're in or near a major city, however. If you're out in a rural village somewhere, expect care to be rudimentary at best. There's a reason the life expectancy in this country is only 67. Most locals can't afford the doctors who paid six figures to study abroad or the gleaming air-conditioned hospital with a high-end clientele. This is a country, after all, where you see dentists who don't look much wealthier than the beggars set up on a blanket on the sidewalk. They have a hand-scrawled sign advertising their ability to yank out your bad tooth on the spot for the equivalent of a couple dollars.

If you're living far from a city you can get to easily, you are better off being young and healthy than retired with failing body parts. If nothing else, keep money aside for a last-minute flight and a MasterCard with a large credit limit. The other option would be to sign up with an evacuation insurance company like MedJet Assist, but you need to really be a tourist (and not a long-term resident on a work visa) for that to apply.

Other Costs
How much things will cost you in India depends a great deal on your bargaining skills. Buying almost any product or service requires a game of negotiation. Without participating in it, you'll get robbed. "The first time I got a taxi in Chennai it cost me 400 rupees," Janet says. "It took 20 minutes, and it was from the airport, so I thought it was very reasonable. By the time I finished living there two years later, I was paying 40 rupees for the same ride. Every time I'd come out of the shopping mall the drivers would all shout '150 rupees for a taxi madam!' Eventually I would ride home for 30."

Liz says utility bills depend a lot of your set-up and how you deal with the frequent power outages. A lot of people have solar hot water heaters so they can shower without being dependent on the finicky electrical grid. "Plus, you always need some kind of backup emergency power," she adds. "Internet is really solid in a place like Bangalore and it's blisteringly fast, but you need an uninterrupted power source. Mobile internet is quite fast as well, but 4G isn't very widespread yet."

She stresses that in local currency terms, inflation is massive. "When I first got my apartment, the electricity bill was usually around 350 rupees per month. At the end it was 675 rupees, for the same consumption. Inflation is so fast that I would go home for Christmas, then come back from the break and prices were higher."

Philippa says was paying $45 - $50 per month for electricity in Delhi in the warm months. Mariellen lives in a housing complex with its own electricity set-up, which enables her to avoid the power outages problem. She says her electricity is pretty cheap normally, running around 800 rupees per month ($11), but "It's been as high as $35 if I have the air conditioning running all the time in the hottest months."

She says India has some of the cheapest internet rates in the world. Because the mobile phone and data landscape is so competitive, you can get rates that seem too low to believe. "I have a plan that's the equivalent of US$8 for 84 days. I get 2gb of data per day for 84 days then I renew and it starts over. So, I doubled down and got that for my phone and for my laptop via a USB stick. Now I have 4 gigabytes per day combined, for $16, which covers me for almost three months."

"A mobile package for one month of calls, texts, and 1.5 gigabytes of data per day is about $3.50 in Goa," says Anna.

Most foreigners spending $800 or more a month here are living quite well because of all the domestic help that income can afford. "You have to *have* a maid," says Liz. "It's a social responsibility to have staff in India, as many people as you can afford. If you don't, you're viewed as socially horrible in a way that doesn't really have a western equivalent. You have wealth, so you must spread it about. My maid's useless, but she's honest. Nearly everyone has a story of a maid who stole from them. You always have to get receipts from supermarkets. You have to be prepared to be fleeced a certain amount, but you must set a limit and don't let it go beyond that."

Liz paid her housekeeper the equivalent of $85 a month to work two days a week, which she says is very high by local standards. "Some expats are paying more than $200 for a cook or cleaner and they think it's grand," she says. "But really that's what a trained sous chef at the Marriott is getting."

One of the great things about living in India is you can afford to have staff," Philippa says, "like a driver or housekeeper." At first, she resisted, but eventually got a housekeeper to come in six days a week and it was only about $60 - $80 per month.

Anna pays around $7 a week for basic cleaning and laundry service. "Yoga classes are plentiful and cost a little more than $5 per class on average," she adds.

Visas

Understand that India loves bureaucracy perhaps more than any country in the world and the civil service is a massive employer in the country. Picture an office with 50 people, desks stacked with papers in triplicate, those papers held down by paperweights since fans are blowing at full speed in the heat. Nobody is in a hurry, nobody is striving for efficiency, and rules are adhered to with glee at every level. Occasionally you can speed up the process with some *baksheesh* placed in the right hands, but otherwise you will need lots of time and even more patience than usual. You must apply in advance and be approved even for a basic tourist visa.

The good news is, the residents of four countries—the USA, Canada, UK, and Japan—can get a long-term visa that allows them to stay for five or ten years, only needing to leave the country every 180 days (for one day is fine) to keep it active. Canadian Mariellen is on a long-term business visa, which is good for five years. "Normally leaving is not a big deal. In the summer I'll go to Canada, in the winter somewhere like Thailand," she says. "They are very serious about it here. If you overstay your visa, it'll definitely put your future status in trouble."

Margot agrees, saying, "Follow the rules closely. "This is not a country where you want to overstay your visa. You may face deportation and never be allowed back in the country again. If you are deported, you may have a difficult time getting visas for other countries in the future."

The citizens of many other countries beyond the four mentioned earlier can get an e-visa that's good for five years, but with more restrictions on the length of stay and how long you must stay out of the country.

If you're not from one of the favored countries though, India is a hard place to move to full-time unless you are Indian to start with (or can demonstrate recent heritage). There is no such thing as a retirement visa here for people with no Indian blood. For a tourist visa, most nationalities get 90 days or 180 days.

Making this even more complicated is that you can't buy property unless you are in the country 182 days in a fiscal year. As you may have noticed from the above, that's impossible to legally do in one stretch, so it takes two entries to accomplish this in a specific calendar time period. You might want to just rent anyway, especially since Indian laws aren't always known for having a strong base in logic and it's not hard to imagine the rules changing again for the worse after you've already invested in property.

There are myriad other visa types you can apply for, but understand that for a business or employment visa you generally need to be sponsored by a local company. "You have to apply for an employment visa under the sponsorship of your country at the embassy of your country of residence before leaving for India." Says Margot. "Employment visas normally last one year and can be renewed in India. You'll be asked to submit detailed contract and employer information along with your visa application. Specific requirements can vary and change, so it's best to check with your local embassy or consulate. You'll also be required to register for a residency permit within 14 days of your arrival in India."

Some retirees have managed to get a part-time local job to obtain a business visa, with the pay they're getting not really being the point: they're doing it to avoid leaving the country every six months.

Trying to come in and set up a business is possible, but it requires extensive paperwork, an attorney, and a pledge to only hire local workers unless you specifically need foreigners for work that can't be done by a local person. It gets much easier if you have an Indian spouse who can be the official owner on paper. Naturally if you marry an Indian person, everything gets much easier for a long-term stay as well. You'll also have less chance of getting fleeced on a daily basis.

Spend some time on your local embassy site and follow the instructions to the letter when applying for a visa. There is usually a private agency in place that handles the paperwork and they will have more information on their site. Take listed turnaround times with a grain of salt and double them to be safe.

Downsides
Some have written entire entertaining books about the downsides of spending time in India. There's probably no country in the world where the touts, the scammers, and the schemers work so tirelessly to extract a few extra rupees in every possible situation. If you've spent a lot of time in Egypt or Morocco, you'll be at least partially prepared, but even the most patient people can end up snapping at some point.

The expats in this country all agree that it's a given you're going to get cheated and ripped off on a regular basis. "You will get fleeced by everyone, all the time, and have to accept that," says Liz. "If you get angry every time you're getting ripped off, it will drive you crazy. You need to have a limit you'll accept and stand your ground on that."

"I often get asked about safety in India by the media," adds Mariellen, "which I don't think is a major concern. Your chances of getting ripped off here, however, are really high. I'm a lot more suspicious of people here, I ask a lot more questions, and I'm a lot tougher than I use to be. Getting ripped off is really the biggest danger here. You can't take it personally though—they do it to each other too! It seems to be in the DNA here."

"Trust is a huge issue in India," says Philippa. "You need to get everything in writing and verified by lawyers for any major transaction and even then, you have to be super careful. I had a business partner and accountant take me for every penny I had—after working with them for 10 and 15 years. If there's any opportunity to cheat you, someone will take it, so you have to be on guard at all times."

It also takes a lot more time and effort to get anything done here than it would in an efficient place like the USA, Canada, or Australia. "When I was in Delhi I would set out for a day of errands and have four or five things on my list," says Mariellen. "In Toronto they would all get done in a few hours. In Delhi if I got one of them done that same day, it was a great victory!"

The infrastructure in this country is seriously overtaxed, with blackouts being common throughout the country. Broadband penetration to the home is the lowest of almost anywhere outside Africa. Most people rely on mobile networks for their internet service. With a population this huge, the more the government builds, the more it falls behind.

"Broadband is still not commonplace here in Goa," says Anna. "Using a 4G hotspot is the best way to get online but there are still many places with poor signal coverage. Most of the restaurants, bars, and budget hotels advertise free Wi-Fi but most of the time its painfully slow at best."

This is a very difficult and trying place to be an entrepreneur. Sure, you see people set up on sidewalks everywhere cutting hair or pulling teeth, but the World Bank ranks India near the bottom of their list worldwide for ease of starting a real, legal business. Expats who manage to get through the bureaucratic gauntlet can do quite well though by offering a first-world level of service. "More and more foreigners are moving to India to start their own businesses and I know of expats who own health clubs, hair salons, interior design firms, travel agencies, and plenty of restaurants," says Margot.

India's weather is greatly impacted by the annual monsoon and it's tropical apart from the high peaks in the far north, so there are really no places where you get some kind of "eternal spring" climate like you have in certain highland towns of other countries. It's certainly much cooler and nicer much of the year in the Himalayas, but winter can turn downright brutal. Kerala during the monsoon can be a soggy mess for months. Delhi or Mumbai in the hottest time of the year will make you sweat a liter of water just walking out the door. It's why you find so many British-era hill stations scattered around the country. So, if you're not on a work permit in a real job, the six-month time limit is not necessarily a bad thing. You just take off when the weather is at its worst, coming back when that part is over.

Last, although India has relaxed a lot of its import restrictions over the years, duties are still high and you can pay more than what you would in your own country for items that come from outside India, whether that's electronics, clothing, or those food items you're craving. "You practically have to take out a loan if you want to buy a block of cheddar cheese," says Mariellen. "One nice development though is a company is now growing quinoa in India. So that's a normal price now."

For More Information
IndiaMike.com
BreatheDreamGo.com
Global-gallivanting.com
MyTripHack.com India section
TransitionsAbroad.com India section
Find Facebook groups for specific cities

Chapter 21:
Malaysia

Pros: good infrastructure, fast internet, wide variety of cuisines, inexpensive rentals, straightforward residency visa, drinkable water, good air connections.

Cons: repressive government, limited press freedom, high alcohol costs, unstable economy, limited sightseeing or culture options.

When Kirsten Raccuia and her husband were getting tired of the rat race in Chicago and wanted to move abroad, they thought that was going to be to Costa Rica. They had made a few trips there and loved it. They were finding that it wasn't really a good value, however, and no place really struck them as having a good expat community to integrate with. "We went to an International Living conference looking for ideas," Kirsten said, "and a guy we met there living in Malaysia really made it sound attractive. We decided to go there on a vacation trip to check it out, but I said flat out I didn't want to live there, being on an opposite time zone and so far away.

Soon after we got there though, I said, 'Oh no, I love it here. I love everything about it.' The food is great, the people are welcoming, there's a big expat community, the price is right, everything. Six years later, here we still are."

She says they intentionally burned their bridges back home. They sold their real estate business, sold their possessions, and took off for a new life in Malaysia. "I didn't want to deal with a house, cars, things in storage—that would make it too easy to go back. I didn't want to have one foot in each place." Now they live in a $650 apartment of 2,300 square feet, ocean views, and "more closets than I have ever had." Kirsten estimates their place would cost $5,000 a month or more in Chicago. Their *total* monthly budget is around $2,000 though without trying very hard. "If I didn't drink and didn't cook, we could spend less." She's able to live a less hectic live as a freelance writer now. See more about her life there on the Sand in My Curls blog.

You don't hear much about Malaysia from the location independent crowd because even though there are an estimated 12,000 foreigners in Penang, most of them fall into two camps: retirees or corporate workers. The former come because of the ease of getting a 10-year visa on the "My Second Home Malaysia" program—more on that in the visas section.

Company executives are there because of the large number of foreign companies operating in this port region and in the capital of Kuala Lumpur. "Then there are a few like us," Kirsten says, "who don't fit into either camp. But we intermingle a lot."

When it comes to the ease of transition into a new life, it's hard to beat moving to Penang. It's a little cooler (a relative term) because of the regular breezes, it's not such a huge city as the capital, and you can get from one end of the island to another for $15 in a taxi. It's quite a paradise for foodies too.

"It has all the comforts of a lively artistic city, it's one of Southeast Asia's most established arts hubs, and yet it has great hiking trails, amazing rainforest, wildlife, and some pretty decent beaches," says Marco Ferrarese, who runs the Penang Insider site. "All within a very short distance on a compact tropical island."

Other expatriates mostly choose to live in the capital, Kuala Lumpur, or the former Portuguese colony of Malacca (sometimes spelled as Melaka). Otherwise you can head to the two Malaysian states on the island of Borneo, where you may need to feel like a pioneer unless you want to mingle with oil workers or environmentalists trying to save the orangutans or dwindling rainforest from awful palm oil plantations.

There are a few bloggers and younger location independent workers who have spent time living in Malaysia and most of them give it high marks. They tout the green spaces, the ease of transportation, the ease of getting by in English, and the bargain living costs. "I couldn't imagine having the same life in London or Melbourne compared to what we have here in Kuala Lumpur," said Sherri "Shezz" Ottova from England on her Travel Mermaid blog, "unless we were on a 6-figure salary, and even then, it would be a struggle."

All of the expats I spoke to and all those who posted online are living on $2,000 or less per month as a couple or $1,500 or less as a single, usually without being very frugal. (Most locals earn less than $1,000 a month, to put that in perspective.) A pretty average wage for a good white-collar job in Malaysia is the equivalent of $700 to $850, so if you're pulling in $1,500—a very minimal income in the western world—you're earning double what a typical office worker does here, and you'll be well off.

Prices aren't rock bottom for any aspect of travel or living, but food, lodging, and transportation all seem reasonable for what you get—and can be lower than some areas in Thailand. Peninsular Malaysia is quite westernized on the western half and while it feels exotic, you can be relatively sure you'll have a clean place to eat and a western toilet in your room no matter where you stay. Transportation is easy and comfortable, a lot of people speak English, and you can even drink the water in most locations.

Housing Costs

If you look around and are patient, you should be able to rent a comfortable and spacious apartment in Malaysia for $500 a month or less, even in good areas of the capital. If you're willing to live on the outskirts of there or Penang, you can pay $250 a month and get something decent. Marco Ferrarese, who runs the Penang Insider site and is married to a Malaysian, spends less than $200 per month on rent including all the utilities. "I live in a low-density local flat, meaning I have no facilities like swimming pool, security, or a gym, and we spend around US$115 a month for our two-bedroom apartment. Yes, it's cheap and yes, it's more than decent to live, but I am on the 4th floor without an elevator. Penang is still full of these deals if you can manage with a spartan life."

Step it up a bit from there and you can really find something grand. "They're constantly building here and I'm not sure why," says Helen Davies, who moved to Penang with her husband Paul for early retirement from the UK. "New buildings keep going up while there's already a wide variety of empty places for rent. There are 600 units over three buildings in our gated complex, but probably only 30% of them are occupied at any given time." They pay around $625 per month for their furnished three-bedroom, 1,600-square-foot condo on the 15th floor with a view of the water. The complex has a big swimming pool, huge gym, tennis courts, and 24-hour security. ("Though I'm not sure how necessary the security is," she says. "Crime is very low in this country.")

Kirsten and Mark don't have as many amenities, but they have even more space, paying less than $650 for 2,300 square feet, terrific views and balconies, all furnished including a dishwasher, oven, big TV, and washing machine. The two of them share four bathrooms, three bedrooms, and a maid's quarters they use for storage. "We have paid between $650 and $700 for six years now," she says. "I know others paying anywhere from $230 for a smaller but still nice and modern place up to $925 for a fabulous penthouse kind of apartment." For that amount, you'll probably get a roof terrace with a plunge pool or a full house with garage.

In Kuala Lumpur, it's a larger and more sprawling city, with the main choices being either living in the city center or going for more space and amenities for the money further out. Living in the suburbs is not a big inconvenience in KL, with public transportation and car services bridging the gap rather easily.

"I lived in a 120 square-meter three-bedroom flat (about 1,300 square feet) in one of the most exclusive expat neighborhoods for the equivalent of US$530 per month," says Shezz. "All bedrooms had an ensuite bath plus there was an additional bathroom. It also had a balcony and 2 allocated parking spaces. The complex has an Olympic-sized swimming pool, 2 additional secluded pools, a gym, tennis court, squash court, badminton court, sauna, Jacuzzi, and an herb garden." She says this is a pretty standard set-up for expats in KL, though they got a better deal than average, for what would normally be more like $650 to $700 in the expat suburbs for a similar size and amenities.

Anya from RoadIsCalling.com decided to rent in the city center instead, where she says the cost of renting an apartment starts from around $310, with plenty to choose from. "Almost all apartment complexes have a gym, pool, barbecue area, cool common lounge, security desk, and office. Renting a home in Kuala Lumpur is easy and quick. A lot of our friends who live in KL use the Mudah.my site to find a flat."

I found basic city apartments on that Mudah site for as little as $150, then at the other end of the scale, huge 4-bedroom furnished places of 2,000 square feet or more with all the amenities renting for $650 to $800 per month. Only a few are more than $1,000 per month, probably rented to corporate workers with a housing stipend. In other cities, there's Craigslist, agency sites, and multiple expat Facebook groups with rental listings. "I think there are four expat Facebook groups here in Penang," says Helen.

Utilities aren't going to set you back much either. Wi-Fi will generally cost between $12.50 and $40 depending on speed. "We pay about the same as we paid in the UK," says Helen, "but it's about 10 times faster here." Water and sewer will be $10 a month or less, gas about the same if you use that. Despite everyone needing to run the air conditioning constantly, electricity costs aren't too bad. Everyone I talked to was paying somewhere between $40 and $70 per month, despite sometimes being in large apartments with lots of windows.

Most apartments come furnished and that includes everything except kitchen items like skillets, glasses, and cutlery. While in many countries you can't expect to have "western" appliances or the kind of bathrooms you're used to, in Malaysia there's not much of an adjustment. You may not have an oven since few locals bake, but you'll usually have a washing machine and often even a dryer.

The furniture will be comfortable and modern, the TV, microwave, and stove up to date.

Foreigners can own property outright in Malaysia, but nobody I've talked to in recent years thinks it's a great investment because there's too much overbuilding. There is an added incentive to buy a home here though: instant residency. If you are looking for a tropical retirement paradise, Malaysia is one of the few Asian countries actively trying to lure more foreigners. If you meet certain requirements on assets and pension income for the "My Second Home "program, there are plenty of incentives on offer. You can accomplish the same thing by putting less than a house or condo would cost into a local bank account though. See the visas section for that.

There is a robust lending system in place for buying property, with low down payments and financing through developers and banks. The negative side of this is that many people, especially ethnic Chinese business families, buy property and just sit on it as an investment, hoping they can flip it later for a better price without incurring much in the way of interest payments. So, check the real occupancy level on any condo building you're considering and see if any lights are on at night.

Food & Drink
Meals are seldom dull in Malaysia because you usually have three cuisines to choose from: Malay, Chinese, and Indian. You could have dim sum for breakfast, a vegetarian thali spread for lunch, and a chicken satay with peanut sauce followed by nasi goreng for dinner.

Street stall or food market meals are 75 cents to $3 with sodas, even in the cities. Local or backpacker sit-down restaurants are only a little bit more. You can go from stall to stall in Penang and have a world-class feast. It's easy to stick to a healthy, well-balanced diet in this country. "We rarely cook because it's so cheap to eat out," says Helen. "Lunch yesterday was 7 ringgit for two ($1.70)."

Even the top-end restaurants are quite reasonable by western standards—until you order alcohol. Beer is expensive for the region: generally, $3 and up in a restaurant for a 12-oz. bottle due to high taxes. You can pay more than you would at home in a nice place. Local commercial whiskey or Arak (a local rice whiskey) is less money if you can stomach it.

"Like most people, we have a smuggler we buy liquor from because the store prices are insane," says Kirsten. "We can buy a bottle of vodka from him for $9 that in a store here would be $20. It's always half or less to go underground." It's especially painful to buy wine at the Malaysian store prices, with a markup of two or three times just to cover the sin taxes.

There's plenty of fresh, tropical fruit juice for cheap wherever you go, and you can safely drink the water in most of the towns and cities. Coffee has traditionally been a letdown outside the large cities, but it's a different story now in the urban areas.

"What we personally like is how many cute cafes there are in Kuala Lumpur that serve delicious breakfast and coffee," says Anya. "There is a lot to choose from and prices range between $3.50 to $8 for breakfast and $2-$3 for a coffee drink."

When you buy groceries, some food prices are subsidized, such as rice, cooking oil, and sugar. Local fruit and vegetables are cheap, and items produced locally like fish and chicken are reasonably priced. Few expats spend more than $100 a week on groceries unless they have a large family or are buying a lot of alcohol.

Kirsten buys most of her food at the market. She says a kilo of chicken or pork is usually around $4. Most fruits and vegetables are a dollar or two a kilo. She says it's cheaper to eat out than it is to cook for yourself. "You can go out to a nice restaurant here and spend 70 ringgit for a couple for a full seafood meal—less than $20."

Naturally, you'll pay more for food from home, but at least here it's available if you're willing to splurge. In Penang you have Tesco, Sam's Club, and Marks & Spencer, while there are even more options in the capital city.

Transportation
"It's very easily to get around for cheap on public transportation, some loop routes are even free," says Helen. "The pay bus in George Town is US 35 cents and the most you would pay to traverse the whole island is on a public bus is a dollar. Taxis are very cheap, plus we have Grab on the phone. A local journey of 5 to 8 kms on Grab is $1.50 to $2.50. The most you would pay is $7, like to the airport. They overcharge to come back from there though, as in $12 for a 30-60-minute ride. So last time we just took the bus."

In Kuala Lumpur, a monthly transportation pass is just $23 and a one-way ticket on the rail service that heads out to the suburbs is 70 cents. There's also a monorail that hits 11 locations in the city center. Most public transportation runs until 11 or 12 at night.

A 6-kilometer taxi or Uber ride will run $2.50 to $6. In theory taxis as supposed to use the meter but some will refuse, thus the massive switch over to Uber and Grab for many riders.

Bus rides within Malaysia are inexpensive and efficient, thanks in part to cheap fuel prices and great highway systems. You can get to most places in the country for $15 or less and it will be a comfortable ride, as long as you bring an extra layer to deal with the extreme A/C. Short hops are just a few bucks. Malaysia has some of the best roads in the world, so buses are faster and more convenient, plus often they are the only option. Almost all of the upper-end ones offer free Wi-Fi.

The train line in Malaysia is not too convenient, but it's good for getting to some places in Thailand from Kota Bahru (on the east side) or George Town/Penang (on the west). One line goes south through the western cities like Penang, KL, and Malacca, while the other starts on the east coast and goes through the forested interior. They meet up south of Malacca and head to Singapore. It is a more romantic way to move about and an alternative to flying if you want to travel to Bangkok or Singapore. You can book online and reserve a seat or sleeping berth. Prices are higher than the bus, but you can get up and move around or sleep better on overnight trips.

Cars can cost 50 percent more in Malaysia than the same model would be in the United States. On top of that, there's a poor market for used vehicles as many won't accept the idea of depreciation; used cars end up being priced higher than they should be. Because prices are so high on new cars, banks give out car loans running 10 years or more. If you really need a car, suck it up and pay, but you're better off using public transportation.

Healthcare
The healthcare system in Malaysia is excellent. The main reason Malaysia doesn't have the kind of medical tourism industry Thailand does is not because of skills or equipment, but rather a lack of marketing savvy. Prices and the quality of care are on par between the two countries. Thailand has just done a much better job in getting the word out.

Seeing the doctor is usually somewhere between $5 and $20—even if it's a house call. In Penang alone there are at least 20 hospitals, all employing English-speaking doctors. They're well-staffed too: no four-hour waits to get treated here.

You won't need to put off your check-up at the dentist's office. A cleaning is generally around $25-$30, a filling less than $20, and a porcelain crown $300 or so. For major procedures, the economics are equally enticing.

Many surgical procedures that cost tens of thousands of dollars in the USA are a fraction of that in Malaysia, even in the top private hospitals. As in $6,000 to $12,000 for a hip replacement, $800 to $1,000 for cataract surgery, or $70 tops for an ultrasound. A night in a private hospital bed will cost you less than a nice local hotel room, not 10 times as much.

If you want to get private medical insurance that allows you to go to any doctor and hospital you'd like, you should be able to find a good policy for under $1,000 per year. A bit more if you travel a lot and want to be covered elsewhere. "My health insurance for the year is $1,200 with terrific coverage, no deductible," says Kirsten. My older husband Mark's is $1,400. In the USA we paid $1,200 per *month* for the two of us, with an insanely high deductible we'd have to cover first."

Up to now we've just been paying out of pocket," says Helen, "because the prices are so reasonable. "We are thinking about getting an insurance policy now though because a friend of ours just had a nasty accident and that's a little scary."

Other Costs

Utility costs are quite reasonable in Malaysia, with most people paying $40 to $70 per month on electricity even if running the air conditioning regularly for a large apartment. Cooking and shower gas will be $5 to $15 a month and fast broadband internet ranges from $13 to $40. Figure on $20 to $45 per month for cell phone calls depending on whether you need unlimited data. A Sim card will be $4 or so.

If you've visited Cambodia, Laos, or Vietnam before coming here, you may feel downright ignored as you walk the streets of Malaysia. There's no real "walking wallet" view of foreigners by vendors here as many of them are foreigners themselves—by bloodline anyway. When you're quoted a price, it's generally the same price any local would pay. On the flip side, customer service is often the opposite of attentive.

Local school costs may be around $100 a month, but you have to factor in uniforms, supplies and other fees. If you want to enroll your child in an accredited international school, however, that can cost as much as $2,000 per month for the ones the children of tycoons and political leaders attend. There are options in between without international certification.

For basic clothing made in Asia, prices are the same or less than they would be in the U.S., in giant air-conditioned shopping malls. The shopping for handicrafts is not great, but you can get Chinese-made electronics for competitive prices, especially in the capital.

Visas

Malaysia has gotten a reputation for being much more welcoming to foreign retirees than most Asian countries because of its *Malaysia My Second Home* program—usually shortened to "MM2H." If you have some money to put into a bank or to invest in buying property in Malaysia, it's quite straightforward for you to get legal residency and be welcomed with open arms. Once approved, you are a legal resident for 10 years and can come and go as you please. You can also import a car duty-free or buy one locally that's free of taxes. You can also import household goods duty-free.

This program has actually gotten less costly since the first edition of this book came out if you're bringing in U.S. dollars (because of exchange rate declines for the ringgit), but the same or more if you're Canadian or British. If you're under 50, you need to invest a sizable chunk of cash in a Malaysian bank and then after a year you can draw that down by a third if you are spending money on education, a home, medical care, or some other approved expenses. The bar is lower if you are 50 or older. At any age you can purchase property with no restrictions under this program.

"When we applied, you had to prove 350,000 Malaysian ringgit (a little more than $80,000) of savings that cannot be property," says Helen. "You also have to show income of 10,000r per month (currently around $2,300) for at least three months, with bank statements. You apply in one person's name for the visa and that includes a spouse, parents, even a housekeeper supposedly. The whole process took two months, but now a different ministry is handling it and we hear it's taking much longer now. The MM2H visa is renewable after 10 years, but of course if your passport renews before that, you have to transfer the visa, which requires another step. Should my husband pass away, I would have to reapply. It should be transferable, but it's not."

You'll see that MM2H income requirement quoted with different figures in different places, but that's mostly because of exchange rate differences. To be safe, find a way to get at least $2,600 coming through your checking account for a few months as they'll be looking at your bank statements and the ringgit could strengthen.

The rules and amounts change every year or two, partly due to exchange rate erosion, plus the money amounts can be different according to where in Malaysia you decide to live. You have to deposit or invest more in the capital city, for instance, than you do in Kuching, which is not on the peninsula. If you invest a large sum in property you can get around the bank deposit, but sale prices aren't as good as rental prices and if you're 50 or older, the amount you have to deposit in a bank is much lower that what you would have to spend to buy property.

If you don't go down the MM2H path and you don't have a work visa, the most common path is a three-month tourist visa. "The first year we had tourist visas and did visa runs," says Kirsten. "We would just take a vacation every three months and go somewhere new. Later we got a business visa because we had plans to run a medical tourism business here, but then that ended up not working out. When Mark hit 50, we got on the My Second Home program, which meant showing income and depositing about $33,000 at the time in a fixed deposit in a Malaysian bank. You are not allowed to work for a Malaysian company, but otherwise the rules aren't restrictive, and the 10-year visa is a huge benefit."

There are myriad other ways to apply for long-term residency, many based on your occupation or skills, whether you're getting a work permit or not. As usual, if you're married to a local it gets easier.

There is some hope that the government is adjusting to the new remote worker reality though. If you are running a legit online business or are getting ready to launch one, the Malaysia Tech Entrepreneur Programme will provide a visa of one year or five years depending on an array of qualifications and fees. The income requirements are a little fuzzy on what is essentially a one-page website as I write this, but it is an encouraging development for Southeast Asia, where tech entrepreneurs who are location independent have traditionally been viewed with distrust or skepticism, despite their ever-increasing numbers and spending power.

Downsides

A kind of voluntary apartheid exists in the country, with ethnic Malays running the government, the ethnic Chinese and Indians running businesses. Many jobs are only open to Malays and this is perfectly legal.

This is a schizophrenic country in many ways, divided between ethnic Malays, Indians, and Chinese. This is great when it's time to eat out, but traveling from one coast to the other can feel like going to a completely different country—a strict Muslim country without alcohol if it's the east coast. This is no Thailand when it comes to permissive attitudes toward sexuality and sexual orientation. It's also not a place you want to settle if you're a regular recreational drug user. You know that *Return to Paradise* movie where Joaquin Phoenix faces execution for some hash found at their beach hut by the beach? Well, it's based on real laws on the books.

There's very little press freedom in Malaysia and the government has shown time and again that it's not afraid to throw around its weight and bend the rules to stay in power.

If you're going to move here, you'd better not have an aversion to sweat. "No matter what clothes you put on, be ready to sweat once you step outside," says Anya on the Road is Calling blog when talking about what it was like when they lived in Kuala Lumpur. "I don't think the temperature ever goes below 30 degrees Celsius (86 degrees Fahrenheit) and humidity never drops below 80 percent."

There's also a major litter problem fed by a garbage-tossing culture, not helped by the locals' love of plastic in all its forms. Any drink you get to go will probably come in a disposable plastic bag and there's no limit on any kind of single-use plastic yet, something that will become quite obvious if you visit the beaches of Penang, where too much of it ends up.

"I'm not sure I'll ever get used to motorbikes riding down the sidewalks," says Helen. The only sidewalks where that doesn't happen are the ones jammed with food stalls.

Marco says the traffic is getting much worse in Penang and the over-development brings a lot of negatives. "The place is losing its authenticity to try to mutate into something it shouldn't become."

Inflation sometimes hits double digits for years, compounded by currency fluctuations. In some regions there are many indications of a real estate bubble and an overbuilt condo market, so take your time if you want to buy instead of rent.

Long-timers who have been in Malaysia for more than a decade keep predicting a collapse because of the increased consumer debt, coupled with a rise in foreclosures and bankruptcy. If you're living off an income in dollars or euros though, this bargain-priced country in the tropics has a lot to offer.

For More Information
PenangInsider.com
SandInMyCurls.com
HappyGoKL.com
ExpatArrivals.com – Malaysia
Mudah.my

Chapter 22:
Mexico

Pros: six-month tourist visa, straightforward residency requirements, wide range of climates, wide range of locations, established expat centers, good domestic transportation options, friendly population, low stress.

Cons: poor waste management, ineffective police, usually can't drink the water, land restrictions near coasts, high income requirement for residency, noisy.

Until my daughter got comfortable going to school by herself when we lived in Mexico as a family, I would take a 10-minute cab ride to her middle school for $3 and listen to podcasts on the 40¢ bus back home. Often, I'd buy a sausage and cheese baguette for 80¢ or two pastries for 50¢ on the walk from the bus stop to my house. I might buy 16 ounces (around a half liter) of fresh-squeezed juice for around $1.

If I go out for lunch in my town, I'll get a pork carnitas sandwich in a crusty roll for $1.50 or a couple *gordita* corn patties with fillings for around a dollar each. A meal of the day at the largest market is under $3, a three-course one at a real restaurant can be found for $4.

For going out in the evening, we've bought ballet tickets for $4, movie tickets for $5, symphony tickets for $6, and performances from major international acts for $15 or less. Most of the time though, entertainment is outdoors and free. If we go for a simple dinner for two, we might spend $10. If we go to a top-tier restaurant and order wine and dessert, we can occasionally top the $50 mark for two—with some effort. A beer is not more than a lemonade, coffee, or juice, usually around $1.25 to $2. Museums typically cost a dollar or two, the most spectacular ones in Mexico City around $6. Much of our furniture is custom made for about one-third of what it would cost stateside. If we need tailoring done, it's a few dollars. Our housekeeper and handyman are both paid roughly $5 an hour and we're paying above-market rates.

We live on less money in Mexico for *everything* added together than we did just on rent before utilities in Tampa, Florida. We have swapped rent for house upgrades and furniture in a house we own outright our second time in the country, but when we rented the first time, we also cut our expenses in half. Your experience could vary depending on where you're moving from: Mexico is not a cheap as Nicaragua or Cambodia, especially in beach resort areas that also require air conditioning. We're in the highlands where utility bills are next to nothing. On average though, most people who make the move cut their expenses by a third even if they're living the high life, but by half is easily doable almost anywhere in the country.

Our life is less stressful than in it was living in the U.S., we spend less time in traffic, and keeping the weight off here seems almost effortless because we walk almost everywhere. Our experience is shared by many, many others. Some are single mothers, some are young couples, some are entrepreneurs, and some are retirees. Mexico draws all types.

This will be the longest destination Chapter because Mexico has more expatriates living in it than most of the others in this book added together. If you add just the Americans and Canadians together the total is estimated to be close to a million and a half now. Granted, some are snowbirds who only come down for half the year, but that's a mid-sized city's worth of people enjoying better weather and lower prices south of the border. You also get a fair number of Europeans, a smattering of Asians, and plenty of people from other countries in South America living in Mexico.

Besides the proximity to the North American neighbors, Mexico has a lot going for it: welcoming people, good food, interesting cities, and plenty of beaches to pick from on 5,600 miles of coastline. You can take your pick of the Gulf, the Caribbean, the Pacific Ocean, and the Sea of Cortez. It works for city people who like culture and the arts. It works for rural people who like farmland or jungle. It works for beach lovers who want to watch the waves and walk around in flip-flops. Plenty of spots have mountain views and highland climates.

With a generous 180-day visa available for the asking upon arrival, this is also one of the easiest countries in the world to live in temporarily or for a year without paperwork: just leave the country once and return to have five days shy of a year in one place. With a large network of expatriates in some areas and at least a few to connect with in others, it's not hard to find guidance on getting a house or apartment and getting settled.

Here's an added bonus: Mexico is cheaper for Americans and Europeans now than it was the first time I stepped off a plane in the country in the 2002. That's because the peso has declined against most other currencies. That drives up the price of imports, of course, but anything made in Mexico is cheaper now, including wages.

You can spend a fortune in Mexico if you would like, of course. There are mansions on the Pacific Ocean north of Puerto Vallarta worth more than $10 million and colonial homes in San Miguel de Allende with price tags above $2 million. Some people who haven't traveled around much are surprised to learn there are lots of rich Mexicans as well. One of the wealthiest men in the world is Mexican after all, and there's a sizable collection of millionaires in every city, fed by a strong industrial base and a middle class that gets substantially larger each year. This is not a country like Nicaragua or Honduras where one or two families hold all the wealth and power—though there are some industries that are duopolies—like the commercial beer and soda ones. There are hotels in Mexico charging $500 a night and up that are filled almost entirely by Mexican families. There are upscale malls full of stores where only those making six figures a year (in dollars, not pesos) can afford to shop.

Many industries have too little competition, no doubt, and ten families have a grip on some near-monopolistic business sectors, but a rising tide is definitely lifting a lot of boats. The middle class in Mexico is for real, with a widening girth being the most obvious sign that most families are in pretty good shape financially. Fewer have headed north to the U.S. since 2008 not just because of tightening at the border, but also because the outlook at home keeps getting better.

It's very easy to live a middle-class life here for less, however, even if you don't have 10 people in the family compound. Many retiree couples live in Mexico on two social security checks and many location independent couples get by on less than $2,000 per month—even in Mexico City.

American T.W. Anderson, who now runs a video game development company remote from Mexico City, has managed to get by for cheap in some of Mexico's most expensive tourist towns: Cancun and Playa del Carmen. "We saved a lot of money by living like working class Mexicans," he explains. "If you live where all the tourists hang out in Playa del Carmen, you can spend as much as you would in Miami, like $800 or $1,000 for a so-so studio apartment. But I pounded the pavement for five days and found a place in a subdivision for the equivalent of $470, a two-bedroom apartment. It was 10 minutes by bus from the beach, or a 30-minute walk." Counting utilities and all other expenses besides travel, T.W. estimates the monthly budget was around $1,000 even in this location that's expensive by Mexican standards.

Mobile workers I know who have lived different places in Mexico have gotten by on $1,100 to $1,400 a month in San Pancho (near Sayulita) on the west coast of Mexico and $1,300 to $1,800 in Playa del Carmen. Just understand you won't be right by the beach at those levels.

For most expats who want to live what would be considered a regular middle-class lifestyle in the USA, with a large house or apartment, it's probably in the $1,250 to $3,000 range for most singles and $1,500 to $4,000 for couples or families (the high end of that being the most expensive areas, like Los Cabos). When you compare these ranges to what it would cost for a city or suburban life in a desirable part of the USA, Canada, UK, or Australia though, this is still easily half for a lot of people—while going out more than they would before.

I live in a historic city in the central highlands at 6,500 feet. There are probably 300 to 600 expatriates here, counting the part-time ones. I have detailed my expenses a few times on my blog (cheapestdestinationsblog.com), but the short summary is that for a family of three we spent around $2,100 per month when we rented. These days my wife and I are empty nesters and we spend far less since we own our house outright and just spend on repairs and upkeep. When we were sheltered at our home during the coronavirus outbreak and only going out for essentials, for a while we spent $800 or less per month. In normal times, we tend to take advantage of the low prices by eating out more, traveling locally, and having a good time.

We're in the interior though, paying prices that aren't inflated for foreigners. Even down the road in San Miguel de Allende it's going to cost more per month for rent. If you decide to settle down in a beach resort town, expect to pay a good bit more for rent, eating out, and taking a taxi. It's hard for us to ever pay more than $4 for a taxi ride, for instance, but in Ixtapa it's hard to get a cab for less than $8, and in Cancun what seems like a ridiculously short trip could cost you double or triple that.

The favored expatriate spots tend to be more expensive, just because foreign retirees with plenty of money in the bank will spend a lot more for property than any local will. They will overtip, overpay, and generally drive prices up—especially if they're trying to get by in English only. Still, while many of us Mexpats think San Miguel de Allende is really pricey, rents there are still a fifth of what they are in San Francisco and restaurant meals are about a third of the cost there. So, it's partly a matter of perspective: those from California think it's a bargain, while someone moving down from small-town Oklahoma may not see where those cost savings are supposed to come from.

Where to Live Within Mexico
Nobody can answer the question of "Where should I live in Mexico?" except you. The country is incredibly diverse geographically, from hot beaches to cool mountains, humid jungles to bone-dry deserts. The best way to figure out which place really speaks to you is to figure out your priorities and do some exploratory trips to try them out.

Here are some of the most popular places for expats in Mexico and whom they're good for:

San Miguel de Allende – Around 25 percent of the growing population here is estimated to be foreigners. Good for those who don't speak much Spanish, who like spring-like weather, and enjoy walkable, picture-perfect colonial streets where everything is nice and tidy. If you want a packed social schedule with a like-minded tribe that speaks English, this is your best bet. Closest cities are Queretaro and Leon.

Ajijic – On Lake Chapala near Guadalajara, another mild climate place where you seem to see as many gringos as locals. Good for those who want American-style homes with garages and don't mind depending on a car for shopping and social life. Close to Guadalajara for flights and medical needs.

Puerto Vallarta region – Full of foreigners who came and forgot to leave, a tourist magnet with lots of beachfront condos and hillside homes with panoramic views. For beach bums and barflies, seafood lovers and those who want multiple flight choices out.

Sayulita region – The coast stretching north from Punta de Mita is full of surfers and bohemians, plus rich people who used to be one or the other. Wilder beaches and mellower towns than Puerto Vallarta, but with the same easy air access.

Southern Pacific Coast - There are pockets of expatriates who are aging surfers or retirees all along the Pacific coast south of Puerto Vallarta. The best-known spots are Puerto Escondido, Zihuatanejo, Trancones (near Ixtapa), and Melaque (near Barra de Navidid).

Los Cabos region – Southern Baja is a very hot place, a desert landscape by the sea. Favored by Californians with lots of money to spend, those who want luxury digs and golf courses. La Paz, two hours north of Los Cabos, and Loreto much further north are the more laid-back alternatives on the peninsula.

Mexico City – The world's second-largest city by population has a strong pull for those who want an urban lifestyle akin to other world capitals but at a lower price. Many come here for jobs and end up staying or they find multiple freelance opportunities through the strong local network. The best bet for culture vultures and foodies.

Oaxaca – A colonial city with a large indigenous population, this is Mexico's finest food destination after Mexico City. It offers a lot to explore in the surrounding region, culturally and for adventure activities.

Merida – Just a short hop by plane from the U.S. in the Yucatan state, this flat colonial city near the coast gets quite hot part of the year, but attracts residents with a gorgeous historic center, easy beach access, interesting food, and great Mayan ruins to explore nearby. Lots of retirees are spread along the nearby Gulf Coast beach towns.

Cancun and Riviera Maya – As with Puerto Vallarta, many come here on vacation and decide to buy or rent something more permanent, especially in Playa del Carmen and Tulum, which have large expat communities. Prices are not so cheap in Mexico's #1 tourist destination and it's a warped version of Mexico, but well-equipped condos and good restaurants are geared to foreign tastes.

Mazatlan – This west coast area offers some of the best beach city values and is probably has the lowest foreigner-to-Mexican ratio of the resort communities in Mexico: most of the tourists are domestic. Foreigners enjoy the tight-knit community, great housing options, a colonial center, and golf.

Morelia/Patzcuaro – While this region has suffered from a reputation for violence in the state of Guerrero, it's still an attractive region of handicrafts, natural beauty, and one of Mexico's most beautiful cities.

If the idea of moving to Mexico only to be surrounded by people from your own country is not appealing, it's easy to find a place where you can do the opposite. This is a very big country with metropolitan cities and gorgeous "Magic Towns" that are more manageable spread from coast to coast. Schools are better in the former, prices are lower in the latter. Naturally, the smaller the town, the faster you'll need to learn Spanish.

Housing Costs

Housing costs in Mexico are all over the map, whether you're renting or buying. This is a vast country that's about as wide as the U.S. or Canada, so just imagine the disparity you see in your own country between different regions. As is normal, big cities cost more than medium-sized ones, small ones cost less than medium ones, and rural areas can be cheaper still. What's different here is that foreign demand has a huge impact on prices. Besides all the free-spending expatriates you have driving up costs, real estate tends to get overvalued quickly if there's more demand than supply for nice rentals that are up to international standards. Therefor, when evaluating a potential place to live in Mexico, it's worth asking, "How many gringos are there already and do they have far more money than me?"

One of my newsletter subscribers sent me this note in mid-2020: "My good friend is driving from New York to Mexico starting today to close on her house that is about 30 minutes from Patzcuaro. It's a little resort spot on a lake and she got a nice two-bedroom, two-bath house with an unfinished downstairs (that will become a one-bedroom apartment) with views of the lake for $38,000. All in with fees it's going to be $42,000."

At the same time, if you tried to buy a house on the water in Los Cabos, Baja Sur, you're probably looking at a million bucks or more for an equivalent size. That's a wide gulf. That range of housing prices also applies to long-term rent prices.

In general, the interior of Mexico is cheaper than the beach areas except for the most desirable parts of Mexico City. I ran a survey of residents renting where I live in central Mexico and half were paying $500 or less per month. Fewer than 10% were paying more than $1,000 per month and those places were sprawling houses with modern appliances and parking. You can find foreigners living in this range in other colonial cities like Queretaro, Zacatecas, San Cristobal de las Casas, or Morelia.

Rosemary Kimani and Claire Rouger, who run AuthenticFoodQuest.com, moved to Guadalajara for three months to have some elective surgery done at a fraction of the U.S. price. They had a bit of trouble finding an ideal rental on Airbnb because it was the holiday season when extra family members need to be housed, but in the end, it worked out, even with a fair number of filters. "Given my criteria for a non-shared place, no pets, and no stairs, this narrowed my options considerably. The place we ended up finding was $500 per month furnished with utilities and internet included. If you are flexible on sharing a home and are willing to go up and down stairs, you can find places for as little as $300 per month."

That's for Mexico's second-largest city. So, you'll find similar prices in Monterrey, Puebla, Morelia, Queretaro, or other urban options in the interior.

San Miguel de Allende and Ajijic are a bit more expensive than most other parts of the interior, however, and it would be tougher to find a cheap rental and live on $1,000 a month there. Go an hour or two in any direction and both the rents and purchase prices can literally drop in half. The same is true on the coasts, where Los Cabos might as well be in California, but Loreto, La Paz, and Mazatlan are not so bad. The Punta de Mita area north of Puerto Vallarta, filled almost exclusively with millionaire foreigners, is in the stratosphere compared to Huatulco, Puerto Escondido, or Melaque. Go further afield to beach towns where you have trouble spotting another gringo and you'll find prices to be closer to what the local market will bear.

In 2014 I sold my two-bedroom vacation home one house back from a Gulf Coast beach in the Yucatan state for just $55,000. It was in a fishing village area where most homes are owned by locals from Merida. Prices have stayed reasonable on the modest homes there. You can even find a sizable house right on the beach for $150,000—the last time that was true in Florida or California was many decades ago.

Merida itself has gotten a bit more expensive since I first started going there from an influx of foreigners and wealthier Mexicans. "Our rent comes out to around $750 per month. That's about midrange for foreigners," says Cassie Pearse, who lives there with her family and runs the Mexico Cassie blog. "We have a large, not very modernized 4BR house with a pool. I have friends who pay $600 per month for a house and friends who are paying $2,000 per month. Most foreigners wouldn't dream of not having a pool in this climate. If you don't get a pool rents can go far, far lower." Tom Williams, who runs a variety of blogs and podcasts with his wife Megsy, appears in the earlier Georgia section, but says they were paying $320 for an apartment in Merida with some garden space. That was on the edge of the historic center when they appeared on *House Hunters International.*

It's nearly impossible for me to tell you what you're going to spend to rent or buy without knowing where you're headed and how much space you need. You could find a nice house or apartment for $200 a month or spend $25,000 a night on a Los Cabos villa if you're a rock star. You can buy a whole house that comes with furniture for $40,000 in some areas, but in San Miguel de Allende that will only get you a building lot a couple of miles from town. In Los Cabos it won't even get you that. Going one city over or 30 miles up the beach can make a huge difference.

In all cases though, unless you want to throw away your money, take the time to talk to people and look around, with feet on the street. If you don't speak Spanish, find a friend fast who does and can help you. If you try to find apartment listings in English, you'll probably only find short-term vacation rentals or overpriced expat homes for sale. In some areas you won't find much online period: the best source of listings where I live in Guanajuato is a quirky local book-sized newspaper that comes out once a week. There you can easily find a two-bedroom apartment for less than $200 and it's hard to spend more than $600 for one with two bedrooms even in the best parts of town, furnished and with utilities included. You can easily rent a whole house with multiple bedrooms for less than $800 per month.

Lydia Carey lives in a nice two-bedroom place with lots of light in the desirable Roma neighborhood of Mexico City. She pays around $500 a month, but "it's a noisy location and I got a really good deal," she says. Many people she knows in the area pay closer to $700 a month.

T.W. Anderson lives near the U.S. embassy off of Paseo de la Reforma and pays an under-market $650 for a one-bedroom furnished place. "We got a steal as most things in this area were going for twice that, unfurnished, when we arrived in February of 2018. We had to negotiate pretty hard on the lease, but it's an older apartment built in the 80s so that worked in our favor."

In even more desirable Condesa, you could pay $1,500 for a spacious apartment. Still, this is one of the largest cities in the world, so compared to London or New York it's a bargain. "We can live a New York City kind of life without the New York City kind of costs," says my friend David Lida, author of the book *First Stop in the New World*.

Food & Drink
Mexico isn't the cheapest place in the world to eat, but it's one of the best. You'll nearly always get a great value for the money and it's hard to point to anywhere in Latin America that even comes close in terms of variety, depth, and intensity of flavors. It's also quite filling food, so you can get stuffed without spending a whole lot. In small towns you'll find dozens of variations of things stuffed into something made out of corn flour, while in the capital and food cities like Oaxaca and Puebla, you'll find chefs that win international awards and are celebrities.

Although Lydia says it's easier to find a cheaper apartment outside of Mexico City, she actually spends a lot less on food and drinks in the capital and "the selection of everything is far superior."

When there were three of us in the house, my family averaged out to $300 or so a month on groceries in Guanajuato, then that again on going out. People who are being frugal spend far less, of course. If you shop at the markets, cook a lot at home, and don't drink wine and liquor much, you could cut the food and drink budget down to $150 - $200 a month for a couple without trying very hard.

I often go to the market and pile up a bunch of fruit and vegetables on the scale, getting kilos of food for the equivalent of a few dollars. In season, it's common to see produce for less than $1 a kilo (2.2 pounds) and oranges can be two or three kilos for a dollar. A lot grows in Mexico with all the different elevations, so good, fresh produce is easy to find and cheap. Most foreigners and many locals soak the things you don't peel in iodine water though. The health inspection regulations aren't as stringent or enforced as they are in developed countries.

It would be harder to get by on this amount at a beach resort area. Grocery prices in the supermarket are standard throughout the country except in Baja Sur. For going out to eat though, the more of a tourist town flooded by foreigners you're in, the more you're going to pay for street stalls and restaurants. Where foreigners come in daily by the planeload—Puerto Vallarta, Los Cabos, Playa del Carmen, Cancun—prices naturally rise to the level of what those short-term vacationers will pay. Plus, in Los Cabos, you have the added issue that's it's a geographically isolated city far from everything. Where Mexican tourists congregate, however, you'll still find Mexican prices.

Street food and "meal of the day" places are quite cheap in Mexico. If you eat where the locals eat, you can stuff yourself for $3 or $4 pretty easily, even in tourist zones if you find the local market. You can easily find a plate of tacos for under $2, tamales for less than a buck each, or a set meal with soup, meat dish, rice, and something to drink or a dessert for under $4. It's actually more expensive to try to buy groceries and make some of these things yourself than it is to just buy them made by a vendor: the sellers definitely don't have fat profit margins.

Nice restaurants can be a great bargain in places without a lot of foreign tourists but can cost as much as at home otherwise. In general, if you can eat where middle-class Mexicans eat and you're not in a resort area, your dinner and drinks tab will be roughly half or less of what it would be in a mid-sized U.S. city.

Beers are usually $1 (happy hour or buckets) to $2.50 in a bar or restaurant (higher for microbrews). Cocktails are about a third or less than what you would pay in the U.S., a quarter of what you would pay in most of Europe or New York City. You can get a good bottle of 100 percent agave tequila for under $10 in a grocery store, or splurge and get the good stuff for under $20. Wine and most foreign liquor types are taxed heavily though and are expensive: both will cost a bit more than you pay now probably except for rum. Domestic wine producers don't get a break: they're taxed just as heavily as the ones from Chile or California.

If you're in an area with a good number of foreigners or well-traveled Mexican, you'll be able to find plenty of organic food and health food. Much of the produce not made on factory farms is organic anyway, just because the families prefer tradition. "One kilo of organic eggs (yes, eggs at the market are sold by the kilo) costs about $3 for 18 eggs," says Rosemary. "I also bought organic Mexican coffee by the kilo and would brew a fresh pot every morning. For about $5, I enjoyed high quality coffee in the comfort of my home."

Transportation
There's no regular passenger train system left in Mexico except along the Copper Canyons in the west, though a very expensive new train service coming to the Yucatan Peninsula may become reality at some point. What Mexico does have is an excellent, comfortable bus system and a competitive domestic airline network.

The buses are not cheap, but they certainly are pleasant. The first-class ones have four seats across, bathrooms, entertainment, and a snack. The luxury ones usually have three seats across, with more legroom, and have (cellular based) Wi-Fi that sometimes works for enough of a stretch to get something done online. The buses have built-in speed limiters that keep the driver from becoming a maniac on wheels. There's no charge to transport luggage underneath. Prices are generally $6 to $8 per hour of travel on the first-class ones, $9 to $10 on the executive/luxury ones. So, a four-hour ride will be $24 to $40 depending on class and an overnight bus of 12 hours can cost you more than $100.

The relatively high bus fares are partly due to Mexico's love affair with toll roads. A short trip of 10 or 15 miles might be $2 or more for the toll and a really long stretch, like Cancun to Merida, can be $25 to $30. If you're weighing the advantages of driving somewhere yourself, take these into account.

Flight prices are quite reasonable on the low-cost airlines Interjet, Volaris, Tar, Calafia, and Aeromar, while on Viva Aerobus they are cheap before you add in all the fees. (They're Mexico's version of RyanAir or Spirit Air.) If you plan ahead and are flexible, you can often find a flight price that's lower than the bus would be. Aeromexico is a different story though, with prices more on par with what you would pay for a domestic flight in the U.S. They also use a hub system, so no matter where you're going, you'll probably have to pass through Mexico City's overtaxed airport. As I write this the airline industry has been decimated by the coronavirus lockdowns, so check the current situation to see if all of these have survived.

Mexico has multiple places to land, with international flights arriving daily at 20+ airports. This is, therefore, a great country to live in if you need to get back to see relatives regularly or just like to travel internationally a lot.

In the cities themselves, taxi prices are quite reasonable once you get out of the vacation resort areas. Where I live, the average fare is less than $3 and it never costs more than $5, even get to the suburbs. Prices in Oaxaca are pretty similar. In most of Mexico, fares within city limits are going to run less than $10. There's seldom a meter, but outside tourist resort areas, few drivers try to overcharge you. If you land at an airport or bus station, you go to a pre-paid taxi booth where fares are regulated by zone.

Uber operates in most Mexican cities now, though where I live it's often not any cheaper than flagging down a taxi. In the bigger cities the difference can be more dramatic though and Rosemary says for Guadalajara, "Local shared rides alternatives like Beat or Didi Ride are even cheaper."

City buses are always a bargain, ranging from 35 cents to a shade under a dollar. Local buses that go from one close town to the other range from one to three dollars.

Healthcare

Throughout the major population centers of Mexico, health care is advanced and of good quality in the private hospitals. With the country being just a quick hop from the United States, many of the doctors have trained there and many hospitals are affiliated with or owned by U.S. ones. Doctors average a salary of $20,000 to $30,000 though instead of 15 or 20 times that. All the way down the line the expenses are lower, from administrator and nurse pay to costs for liability insurance and paperwork processing. Some retirees have found that paying all their medical expenses out of pocket in Mexico is less than their 20 percent co-pay would have been at home.

Mexico is a major medical tourism destination, from basic dental work up to major surgery. "My surgery at the best hospital in Guadalajara cost a little under $6,000 out of pocket," says Rosemary. "This included medical tests, surgeon and anesthesiologist fees, one night in the hospital, medication, and follow-up visits. Similar surgery costs in the US are between $60,000 and $125,000."

A visit to the dentist for a check-up and cleaning will run you $25 to $50, a filling about the same. I got a $3,000 estimate from my Tampa dentist for a bunch of dental work to be done. I got it done in Mexico instead and it was $600. The care was better than I would have gotten too. My dentist actually sent a crown back and had them redo it when I came in for the permanent one because it wasn't as perfect as he wanted it to be. He's the one that does all the serious work also; he doesn't just pop in to supervise.

A friend of mine has a house in Merida and whenever he has a dental or medical issue, he hops on a plane from North Carolina to get it treated where his second home is located. Even with the cost of plane tickets and airport parking figured in, the total is always half or less. Some retirees have done the math on knee and back surgery and found that getting it done in Mexico would be cheaper than just their costs not covered by Medicare in the USA. For Canadians, they might pay slightly more after factoring in travel costs, but they can get it done tomorrow instead of months from now, with better service.

For each location in Mexico with some foreigners, you'll find plenty of stories like this that involve fractions. As in "I paid 1/5 what my doctor quoted me in Cleveland" or "my father's hip surgery with two days in the hospital was 1/3 of just what my out of pocket costs were going to be in L.A."

You'll often pay less than $50 for a visit to the doctor, even to a specialist, and follow-up visits are often included in that price. If you just want a quick diagnosis, you can go to a little storefront next to a pharmacy and the doctor will check you out for $3 or so.

If you're a legal resident, you can apply for the national IMSS health care program and after filling out the right paperwork and getting a physical, you're in for a few hundred dollars a year. This option can mean more waiting around at clinics and government hospitals, but if funds are tight, you'll be covered in case of an accident. Many expats just pay out of pocket or buy an international insurance policy that covers catastrophe anywhere—including Mexico and the USA on visits back. That's what we are doing now, at close to $5,000 per year for a couple in their 50s. If we didn't have to include the USA because of trips back for business and visiting relatives, it would be far less. (If you're going back to the USA for less than two weeks at a time, check out SafetyWing for an economical option you can switch on and off.)

Medicare is not accepted in Mexico. Neither is the Canadian health care plan. On top of that, Canadians can lose their coverage if they're out of the country more than half the year, so you see a lot of snowbirds going back and forth. There are some whole beach communities that are packed with Canucks in the winter and are more like ghost towns in June. Don't move to one of these if you want year-round action!

Other Costs
Costs for electricity and gas are going to depend a lot on two factors: how hot it is where you choose to live and how big your home is. Mexico has progressive electricity costs: if you use more than a certain tiered amount, your bill goes up to a higher rate per kilowatt hour. Some people who have a pool and lots of air conditioning spend more than they did in Texas or Arizona. On the other hand, if you live in a highlands town where the summers aren't all that hot and the winters aren't all that cold, you may find you need nothing but a couple weeks of using a space heater.

I have yet to get a monthly water bill that has topped $15 or an electric bill that has topped $20 in my highland location. Propane tanks for hot water and cooking are delivered to our door for about $25, and one will typically last two or three months.

Those in a tropical climate closer to sea level will need air conditioning at least part of the year and that can drive the electric bill up past $100 even if you're careful. If you get a good sea breeze and have ceiling fans, that helps a lot in keeping the costs down.

"Our electricity bill is around $125 for two months," says Cassie in Merida. "We don't use crazy amounts of electricity because we don't have air conditioning downstairs and we live in a well-ventilated house. Many are choosing to get solar panels at the moment and reduce their bills to practically zero. If you run aircon all day all year then you could end up paying $200 or more per month pretty damn quick."

There's long been a monopoly on land-line phone service, though you get a few more choices with cell phone service and internet service. Remember that Mexican who's one of the richest men in the world? He owns the most popular option for all three. Prices are finally coming down due to healthy competition and internet speeds are going up. The first few times I lived in Mexico; I couldn't get more than 5 mbps at my house (for $30 a month) no matter how much I was willing to pay. I was finally able to get cable service a couple years ago though, and now I get 30 mbps internet, a slew of TV stations (almost all in Spanish) and a land line for around $26 per month total. I could get speeds as high as 100 mbps if I were willing to pay $50. The bigger and denser the city, the more options you have.

Pre-paid cell phone services are relatively cheap if you don't need loads of data, with $20 a month being enough for most people. Double that though if you're on your smart phone all the time sending status updates from outside the home. Then it becomes worth it to get a monthly plan. Usually you can call the USA and Canada at no extra charge and some social media services don't count against your data plan.

This time I've hung onto my T-Mobile family plan ($133 for unlimited data and calls for 3) since my daughter lives in the USA and is on our plan. I can roam internationally with it and pay no data or text charges, plus I can call the USA and Canada for nothing from Mexico. It also makes all the security verification texts easier. If I got local service again, I don't think I could spend anything close to that much if I tried, so if I didn't travel so much, I would just go local again.

Anything that takes advantage of cheaper labor costs will be dramatically lower than you're used to, from getting your house cleaned to getting some pants hemmed. Typical pay for a skilled handyman or a good housekeeper is $3 to $6 an hour, for a basic laborer or house painter it's less. Much of the attraction for moving here for retirees with a bit of money saved is they can hire a cook, gardener, or maid without having to spend a whole lot. Here you can actually get things fixed too, whether it's a pair of shoes or a blender—for a few dollars. I once had a faulty computer cord repaired for $2.25 that saved me having a new one shipped from the states.

Museum admissions and entertainment are very reasonable in Mexico, with some of the best museums in the world having ticket prices between $1 and $6. When we go to the symphony in my town it's $6 each, some other performances at a beautiful historic theater are less than that. Archaeological sites are very reasonable, seldom costing more than $8. We pay $2 or $3 for a movie (or a buck for a bootleg DVD to watch at home).

The things that cost more are the usual expat suspects: electronics, small appliances, tools, clothing, and toys. There's no free trade agreement with China, plus the distribution system has more layers and competition and is less robust than in the USA. The gap has gotten narrower since I first moved to Mexico though and the selection is better as well thanks to the proliferation of foreign chains like Home Depot, Office Depot, and Costco.

Your private school choices are dependent on how big your city is and how many expats live there. We only had a few choices in Guanajuato—all in Spanish only—and paid around $300 per month at two different ones. If you go to an accredited international school with classes in English in Mexico City, you could be looking at more than $1,000 per month. Check the American Schools resource site listed at the end, as well as ones for Waldorf, Montessori, or International Baccalaureate.

Visas
Mexico hands out six months for the asking to many nationalities on tourist visas, so this is a great place to be a snowbird who flies south for the winter. The first time my family came for a year we stayed on tourist visas: we just took a vacation in Costa Rica in the middle and started fresh with six more months when we returned. If you want to try Mexico on for size, just waltz in and unpack for six months. This is not always going to work for families though. Most schools want your child to be a legal resident in order to accept him or her and will ask for the ID card. (The Waldorf school was more lenient in our city, though I'm not sure that's the case everywhere.)

Those who want to put down more permanent roots get a temporary residency permit that's good for a year. Provided you haven't run afoul of the law, renewing it should be easier than getting it in the first place. You just have to cough up the fee, which is around $275, and get your fingerprints done again. There is a working version for those who have a job with a local employer, or the non-working version for everyone else. After you've had a temporary permit for four years, you can apply for permanent residency. Lately, some people I have interviewed have been able to secure a permanent visa from their home consulate right off the bat by paying more money. That's worth splurging the extra $100 or so if you can pull it off since it saves a lot of annual visits to the immigration office.

Mexico has a higher bar for its residency visa than other Latin American countries and it can be difficult if you don't have sufficient income you can document. Thankfully, just as this book was going to print, the government recalculated how this minimum is determined and now the bar is lower. Officially, the requirement was around $2,000 per month for the applicant and $500 for each dependent, but now it has dropped to under $1,400 for a single person and under $350 for the others. (This can vary based on exchange rates and the Mexican wage figure the formula is based on.) Local embassy or consulate personnel were just getting the ruling on this in late 2020 though so expect some inconsistency for a while. This is still more than you really need to live in Mexico, of course, but at least now the retirees who didn't manage to save much in their working years can qualify just with social security earnings. Embassies have known to cut retirees some slack anyway if they can show some savings or local real estate holdings on top.

You must apply in your home country before departure. You can't come into Mexico on a tourist visa and then decide to become a resident. You must apply at a Mexican consulate or embassy abroad and that's where you'll need to show up with notarized bank statements proving you have adequate income. They will also want to see a whole stack of other documents like a marriage certificate, a birth certificate, and proof you're not a felon. Check the embassy site and as always, it's better to bring too much than not enough.

Once you're approved on that step, you do the rest at the closest immigration office to where you're moving in Mexico, right after arrival. This will take several visits to the office for applications, payments, and fingerprints before you get your ID card and you're all set. You can hire someone who will be situated in a nearby office to help prepare documents for less than $100, or you can spend more to hire an attorney who will take care of everything and you just have to show up and sign.

There is no special visa/permit for retirees in Mexico and no real incentives either for foreigners of advanced age (though you can get some regular senior discounts if you're a legal resident, such as discounts on bus tickets, admissions, and some cultural events). You simply hang around long enough and eventually you can get permanent residency. You can join the public health care system when you become a permanent resident, but most foreigners don't bother.

You can acquire a business visa in this country by setting up your own corporation. It's a convoluted affair because first you have to set it up through an attorney, then hire an accountant, then the accountant can petition for the president (you) to get a business visa. Once you have that, you're a legal resident who can get a driver's license and do most things besides vote. You can request your own visa extensions from then on out. As you can imagine, this process is ripe for fee padding and abuse, so ask around to find a trustworthy attorney and accountant and be prepared to lay out a few grand in the process. It's a way to essentially buy your way in, however, because you'll get a few years' grace period before anyone even looks at whether your company is earning money or not.

Downsides
Half my relatives probably expected me to be dead by now from moving to Mexico. If you watch enough TV, you're bound to think Mexico is a lawless failed state full of brutal drug gangs and murderers. In some ways, that's all true, but in the same way the USA is a corrupt political system with lawless inner cities, police brutality, and rampant gun deaths from mass shootings. You can read my broader take on this in the safety Chapter toward the end of this book, but the short explanation for Mexico is that "some parts are bad, some parts are perfectly fine, but most violence is the gang-on-gang kind."

This is probably true in your own country too, or your own city. You know which neighborhoods to avoid, especially at night, and which ones pose no worries. There are parts of Mexico that are best avoided, mostly on the border with the U.S. but also some interior states where drug cartels are headquartered. Most expats who read the news and are aware of what's going on can tell you more and the U.S. State Department advisory keeps getting better about discerning which areas pose zero worries and which are best avoided.

In all fairness, there are valid crime worries in the bad areas. Throughout Mexico, the police are too few, are underpaid, and are easy targets for corruption. Parents are also notoriously lax with their teenage kids and it's easy to become a graffiti-spraying, pothead punk whose mother still thinks you're an angel. If you're a big fan of law and order and well-enforced rules, you may be better off in Canada or Switzerland—or at least in a gated community somewhere around Lake Chapala. In terms of safety though, Cancun has fewer murders most years than Edmonton, Canada. Mexico City has less than half the number of murders per 100,000 people as Washington, D.C. and Puerto Vallarta has far fewer annual murders per 100,000 people than the port of New Orleans.

A more universal annoyance is the lack of quiet, which is going to be a problem almost anywhere in the country. Mexicans have a very high tolerance for noise and seem to feed off of it like an energy field. It's not at all unusual to hear fireworks going off at the crack of dawn or a mariachi band one house over playing full blast at two in the morning. It's also not unusual to be sitting at an outdoor restaurant or cafe and hear three stereos and a TV playing at once, all different. I once stayed at a fancy resort on the Pacific coast where the wedding band played until 4:30 a.m. and then the lawn maintenance guys started running their mowers and trimmers at 7:00 a.m., on a Saturday morning. If I had complained, they would have looked at me like I had just walked off a spaceship. That's generally how a restaurant waiter will look at you if you ask them to turn the TV or music down. They'll be baffled.

Speaking of service, don't count on it being efficient or quick. I've seldom managed to get out of a rental car office in less than a half hour—if they actually have the car I reserved—and every time the clerk makes it seem like it's his or her first day on the job. Eventually, the guys doing work in your house will do a good job, but if you're in a hurry be prepared to stay frustrated. Patience is not just a virtue in Mexico. It's required.

For More Information:
Mexiconewsdaily.com
Mexperience.com
MexicoMike.com
MexicoCassie.com
People's Guide to Mexico book
Association of American Schools in Mexico (Asomex.org)

There are multiple books out on moving to Mexico. One that's not a decade old is *The Move to Mexico Bible*
There are multiple Facebook groups like Expats in Mexico, but also at least one for each city where expats live

Chapter 23:
Nicaragua

Pros: cheapest prices in the Americas, low bar for retirement visa, variety of landscapes, clusters of expats, relatively cheap airfares, lots of opportunities to start a business.

Cons: still a lot of poverty, very basic public transportation, unattractive capital city, internet is mostly wireless, advanced health care limited to Managua, "dictator for life" government for now.

"If you make $1,000 a month, you can drive a small car, take your family out to decent restaurants sometimes, and visit a place like this on the weekends." That was an offhand comment from my Nicaraguan guide Pablo when we were at the overlook area checking out Lake Apoyo between Managua and Granada. "On that salary, you are middle-class here."

A lot more local people were stepping up to that level in Nicaragua when I put out the first edition of this book, as the economy kept improving and its relatively low crime rate made it a place where international companies wanted to invest. Anti-government riots in 2018 and the brutal crackdown killed tourism for the next two years though and then the COVID-19 shutdown hit just as things were starting to recover.

Because of the political situation, I have mixed feelings about recommending Nicaragua. It's one of the best bangs for your buck in the world—most couples spend less than $1,400 per month and many singles less than $800—but with Ortega trying to become a ruler for life in the manner of those in Cuba and Venezuela, and doing anything to hold onto power, the future may turn just as bleak as it is in those two troubled nations.

As one person said on the ExpatExchange message board for Nicaragua as I was writing this, "The next election is November 2021. If it is clean, Nicaragua will prosper. If it is dirty, we are screwed."

Until things improve politically, it is probably best to just rent where you're going to live unless you can afford to lose whatever you have invested during an implosion.

In most respects, Nicaragua is the cheapest place to travel in Latin America, which makes it the cheapest destination in the Americas period. Since it's also normally easy to get to and from for a reasonable airfare from North America, moving to Nicaragua and getting set up here is not going to set you back very much.

When it's time for a break, you've got a lot of options in the country or you can make a quick hop to Costa Rica.

If you're American or Canadian and you ask me where you could pack a few suitcases and take off with just a grand or two in your bank account and still live well, this is where I'd tell you to go. You can stay a while on a tourist visa, there's a good expat support critical mass in place in a few spots, and you can coast along for cheap while you get established. You'll probably pay more to fly your surfboard down than you will for your first week's meals and groceries. The average after-tax household income in this country is around $600 a month, so if you've got just an average social security check to live on, you're still going to be well-off by local standards.

"My pension alone is 3-4 times what the average Nica makes," American Jim Lynch told me over coffee in Granada. "We spend around $1,800 a month, which is extravagant by local standards. We live in a big air-conditioned house with a swimming pool. We eat out whenever we want, wherever we want. Medical care is so inexpensive here we don't even have insurance. We just pay for things as they come up. I had to go to the best hospital in Managua for surgery and it was cheap enough that I put it on a credit card."

This is also a country on the rise—from a low base to be sure—but there's no denying that the government has poured a lot of money into improving infrastructure. "In San Juan del Sur we saw the completion of a new hospital, police station, fire station, and courthouse, plus a refurbishing of city hall," says Gord MacKay, who lives in Nicaragua with his wife Elisha. "Some streets in town were torn up and new sewer and water pipes were installed before resurfacing the roads. We also have a new power substation for the region to help regulate our electricity. All of this happened in the last year and a half."

Don't come to Nicaragua to enjoy ruins from ancient civilizations or go sightseeing in the traditional sense though. Come to take pleasure in the great, unspoiled outdoors and explore a land where there are few signs of mass tourism. If you're the type that yearns to be a pioneer and don't like being tied down by a lot of rules, Nicaragua is a great "blank slate" destination. If you're looking for a laid-back lifestyle, it's hard to beat San Juan del Sur. "There are people here from their early 20s to their 70s from all over the world," says Gordon. "There's a very relaxed vibe. Even the real estate agents are surfers; it's hard to find them in the office."

The main expatriate center is the colonial city of Granada, which is a short drive or shuttle bus ride from Managua, where most of the business population lives. Granada is a clean, picturesque small city that's easily navigated by foot or bicycle. It is by the country's largest lake and has plenty of outdoor recreational opportunities nearby. With a fairly large number of expatriates established there, you can find good restaurants, coffee shops, a bookstore, and holistic health centers.

Leon is the other city attracting a fair number of foreigners, though the number is much smaller. This is a university town closer to the coast, north of Managua. Apart from San Juan del Sur and some nearby communities, no other locations have more than a handful of foreigners in place. You'll have to be a pioneer in those, but you'll also benefit from the lack of a "gringo effect" driving up prices.

Maryanne Tranter lives in Jinotega, about 2.5 hours north of Managua in coffee country. She is a pediatric nurse practitioner and founder of The Healthy Child Concierge (healthychildconcierge.com). She originally went there a few times for a research project but eventually stayed on. "I love living without so much consumerism. Living slower, more deliberate. I have visited many places in Nicaragua due to my research and travels for music. I stayed in Jinotega for the cost of living, climate, small-town feel, and people. I have the gift of time, to think, to cook, to rest, to talk with friends."

Housing Costs
The price of renting an apartment or home here is probably going to make your previous place look like Tokyo in comparison. The crowdsourced site Numbeo.com says the average price a local pays for a one-bedroom apartment outside the capital is $190 and the average for a three-bedroom is $343 (about the same prices as they were in 2014). On their cost scale where New York City is 100, Managua is a 10.

Gord and Elisha MacKay have a better perspective than most because they have lived in Leon, Granada, and San Juan del Sur. They've detailed their living expenditures to the penny each year on their InNicaNow.com blog. They paid $300 for a one-bedroom apartment in Leon and $550 for a swanky furnished apartment in a building with a pool in Granada. When I spoke to them in 2014 there were paying $300 a month in San Juan del Sur—but for a two-bedroom furnished house that included cable and water in the rent. Since then they've bought their own house and own it outright, so there's no rent cost. They estimate that the rental range throughout their region is between $350 and $1,500: the latter being a big beach mansion with a pool facing the water.

Jim and Carol pay $650 per month for a big house in Granada. They pay another couple hundred in utilities, much of that electricity for the air conditioning, pool, and "a 55-inch flat-screen TV."

In areas with fewer foreigners, there's not much demand at the high end. "Expats here in the city pay between $100-$500 a month for rent, " Maryanne says of Jinotega. "$100 would get you a room with private bathroom and shared eating space, $200 will get you a studio apartment, $350 is enough for a basic two-bedroom small house, and for $500 you'd probably be renting a well-made two- or three-bedroom home with space outdoors."

As is usually the case, you're going to find much better deals after arrival than you will if you're trying to set up something in advance. This is a country, after all, where less than two-thirds of the population has internet access anywhere besides their phone, even in urban areas. It's best to get a short-term rental or hotel room at first and start asking around locally about long-term rentals. With tourism in a years-long slump and some expats lukewarm on the idea of returning, however, there are plenty of great deals available through the usual home rental services.

Despite the previous non-stop promotion in the likes of *International Living, Live and Invest Overseas,* and *House Hunters International,* not enough foreigners ever arrived in Nicaragua to drive prices to crazy levels. When the housing crisis hit in the United States in the late '00s, home prices declined due to lack of buyers and still haven't recovered. Sure, if you want a beautifully restored colonial home in the heart of Granada, you may have to cough up a few hundred thousand dollars. Those are the exceptions though, not the rule. When a luxury travel website my media company owns did a story on high-end real estate in that city, we had serious trouble finding homes listed higher than $500,000. There are more luxury places for sale in beach areas, but some have been on the market for years.

For the most part, Nicaragua hasn't attracted a lot of high rollers. Whether they were scared by the political climate or felt more confident investing elsewhere I don't know, but fortunately for anyone heading there now, prices are still quite attractive—and have good upside potential in the future if the country ever returns to a real democracy. Prices are highest in Granada and the coast near San Juan del Sur. If you're willing to look beyond those areas, you can really find some rock-bottom bargains.

Condo prices, where there is such a thing, are only $400 to $650 per square meter, so we're talking an average of $50,000 to buy a 1,000-square-foot apartment. The average cost per square meter for a house is around $50, so you have to get to around 5,000 square feet before you cross the $250,000 mark. You can find building lots for under $30K with a sea or lake view. You can own property free and clear here with no restrictions. Just do the usual due diligence with an attorney to ensure there's a clear title. Because of the civil war and the Sandinistas appropriation of property, the ownership history of some buildings is murky to say the least.

Food & Drink
This is one of the cheapest places to eat in all of the Americas. You can get a market stall lunch with several items for $1.50 to $3, a simple restaurant lunch for $2.50 to $7. Often, you'll find all-you-can eat buffets meals for as little as $4. A fancy restaurant meal with cloth napkins will seldom top $15 and if you spend $20 per person, you're really living it up. "Currently a whole fried fish dinner is the costliest meal we eat out. It usually runs us $8 or $9 per plate," Gord says.

The good Flor de Caña rum will only cost you $3 - $10 for a bottle (the high end is for the 7-year version) and a rum cocktail in a bar is often $1- $3. Dollar beers are more common than not in bars and restaurants. A cup of coffee from good export quality beans will be 50 cents to $1.50.

Seasonal fruit is often $1 or less per kilo, so if you go to the market alone with $10, you are going to need strong arms and a taxi. (Probably not a problem at your local farmer's market, now, right?) A buck will get you a meal or two's worth of tortillas or baguettes for a large family.

"Anything Nicas use often themselves is going to be cheap," says Gord. "Rice, eggs, beans, oil, vinegar, and beef are bargain priced. You can get a really nice filet that's good for eight steaks for $10. And it's excellent, grass-fed beef. The steak was probably butchered that morning. The seafood you buy was caught that day. The fruit and vegetables were probably on the branch or vine two days ago."

Many expatriates in Nicaragua talk about how healthier they feel, about how they've lost weight without really trying. "I am much happier with the quality of my life now," says Maryanne. "I eat more whole foods and get fresh vegetables at my door daily. I walk everywhere. I sleep how my body needs."

It's not that the Nicas are all eating health food, but there's far less processed food, packaged food, and fast food here, especially outside Managua. People eat what's fresh and local because it's less expensive to transport, so those who move here often follow the locals' lead, at least part of the time.

Transportation
Probably a higher percentage of expatriates own a car here than most other destinations in this book because while Granada and central San Juan del Sur are easy to navigate on foot, getting from city to city in Nicaragua is not so easy. You either pay next to nothing to endure a "chicken bus"—a retired school bus from the USA now jammed with intercity passengers—or you pay a hefty $15-$30 to take a tourist shuttle for a ride that's only a couple hours. You can only find these on a few routes though, running just two or three times a day.

There is a middle ground on some popular routes. Sometimes you can find an "express bus" that still stops to pick up anyone who waves, but it's only 60-80 cents per hour of travel. It's around $1 from Managua to Granada, around $2 Managua to Leon.

On the plus side, car prices don't seem to be as inflated here as they are in Mexico or Belize. If they were, hardly anyone local could afford one. Gasoline is on par with U.S. prices or less, depending on what kind of deal is in place with Venezuela at the moment.

Taxis are very inexpensive. Except for an airport ride, 50 cents to $4 will get you around most of the time—$6 would mean a long ride across Managua. A city bus will be 10 - 25¢.

Internal flights run from $40 to $140 on a puddle jumper prop plane. A flight out to the gorgeous Caribbean Corn Islands is usually around $70 from Managua.

Health Care
Nicaragua is one of those countries where even elderly retirees often don't bother with insurance. Costs are so low they just pay out of pocket when something comes up. When a doctor's visit or dental appointment is $15 to $25, it's not going to tax your budget much. The doctors will often give you their cell number in case a problem comes up.

Residents of San Juan del Sur have a better hospital in Rivas to go to for simple things now, but most expats head to Managua for anything serious that can wait. "My wife had to go to the hospital for two days at one point," says Gord. "She had a private nurse just for her. They ask you what you want to eat there and will prepare it. There are flat-screen TVs on the wall. For all the extensive work she had done and the recovery it was only $1,300."

For more routine things, even a specialist is not pricey. An appointment with the gynecologist at the best hospital costs $40, maybe $45 for a visit with a diabetic doctor or dermatologist.

The good news is, Managua is not very far from Granada, Leon, or San Juan del Sur, so it's not difficult to get to a good hospital from one of these three locations. Both the service and the amenities you will find there are excellent and there are some doctors who speak English. Ask around or check the message boards. If you're in rural coffee country though or out in the Corn Islands, try to stay healthy and maybe get some kind of medical evacuation insurance in case of a bad accident.

If you want to buy national health insurance, it won't set you back much. Figure on $50 to $120 per month for the very best plan, depending on your age.

These are all costs for private hospitals up to wealthy country standards. The local public health care system is free to everyone, including tourists.

Other Costs

Any costs that are labor-based are quite cheap in Nicaragua, from getting custom furniture made to having someone clean your house regularly. The per-capita GDP is around $3,000, which is the lowest in Latin America apart from Haiti. Things are improving each year, but you won't have to pay much to exceed the local norm for a maid, gardener, babysitter, or caretaker. A single visit from a housekeeper is generally around $15. A full-time housekeeper or gardener will set you back less than $300 per month including the required taxes, vacation pay, and one-month bonus at the end of the year.

Admissions, cultural activities, and entertainment are all bargains, with prices in the low single digits in dollar terms. Maybe $3 for a baseball game, $4-$6 for a movie, a few bucks for a concert by a local band.

Mobile internet charges are low, but the whole country initially bypassed the fixed line system and went to mobile only. Outside the capital, it's hard to get a wired broadband connection and you'll be waiting quite a while for someone to install it. If you can rent a house that already has this, it's a big plus. "Our reliable land line internet is $45 per month," says Maryanne.

"Our monthly internet plan costs $57.20," says Gord. "It includes 200 GB of data at an average speed of 15 mbps. Initial setup involved the purchase of the router which cost us a little more than $100." By developing country standards, this is quite high, 2.5 times the price of faster service in Mexico. Pre-paid cell phone charges are a bargain though: Gord and his wife average $23 per month for voice and 2 GB of data each, Maryanne pays half that for one person.

Gas for cooking and hot water is $10 a tank and lasts 2-3 months for a couple. Electricity costs can vary wildly depending on whether there's air conditioning in use. I've gotten figures from $7 per month in a temperate climate to more than $100 for a family with A/C and a pool at the beach. It's the same with water, which can vary from $2 per month to $40 depending on the area and usage.

Electronics are costly and not high quality. "If you're looking for a TV or computer, it's what you would have bought in Canada two or three years ago, and costs 30 percent more," says Gord. The local clothing that's available is either cheap and poorly made or imported name brands that are very expensive. There's not much middle ground, so most save the wardrobe upgrades for when they return to their former home for a visit.

To import a vehicle requires a 50 percent duty unless you have a retirement visa. With that, every six years you can bring in one vehicle worth up to $20,000 in value, not more than 10 years old.

Visas
If you come in on a tourist visa, you're allowed to stay three months before you have to leave. For those in San Juan del Sur, this means a short hop to Costa Rica and back. "I was there for five minutes and I would come back with five bottles of duty-free booze," says Gord. He stayed with this arrangement for years before getting long-term residency and it's what a lot of expats do for years without anyone raising an eyebrow.

"Legally you can't work with that though," he adds. "There's 20 percent unemployment here and probably most of the other 80 percent are under-employed, so they don't want people coming in on a tourist visa from other countries to do short-term work. He says that most of the foreigners working in San Juan del Sur have gotten a business or investor visa, which just requires you having hired at least one person.

Technically the investor visa requires a real investment of $30,000 or more, but housing counts if it has a commercial aspect and once you get approved you have permanent residency. I've been told having one room that's an office, a yoga studio, an art gallery, or some other aspect would qualify, though a mixed-use building would obviously be easier. You do have to stay in the country for six months of the year, however.

If you do want to stay long-term, Nicaragua doesn't put up a lot of obstacles, assuming you're not broke. They're glad to have you and your money come stick around for a while. You can get a temporary resident permit that's good for a year at any age, or if you're just 45 or older you can get a retiree/pensioner visa. You only have to show $600 in income per month as a retiree, plus $100 per dependent. There's no tax on earnings from abroad and you can bring up to $20,000 worth of household goods into the country without paying any duties. You can also ship or drive your own car down for personal use with no duty and as long as it's not more than 10 years old, you can sell it locally after five years with no taxes to pay.

There's also a "rentista" visa for those living off investment income they can document. In terms of perks, the deal is similar, but the required proof of income is a bit higher: $750 per month.

After three years of temporary residency, you can apply to be a permanent resident. Once you have that, you're set for five years before you have to renew again.

Downsides

Nicaragua is slowly but surely growing its middle class as the dependence on Venezuela's help dissipates and formerly reluctant foreign investors are more confident in dipping their toes in. This is still a nation where the wealth is concentrated in very few hands, however. The middle class may be growing, but the family behind the Grupo Pellas conglomerate—best known for owning the Flor de Cana rum empire—supposedly has an asset value equal to half the country's entire gross domestic product.

Internet penetration is reportedly the lowest in the Americas and the best you can get in some areas is 3G-wireless.

Nicaragua falls somewhere in the middle in terms of environmental protection. It's not as trashed as Mexico or Honduras, where it's hard to look anywhere without seeing garbage and graffiti, but it doesn't have the resources to be as diligent as Costa Rica. The reasonably clean state of the towns and countryside are due more to cultural norms and a still comparatively low prevalence of throwaway packaging than to any government recycling and waste disposal initiatives.

The government has successfully kept the country off the drug smuggling corridor for the most part, but they have done it by cracking down hard on anyone selling or possessing even small amounts of drugs. If you're a stoner, this is not a good place to live. It's also not a great environment for gays, with a generally intolerant society and no legal protection for partners.

As in much of Latin America, patience is an important virtue. "It is very difficult (and at times frustrating) if I want to be productive here," says Maryanne. "Meetings are not set in stone; time is only an idea." She once waited for hours per day outside someone's office she needed permission from for research. "When I have a question, it really needs to be done face to face: not email, not phone, not texting."

The food is tasty and filling, better in most respects than what you'll get in Panama or Costa Rica, but it's not going to win any culinary awards for complexity or variety. You'll probably want to hone your cooking skills and have a healthy budget for some better restaurants now and then.

For More Information:
InNicaNow.com
TodayNicaragua.com
Expat Exchange Nicaragua forum
Search "Nicaragua expats" or specific places on Facebook for several groups

Chapter 24:
Panama

Pros: top retiree benefits, easy visa process, great air connections, business-friendly, good banking system, low import duties, good health care, beaches, nature activities, dynamic economy, welcoming people.

Cons: pricey capital city, hot and humid in most areas, very wet rainy season, boring cuisine, inconsistent customer service.

Kris and Joel Cunningham were living in Sarasota, Florida, the kind of place many northern Americans dream of retiring to. They had no idea how they were going to make it on their earnings, however, when retired. They were paying $1,200 per month on their mortgage and taxes. Selling it and renting wouldn't help much. "The house next to us, similar to what we have now in Panama, was renting for $1,500 per month," she adds. They're not paying anything close to that though: their rent in the city of David is $385 instead. With lower utility bills, food bills, and medical costs, they are very happy with their new life and feel much more confident about their finances.

Panama perpetually comes out on top as the world's best retirement haven in publications that write about this subject every month. Most of those publications have editors with Panamanian business interests or partnerships though, so take those recommendations with some skepticism. Still, Panama is a winner in almost every category except costs—and those go down drastically if you don't settle down in a waterfront condo in the capital city. Its *pensionada* program for retirees is superb, with a long list of perks and discounts I'll get to later in this Chapter. The threshold to earn those perks is low from a proven income standpoint and with the permit in your hand you get lower prices on services that are already cheaper than your home country's to start with.

Panama is incredibly welcoming to foreigners. It doesn't tax money earned outside the country and a lot of items (including booze) have some of the lowest taxes in the world. This country also has one of the best banking systems in the world, a stable political situation, a good business climate, and uses U.S. dollars as its currency. Recession? They were having none of that. Try 5-10 percent annual growth while the U.S. and Europe were reeling.

American Jim White worked in IT for many years, slogging it out until about four years after his daughter was born, when he discovered the retire early movement. He and his wife Lisa eventually realized they could speed up the process if they moved somewhere cheaper. They eventually went on "an exploratory recon mission" to Panama in 2017 and hit a few different locations that sounded interesting. They ended up in Boquete, where they loved the climate, the driving distance to the beach, and the expat community. Two years later, after putting some more money away, they sold everything and headed south. Now they live in style on around $3,500 per month for the three of them including expat health insurance and a small storage unit back home. (See more on his expat life at RouteToRetire.com.)

The health care system in Panama is excellent, to the point where it is a medical services destination for many foreigners who don't live there. Many fly in to get surgery, have major dental work done, or spend time in a hospital for one-quarter the price they'd have to pay otherwise.

You'll make fewer sacrifices here than you will pretty much anywhere in Latin America if you want what you had at home. There's fast internet, good prices on electronics, reliable electricity, a competitive cell phone climate, and a lot of the shops and services you're used to. Of course, you also get some of the same side effects of all that: consumerism, strip malls, and a culture that revolves around the automobile in most areas.

You're never too far from a beach here though when you want to go unwind. Here you could swim in the Caribbean in the morning, hop in a car, and swim in the Pacific by lunchtime. This is also a paradise for bird watching, nature exploration, and adventure: Costa Rica without the crowds and at lower rates.

As I said though, you may have to take Panama City out of the mix if you're on a strict budget, though it can be easier if you're a dual-earner couple or you're a single willing to share a large apartment with others. Rosie Bell is a British freelance writer who has covered Panama a lot for major publications. "Overall, I rarely spend more than $1,200 a month on my living expenses, even though I live in the capital. My rent is a quarter of what it would be back home and every condo I've lived in has a communal gym and swimming pool included." She took her time and got the word out each time she was looking, however. If you just search the listings geared to expats, it's hard to find a nice place to rent in a good part of the city for under $1,000 per month.

As you can probably tell already, there's no "typical expat" in Panama. You've got people from all over the world, liberal and conservative, those on a strict budget and those with a net worth in the millions. You've got people on corporate transfers, backpackers who forgot to leave, retirees, and ex-military families.

Panama has a high diversity of places to choose from where there is already a sizable foreign population in place. Here are the main ones, but there are plenty of other beach and mountain towns to check out.

Panama City – The closest thing you'll get to Miami after heading south (good and bad).

Coronada – A beach resort community town an hour south of the capital.

Valle de Anton - Just 120 kilometers from the capital, this highland interior area has cool evenings, hot springs for soaking, and relaxed living.

David – The second-largest city, but a bit higher in altitude and not as congested.

Boquete – A popular highland area of flowers, coffee, adventure activities, and cool air.

Bocas del Toro – A string of islands popular with tropical paradise seekers, rebels, and outcasts.

Housing Costs

If you pull up apartment prices online in Panama City, you may think I'm out of my mind to even include this country in a book about living abroad for less. Most of these $5,000 a month penthouses in high-rise buildings on the water are not aimed at you though. Their target markets are people like corporate VPs working for international companies or escaping Venezuelans, Brazilians, and Argentines making banking deposit trips. Yes, there are probably a few drug kingpins and shell company shufflers here and there too. For many "nomad capitalists" who roam the globe looking for business opportunities and wealth sheltering schemes, Panama is seen as nirvana. It has low taxes, limited regulations, a strong banking system, and limited bureaucracy (as long as you hire some legal help). So, there are a lot of takers for expensive condos, whether renting or buying.

That's just one side of the city, however. After all, $1,000 to $1,250 a month for a local is a good white-collar salary, so they're certainly not paying $2,000 per month for an apartment. They are living in less ritzy neighborhoods outside the central business district, with more than two people in a big apartment or house with multiple bedrooms. If you live on the outskirts of the capital, it's not difficult to find a nice apartment for less than $600. That may still seem like a lot, but the closest comparison to Panama City is Miami, where costs are easily double or triple.

Once you get beyond the capital and the prime beach developments, prices drop drastically. Kris and Joel pay $385 per month for that house in David, in a nice middle-class neighborhood on the edge of town, and they love it. "One agent's name kept coming up when we were doing research, so we booked an appointment with him to go see some houses," Kris says. The very first house he showed us was ideal. We took it right away and didn't even look at the others. We have woods and a river behind us, plus there's only one way into the neighborhood so it feels really safe. We're surrounded by local professionals who are just lovely people."

At first, they were living on her husband's social security payment and had a little savings from selling their house in Florida. When I followed up for this edition though, Kris was receiving her own social security payment too, which enabled them to meet the income requirements for the *pensionada* program: $1,000 for one person plus $250 for each dependent (or a spouse). Now they're able to take more advantage of Panama's status as a travel hub and find it relatively cheap and easy to fly back to the USA to see relatives.

A cursory look online at housing rental prices around Panama turned up plenty of affordable places in my search. I found a few one-bedroom places and large furnished studios in Boquete for $450 or less per month including utilities and a large two-bedroom furnished townhouse in the same city with a gourmet kitchen for $900. A three-bedroom furnished apartment in Volcan was going for $650. A two-bedroom beach house in Puerto Armuellas (near Costa Rica) was listed for $450 while an American-style house in a gated community with a pool in Cocle, about 15 minutes from the coast, was listed for $650 per month furnished. I found a 3BR house of 2,100 square feet going for $300 in David. I also found a variety of spacious apartments in prime areas of Panama City for $1,000 or less per month.

If you're in an area that's full of expats and wealthy Panamanians though, naturally you're going to pay whatever that market will bear. It's rather difficult to find a two-bedroom house or apartment for rent in Coronado or the center of Valle de Anton for less than $1,000 per month and you can easily pay two or three times that for a larger place. In more mixed locations, prices drop quickly.

Former Texan Richard Kongable lived in a few places in Panama before settling in a rural area near Volcan, on the side of a mountain. "I like that I never need heat, I never need air conditioning, and there's always a gentle breeze. I'm on the edge of a valley, with a volcano on the left and two rivers. I can see islands in the ocean even though it's an hour and 20 minutes away by car."

Richard rented his house for years for $300 a month and thought he was going to have to leave eventually when the American owner put it up for sale. Instead, the owner fell into health problems and needed to sell in a hurry, so with no buyers in sight Richard got the house of 1,600 square feet for just $25,000.

Prices in prime areas keep creeping up though as Panama's economy continues to grow at a rapid pace. "A lot of what you read in *International Living* and publications like that is out of date on prices," says Richard, "or they're only showing you the outlier situations to get you hooked on coming to a conference. In most cases you're only going to find a terrific deal by being here a while and looking around. In places like Boquete there are a lot of unadvertised rentals from expatriates who are returning home or moving and don't want to leave their house empty. You're only going to find out about these by word of mouth."

When Jim White moved to Boquete from Ohio, his family first secured a short-term rental in a nice complex for a month to stay in while they looked around. They thought they would end up in a house, but they couldn't find one they liked. Eventually they found a fully furnished three-bedroom, two-bath apartment in a gated community for $1,100 a month. Water and internet are included, plus the complex has a great gym, a racquetball court, and two swimming pools. They pay $80 for a propane tank that lasts for months, around $80 per month for electricity. "We have beautiful grounds, the mountains beside us, and some other expats to talk to in English," he says. They're close enough to town to walk, so they don't need a car. "We're paying on the high end for here though," he says. "The average cost of an apartment in Boquete is probably more like $700 to $900 for a nice-sized place."

If you are looking to buy in Boquete, prices are creeping up again after hitting a wall and dropping for years after the housing crisis in the U.S. Most fall in the $80 to $200 per square foot range, the top of that range getting you into luxury level.

Other areas appeal to wealthy retirees looking to build their dream home for less. This is especially true of the Azuero

Peninsula region on the Pacific coast. Avoid that area if you're on a budget or plan to spend a long time searching.

Chuck Holton eventually settled in Valle de Anton at 2,500 feet in altitude with his wife and two kids. He was in the military, then worked as a stockbroker for 10 years and realized that all his older wealthy clients had one regret: they didn't spend enough time with their kids. So, he started looking for ways to restructure his life. He became a writer working at home, a book author, and since 2004, a war correspondent and videographer. He realized he could be based anywhere with good air connections and reduce his tax bill significantly by moving abroad, so the family of seven moved to Panama. "I save more in taxes compared to what my U.S. bill was than what we spend here, total," he says.

"We had spent a year in Panama before when I was researching a book, but we wanted to be somewhere a little cooler, where we didn't need air conditioning all the time. Valle de Anton is a walking town and culturally it's like going back to the 1950s—kind of safe and boring. No crime to speak of and the kids can ride their bikes all over with no worries." They rented for a year to be sure they had a good feel for the market. They then bought a fixer-upper from the local market and renovated it to American standards. Eventually they sold that and bought another house right in the center that was move-in ready. Chuck calls their area "the Aspen of Panama," a place where the elite have their summer homes. As a result, their house of more than 5,000 square feet was $330,000. "You could buy a place a half hour away for a third of that," he explains, "but we're in a prime area with high resale values. There's not much here below $300,000 unless you're willing to do some upgrades."

One big advantage of Panama is that this is one of the few Latin American countries with a banking system that will extend mortgages to foreigners. It takes some patience, but you can finance a home with as little as 20 percent down and interest rates are not as high as in most of the region. Also, many developers have set up financing for new projects and they will have an interest in guiding you through the process.

Food & Drink

You can drink the water from the tap in most of Panama, so that means you're less likely to get sick from the food here than you are in many other developing countries. Unfortunately, the food is definitely not the reason you're going to move here. While there are good gourmet restaurants at the high end, especially in areas with lots of expats, the everyday cuisine is boring and uninspired. Expect lots of fried plantains, beans, rice, and meat stews.

Even where there are a lot of restaurants, like in Boquete where there are at least 75 for a city of 35,000, the variety is rather limited. "For some reason Italian food is all over the place here," says Jim White, "but there's only one Mexican place and not much Asian food."

If you cook for yourself though and have more imagination, you'll find a bounty of fresh ingredients to work with. The varied altitude in Panama means you can buy both tropical fruit and mountain berries, coconuts and fresh coffee. In the Chiriqui province of David and Boquete, you'll be very close to where much of the country's fresh food is produced. I saw people beside the road there selling ten-kilo bags of mixed fruit and vegetables for $5 and it would take you quite a while to get through them all without a big family. It's easy to find good fresh fish everywhere.

According to Numbeo.com, costs for groceries in Panama City are about 60% that of New York City and restaurants are roughly half the price. Both will be far less money outside of the metropolis. Expect to pay $3-$5 for a meal of the day in a place where working class locals eat, up to $30 for a nice non-hotel restaurant. "We might spend $45 or $50 for three at a pretty nice place in Boquete," says Jim, "which is not bad compared to the States. You can easily spend that much at Applebee's. But last week three of us went to a local Panamanian food place and stuffed ourselves with giant portions for $11 total."

Kris Cunningham says she has been pleasantly surprised by low costs in Panama, particularly groceries. "Food is definitely a great deal, especially fruit and vegetables. If you spend $20 on those it will be more than you can carry. We paid two or three times more for almost everything at home, including meat and fish. If you buy what the locals buy and cook, living here is very cheap."

You won't pay much to have a drink with your meal. This is one of the few countries in the world where alcohol isn't taxed at a higher rate than other items. Since taxes are so low here anyway, prices in Panama's liquor stores and supermarkets beat out the lowest duty-free prices you'll see anywhere in the world. This is one of the few countries where I've seen Chilean and Argentine wine selling for less than I could buy it on sale in a low-tax USA state. Liquor prices are the lowest I've seen anywhere on the planet in my travels: from gin to bourbon to Scotch to sake.

"I regularly dine at glittering rooftops with obligatory sea views, which sets me back $20," says Rosie. "A mixology masterpiece at a cocktail bar ranges between $5 and $12." Last time I was in Panama City, I found my own rooftop spot in Casco Viejo and we sipped two mojitos for $8.

"We do spend a lot on food because we buy a lot of imported things at the Pricemart warehouse store," says Chuck. "I also go back to the USA every couple of weeks for work, so I do a lot of shopping back in the states and bring it down in a suitcase. If you're coming here to live on a budget, food is where you'll probably blow the budget unless you can stick to a Panamanian diet with a lot of rice and beans and chicken."

Transportation
Maybe you can blame it on the USA's long domination of the country, but this is not an easy place to get by without a car. The good news is, it has the best roads in Central America. When there are bus connections available between cities, they're not very expensive. The two-hour trip from Panama City to El Valle is less than $5 and an express bus from the capital all the way to David is less than $20.

The big Panama City infrastructure change in this century (besides the canal expansion) was the new metro in the capital. It was finished on time in 2014, roughly within budget, and is working well. A second line opened in 2019, running 13 miles, and more lines are in the plans. The fare is a very reasonable 35 cents per trip after you buy a fare card.

There is only one train in the country, plying the route between Panama City and Colon along the Panama Canal. It's not of much use for residents except to hit the duty-free mall.

Domestic flights are relatively inexpensive, with the one from the capital to David being $120 or less. Because Copa Air is based here, you also have lots of options for getting to other countries, including in Europe and Asia.

The smoke-belching city buses have been getting phased out, replaced by more efficient ones. Taxis in the capital are supposed to run $1-$4 depending on distance in the central area, but you'll have to ask about the fare before taking off if you don't see a meter in use. You can rent a taxi and driver for $8-$10 per hour. "Uber is my main form of transport," says Rosie Bell. I usually pay around $3 for a 30-minute journey, less for short hops." Jim pays $3 to $8 for a taxi trip in Boquete.

Rosie also loves the island getaway options from the capital city. "An overnight trip to the beautiful San Blas Archipelago may cost between $100 and $150 including food, island hopping, world-class snorkeling, and door-to-door transportation in a 4x4." You can also get a public bus to the beach at Coronado for as little as $3.

Chuck has to travel two hours to the Panama City airport on a regular basis and he pays a private driver $100 to $150. "If I didn't mind taking the bus," he says, "that's $4.50."

Healthcare
Nearly all the expatriates in Panama rave about the healthcare they receive. From the time they book an appointment (or get a same-day house call) to the invoice they receive after a hospital stay, it's all a pleasant surprise, especially for Americans. You get the good parts of the American system—well-trained doctors who speak English, the latest equipment, and gleaming clean hospitals—but without the for-profit incentives and layers of insurance executive riches that come with all that up north.

The four largest hospitals in the capital are all affiliated with major U.S. ones, including the Punta Pacifica one with John Hopkins. By most measures, it's the best hospital in Latin America. "But at 1/10 the cost for a lot of procedures," says Chuck Holton. "As one example, I got a gall bladder treatment in the USA that was basically a sonogram and some pain meds and counting the emergency room visit fee, it was something like $2,500. My wife had the exact same treatment here later at the best hospital in the country, same sonogram and pain meds, and it was $139. Plus, she got much better service, with more personal attention."

To give you an idea of what medical prices are like in general, here are some typical ones:

General doctor visit - $20 to $40 (not a co-pay, the whole cost)
Specialist visit - $30 to $60
Doctor house call - $50
Dental cleaning - $35 to $40
Tooth filling - $50
Porcelain crown - $350
Hip replacement surgery - $12,500 total

You will get far better care than you're used to with all this as well. The doctor or dentist won't be in a rush to move on to the next patient. There will be more nurses around. You won't have to worry they're going to charge you $5 for a Q-tip or an Advil. People will actually take the time to explain what's going on and make sure you understand. Since a lot of the doctors and dentists received their education in the USA, it's not hard to find one who speaks English.

When Jim, his wife, and daughter went to the best dentist in Boquete the first time, the total cost for their cleanings, checkups, and his daughter's panoramic dental x-ray was $170. The adult cleanings took around 25 minutes each—very thorough and done by the dentist herself. A follow-up appointment for his daughter to have an orthodontist look at a crooked tooth was $25.

You don't need a prescription for medicines you can't abuse and in most cases those medicines will be a quarter or fifth the retail cost in your home country. Many expats in Panama joke that the price they pay out of pocket for medicine in Panama is less than what their insurance co-pay was before. It depends a lot on the particular drug though and whether a generic version is available, as Kris' experience in David illustrates. "I think my medicines are as expensive here as in the USA, so there isn't much savings there. Anyone taking meds needs to check costs and availability before moving here if that's a major part of their expenses."

Naturally if you're moving from a country with a more civilized single-payer health care system, like Canada and the UK, you won't save as much on health care. You will get far better service though, faster, and with the doctor or dentist of your choice. There's no waiting list or mandated delay.

There is a national healthcare program legal residents can tap into, but it's too low-grade for most of the foreigners I have interviewed over the past decade. Costs are as low as $2 for an appointment, but the service often entails longer waits at public clinics and few choices. Another alternative is a private insurance program, especially good to avoid catastrophic care charges, or a discount program where you pay a monthly fee to get deep discounts across the board when you need care. Those retirees in the *pensionada* program also receive discounts automatically of 10 to 20 percent by showing their ID card.

Keep in mind, however, that the major hospitals are in the two largest cities: Panama City and David. Boquete and Bocas del Toro are not too far from the latter, but if you're on a beach in the far north, or in a hut on the San Blas Islands, you may have to travel quite far for non-routine care. "They're building a new clinic here in Valle de Anton," Chuck says, "but right now we have to be self-sufficient and be our own first responders. The local fire department didn't even have a first aid kit until I gave them one."

Other Costs

The pensionada program for retirement age foreigners in Panama is in most respects the best in the world. Foreigners who can show an income of $1,000 per month (or buy property worth $100,000 or more) get the same discounts and deals that locals get. "I paid back the visa processing costs the first year just from airline discounts," says Richard. As in most countries, this doesn't allow you to work locally though. You need a work visa for that.

Residents that have passed the minimum age level get the following lost list of (sometimes unbelievably generous) discounts:

- 50% recreation and entertainment activities, such as movies, theaters, and sports and other public productions
- 30% off inter-city buses, trains (well, the train route), and ferry boats
- 25% off flights of national and foreign Airlines
- 50% off the rack rate of hotels from Monday to Thursday, 30% on Friday, Saturday and Sunday
- 25% discount of food in licensed sit-down restaurants
- 15% off in fast food establishments
- 15% off the total cost for services of hospitals, dentists, and private clinics, plus
- 20% off doctor consultations
- 10% discount in pharmacies for prescription medicines
- 25% discount in monthly electrical consumption up to 600 kilowatts
- 25% discount in the water bill

The Cunninghams pay $46 a month for a bundled internet and cable TV package, $10-$20 a month or less on their prepaid cell phones ("Everyone seems to use WhatsApp here" she says), and around $45 a month on electricity. If they ran the air conditioning constantly that could triple, however. Richard Kongable estimates that he spends about $160 a month on utilities, including a satellite TV package with lots of English channels, and spends $300 a month on a son's private school. "All in, counting car and gas expenses, the three of us probably spend around $1,700 a month," he says.

"Anything that is labor-intensive is far cheaper here," says Chuck. "So household staff is a bargain, say $20 a day for a maid or gardener. The great thing is if there's anything you don't want to do, you can just hire somebody to do it: to get the car fixed or to go stand in line for paperwork. We paid somebody to camp out all night to be first in line at the immigration office and get our residency paperwork sorted out. He charged us 15 bucks."

Visas

Panama is one of the easiest countries in the world to get a retirement or residency visa and it's a big reason the destination is so popular with expatriates. You only need an income of $1,000 a month to qualify, plus $250 for each dependent or spouse. (Reduced to $750 for you if you own property worth at least $100,000.) You get all those juicy discounts outlined in the previous section and there is no minimum or maximum age requirement. If your pension/social security is low and you want an easy path to residency, it's hard to beat Panama.

In just three months, you can convert a temporary residency visa to a permanent one, a sharp contrast to many countries where it takes years. In addition, foreign residents on the pensionada visa can import up to $10,000 worth of goods tax-free.

If for some reason this option is not a good match, you can still apply for a permanent residency visa from the get-go, with other options to qualify. You have to deposit $5,000 in a local bank, but that's a low hurdle for most people. Then you have three options. The most complicated way to gain residency is to set up a local corporation for a business. Another way is to have a formal offer of employment from a Panamanian company—which generally requires a skill a local does not possess. The easiest way is to buy a piece of property. It doesn't matter if this is a building lot you never manage to build on or the cheapest condo you can possibly find. When you're a property owner (of something worth as little as $15,000), you're on the easy track to residency.

There's another unique option in Panama. You could invest in a teak farm plot and then with that small investment you're a property owner. Done right, this could even be accomplished through a self-directed IRA. Sure, there's some risk involved if the price of teak goes down before the trees mature, but the world is not exactly awash in hardwoods that aren't in endangered forests, so it looks like a low-risk investment.

Chuck Holton and his family are on a "Friendly Nations" business visa that requires starting a local company. This is available to citizens of 48 countries. "None of the single things required were all that daunting," he says, "but we kept running into delay after delay getting through the whole process. As in much of Latin America, red tape and bureaucracy are like national sports here. "They *relish* the chance to make your life difficult when you need that stamp or additional piece of paper to submit," he says. "If you're not fluent in Spanish, it's well worth the money to pay someone who knows how to play the game already."

If you're interested in living here, do some poking around to find the visa/permit that is right for you. There are others where you can buy your way in by investing $300,000 to become a full citizen, a business investor visa that requires an investment of $160,000 and employing locals, or an agricultural visa that requires an investment of $60,000 for a six-year residency permit.

Since it's relatively easy to get residency here one way or another, the government doesn't take too kindly to foreigners trying to stay permanently on a tourist visa. "They have tightened things so you can't cross the border for the weekend and come back over and over, actually living here as a tourist," says Kris Cunningham. "Now you really need residency to live here."

Downsides

It's not all rosy in Panama, no matter how many gushing articles you read about it. This is still the developing world, with a lot of the same problems you'll find elsewhere in Latin America in terms of public services, pollution, traffic, garbage, and inefficiency. There are still corruption cases exposed on a regular basis, despite a muzzled media that has to operate under really strict libel laws.

Unless you love stifling tropical heat and insects, you may not like the majority of the country that sits near sea level. At a higher elevation, you've got the opposite problem. Some think Boquete in the highlands is perfect. Others think it's way too cold. Then when rainy season hits, "We never, ever leave the apartment without our umbrellas because you just never know," says Jim. Try it out during the worst time of year to judge for yourself.

While Panama City has a lot going for it in terms of business opportunities and nightlife, the new subway has only partially relieved the horrendous traffic and the taxi drivers here may just be the most unpleasant you'll ride with anywhere. You can find good dining spots in the capital and Boquete, but overall the Panamanian diet is pretty bland. It definitely doesn't take advantage of the bounty of the land and sea.

The poor customer service you'll receive from cabbies is just the introduction. "Count yourself lucky if your restaurant server looks you in the eyes, not to mention mustering a smile," Rosie says.

If you're a woman under 50, you'll get propositioned on a regular basis in this macho culture.

While the Casco Viejo section of the capital is a nicely renovated version of history, there's no lovely historic city in Panama where you can stroll for hours. There's nothing close to Antigua, San Miguel de Allende, Salta, or Arequipa. The Spanish treated the country as a transit point. Then the United States had a lot of influence in Panama while administering the canal and the banana plantations. That means this is a country often better suited to cars than sneakers.

Overall, Panama has more pluses than minuses. Its easy air connections, light taxes, good health care, good banking system, easy visa process, and dollar economy make it a no-brainer for many retirees who don't want to deal with a tougher adjustment in a place like Guatemala or Ecuador. Chuck Holton loved the array of outdoor adventure activities so much he bought a local tour company. "Between where I live and the Caribbean it's mostly wilderness, so there's no shortage of places to explore."

For More Information
PanamaInfo.com
LivinginPanama.com blog section
Expatexchange.com/panama/liveinpanama
RouteToRetire.com
Boquete.ning.com
ThePanamaNews.com
Panama sections of International Living, Live and Invest Overseas

Chapter 25:
Peru

Pros: gorgeous Andean scenery, varied climates, interesting food, good medical care in the capital, good handicrafts and crafts workers.

Cons: usually gray capital city, expensive internal flights, wide gulf in wealth, poor environmental protections.

"Peru has long lines, every task is far more complicated than it needs to be, and the men can be terribly rude. But I think, just maybe, the best relationships happen when you can love someone (or a country) deep enough to see past their faults. I know I love Peru because when I reflect on my past year, it's hard to remember what was difficult. All I can think about is what I've gained."

That was the opening quote from Danielle L. Krautman on the GoMadNomad.com blog after spending a year in Lima. Later she and her partner moved north to a town outside the mountainous city of Cajamarca and she started liking it much better.

Peru often pops up as the favorite of travelers who have spent a lot of time in South America. The scenery really is as spectacular as any glossy travel magazine spread and the prices are low enough to allow the average tourist to do and see everything. And "everything" is a lot here: desert canyons, mountain cities, the Amazon rain forest, Andean peaks, and of course those Inca ruins. Peru is the home of Machu Picchu, the continent's most popular tourist attraction, but still arguably one of the most magical sites on Earth.

The central hub for most travelers is Cusco (or Cuzco), a stunning city perched at over 11,000 feet/3,500 meters above sea level. From here, travelers can set out for Machu Picchu or many other Inca ruins in the Sacred Valley or just wile away the days in a beautiful, historic Andean city.

Nora Dunn, who runs The Professional Hobo blog, decided to unpack for a while in Pisac, in the Sacred Valley between Cusco and Machu Picchu. "My 'move' to Peru—for me—signified a shift in my travel mentality of being 'homeless.' After more than seven years of transient wandering, I was ready for a place that I could call mine (even if it's rented), that I could use as a base for other travels, and also as a retreat to simply do my own thing. And Peru—specifically Pisac—resonated with me very much as a place I felt comfortable enough to call home, and yet exotic enough that I felt like I was still traveling every time I left the house!"

The colonial city of Arequipa is another highlight, with white-capped mountains in the background of the main plaza and a rambling monastery that is a photographer's delight. Travelers with more time can tour nearby Colca Canyon, see the mysterious Nazca desert drawings, take a boat trip on Lake Titicaca, or visit the "poor man's Galapagos" of Ballestas Islands near Paracas. And that's just the south. There's plenty more to see and do off this main tourist route in the rest of the country and more interesting ruins up north in the Amazonas region that get very few visitors.

A lot of travelers come to Peru and spend a fortune. There are hotels, after all, starting at more than $600 a night, and they fill up sometimes. That $600 is about the annual average monthly salary though, so unless you're living in the poshest part of Miraflores, Lima, you should easily be able to live a half-price life in this South American country without trying very hard. Some NGOs tell prospective volunteers that they can get by here from $400 at the most frugal end to $800 going out a fair bit and eating at nice restaurants now and then. Therefore, if you're coming in with monthly earnings of $1,200 or more you should be able to live an upper-middle-class lifestyle rather easily, not counting travel.

Peru is one of those countries where the largest city is not the one that enchants and pulls in foreigners. The nightlife, art scene, and culinary scene all get high marks, but the historic section feels neglected and the weather sucks. I've been to Lima five times now and have seldom seen the sun more than an hour or two at a time. "You need to come in January" was one resident's reply when I told her this. There's a constant haze and cloud cover over the city most of the year and unless you like the color gray, it can get old fast. Unless you're transferred there for a job or marry someone who lives there, you'll probably want to settle down somewhere else instead unless good restaurant food is at the very top of your priority list.

Housing Costs
There are several clear strata of housing prices in Peru, from dirt-cheap in the countryside to first-world expensive in the heart of Cusco or in the best neighborhoods of Lima. In general, you can find a two- or three-bedroom apartment or house in most parts of the country for $400 to $800 a month quite easily, less for smaller quarters. The smaller the city, the less it will probably cost. Where things get out of whack are the most elite neighborhoods or the heart of the historic center. As always, if you get feet on the ground

and look around, you'll find a better deal than if you try to set it up in advance. Just get a cheap hotel or vacation rental apartment while you put out some feelers.

To give you an idea though, the site Numbeo.com has the average rent in Peru at 70 percent lower than rent in the USA. If you can read enough Spanish to figure out the local classified ads in Cusco, you can easily find a one-bedroom apartment for $300 or less and it's not a whole lot more to step up to a two-bedroom one. Even in Miraflores or Barranco in Lima you can find a deal if you're patient enough.

Foreigners cannot own land within 50 miles of the border, but that only really impacts Puno near Lake Titicaca, so it's not really an issue for many foreigners. Closing costs are reasonable but as in most developing countries, mortgage options are minimal, with rates at 10 percent or more. Expect to pay the full amount unless you arrange seller financing. There are terrific bargains in the countryside, but prices in the desirable parts of Lima are ones better suited to executives on a fat banking salary than those trying to cut costs.

Freelance writer and memoir coach Wendy Dale moved to Cusco with her Bolivian husband and found a hotel building for rent. In a fateful turn, it was the same hotel they had stayed in on their honeymoon, which they took as a sign it was meant to be. Their new Hotel Artsy Fartsy (HotelArtsyFartsy.com) has eight rooms and a terrific view of the city from the rooftop terrace. So, there's another option if you want to start a business in a foreign city: you can run a hotel or bed and breakfast without tying up all your cash in purchasing the building. You rent it and run it instead, keeping the profit that's left.

Food & Drink
Peruvian food has gone from completely unknown to "hot cuisine" since the first time I visited in the early '00s and generally the hype is well placed if you're dining in a nice restaurant. Some local dishes are not for the squeamish, as in roasted guinea pig, bull penis soup, and another soup made with boiled cow hooves. Get away from the sensationalist TV show fare, however, and the food is quite impressive overall, especially at nice restaurants on the coast and in the capital.

More standard fare includes pastries stuffed with meat, the world's biggest variety of potatoes, corn, rice, chicken, plenty of fruit, and lots of seafood, especially ceviche. The food varies widely from region to region, however, and you'll actually have an easier time finding pizza these days than you will finding a roasted guinea pig. For most travelers, the food ends up being a pleasant surprise. At the cheap places it's not amazing, but it's consistently good and filling, and a nice break from the beans/tortillas/rice diet of much of the Americas. Quinoa is now getting too expensive for locals because of heavy export demand, but it's still common in tourist restaurants. Otherwise, expect lots of rice. You can eat healthily here without trying too hard, especially in the Sacred Valley, since there's so much farming at different altitudes.

The street food is cheap and filling, with kebabs, fried potatoes and sausage, and empanadas being the most common. You can always get a cheap meal at local markets, or stock up for a hike or picnic. Mild cheeses and sausages that can be sliced like salami are easy to find. In the cities, there are plenty of cheap set meal places for as little as $1.25 and local fast-food options outside the tourist areas. Spit-roasted chicken restaurants are also numerous.

In the mountains, expect plenty of vegetables and rice, with a bit of meat thrown in for flavor. In the jungle, bananas, plantains, yucca, rice, and river fish are the staples. Along the coast, you'll find plenty of ocean fish and scallops, though the preference is often ceviche preparation (not cooked but cured in citrus juice).

You can generally find a set meal in a locals' restaurant anywhere for $2 to $4, or $3.50 to $9 in a tourist restaurant. This will include a soup, main dish, bread, and tea or coffee. The dining scene is so competitive in Cusco that even the smallest tourist restaurant will usually throw in a free glass of wine or pisco sour to get you in the door. Chinese food is available in most towns and there are ample vegetarian choices in the cities and tourist areas.

Going up a notch, spending $8 to $14 per person on a meal will enable you to eat almost anywhere, with pretty surroundings, maybe a fireplace, and cloth napkins. There are only a handful of restaurants outside Lima where a couple would spend over $70 on dinner, almost none outside of the five-star hotels. You'll be expected to leave some change for a tip if a service charge isn't included but in nicer places, 5-10% is common. If there's a music performance, you'll find an additional charge tacked on and fancier places also levy a hefty tax.

Fruit juices, bottled water, and sodas (including bubble gum flavored "Inca Cola") are everywhere. Peruvian wine is a hit and miss affair, but it's seldom more than $10 a bottle in the stores and $3 a glass at a restaurant. Better stuff from Argentina and Chile isn't much more. Most beers are similar regional lagers that are good enough, but you can also find a malty black beer here and there. They run from $1.25 a bottle at happy hour to $1.50 or $3 other times, sometimes for a large bottle that's actually double sized. Peru is proud of its pisco and this clear grape brandy is sipped straight or mixed in cocktails. It'll sneak up on you, especially at high altitudes.

Coca leaf tea is not only legal but encouraged. It provides stamina on your treks and helps with altitude adjustment, without giving you any real buzz: think coffee without the shakes or the comedown afterwards.

When shopping for your own food, if you buy what's local the prices are particularly good. Seasonal fruit and vegetables average 75 cents a kilo and year-round staples like rice, potatoes, and beans are about the same.

"I think food in Peru might even be cheaper than in Bolivia if you're cooking for yourself," says Wendy. "We arrived three weeks before the COVID-19 lockdown, so we were soon eating at home every meal. Still, we were only spending about $50 a week at the grocery store, not including alcohol."

Healthcare
While not quite up there with Panama and Mexico, Peru is becoming a major medical tourism center and Lima has a variety of gleaming modern hospitals with English-speaking doctors. Costs will vary by procedure, but you can often expect to pay one-fifth to one-quarter the price of a similar treatment or operation in the United States if you go to the best facility. You may pay all of $35 to see a specialist (who will take his time and not rush off to another patient) and $15 an hour at most for a physical therapist.

You can buy an insurance plan in Peru that's kind of hybrid between insurance and a discount card. You pay $300 to $400 per year and get at least 20 percent off and up to 100 percent reimbursement on some services, like an ambulance. With one of these plans a doctor's house call can be as low as $20.

Dental care in Lima is quite good and if you need some serious work done it'll cost a small fraction of what you're used to. I've seen prices posted online of $120 for a crown or root canal and a check-up/cleaning will probably cost you $40 or less—at the nicest office in town. This is a popular medical tourism destination for crowns and implants, with a faster turnaround than what you'll often get in your home country as a bonus.

Service and English fluency both decline quite a bit as the size of the city gets smaller. There will be at least one international-level, modern hospital in good-sized cities like Cusco, Arequipa, and Trujillo, but in small towns you may be limited to a basic public clinic. These clinics may think things like rubber gloves, sterilization, and general hygiene are optional. Spending money to get to a big city (or buying evacuation insurance before moving) will be money well spent.

Transportation

In general terms, getting around within a city or town in Peru is cheap. Bus travel prices are affordable, but the trips can be quite long. Where you'll really get socked though is when you buy a domestic flight. There's a legal two-tiered pricing system that soaks the foreigners.

A local bus in Peru will generally cost you 25 cents to a dollar—the latter being from a far-flung suburb to the center of town. When you take a taxi in Lima, Cusco, or Arequipa, a three-kilometer ride will usually be under $4 if you're getting the right price. This makes the trip from the Cusco airport to the center one of the cheapest in the world, at around $7. You have to haggle sometimes though, especially in Lima, where the driver may be quote you $20 just to see if you're gullible enough to pay it. The arrival of Uber was a welcome development for those who hate to haggle.

Long-distance buses come in a variety of classes and companies, with the one from Lima to Cusco running anywhere from $29 to $80 depending on how luxurious it is. The ones running up and down the coast are significantly less as they don't have to cross the Andes. Many people just suck it up and buy a flight to cross the mountains, but if you're not a legal resident you'll probably pay twice as much as you should for a domestic flight. It can often top $200 for a very quick jaunt that's barely long enough for drink service.

In many towns and cities, you can easily get by with public transportation, but if you're an expatriate living in the outskirts of Arequipa or in the Sacred Valley, you might want to keep a car to get around in. You'll pay more than you would in the USA for one, but maintenance will be much cheaper.

Peru is one of the few countries in South America that has a network of passenger trains you can ride between cities. Most of the classes are priced for tourists and are going to cost you more than riding a bus, but they're a more romantic and interesting option to get between Cusco, Machu Picchu, Puno and Arequipa.

Visas
Peru makes it quite easy to stay for six months, but "getting residency as an American is quite difficult," says Wendy. For her it was easier because she has a Bolivian husband covered by a reciprocal agreement, but normally it's a long, tough process for most foreigners from abroad to stay on longer.

When you land in the country, you can get a visa for 30 days or in various increments up to 183. For the latter, you just have to ask (assuming you're from a country on the right list, like the USA, UK, Australia, or Canada). Immigration can ask for proof you have sufficient funds to support yourself. You can't extend this beyond that six months though, and it's only good for six months within a year. Back when I put out the first edition of this book you could leave the country and then come back again, immediately getting another 183 days. Some people went on like this for years. If you overstayed your visa by a few days, the fine was just $1 a day. That all came to a halt though and now you have to leave for at least six months before you can return for another six. That's fine for those who don't mind traveling or living somewhere else half the year, but a deal breaker for those who want to stay put.

Nora eventually moved on but said while she was there that if she wanted to stay, she would either buy land or get sponsored for a permanent visa by being employed by a local company. Getting a work visa is relatively straightforward if you have a job. You can upgrade a tourist visa to a work or resident one without leaving the country by just paying up and showing the proper documents. You'll get a visa that lasts as long as what's on your employment contract. As long as you have the job, it'll keep getting renewed with no hurdles. There are probably tens of thousands of foreigners working in Peru right now, in industries including mining, hospitality, oil, agriculture, tourism, and charity. (Yes, that last one is a very large industry too.) If you do a little legwork ahead of time, you'll find plenty of networking opportunities, though be advised these are mostly centered in Lima.

There is a freelancer "rentista" visa available here for those who can easily demonstrate more than $1,000 per month income from elsewhere and document their "professional standing." The difficulty with this rentista visa is that the income must be from a non-employment source like rental income, so you could be a self-employed person pulling in $5K a month that they don't think qualifies because it's too irregular. I would presume it's better to be getting regular payments you can easily divert into a Peruvian bank than erratic monthly payments from one company freelance client deposited into PayPal. I haven't managed to track down anyone who has received one of these, however, so I don't have any examples of approval or rejection.

You can get an investor visa for sinking an amount into the local economy by way of real estate, investment in a Peruvian company, or starting a business. It's listed in soles and can change with the exchange rate, but as I was putting this book together the amount was $154,000 in U.S. dollars.

After two years on any temporary residency visa you can apply for citizenship if you speak Spanish well and know plenty of Peruvian history for an exam.

Most of the expatriates I've run across who are living in Peru have a work visa or are married to a Peruvian. You don't see nearly as many foreign-owned businesses here as you do in many other Latin American countries, which is probably a testament to the difficulty of doing it. You can't just roll into town with some cash and have a coffee shop or tour company running a few weeks later as you can in Colombia or Panama.

Other Costs
In theory at least, you owe taxes on income as a resident, even if that income is from outside the country. If you're American that's no big deal if documented correctly because unless you earn six figures that will shield you from owning U.S. taxes if you're permanently away. For some other nations though, or big earners, this could mean double taxation.

If you're in Lima, you can find a good bilingual school for your child for $350 a month or less unless it's part of a major international network. In other cities there will be private schools for the same price, but they may be Spanish only. The site ExpatPeru.com has listings for different cities.

Most utility costs are reasonable, with $50 to $100 per month covering electricity, water, and gas. Tropical areas that need air conditioning will cost a bit more for power. Areas that have high-speed broadband to the home will pay $30 to $40 per month for 60 mbps or more. In rural areas you may have to rely on a wireless signal, but there are four major players competing, so the prices are good. Assume you can get a SIM card for less than $2 and 3 gigabytes of data (plus phone calls) for less than $10. For most people, that's enough for a month or more of use. Often these plans include calls to certain international countries, such as the USA, plus unlimited use of WhatsApp and Facebook.

Downsides
This is still a poor, developing nation overall and there's a lot of very real poverty in the shantytowns and the rural areas. A lot of export wealth is generated in Peru from mining, agriculture, and oil, but very little of that is trickling down to the people at the bottom and there are constant protests against extraction companies taking over indigenous lands. Sustainability and environmental protection are seldom near the top of the list when planning business ventures or how to run tourism programs.

There is a good bit of petty crime throughout the country and more than a few cases of muggings and assaults in Lima and Cusco. You also get the typical Latin American annoyances like machismo, widespread graffiti, public urination, litter, a lack of change for purchases, and stray dogs.

The political situation looks like a circus to many outsiders and there's plenty to complain about in terms of corruption, an unfair judiciary, and poor infrastructure. Peru has a strong pull on many who visit though and there's no country quite like it to substitute.

For More Information:
ExpatPeru.com
PeruForLess.com/blog/
HowToPeru.com
PeruReports.com (news in English)
LimaCityKings.com
Plus see expat boards on Facebook

Chapter 26:
The Philippines

Pros: english-speaking, hundreds of location options, good transportation system, easy retirement visas, cheap booze and beer, great diving and snorkeling, good flight connections.

Cons: disappointing food, ugly architecture, lax building regulations, messy politics, autocratic leader, unbelievable traffic in the capital, pollution and garbage, frequent typhoons.

Few countries provoke such a love it/hate it reaction from travelers as The Philippines, so naturally the decision is a split one on living there as well. It's not as good a value or as attractive as many other countries in Southeast Asia and I've yet to hear anyone rave about the food. The cities are downright ugly throughout and Manila has some of the most traffic-clogged streets in the world.

This country deserves the "land of smiles" moniker much more than Thailand does though. The people here are constantly smiling, friendly, and welcoming. Anyone who has been to school speaks fluent English also, making this a super-easy place to get around and take care of business. Prices are reasonable across the board and there are thousands of "toes in the sand" bars and restaurants with a view among the thousands of islands. It's easy to get from place to place once you get out of jammed Manila.

This can be a tough place to gain residency or own a business though if you're not retired unless you marry a local. For the gray-haired men with a paunch that easily find a hot Filipino wife, that's not considered an obstacle. This is the main group you hear championing the country as paradise on Earth. I'm not being judgmental since both parties get something they want out of that arrangement, but more than a few would-be expats find the prevalence of this a bit too creepy.

The others that love the place though are (mostly male) entrepreneurs who come here for the great business environment. It's easy to find English-speaking workers at bargain prices and you can live for cheap while you're ramping up your operations. Internet access is fast in cities, flight connections are good, and a nice beach is always just a short hop away when it's time to recharge.

There's no one certain place that gets the bulk of the expats here, so it's best to travel around a bit and get a feel for the different places to find the right fit. There were some areas in this country I loved, others I couldn't wait to get out of, even after just one day.

So much of your choice is going to be subjective, not something you can map out on a checklist. You'll find expats in areas stretching from northern Luzon all the way down to Davao in Mindanao, with plenty scattered around places in between like Palawan and Cebu.

Others settle down because of perfect beaches or a chance to indulge in regular snorkeling and diving trips. Justin Carmack is an underwater photographer and videographer who runs the Critter Hunter YouTube channel. "I'm based here in Dumaguete because this area has some of the rarest underwater species on Earth."

Digital Nomad and Alajode.com blogger Jodie Dewberry lived in Manila for a while and used it as a base to explore other parts of the country she didn't see during her first visit. Apart from the lousy internet connections in some places (more on that later), she says it's a great base in Southeast Asia with very attractive prices.

This is one of the many countries in this book that is cheaper now in U.S. dollar terms than it was when I researched the first edition in 2014. Thanks to a steadily declining currency, some goods and services are cheaper than when I first visited as a backpacker in the mid-1990s!

The average monthly salary in the Philippines is less than $400 per month, which is why there are so many call centers and staffing firms here. There's nowhere else in the world where companies can find educated English speakers without a thick accent for such a reasonable rate—plus they can work what is the night shift in the USA and it's their daytime. That shows you though that if you land in the Philippines with just two government retirement checks going into your bank account each month, you can live two or three times better than a fully employed local couple can. Add some savings or online income and you can have a sweet life in paradise.

Housing Costs

The Philippines is a nation of 2,000 inhabited islands, so naturally costs are going to vary quite a bit depending on where you settle down. Rent prices in Manila are on par with Bangkok, a range of $300 to $800 for a one-bedroom place in the city center. You can easily pay more than $2,000 per month there in a modern high-rise where executives live. Rents go down quite a bit in most other areas of the country, however.

American Justin Carmack pays $400 per month in Dumaguete, on the island of Negros near Cebu. For that he has a one-bedroom house with a pool that's near a beach. He and his wife spend another $100 or so for electricity each month, then "The water bill is maybe $2, buying drinking water is around $10 a month."

Katie Lamb, a freelance writer who also runs the EarthCrusin.com blog, has opted for staying in hotels for months on end to avoid the hassle of signing a lease and getting utilities set up. After she was in, she started negotiating. "I stayed at the Forever Blessed Inn in El Nido, Palawan for about 6 months. I started paying $940 a month (which was during high season) then got it down to $630 a month. When the virus lockdown happened, I paid about $380 a month. I had no costs for utilities."

When she moved on to Puerta Princesa on the same island, she rented her own space that was part of a hotel in a good area. "I got a decent-sized bungalow with a pool. I paid 750 Philippine pesos a day which is about $16. It worked out to $480 per month."

When Jodie lived in Manila, she found a nice apartment with a view for $650 per month on a short-term rental basis. "We found ourselves on the 50th floor with a view across the city, two balconies to enjoy it from, and a rooftop pool and gym to escape to."

You can't buy property here as a foreigner and if you have a local spouse, the house will go in his/her name, even if you put up 100 percent of the money. On the plus side, it's quite easy to find a condo for less than $50,000 and you can own that outright. If you form a corporation though, you can't own more than 40 percent.

Ron Meyers is one of those happy guys who married a lovely local woman and settled down on the island of Cebu. "You can still buy land for cheap here, like beachfront under coconut and mango trees for under $43 per square meter. Building a nice new house will cost around $580 per square meter. He admits though that, "If it were not for the younger wife, I would not be here for the living experience. I have a child now. I had no children before and now I'm living life in reverse of most guys; that part I really like."

Condos in the big cities where executives live can easily start at $150,000 in new complexes, or $2,000 per square meter, but you can find ones for sale for under $50,000 in secondary beach locations.

Food and Drink

Perhaps because it's such a hodge-podge of different influences, Philippine food gets a bad rap and is definitely not the reason most people move here. Food often sits out in the tropical heat all day at cheap places and hygiene isn't always what it should be. "Nearly everybody who visits the Philippines gets sick at some point," says

Jodie. There's also probably more fast food consumed here than in any country outside the USA. If you like seafood, nuts, and tropical fruit though, you're in luck.

This is a country where most expats quickly tire of the local cuisine and end up spending more to get some variety. That doesn't mean it'll cost a fortune though. "We spend around $450 per month on food for 2 people," says Justin, "and that's eating steak and seafood—not the cheapest meals."

As with anywhere, eating out in prime tourist areas costs more. "El Nido is on the more expensive side of places to stay on Palawan. A breakfast of eggs and toast would be $2 to $3," says Katie. "If you go to a neighborhood restaurant for a local dish like Tapsilop or some sort of fish/rice buffet meal it's as cheap as a dollar. I ate mostly at western restaurants though as I'm a pescatarian. I found a great local fish restaurant on the beach with dishes around $3. Pizza, pasta, and western dishes are more expensive at around $4. I would say I spent about $12 to $20 a day on food when I was there."

Local brew coffee is often a dollar or so, but "expect to spend $2 to $4 for a latte at a nice coffee shop," Katie says.

Jodie spent a lot of time going out or ordering in when she lived in Manila. "The cost of eating out would vary. If you ate street food, you could fill up for $1.50 to $2.50 per person. If you ate in the upmarket areas like Makati, or in a mall, it would be around $5 to $7.50 for a meal. You can order food through Grab (like Uber Eats) and most of the food on there was around $5 to $7.50 per person for a meal. The only issue with delivery in Manila is that it rarely takes less than an hour because of the traffic!"

If you like to drink or go clubbing though, this is one of the best bargains in the world if you stick to what's produced locally. It's easy to find dollar beers in basic bars, even on touristy Boracay, and rum cocktails made from the abundant sugar cane will only cost two or three dollars in a lot of places. You can spend a lot more getting bottle service in a fancy Manila club, of course, but even that will cost a quarter of what you would spend in London or New York, with a smiling waiter or waitress taking care of you.

Going grocery shopping here won't hit you too hard if you stick to what the locals eat. For a dollar or less you can get a pound of rice, bananas, mangoes, potatoes, tomatoes, peppers, pasta, and much more. Meat isn't such a bargain except for pork, but fish and seafood sell for great prices near the coast—which is almost everywhere.

Transportation

The Philippines is a land of islands, which means you'll probably get on a ferry or plane on a regular basis. Then on the island where Manila is located—Luzon—there's an extensive bus service that will make you think half the residents are on the move at any given time, with half their belongings coming with them.

In this nation of islands, the ferries are a major form of transportation. Sometimes it's a quick hop across the strait in an open outboard motorboat for a couple of dollars, other times it's a big ship with sleeping cabins that can take two days. Prices are reasonable across the board, so it's prudent to choose the safest option available. Philippine ferries have capsized on a far too frequent basis. Sometimes they are quite nice though, like the big catamaran between Cebu Island and Bohol island, which is as little as $6 for the three-hour trip. To give an idea of the long-haul options, the trip from Cebu City to Manila ranges from $28 for an open-air bed to $52 for a bed in a 4-person cabin with A/C, a desk, dividers, and TV. A ferry from Cebu City to Palawan will cost $25 to $60, but it takes more than 24 hours to complete.

Flight prices on busy routes are sometimes in line with ferry costs if you're traveling light (which very few locals do) and you plan ahead. You'll often find promotional fares under $50 one-way. It's kind of a no-brainer for some routes, like that Palawan one mentioned above. You shave at least 22 hours off your travel time by spending $40 to $120 on a ticket. You can find flight/hotel packages for quite cheap too as they are priced for the domestic market. Expats living in Manila think nothing of flying to somewhere like Boracay for a 3-day weekend.

Bus prices are all over the map, from $2 for a bumpy jeepney ride across a mountain range to $50 for a nice overnight bus from Manila to the far north of Luzon. Often you do get what you pay for, so check all the options carefully.

Getting around in Manila is not expensive, but what is your time worth? Official taxi, Uber, or Grab prices start at around a dollar for a short ride. The last time I was there I spent just a few dollars getting from point A to B each time, but except in off-peak times, even a short trip would routinely take an hour or more. Bring something to read. Waiting time stuck in traffic will add a few dollars an hour to the fare.

In most of the country this is not such an issue though and while the rides aren't always comfortable, they're generally cheap. "To get from El Nido to Puerto Princesa in Palawan in a minivan is $10," says Katie. "Moto tricycles around both places are dependent on your haggling skills. They always try to up the price for foreigners like everywhere. In El Nido when I first got there, I paid a tricycle driver $2.50 from the bus station to town. When I knew how far it was, next time I paid 40 pesos—82 cents! In Puerto Princesa, some tricycle drivers have a fares list in their cab. Some don't and will try to overcharge."

Few foreigners own a car here (though purchase prices are better than in most of Southeast Asia), but a lot of them will buy or rent a scooter. Justin rents his and pays around $150 per month.

Healthcare
As in many developing countries, health care can be first-rate in the cities, but is rudimentary in the rural areas. If you're not living near a city like Cebu City, Davao, or the capital, it's best to have some kind of plan that covers evacuation insurance. Or be ready to hop a flight to get to a gleaming modern hospital when it's necessary.

The Philippines is on the map as a medical tourism destination, with well-trained doctors performing elective surgery for a fraction of what it would cost in the USA—or with no waiting time for others who have the money to get the procedure done now. Since all the doctors and nurses speak English, there are no communication issues.

Jodie ended up going to the hospital twice while in Manila. "The two hospital visits only came to about $120 ($32 for the initial consultation and $88 for an ultrasound and follow-up). I didn't bother to claim it on my insurance."

She was hesitant about going to a foreign hospital but was pleasantly surprised. "I simply can't fault a single member of staff at the clinic I was in and out of. I was seen instantly, the doctors and surgeons were incredibly friendly and efficient, and the whole thing couldn't have gone better."

Fortunately, there's a robust internal flight system in The Philippines, so it won't take you long to get to a major hospital if your problem is not immediately life-threatening.

Other Costs
Staying in touch won't cost you much here and mobile coverage is widespread and fast. The cellular space is competitive, and many companies will give you a SIM card for free. Then you get a pre-paid phone plan you can top off for a few dollars. "I paid around $5.25 per month for 4 gigabytes of data," says Jodie.

Unfortunately, the country continues to lag behind in broadband connections to the home, as well as the speed you can expect if you're lucky enough to get one. "I fell in love with Palawan last year, but the Wi-Fi was appalling there," says Jodie. The national average is still below 10 mbps outside of the big cities. Rates are no great bargain either, starting at $35 and rising to $60 if you are lucky enough to live in an area with 100 mbps fiber to the home. Most people make do with some kind of mobile USB stick to supplement a home or hotel connection that's often still DSL on copper lines.

Electricity costs are quite high on all the islands, so many expats report a power bill that tops $100 per month. Many locals do without air conditioning because it drives up their monthly costs so much, or they only use it in their bedroom at night. Water, propane gas, and other utility costs are negligible though.

Visas

You can get a six-month tourist visa here if you apply in advance and can document income or savings to support yourself. Then you can extend it for 60 days by paying a heap of Philippine pesos. Some report being able to re-up that again if they travel elsewhere for a while and return. That's what Justin does, and he says it costs him about $75 for visa costs with extensions.

Technically though, if you're not on a retirement visa and you want to stay longer, you have to get a work permit, marry a local, or buy your way in, by investing at least $75,000.

If you have a bit of cash put away, the Special Resident Retirement Visa is refreshingly welcoming by Asian standards. There are four options, with the names "Smile," "Classic," "Human Touch," and "Courtesy." These range from one requiring a deposit of $20,000 into a Philippine bank to $10,000 into a condo purchase, to a deposit and a local health insurance policy (for "ailing retirees"). The Courtesy category is for returning Filipinos. See pra.gov.ph for the latest requirements.

One of the best ways to get around all this is to open a local business, like a call center or a place outsourcing virtual assistants. If you have 10 or more employees, you can get a permanent residency visa. Some expatriates who have put this into practice run companies such as Virtual Staff Finder and Empire Flippers.

Downsides

This country is tropical hot and has a long history of being the victim of natural disasters. "Unless you like the jungle heat and humidity, I think it's hard here for the average foreigner," says Ron. "Without A/C I would have already been dead. Also, I lived through a couple big typhoons. During one of them we were without power for 22 days. My friend who lives just outside of Tacloban was without power for seven months."

If aesthetics are really important to you, urban areas of The Philippines are going to be an affront to your senses. While there are flashes of good interior design here and there at resorts and nightclubs, most exteriors are functional at best, downright ugly at worst. Zoning and development laws are improperly enforced, which leads to dangerous construction and additional pollution. The government had to shut down the island of Boracay for six months so it could recover from untreated waste while officials shut down hotels that were not in compliance.

The government in this country is a perpetual mess and the population has a decades-long tendency of electing people who either soak the system for all its worth, are inept, or seem just plain batshit crazy to outsiders. If you're looking for a smooth-running government where everything makes sense, this is not your place.

Resources
LivingInThePhilippines.com
Philippines-expats.com
ph.usembassy.gov
ExpatsInManila.com
Search "Critter Hunter" on YouTube for Justin's underwater videos
See Philippines sections of ExpatExchange.com, Expat.com, and Internations

Chapter 27:
Portugal

Pros: sunny weather, mild winters, low crime, low pollution, classic European feel, good wine, inexpensive food, geographic variety, abundant local produce/meat/cheese, foreigner-friendly, welcoming/progressive politics.

Cons: high import item costs, expensive toll roads, tough language, limited English outside cities & Algarve, limited restaurant diversity, expensive visa process for non-EU citizens.

When Susan Korthase and her husband were looking to move abroad from Milwaukee, Wisconsin, they had already lived abroad and moved 17 times. They started diving into the options and considered all the touted suspects like Panama, Uruguay, Ecuador, and Belize. "We looked at a lot of spots highlighted by *International Living* and books on living outside the U.S.," she says." Portugal only came up once; back then it wasn't really discussed." They decided to go traveling around and check out different options, but they started in Europe, with plans to begin in Portugal and make their way east.

"The first place we started with was Portugal, but we went to the Algarve and really disliked it quite a bit. We went to Lisbon, and that was better, but at the very end of our two-week trip we got on a train and went to Cascais and said, 'Wow, this is it!' We had planned to move on and check out other places, but we never did. We just stayed. We rented out our condo back home and eventually took a trip back to get new visas, but we have been here since January of 2011."

While many fantasize about moving to a western European country like France or Italy, the dream of living in most of Western Europe can be hard for the average person to attain. High taxes, high labor costs, high fuel costs, expensive real estate...it all adds up to make nearly everything cost more than it does in the United States or Canada. So, unless you're loaded, it's hard to imagine moving there unless you're working for a big company that's posting you there on a job transfer.

Portugal is the odd man out though. Even before the financial crisis of the late '00s, it was a country that was drastically less expensive to travel in than its other euro-using counterparts. When the crisis really took hold, prices flatlined for anything not imported and have remained low. When I visited Lisbon and then did a week-long bike trip through the rural Alentejo region of

Portugal, I found the prices on many things comparable to what you would find in Eastern Europe. But you get those cheap prices in a warmer climate that borders the ocean. And if you learn the language here, you can at least use it later in huge Brazil.

This is a country in transition though on the housing side. The buyer's market for real estate and the renters' market for apartments have swung more to the seller/landlord side in recent years. Still, with unemployment stubbornly high, there's little opportunity for other living expenses to rise but so much for the locals. For those who do have a job, the minimum wage has only climbed up to €700 per month and many Portuguese people live on that amount. Sure, several family members will generally pool resources in one home, but still, if you move here as a couple that can bring in $3,000 a month—nearly twice what many local couples earn, you're going to be considered well-off by local standards.

The secret is out for expats and tourists alike though, with more and more foreigners moving to Portugal. This is driving up the cost of living in some coastal areas, says Lonely Planet writer Kevin Raub. "We pay €672 per month rent for a nice two-bedroom apartment 500 meters from the beach in Parede, halfway along the coastal route between Lisbon and Cascais. We have both sea and river views from our terrace. We beat the expat rush and consider our rent a steal at this point—it could easily be €1,000."

Julie Dawn Fox had been teaching English as a second language for 12 years, mostly for the British Council. After living in Spain, Tanzania, and Venezuela, she was getting tired of the transient lifestyle and wanted to settle down somewhere in Europe. "I missed the boat on buying a house in the UK; I had an opportunity when I was younger but passed on it to go traveling instead," she says. "While I was gone, prices skyrocketed and there was no way I could afford it.

I looked at Portugal and the prices were much more affordable. I knew I could buy a house there on my own. I got a job teaching, but then I met my husband (also English) there. We only pay a couple hundred euros a month for his place. The drawback of that is we needed two cars before I started working at home. We're about 35 kilometers from Coimbra city where we worked. We spent €200 - 250 a month on petrol—usually more than our mortgage"

Julie and her husband regularly put €1,200 a month (around $1,500) from their earnings into a joint account and that covers all their expenses. He still teaches, she runs an online travel business and blog. "If you aren't extravagant, you can live well on a decent wage. Occasionally there's enough left over for eating out and a bit of travel. We could probably could do it on €1,000 a month if we had to." They are living in a modest three-bedroom house, but the low mortgage cost definitely helps. "This house would cost a fortune in the UK," she estimates. "We wouldn't be able to afford it."

The great wine here is a terrific bargain and there's a tremendous amount of inherent beauty. The big drawback for Americans is this is a full member of the EU, with the same residency difficulties you will face anywhere else in Western Europe. It's much, *much* easier to move here if you're from the EU than it is from Canada, the U.S., or Australia. There's a new visa option for self-employed people and professionals though that has opened up residency to more people who can show a steady income stream.

There's not the huge gulf in prices between the capital Lisbon and the countryside like you find in some countries. The main difference is selection. It's harder to find cheap eats like street food in the countryside and in smaller villages the locals don't really seem to eat out that much. They may hang out at a cafe all day nursing an espresso or a tiny beer, but restaurant choices get pretty slim sometimes.

Gail Aguiar has plenty of places to compare with her new home in northern Portugal. She was born in the Philippines but moved as a toddler with her family to Canada. "I grew up in several regions of Canada, where she spent time in Saskatchewan, Winnipeg, Vancouver, Toronto, and Banff. In between there was time in Australia, the UK, and the semi-rural northeastern U.S. This is it, though," she says. "I have no plans to move anywhere else unless my Portuguese husband suddenly decides he wants to try expat life for himself, in which case I would join him."

Hers is a fairytale story of falling in love, first with the man and then the place. "I was first in Portugal in mid-2011, on a birthday trip. It's a tradition of mine to visit a new country on my birthday, and I traveled solo using Couchsurfing to stay with locals. I had three hosts in Portugal, and I stayed in contact with them all after the trip, but especially my host in Porto, where I stayed for one week. We were in regular contact mostly by phone. More than a year later (2012) he visited me, we were a couple by the end of the trip, got married the following year, and a few months after that I landed in Portugal. There was, of course, a lot of paperwork, arrangements, planning, and coordinating in-between but that's the basic timeline."

Author Alicia Sunday grew up in the Leicestershire countryside in England, moved to London for fifteen years, then to Cambridgeshire for twelve years. "We were attracted to the warmer weather and being able to lose the mortgage and buy something with the equity from the house yet have more space and land," she says. "We had to move anyway as we needed more space, so when we sold the house thought we would give a foreign adventure a go. We had a similar experience in Spain a few years ago but rented. The friends we made in Spain had moved to Portugal and recommended it.

With Portugal we also liked the fact we could still afford to be less than an hour away from a fabulous capital city. Since coming here, we have also discovered that expats are being encouraged here by lower taxes via the non-habitual residency scheme. The health care is good. Foreign investment is going into the area. School fees are reasonable. People are generally friendly and helpful. The scenery is stunning and there is so much beautiful coastline it's easy to live near the sea and have spectacular views. To know that within half an hour of where we live is the opportunity to go surfing, swimming, sailing, etc. Is just wonderful."

Portugal has a lot going for it. The country appeals to two broad kinds of expatriates: those who want to live a "civilized" European lifestyle without paying anything close to what it costs in France or Italy, and those who want to stop thinking about how much they're spending and just enjoy life to the fullest. Susan and her husband fall into the latter category. They were pulling in half a million dollars a year on their two salaries before, so they weren't moving abroad to scrimp and save. They've drastically lowered their expenses though by relocating. "Rent and utilities cost us about $1,700 a month, for a two-bedroom, two-bath home right in the historical center of Cascais. We do not inhibit ourselves on eating out and groceries, and we drink good wine. We probably spend another $2,000 to $3,000 a month more on everything else, including trips to Spain and elsewhere. For us, all this seems very cheap, but of course it depends on where you're coming from and what your income was before. We've moved up to the 10-euro bottles of wine now, but to get that same level of quality where we came from would cost three times as much. The same goes for fine dining or nice hotels in this country."

This being Western Europe, infrastructure is good as well. "You can usually get broadband or Wi-Fi anywhere so if you can work on the internet then Portugal is a great place to be," says Alicia. "You can realistically 'live the dream' here, be working on your laptop under a palm tree and then a quick dip in the pool in a property that can cost less than €100,000 to buy."

You can drink the water, crime is low, and infrastructure is very good.

There's another category where Portugal is at the top of the list: liberal drug laws. Holland may get all the attention, but Portugal quietly dropped penalties for purchase and possession of any drug and has stuck with it. Despite the conservatives' fears, crime hasn't gone up and cities haven't turned squalid. What's defined as enough for "personal use?" That would be a 10-day supply. If you want to cut your costs while living in a progressive country with a real democracy and no harsh winters, here's your spot.

This is a good country for families, with a safe climate and good schooling options, at least in the cities. "The main reason why we decided I would move to Portugal was because we want to raise children here," says Gail. "Portugal is much more child-friendly than Canada."

Housing Costs
Of all the countries profiled in this book, Portugal has seen the most changes in the housing market. A combination of an improving economy and a big increase in the number of incoming foreigners (especially Brits post-Brexit) has led to widespread price increases in the favored spots. An increase in tourists also meant some long-term rental properties became vacation rentals instead.

James Cave from travel site The Portugalist says the popular areas are definitely seeing an uptick. "Lisbon has been experiencing a tourism boom, and this has had a negative effect on the property market. One-bedroom apartment rental prices start from around €650 per month, but average closer to the €1,000 mark.

Susan says housing prices have been rising at a rate of 6% per year for a while, in 23 of the 24 largest markets. "Portugal had the second highest increase in property prices in the European Union (Ireland was highest)," she says. "With the increases in house prices goes the increases in rental prices, which found 19% increases year-over-year in the more popular city centers."

Still, that's from a low base and it's worth keeping in mind that these are still some of the most reasonable markets in Western Europe plus the rises vary quite a bit by region. Porto actually saw an increase of nearly 16% a couple years back, while prices only rose half that amount in Lisbon. The average price per square meter to buy something is around $1,400, still quite good by European standards. "From the perspective of the foreign buyer, Portuguese property is an astonishingly good value," Susan says. "Portugal's house price to GDP per capita ratio is one of the lowest in Europe. Portugal has some of the lowest prices for city-center property in Europe, according to Global Property Guide research. Rents in this country aren't as dirt cheap as in Eastern Europe, but you get warmer weather, lots of sunshine, and plenty of historic architecture. You also have a lot of inventory to choose from these days."

Gail lives about 10 miles from the center of Porto and while her husband already owned a place, she says rental for a two-bedroom apartment like she's in starts at around €400 per month ($480). In the center of Porto prices would be similar, but the apartment might be older and smaller.

Retired American Bill, who sometimes writes about his experience on FourLetterNerd.com, lives an hour north of Lisbon in Caldas da Rainha, a city of about 60,000 people. He pays €500 a month (around $600) for a 3-bedroom, 2-bath apartment that he sorted out locally after renting two Airbnb places the first month. "I ended up paying 50 euros more than I wanted but I'm across from a park and walking distance to food, grocery, cafes, and the bus station."

Jonathan Look lived in Asia for years before doing a 30-day house hunting trip through Portugal to find the ideal spot. "We rent a big, modern, 4-bedroom, 3-bath house, with a swimming pool for €1,000 per month. The house overlooks the Atlantic Ocean in an area known as the Silver Coast, about an hour from Lisbon. I would say that I would have to spend at least a third more than I spend in Portugal to live a comparable life back in 'Middle America' United States. Living directly on the coast, as we do here, would be substantially more than that, maybe double or triple."

Alicia and her husband paid cash for their home from a sale in England and had enough left over for a fixer-upper project on top. They live near the Silver Coast in Central Portugal, half an hour from the ocean and an hour from Lisbon and the airport. "We have a pool and an olive grove, and gorgeous views. We also bought an incredibly cheap village house in Castelo Branco which is a stunning area," she says. "We get to experience real village life and the neighbors are very friendly. We are renovating the house and its slow going as we don't live there now but we plan to rent it out for holidays.

They don't have rent or a mortgage since they own the house outright, but Alicia says prices are still quite attractive in Central Portugal and on the Silver Coast. For their five-bedroom house near Lisbon they pay €890 per annum in property taxes. For the two-bedroom house in the countryside it's only €100.

Entrepreneur Natalie Sisson of New Zealand purchased a 3-bedroom house in a town near the ocean several years ago for €107,500. (They threw in most of the furniture she wanted for another €1,000 because they didn't want to cart it away.) She has her choice of several places to go surfing when she's done working for the day on her laptop. In general, the cheapest places to live in Portugal are where you don't see hundreds of other foreigners. In rural villages you can buy plots of land for the price of a car.

She was able to get a mortgage too. She put 20% down and secured a long-term interest rate of 1.95% for her choice of 25 or 30 years. That's probably less than the rate of inflation long-term. You have to have a life insurance policy to get that rate (easy and not all that expensive), but otherwise the rate is barely over 3%—still cheap.

She says having a real estate agent used to working with expatriates was a big help and he also recommended an English-speaking attorney who made sure everything was in order and fast-tracked the paperwork. She paid out a few thousand euros in closing costs. Foreigners can own real estate outright in Portugal, but closing costs can be high: figure on 7-8 percent.

Food & Drink

Do you get excited about drinking good wine? Do you get even more excited when it doesn't cost you much? Portugal is much like France, Italy, and Spain in the sense that a glass of wine with lunch or dinner is considered a God-given right. So, if you get a meal of the day at a lunch cafe, it will often come with a carafe of house wine that's surprisingly large. If you want to order a bottle with dinner, it will likely cost the same or less than most of the food items on the menu. Plus, it'll usually be quite good. "For two euros in a store, you can be confident it's going to be a drinkable bottle of red wine," says Julie. It could take you a lifetime to figure out which labels from which region are the best as production here is very high, but most wines are blends and don't depend on a specific grape from a specific place having an especially good year.

Drinking good local wine in Portugal is not something you do for a special occasion. Prices are low across the board from the vineyards dotted around the country. This is one of the best values in the country when looking at all the costs to live in Portugal.

Kevin Raub enjoys not having to think about whether or not to order his *vinho* with dinner in Portugal. "Wine is super cheap in Portugal. We don't even usually ask the price. A great bottle is €10 - 20 at any place besides a Michelin-starred restaurant!"

"Wine is very affordable, and a pleasant bottle of wine typically costs between €3-€8 in the supermarket. There are wines above and below that price, but that's the average," says James. "A lunch menu in a Portuguese *tasca* can cost as little as €5 - 6, particularly in non-touristy parts of the country, but on average is somewhere around €10. This typically includes the couvert (bread, butter, sardine paste), a main meal, wine, and either coffee or dessert."

Portuguese restaurants are much cheaper than the rest of Western Europe. Lunch is usually less expensive than dinner, especially if you get the *prato do dia*. "That's usually six or seven euros in the rural areas, more like eight to ten euros in cities," says Julie. "That gets you a starter, soup, main dish, and then maybe dessert or coffee. There's always wine of course."

Typical main dishes for dinner at a basic restaurant are €2.50 – 10, in a really nice restaurant, €5 – 18. "Coffee and cake in a cafe are also reasonable," says Alicia. "A round of lovely pastries and drinks for four can still only add up to €5. We go to cafes far more than we would in England."

"Our weekly shop tends to be around €120, including wine and beer," says Julie, "and that's always more than we need. It pays to keep full cupboards when you live in the sticks as we do. We could cut back if necessary."

Here are some other typical prices:
Coffee: €0.50 – 1.50
Wine in a store: €1 (really!) – 12 for most, "Reserve" brands €10 and up
Beer: €0.50-0.75 each in store, €0 .75 – 2 in restaurants (liter draft €3-4)
200 grams of cheese: €0.79 – €3
200 grams of dry sausage/pepperoni: €0.89 – 3.50
Baguettes: €0.30 – 0.60
Can of tuna or pate: €0.59 – 1.50

Seasonal fruit and vegetables: €1 – 2 per kilo for most, €3 for berries
Oranges in season: €0.50 – 0.80 per kilo

At a local market in Estremoz we bought a wheel of aged cheese (enough for two to share) for €2 and a bottle of olive oil for €3 – both from local farmers.

One oddity here is that nothing placed on your table that you didn't specifically order is complimentary. If you don't want to be charged for bread, butter, soft cheese, or olives, you have to ask the waiter to take them back or push them over to the side so you won't get charged.

Transportation
The cost of getting around in Portugal has a lot to do with whether you're driving a car on the highways or not.

Gail says in Porto a monthly public transit pass for their (outer) zone is €36, with individual trips as needed into the city being €1.50 each.

A taxi in Lisbon for two people is officially €2.25 to start, then €1.60 per km. This can vary a lot across the country though. When I was in Evora it was €3.25 to go two blocks, but only €0.80 per km after that.

"Public transport in Portugal is very affordable, James says. "In Lisbon, a journey on the bus, train, tram, or ferry ticket in Lisbon costs €1.40 (using the rechargeable Viva Viagem card). Cross-country train travel is also very affordable, and there are generous discounts for booking in advance. A single train ticket from Lisbon to Faro in the Algarve costs as little as €11, while a single ticket from Vila Real de San Antonio to Valenca (a 715km journey) costs as little as €38.10."

Bus routes in rural zones are not very frequent, but between the larger towns and cities it's a different story. The 1.5-hour bus ride from Lisbon to Evora is €12.50 one-way. A 2.5-hour bus ride (Lisbon-Western Algarve towns for example) will run around €20 one-way, while the three-hour one between Lisbon and Porto is €24 to €42 depending on how luxurious it is.

Gail just relies on this reasonable public transportation most of the time, renting a car to go exploring further now and then. Renting a car for a week ranges between €150 and €260. Besides the hefty fuel costs Julie and her husband pay—about double U.S. prices—they also pay a few hundred euros per year to insure each of their not-so-new cars.

You have to factor in tolls on the expressways, however. "The highway tolls can really have a big impact on the cost of your trip," says Julie. "Below Lisbon to Algarve, there's a short stretch of road that's 20 euros, for example. But it saves loads of time, so people pay it if they can afford it. The good thing is, the motorways are pretty empty when you're on them because of the high cost."

"Motorway tolls are a definite minus," agrees Alicia. "They are far too expensive and thus not well used."

You need to check the routes you don't know in advance because you don't stop at a booth and pay: you get charged automatically via a sticker on your windshield. You could return from a jaunt around the country to find a hefty bill on your account.

Healthcare
The World Health Organization ranks the effectiveness of care in Portugal at number 12 in the world, well ahead of the United States, England, and Canada. Portugal also has the 10th-highest life expectancy for women in the world, at 84. Pregnant women get 120 days of paid leave at full salary and you won't get stuck with a hefty bill if an ambulance picks you up at the scene of an accident.

Julie and her husband both have health care through an employer, but says if you're on the national health scheme, you pay €5 to see the doctor and €10 for emergency care. You pay out of pocket for lab tests and x-rays, but then you can charge them back to insurance and get reimbursed 60 to 80 percent. "The health programs are all pushing more generics on patients because the name brand drugs are rather pricey. It seems to me that the doctors all over-prescribe medicines too."

In general terms, you will be treated like a local in terms of the health care system. Some costs are free, while others require a token payment. Dental costs are mostly covered by taxes, plus children, pregnant women and pensioners have the right to receive dental care for free.

"The National Health Service of Portugal is available to citizens as well as both temporary and permanent residents," says Susan. "As an expat or immigrant, you will receive a user's card with a *Número Utente*. This allows unquestioned access to the state medical system. If you are a citizen of a European Union country with a European Health Card ('Blue Card'), your ID from that country is honored in Portugal, entitling you to the same medical care available to Portuguese residents."

To choose your own doctor or hospital outside the national health care system, various insurance schemes are available at a reasonable cost. "My medical expenses have gone down $139 a month from what I spent in Thailand," says Bill. "Part of that has to do with the meds I am taking. Also, insurance is cheaper than Thailand and I have better coverage, $56 less per month."

In Lisbon, the care is excellent and if you ask around, you'll easily be able to find an English-speaking doctor. This also applies to tourist zones like the Algarve and larger cities such as Porto. In smaller towns you may just have a local clinic, which is fine for basic problems, but then you'll likely want to travel to a larger city for surgery or serious tests.

Private health care costs are still reasonable to pay out of pocket. Expect to pay around €15 for a doctor visit, €50-80 for a dental check-up and cleaning, €75 for a mammogram, and €8,000 or less for hip surgery. "I had a check-up with four sonograms, a prostrate exam, and more for €150," says Bill. "That probably wouldn't even cover the cost of the gel in the USA."

Other Costs
For utilities, Julie says the two of them average €16 or €17 for water and almost €50 for ADSL internet that's not all that fast. "You can get better broadband for a better price in the cities," she says. A propane gas bottle is €100 and that's good for around six months of hot water and cooking on the stove top for them. "Electricity has gone up a bit since we installed air conditioning—probably around €65 per month now. We also pay around €500 a year to keep our pellet stove running."

"As for utilities, for us they are not bad at all," says Kevin. "I'd say gas ranges from €15 - 25. Electricity from €25 - 45. Internet/mobile/cable TV combo for two is around €120."

Alicia says gas is their biggest utility bill in the winter, running them about €100 a month as sometimes both of them are working at home all day. "That heats our large living room, cooker, and supplies the hot water. Summer is about half that amount." They spend around €100 for a package that includes phone, internet and a premium batch of TV channels. Their electric bill averages €60 a month and "It is cheaper per unit than the UK." Their water bill is estimated at €12.50 a month.

Gail works at home, but her electricity bill doesn't rise above €50 for two until the winter hits and they need some heat from their electric system. Their water bill is around €20, and the gas bill averages €10-30 per month. Their bundled cable package of internet/phone/TV is only €36.

"Our cable TV, fiber internet, and phone package cost about €35 per month," says Jonathan. "Service for our smartphones is €17 per month with 3GB of data and more texts and phone minutes than we ever use."

"Services such as shoe repair, hairdressers, auto mechanics, and such have lower labor rates compared to the rest of the EU," says Gail. "Portugal is also known for textiles, so clothes and especially shoes are cheaper. Camping is cheap (even private campsites), so is all other lodging around the country when you go exploring."

Natalie was pleasantly surprised about the cost of labor when she needed work done on her new house. "A crew painted the whole interior of the house in two days for €300. The plumber was here for a half hour and he charged me €15 including the part he needed. I'm finding people to be a lot more helpful than I expected. I think the cleaning lady works out to €7 or 8 an hour. There are places in the world where it's far cheaper than that of course, but Portugal is certainly affordable."

Going to the movies is also affordable at around €5 an adult ticket and entrance fees to galleries and events are much cheaper than in most of Western Europe.

The expatriates I spoke to agreed that cars are more expensive than in many other parts of Europe, while gasoline (petrol), non-domestic food products, and clothing costs were about the same.

Visas
Bill moved to Portugal less than a year ago and says the procedure is ongoing but not that difficult. "I got a resident's visa outside the country, then turned that into a one-year temporary resident's permit, then when that expires, I can get a two-year permit. Finally, after that I can apply for permanent residency. I mostly did it myself, but you need a taxpayer identification number and for that you need a resident to be a middleman (or woman) and be responsible for forwarding any communication to you. She went with me to get the NIF or you pay 100 euros to give someone power of attorney. There is a Facebook group called "Americans & Friends PT" and their immigration file section is kept up to date. It's the best source of information on getting set up in Portugal. If you use their files, the only reason to pay someone is if your time is more valuable than money or you don't have the confidence to deal with bureaucrats."

"I married a Portuguese citizen in the Azores (which is under Portuguese law), and to enter as a spouse it couldn't have been easier," says Gail. "We made an appointment for the residency permit before I arrived for the nearest date available (five days after I arrived), and two weeks after that interview I had a letter confirming my five-year residency permit, which I picked up right away." She says this was the fourth expat visa she has applied for in her life and this one was by far the most straightforward. "The fees were also very low, especially compared someone pays in the USA."

"For EU residents, the visa situation quite straightforward," says Julie. "The most important thing is to be able to prove income, to show that you can support yourself. You need to have ample documentation to show them. Assuming that's in order, you go to the foreigners service desk and soon you'll have a residency permit for five years, which you can then renew."

For those without a local spouse or EU citizenship, it can be much tougher. "Almost all the articles you read about moving to Portugal talk about Brits or other Europeans," says Susan Korthase. She and her husband spent around $400 in fees to get their residency visa, then another $3,600 for attorney fees. Each time they renew, they have to do it all again, though the second time they got two years instead of one. "There are a set of steps, with very explicit requirements," she says. "Then you have to overcome the language barrier, which is where the attorney comes in. You quickly forget how painful it was when it's done, but it was. Start to finish first time was about six months. If we had tried to do it without an attorney, it would have taken longer, and they treat you differently. You have to accept that bureaucracy will be a lot more complicated than you're probably used to and people in the offices will be asking for things they don't really need." Eventually they got a five-year residency permit. At that point, the big renewal bill they faced each year from the attorney went away.

Others have reported drastic inconsistencies in how they were treated and which documents were required, even in the same immigration office. One person said his lawyer told them he needed to watch which window they got when their number was called: if it was a person the lawyer felt was going to give them a hard time—based on experience—they would take a different number and wait for a better option.

As the experience of Americans Bill and Susan shows, the prevailing assumption that you can only get a three-month visa is not true. Susan and her husband applied for six months at the embassy in Washington, D.C. before they left and after showing the means to support themselves, it was granted easily. In theory anyway, you could return to the USA for a bit and then do it again if you still didn't have residency sorted out.

Susan writes about living in Portugal for ExpatExchange.com and also does consulting for people considering a move to her adopted country. "For those of us who seek a first-world, high-culture experience, Portugal is among the most accessible." Fortunately, this country's government is more enlightened than most when it comes to attracting foreigners who are self-supported, and they are making progress on easing the application process for non-Europeans. There's a new residency visa option that didn't exist when I put out the first edition of this book. Here's how Susan sums it up:

Portugal's population is declining and aging. Young professionals leaving the country for better earnings and young couples limiting themselves to smaller, single-child families are depleting the earning-age and next generation population numbers. Attracting more immigrants with highly desired professional training and entrepreneurial skills is the goal of streamlined processes under the Type 1/D/D7 visa called the 'Entrepreneur, Employed and Self-Employed Program'. Easing this group's entrance to Portugal started in 2017 and saw renewed emphasis in 2019 and 2020. This program exists to attract and fast-track highly qualified, educated professionals to work and invest in Portugal. Skilled professionals currently working in or who retired in the US might follow this approach to start a business or be self-employed in Portugal.

The income requirements for this D7 visa are surprisingly low, just equivalent to the Portuguese minimum wage. If you have a spouse, add 50% and it's still less than $15,000 annually for a couple. (Naturally though, if you can show a higher amount and some savings, it'll make approval easier.)

You can also buy your way in and get a residency permit that requires less time in the country, but with a price tag that starts at 350,000 euros. If you've got that much to toss into a local bank account or business, however, you can probably live anywhere you want in the world.

Downsides
The online publication *Live and Invest Overseas* has named Portugal its top retirement haven for five years in a row, saying

that "There are very few negatives to living in Portugal." This country has far fewer downsides than most.

The most obvious one is the language. Bring a phrase book or good language app! English is not widespread outside of the cities and resort areas on the coast. If you speak Spanish it helps when reading a menu and some people can speak Spanish. While many words are the same, however, the pronunciation of Portuguese is completely different.

"Although most Portuguese speak a little English, not all do," says Alicia. "I worry particularly when I have to make a phone call to deal with utility services. It's quite a difficult language to get to grips with but there is usually someone around to help."

The economy in Portugal has been down far more than it's been up, and the local population is understandably frugal, so don't expect to earn much money providing services for locals. Some things you would consider normal consumer goods are priced like luxury goods here. "Anything imported, like cars, electronics, technology items, and fuel are more expensive than in the USA," says Gail. "Portugal also doesn't have enough consumers for a big used market like what I've had with Craigslist in other countries."

The shopping choices are quite limited as well. "We always stock up when we go shopping," says Julie. "If you see something you like, you'd better buy it then as it might not be available next time. There is absolutely nothing in the village where I live. There's actually a bread van, a fish van, and a mobile supermarket and if you catch it at the right time you can buy from one of those. Otherwise, there's a small town 15 minutes away that has small supermarkets. We really need to do most of our shopping in the city where we work, 35 kilometers away."

Many complain about the poor customer service and broken promises on contracted services, especially in the Algarve. It's essential in Portugal to get unbiased references for past customers (who are not their relatives) before hiring someone to add onto your house or be your immigration attorney. Then after that, expect anything to take twice as long as promised.

You may not have the same constant temperature level in your home that you've gotten used to elsewhere. "Portugal is warmer than England, but it can still get nippy in winter and the older houses are built to keep heat out," says Alicia. "So realistically you need central heating in winter to be comfortable, but most houses don't have it."

For every downside though, there are at least two upsides here, including a safe environment. "Rates of violence and terrorism are lower than in almost any other European country, including Italy, France, and the UK," says Susan. "While you will want to look out for pickpockets, you can feel safe walking alone, day or night—that goes for big cities like Lisbon or Porto too."

For More Information
"Americans & Friends PT" group on Facebook
Portugalist.com
JulieDawnFox.com
LivinginPortugal.com
Portugal.Angloinfo.com
Portugal info at ExpatExchange.com
Portugal message board of ExpatForum.com

Chapter 28:
Thailand

Pros: sunshine and beaches, great food, fun atmosphere, good infrastructure, fast internet, good social life, great air connections, good public transportation in the capital.

Cons: difficult visa situation, rising prices, political instability, corruption, always hot, tropical diseases/insects, traffic and pollution in Bangkok

"I've traveled to 100 countries and seven or eight non-sovereign territories, always with the question of whether or not I could live in the places I visited. Thailand isn't perfect, no place is. But suffice it to say that I've never found another place that resonated with me so strongly or another culture that I loved as much," says Barbara Weibel, full-time blogger at HoleInTheDoughnut.com. "I've now lived here permanently for the several years, but I wintered here for five years prior to moving here permanently.

Thailand is one of the most popular countries in the world for travelers and many of them decide they'd like to stick around. Thailand has a lot going for it and it's a beautiful, fun place, with one of the world's most interesting cuisines.

They don't make it easy for you to stay on, however, plus this is one of the few countries where the prices have risen across the board since I put out the <u>first</u> edition of this book. "Prices haven't really gone up much the past five years in Thai baht terms," says Matt Gibson, who runs several online companies and blogs at XpatMatt.com. "The baht has gotten stronger against the dollar, pound, and euro, however, so many expats on a strict budget had to move away because they just couldn't afford to stay there anymore."

As prices have gone up, Thailand has lost some of its allure when it comes to the cost of living. While Chiang Mai used to be the place backpackers on a budget could hang out for months on a strict budget, costs in that city are now on par or even higher than Penang, Budapest, or Mexico City. Bangkok is even costlier if you live in a convenient area. While one dollar would get you between 33 and 35 baht for years, since 2018 it has been more likely to get you 31. That's not a huge difference in percentage terms for those earning in dollars, but if you rented a Bangkok apartment for 15,000 per month at an exchange rate of 35, your $429 rent went up by $53 per month and your costs for food, utilities and transportation also rose. It has been even worse for Canadians, with the baht rising by 20% against their currency. When I first started visiting Mexico, costs were significantly higher than they were in Thailand. Now when you compare them on Numbeo.com, Thailand averages out to 40% more expensive than Mexico, including for rent.

For everyone who leaves, however, it seems at least one foreigner replaces them. Bangkok was an expatriate hotspot before anyone else even knew there was such a thing. Men especially, lured by thousands of beautiful women that they could successfully hit on (sometimes for a price), found the sultry climate and people hard to resist. "I came here on holiday and never got around to leaving" has long been a typical refrain.

By percentage of population, Chiang Mai still probably has the greatest number of expatriates in the world who can live wherever they want; by some estimates 50,000 of the million or so residents and workers there are foreigners. This means a major support structure and a long list of activities for expats, which run the gamut from 20-somethings to families to retirees. For many, life here is less stressful than in Bangkok. "It is still a small city which takes half an hour, at most, to drive across," says Pim Kemasingki, who lived in six countries before returning to her once-home and mother's birth country of Thailand. "A mere 30-40 minutes' drive in any direction will have you in near-pristine nature: waterfalls, jungles, lakes, and resorts. With six major universities in the area, it's a young and vibrant city that's very socially tolerant and packed with cultural activities." She keeps tabs on it all with the local publications she runs, including Chiang Mai City Life.

Other popular areas with smaller pockets of foreigners include beach resort areas Phuket, Koh Samui, Pattaya, Krabi, and Hua Hin. Those who are willing to go all in and learn Thai could find a lot of smaller, cheaper towns and islands to call home.

Thailand is not the Wild West anymore though and the days of finding $5 per night beach bungalows in an island paradise you could live in for months are long gone. The tourism numbers have grown exponentially the past two decades, edging close to 40 million visitors in 2019 (counting the many who leave and come back on visa runs). The population has grown steadily wealthier as the economy keeps growing. Apart from some political hiccups here and there, Thailand has marched onward and upward.

The country is still a great value though to visitors and residents and lately it has also become one of the key hubs in Asia for entrepreneurs. With reasonable rents, fast internet, and good air connections to almost anywhere, this is a good place to use as a base for running an online business. Chiang Mai is the most popular spot for this—and for expats trying to live in a cheaper place than Bangkok—but there are also plenty of digital nomads in spots like Ko Samui, Phuket, and the capital.

There are some English teachers and vagabonds living for $600 a month still in Chiang Mai, but that's tough to pull off long-term for most people. As Pim Kemasingki says, "If you live in a small room, drink Thai whiskey, have no insurance, stay healthy enough to avoid hospitals, ride an old motorbike, and eat mainly Thai food, it is possible to live here on $600 per month. You can actually enjoy a lot of what Chiang Mai has to offer for that, but I think it is only for the really young to handle, and most are doing that as they stop over here to teach or volunteer. However, if you aren't a spoiled brat like me, I would say that $1,500 - $2,000 could be easily doable. A one-bedroom apartment would cost around $250 - 350, rental or lease of a car would be around $300 a month, a Thai lunch would be $3 each, a good dinner around $10 each...though a fine one wouldn't break the bank either at around $30 - $40 dollars a head. Water, electricity, and other utilities are still cheap except for air conditioning costs during the hot seasons."

Of course, if you're not trying to be on a strict budget and you routinely spent $5,000 a month at home, Thailand can feel like paradise at half the price even if you're living it up. Some Bangkok expats say a monthly $2,500 budget can set you up quite well there, including a cleaning lady, a gym membership, a motorbike, visa runs, $600 or $700 for "going out" and at least one big trip out of the country to visit the relatives or go on a major vacation.

There is one huge negative to Thailand though that eventually becomes a deal breaker for many non-retirees who live here: the foreigner-unfriendly visa policy. It is next to impossible to get long-term residency here without setting up a corporation, marrying a local, being retired with loads of cash to put into a local bank, or getting work sponsorship. Even then you'll have to jump through quite a few hoops and spend a lot of time waiting. For the vast majority of foreigners, living in Thailand means making runs for the border as soon as the tourist visa runs out. The rules were in flux again as this book went to press, but normally that tourist visa is only good for 60 days if secured in advance, 30 days if stamped upon arrival. Despite a one-month extension done locally at immigration, you're still forced to travel to another country at least four times per calendar year. Even for people who like to travel, that's a lot of forced trips you can't postpone.

On the plus side, at least there are a lot of neighbors to choose from. You can travel by train or bus to Laos, Myanmar (Burma), Malaysia, or Cambodia.

Life is pretty easy in much of Thailand without learning a lot of Thai and the shopping is some of the best in Asia in terms of availability. "Many merchants speak English, so communication is never really an issue," says Spencer Montague, who moved from land-locked Knoxville, Tennessee to Thailand and settled on the island of Ko Samui. "I have traveled extensively and chose Ko Samui and specifically the Lamai area because it has everything I need in terms of shopping, entertainment, good hospitals and overall quality of life. I'm three minutes by motorbike from one of the world's most beautiful beaches, Lamai beach. Yet, there is a large Tesco Lotus grocery store here and 15 minutes away in Chaweng you will find malls, a cinema and even bowling! No one place is perfect, but this place is about as perfect as I could ever ask for, though you will need to enjoy very warm and usually quite humid weather. Considering I have air conditioning, I am a happy camper here on my little island in Asia."

Pim says this is also a great country for parents with school-aged kids. "There are six international schools in Chiang Mai preparing kids for all the standardized tests. Then there are numerous bilingual schools as well." With so many foreigners working in Bangkok, there's a large selection of quality schools there as well.

Housing Costs

Bill, an expat I interviewed who has lived in Thailand and then Portugal, chose Hua Hin to stay away from the hard-drinking expat crowd you find in more popular areas. "It also has one of least rainy seasons in Thailand and the hot season doesn't get as hot there" in this beach location. It's the second home area for the king and has been for close to a century. He paid around $200 there for his apartment and another $40 to $100 per month in utilities, including internet. "For that I had a huge studio apartment that stretched the whole width of the building, fully furnished. I was close enough to walk to the beach if it wasn't too hot, about a mile away."

He averaged around $1,600 a month total for his living expenses there over several years, not counting travel. "Without travel, in Thailand I could have lived off social security alone if I needed to. But I liked to take trips to Australia, or Europe and fly in business class."

Matt also lived in Hua Hin and only paid $230 per month for rent, furnished, "But that was a pretty basic place," he says. "I also rented an office for about $400 per month and that was much nicer." He estimates that a nicer apartment near the beach in his Thai neighborhood would be twice as much as he paid and in the popular tourist areas, maybe $600 or more.

Christa Romera, a person I interviewed for the first edition, worked at Thailand-Property.com, a site meant to help expats find apartments in Thailand. Her 2-bedroom apartment she shared with a friend while there was brand new. It had a big living room, a small but separate kitchen, two balconies, and bedrooms big enough for king sized beds. Rent plus electricity, water, and internet costed her around $360 per month. In New York City about half of her salary went to rent, even though she was sharing with two other people. In Bangkok she was making less, but spending just a fifth of it on housing.

That's in Bangkok, the big capital city. There are some people paying more than $1,000 a month there for sure, but you can easily find a nice furnished one-bedroom or two-bedroom apartment on that Thailand property site for under $650 (20,000 baht) very easily. There were more than 200 of them to pick from as I was writing this Chapter, many spacious places in a building with a swimming pool. Some one-bedroom places are available for 7,000 baht—around $225. And that's what you can find in advance online. Someone I interviewed for the first edition based there said, "If you search long enough, 15,000 baht will get you a really comfortable place to live in. I know many people who rent spacious houses or impressive apartments in good locations for that amount." That comes out to around $500 when the exchange rate is at 31 to the U.S. dollar, less when the local currency drops.

Once you get into other parts of the country, prices usually go down substantially unless you're oceanside. Even in the second-largest city of Chiang Mai, expect to pay $200 to $400 for a nice air-conditioned studio or one-bedroom apartment. If you've got some friends, you can get a whole huge house for $350 to $900—the top of that range often coming with a pool.

"I've chosen to rent a one-bedroom apartment in a more upscale, expensive high-rise in Chiang Mai, simply because it makes my life easier," says Barbara. "It's a serviced residence, which means the housekeepers clean it twice a week and all my linens are provided, right down to beach towels. It's staffed 24 hours a day, has a gated entrance, rooftop pool, gym, and covered parking. Fast, reliable Wi-Fi is included. Electric and water are separate, but billed by the management, so I don't need to go to the electric and water utilities each month to pay the bills. Perhaps best of all, I can leave for months at a time and not have to worry about anything, as the management will inspect the apartment each week to make sure nothing is amiss. My rent and utilities amount to between $750 and $800 each month, depending upon currency exchange and utility usage."

Spencer Montague likes his cost of living on the island of Ko Samui. "I rent a lovely, partially furnished one-bedroom house with full bathroom, kitchen area, and a living room area plus a nice balcony. I have at my own expense added the additionally needed furniture including a second AC unit, stovetop and washing machine. I pay about $420 a month. That includes my Wi-Fi, water, and electric. There is a large pool, which is big enough for me to do laps. No one but me ever seems to use the pool so I almost always have it to myself. The pool is lit at night and even has a Jacuzzi and waterfall!"

Robert Holloway lived in a smaller town outside the usual expat circuit and paid around $500 per month, furnished and including utilities, for a 3-bedroom, 2-bath house. He later went for a significant upgrade and paid $825 per month for a "large and lavish" 3-bedroom house in a gated community with a gorgeous swimming pool, gym, and the works.

When Alexandra Baackes of the Alex in Wanderland blog lived on the small island of Koh Tao for seven years, she first shared a small wooden bungalow with a boyfriend for $300 a month. Then she moved into a larger space, a nice furnished apartment for $425 per month including cleaning once a week. She estimates her non-business expenses came out to around $1,500 per month the last few years before she left the island in late 2018.

Technically foreigners can't own land in Thailand, so it's much easier to buy a condo if you want something permanent. Most are in the $50 to $200 per square foot range. So, a two-bedroom condo of new construction, 1,000 square feet, could be between $100K and $200K in a prime area. If you're willing to buy something a bit older or less ideally located, you can find quite a few listed for five digits. Of course, there are some priced much higher than this too, especially in Phuket or Bangkok.

Food and Drink
All those great dishes you're used to sampling at your local Thai restaurant are as good or better here, but at a fraction of the price. Coconut curries, pad Thais, big noodle soups, and the like run 75

cents to $2 on the street, $1.50 to $6 in simple restaurants, even with seafood. The variety is excellent, the quality is uniformly high, and most street stalls are extremely clean and sanitary—just don't drink the tap water. There is a serious street food culture here: it is common for office workers to grab something from a sidewalk stall and few "brown bag it" since the cost to get a real meal is minimal. Some expatriates living in Thailand don't even have a kitchen where they live: they eat every meal out since the food is so tasty and inexpensive.

"Thailand is great because you can easily find international food or go to place with a nice atmosphere that won't cost you all that much, but you can easily get food that's just as good on the street in a real Thai neighborhood for 35 baht—just over a dollar," says Bill.

"Most locals get by on the equivalent of $300 per month, which is how much I spend just on food and eating out," says Robert. "I can still get a local meal for less than $3 with something to drink and a nice restaurant will be under $10, with a glass of wine even."

If you like to party, that will drive your costs up significantly here because of high taxes on alcohol, Thailand is not a country where you can drink for cheap. You might want to stock up every time you come through duty free and treat your visa runs as catch-up time. One beer or glass of wine can double the price of a simple meal. A night of partying in Bangkok can cost more than a cheap hotel room. The local rice whiskey (which really tastes like rum) is much easier on the budget at less than ten bucks for a 750-ml bottle. "There are some expats who choose the Philippines over Thailand just because the cost of alcohol is a lot lower," Bill says.

"Beer is no bargain in Thailand," says Matt. "I feel like it's cheaper to go out drinking in Europe than it is in Thailand."

It must be said that drugs are easy to find and are inexpensive, but lots of discretion and personal recommendation is required. There are more than a few foreigners in not-so-nice Thai jails.

If you're a hedonist with some cash to throw around though, Thailand is one of the most permissive countries in the world. Whether this titillates you or disgusts you will greatly influence how excited/bothered you get about the sex, drugs, and debauchery.

Transportation
Many foreigners don't own a car in Thailand and have no desire to deal with one. You can get to most parts of the country by bus for $1 to $3 per hour of travel and though the train costs more in first

class, it's still very reasonable and you can sleep on the way on longer trips. The train goes to the Laos border, up to northern Thailand, and down through Malaysia to Singapore (with a change of train cars).

Internal flights are often under $100 and can be super cheap if you purchase far enough in advance.

Bangkok now has an excellent metro and sky train system that can help you avoid traffic on many routes. Most rides are $1 to $2, or you can get a monthly pass for around $32. If you do need a taxi though, it'll only cost you three to five dollars for a trip of half an hour. All of this can add up if you live in Bangkok though and go out to events or to see friends. Plus, you'll invest a lot of time waiting in traffic if the metro or sky train don't go to where you're headed. It's a spread-out city that can get choked with traffic.

In other cities and towns, those who don't want to depend on taxis will rent a motorbike to run errands and get around, at a rate of $60 to $100 per month. An uncomfortably large number of foreigners get in motorbike accidents though. "Don't even think about renting a scooter until you've observed traffic long enough to know what the local conventions are," says Bill. "If you can't ride a motorcycle without thinking about what you are doing, you do not want to be riding one here. It's not a good place to learn."

In smaller towns and some neighborhoods of Chiang Mai you could get around by bicycle, but not in Bangkok. There you may need to take a bus sometimes to get to where you're going, at prices at or lower than the metro.

Healthcare

Thailand actively promotes its health tourism sector and sends its doctors to top-tier international medical universities for training. You'll get excellent care here and in the major cities and tourist centers you'll usually be able to communicate easily in English. Costs are a fraction of what you would spend in Europe or the USA though, and you'll probably have more people waiting on you. In Bangkok, some of the hospitals look as nice as a high-end hotel and people who live in neighboring countries will often come here for serious medical needs.

Many round-the-world travelers will wait until they get to Bangkok to get all the vaccinations they will need for the rest of their travels. The costs are significantly lower, and you can just walk into a clinic or hospital to get them knocked out.

To get an idea of costs, here are some Bangkok averages you can compare to where you live now:

Lasik surgery (both eyes) - $1,850
Cataract surgery (both eyes) - $3,500
Angioplasty - $3,800 to $4,200
Hip replacement - $8,000 to $17,000
Knee replacement - $7,000 to $14,000
Liposuction - $2,300
Breast Implants - $3,000
Face Lift - $4,000

"I had a heart attack a few years ago," says Bill. "For being stabilized here at the local hospital branch in Hua Hin, transport to Bangkok hours away with the sirens and lights running, 5 nights in intensive care, 4 nights in regular care, it was $30,000. I was glad I had insurance, but that's nothing compared to what you would spend in the USA." (The average cost of a heart bypass surgery in the United States is $123,000.)

"Just do some research to find the best hospitals," he adds. "Also, doctors here love to overprescribe medicines, so just get a one-week supply of what they tell you to take so you can figure out what you really need. For most drugs, you don't need a prescription anyway, so you can always get them later."

His health insurance charges in Thailand were $200 to $300 per month. "That included eight countries in Southeast Asia, excluding Singapore. The cost went up as I got older and added coverage, but the later version I was on covered Europe as well."

Other Costs
Thailand is a great place to stay loose and limber. You can get a massage in a place that's not fancy for $5 to $10 for an hour. If you go to a real spa, it can still be $20 or less. "When I lived on Koh Tao, I got an hour-long massage every week for $6," says Alexandra. "It was an affordable indulgence." You get similarly great rates on manicures, pedicures, and facials. A whole spa package in a place that caters to locals will cost about one-tenth of what you spend in the U.S. or Western Europe.

If you're looking for the kind of sex you would pay for, this has long been a magnet for that kind of transaction, with any type of partner. This book is not the place to find details on that, but it's a key attraction for one subset of expatriates.

In cleaner pursuits, you can get your laundry done for about a dollar a kilo, get your apartment cleaned for $10, or get a nice suit custom made for $80 to $200.

Utility costs are reasonable across the board in Thailand and you'll probably pay less than you did in your home country for everything from mobile data to TV cable. Most interviews and online estimates have put all of them together in the $40 to $150 range for a decent-sized apartment or house, less for a studio. That's electricity, gas, and water. If you use air conditioning all day every day, figure on more like $200 to $250 total. "In the cooler seasons, my electric and water are usually about $30 per month," says Barbara. "In the hottest months of April and May they can be as much as $120 per month."

Internet speeds keep getting better all the time and you can expect to get fast home service now for less than $25 per month, a bit more with TV service. Cellular calls and data are competitive and cheap.

A movie ticket costs around $6, but the ones in Bangkok are twice as nice as what you're probably used to. Going to the movies is a real experience.

This is one of the easiest countries in this book for finding a good international school if you're moving here with a family. Since the Thai language is so useless outside the country, most are in English by default. Because of all the expats in Thailand though, plus a good number of local elites, prices are no bargain. Expect to pay $600 to $1,000 per month for tuition.

Visas

There's one factor that keeps the long-term expatriate population in check in Thailand: the awful visa situation. For the vast majority of foreigners living here, life in Thailand means a lot of trips on buses, trains, or planes to neighboring countries. The visa run is a regular ritual here, one that wastes an incredible amount of time and money on trips that serve no other purpose than to get a new passport stamp. To make it worse, the rules change at least once a year it seems, making this the country in this book that has seen the most instability over the past decade.

As this book was going to press, Thailand was introducing a new 90-day tourist visa that could be renewed twice, potentially giving you 270 days in the country. This would be a godsend compared to what's been on offer before, but it comes with a lot of pandemic-era rules, including a 14-day quarantine, a criminal background check, and medical insurance that covers costs up to $100,000. Assume the rules have changed by the time you read this.

"Thailand has changed their immigration rules for retirees now three times in as many months," said Robert Holloway when I interviewed him. "There are ever-changing rules about how much money you need to deposit, how long it needs to stay in the bank and what percentage, and how much you need to be earning. There is still the combination of income and deposit option, but it is too complex and ridiculous for even the immigration people to figure out. Now they are talking about forcing all long stay pensioners to have a minimum of 400,000 baht in health insurance coverage medical care, which they are saying will have to be purchased only from a Thai company." A few months after I interviewed him, Robert left his home of several years and moved out of the country because of medical conditions.

"There was an enormous upheaval in 2019 when the government decided to change many of the existing visa rules for expats," says Barbara. "Previously, we could swear out an affidavit at the U.S. Embassy/Consulate that we received an offshore income of at least 65,000 baht (slightly more than $2,000) per month. Or we could present bank statements from an account in the U.S. to prove that we had at least 800,000 baht (about $25,000) in an account. Or we could deposit 800,000 baht (about $25,000) into a Thai bank account. Most of us, including me, used one of the first two options. Thai government decided they would no longer accept proof form foreign banks and required us all to either deposit the 800,000 baht in a Thai bank or arrange for 65,000 baht per month to be deposited from an offshore source to a Thai bank account each month. That was a bad situation for me because funds in Thai accounts had to be 'seasoned' for a certain number of months. We have to renew our residence visas every year and by the time the government announced the changes, there wasn't enough time for me to meet the seasoning requirements.

I had no choice but to leave the country, return with a new Non-Immigrant 'O' Visa, and go through the entire approval process for being granted the Retirement Extension attached to the Non- 'O' Visa. It was costly and aggravating, but I got it done. Barring any more changes, it should be relatively easy to renew it year to year from now on, especially since the country's economy has been hard hit by COVID. But in Thailand, you can never be too sure."

"It's very easy to get a tourist visa to come to Thailand for up to three months," says Christa. "Just go to your consulate with some form, pay them the correct amount of money, and pick up your passport the next day. I did that and then found a job before the three months ended. Then they helped me take care of processing my work visa, which required me to leave the country. Visa runs can be exhausting if you are only going to process the visa, but if you can time it right and stay in the other country for a few extra days you can turn it into another travel opportunity. I got an incredible little trip to Laos out of it!

There's no denying though that the immigration office totally sucks," she adds. "It's 10 times worse than the Division of Motor Vehicles in the U.S., but you deal with it because everything else is worth it." Understand that you're probably not able to do this indefinitely. The first couple times are no problem, but as your Thai passport stamps start increasing in number over a year or two's time, immigration can limit or deny renewals. If you have to renew your passport though, you'll start with a clean slate.

There is an option to get a six-month visa though if you apply in your own country before heading to Thailand. This works well if you're not planning to stay there permanently, or you want enough time to sort out a residency visa without having to make a run for the border halfway through.

There are a few under-the-table methods you hear about sometimes for avoiding these visa runs, but you'll have to investigate those on the ground with some long-term residents. Officially, here's how you can get a longer-term visa.

- Marry a local
- Form a corporation with a local (real or shell)
- Acquire an education visa by enrolling in formal study
- Work for a company that will secure a work visa for you.

"If you are too young to retire, then you have to start playing clever games with the law," says Pim. "Some people set up shell companies to get work permits, others do things with marriage, some get jobs. But it is not easy. Otherwise it is the regular schlep to the border every two or three months."

If you're moving to Thailand because you or your spouse has a job offer, then pop the champagne and pack the suitcases without thinking. All the visa hurdles most people have to deal with should evaporate for you and you will be living a very comfortable lifestyle even if there's a pay cut.

If you're self-employed or living off savings, however, build visa run weekends into your calendar and budget and assume this won't be your long-term home. Don't pile up too many possessions unless you're retired because it could all come to an end at any time.

"Thailand has a true retirement visa with a path to real residency," says Bill, "but most people I talked with when I lived there were on the non-immigrant type O temporary residency visa. You have to put a serious chunk of money in a Thai bank or you have to have some kind of steady pension—or a combination of the two. When I left, they were changing the requirements yet again and that's part of the reason I moved on to Portugal. It's best to go to Thaivisa.com to get the right current information, though be advised you're going to get snide answers from the jaded people on there who don't have anything better to do than criticize."

Specific requirements for long-term visas are in a constant state of flux, but for the moment you need to deposit 800,000 baht (close to $26,000) in a Thai bank and ideally show a steady income from a pension or other source of around $2,200 per month—though that income might not be considered "verified" unless it goes into a Thai bank. These figures vary depending on the exchange rate and the whims of the government that month. In general though, after you meet the requirements and get approved, the renewals are just a formality—they don't keep checking your income. At some point you can draw down that bank amount by half to 400,000 baht. What's left is stuck there until you leave or die though if you want to keep renewing.

That's exactly how it worked out for Spencer. "I'm on a retirement visa so I report every 3 months to immigration (only to provide an address), renew my visa yearly, and at the end of the first year I had to meet and maintain the financial requirements. I just left the 800,000 baht untouched in a Thai bank account because the interest rate is good."

There is a way to buy your way in, but you reportedly have to invest at least $300,000 on a property purchase, keeping in mind that foreigners can only buy condos unless they form a corporation and give up part of the ownership. It's not hard to find condos going for this much of course, especially in prime areas of Bangkok, but it's high for the local market when that's about 40 times the average Thai annual salary.

Downsides

Thailand's political situation has been a mess for decades and seems to go through a new round of protests, coups, and curfews every year or two. This invariably looks worse in the news than it is on the ground, but a country without a functioning government is always a bit unnerving. Many of the government problems have corruption at their heart and there's still plenty of it at every level in Thailand. Oh, and you can also get thrown in jail for criticizing the king, so watch what you say on social media.

Environmental protection has been an afterthought at best in the country, so in a few short decades the beaches and rivers have gotten polluted in many areas. There's not much serious effort to recycle and garbage is a problem everywhere.

Air pollution has dogged Bangkok for decades and there's often a haze over the city. Don't move to the capital if you have respiratory problems. Also, "We have awful air pollution between March and May each year in Chiang Mai," says Pim. "Many people time their visits back home then. Traffic is also becoming a bit of an inconvenience, but not as bad as many parts of the world. There are issues such as over-building. The sleepy backwater town of old is no more in Chiang Mai; instead, it is a thriving city. With this rapid growth comes other issues people don't like: horrid signs up everywhere, tall buildings, ugly streets, etc."

Overbuilding is a big problem in many areas, with few regulations or formal building restrictions enforced. On many islands, haphazard construction and too much density have quickly taken former paradise areas like Ko Phi Phi to the point of near collapse. The Phi Phi islands were actually shut down for an extended period to give them a chance to at least partially recover.

Sex tourism is a major industry in Thailand and for some that's a big draw. For others it's a huge turnoff. No matter what you think about it, there are clear side effects in the form of human trafficking, organized crime, and exploitation.

As in many countries profiled in this book, buying electronics is probably going to cost you more than what you're used to in a richer country. The cost of electronics in Thailand relative to the quality is not good," says Bill. "They're taxed like luxury goods, especially camera gear." Also, while internet speeds are great in the cities, that's not always the case on islands and in rural areas.

Tens of thousands think the trade-offs are worth it and Thailand will probably always be a popular destination for foreigners to live. "I must say that the visa requirements are the only thing I don't like about living in Thailand," says Barbara. "On a day-to-day basis, I rarely feel the impact of government and I have to say they did a good job during the COVID-19 pandemic. I love Thai culture, which values the whole of society over the individual. Especially in the north where I live, the Lanna people are gently, smiling, and welcoming. And frankly, my age is a factor as well. I'm now 68 and completely healthy, but some years ago I decided to let my hair go naturally white. The moment I did that, people in the U.S. (especially the younger ones) began treating me differently. It's as if I suddenly had become invisible. No one wanted to talk to me. No one seemed to value my opinion. Here in Thailand, people revere the older generation. Younger Thais appreciate our knowledge and experience. I love the way I am treated here."

For More Information
ThaiVisa.com
TheThaiLife.com
ChiangMaiCityLife.com
TheThaiger.com
BangkokPost.com
U.S. Embassy Thai visa information

Chapter 29:
Vietnam

Pros: cheap prices, three-month tourist visa, ample short-term rentals, great food, decent internet, easy air connections.

Cons: communist bureaucracy, heavy traffic, heavy rainy season, polluted cities, hot and humid, no retirement visa.

After spending a year in Chiang Mai, food writer and recipe tester Halona Black decided Danang would be a good spot to settle down next. She has been happy she made the move and is living well without spending a lot. "I'm spending less than $1,000 a month here not counting leaving every three months for the visa renewal. It's very affordable. Maybe housing is a little more expensive than in Chiang Mai, probably because we're by the beach, but food is cheaper in Vietnam than Thailand. Groceries are a bit cheaper here, with a lot of good fruit, vegetables, and seafood. You can spend $20-25 per week and eat great."

For many potential expatriates, Vietnam is not the first place that will spring to mind. For digital nomads though, this has become an entrepreneurial hotspot. In Ho Chi Minh City (Saigon) especially, there are lots of people with laptop jobs you can bounce ideas off of and get advice from about settling in. Vietnam has a lot of similarities with Thailand, but it offers an easier visa situation if you're not retired.

This country is one of the best values in the world for travelers, especially when it comes to lodging and food. Naturally that makes it a great value for residents too. You can land one day and have a short-term apartment for a good price the next. Many foreigners who live here don't even care if there's a kitchen or not. They eat out every meal and just use the fridge for beer and sodas. (For juice, they just get it fresh squeezed from a local stand.)

Forget the image of a war-torn country or a bleak communist wasteland. This is not some sad and downtrodden place anymore where a lot of people are struggling to get by. It's a thriving economy where motorbikes seem to sprout from the ground each time it rains. When you say, "Everybody and his brother has one," it's really true. This is a business-friendly country where regulations are lighter than you would expect, though the "soak the rich foreigners" attitude is unfortunately still alive and well in some sectors of the economy. Getting the local price for goods and services here sometimes takes a lot of effort and patience—and the willingness to walk away when the difference is really blatant.

With a coastline as long as the US west coast, there are plenty of beaches to choose from—with water warm enough for year-round swimming. You'll also find soaring mountains, waterfalls, jungles, and hill-tribe trekking areas that aren't as commercialized as Thailand's. Most of the beauty here is of the natural type: the older architecture was wooden, and most has long since vanished, outside of Hué anyway.

Many educated locals speak English in Vietnam, especially in the south. The local language is tonal (like Chinese or Thai), but the writing uses Roman letters with accent marks. With a little effort, you should at least be able to learn to read menus and navigate street signs.

Despite the madness you'll encounter on the streets and barely passable sidewalks, there's a lot to uncover in Vietnam, the food is interesting, and one study found the locals to be the second-happiest people in the world behind Costa Rica.

Here are some of the most popular spots for foreigners to settle.

Ho Chi Minh City (Saigon) - Huge, spread-out, chaotic, and hot, this is also clearly the business center of Vietnam and a hub for virtual entrepreneurs. This is the city with the best health care, shopping, and air connections.

Hanoi - The second largest city is calmer but more compact, with architecture from the French and an old quarter great for strolling. This is a traveler base for excursions to Ha Long Bay and the northern hill tribe areas, so there is plenty to do and see nearby. The capital city is cooler than in the south much of the year, though summers are equally brutal.

Danang - Vietnam's cleanest city strikes some as boring, but it was named the top city in the world for digital nomads in one report because it met so many criteria. It's close to beaches, islands, Hoi An, and beautiful countryside. Two golf courses are nearby, one of them frequently tagged as the best in the country.

Hoi An - This popular tourist spot is the center for getting clothes custom tailored, so you'll be well-dressed if you live here. Historic Chinese and French buildings vie for attention and there are stunning beaches nearby. Danang is about 30 minutes away to hit big supermarkets.

Hué - Vietnam's most interesting historic area is an easy city to navigate. It sits on a large river and has train connections north and south.

If you want to live a frugal life, it's quite easy to do here. Blogger James Clark, who runs NomadicNotes.com and LivingInAsia.co, says he routinely gets by on $800 or so per month in Ho Chi Minh City, a bit more if he buys a plane ticket to leave the country. "It's pretty easy to get by on $1,000 a month or less here if you're living a normal traveler kind of life." Even if you get a really fancy apartment, it would be hard to spend anything close to what you do in Australia, Western Europe, or the USA.

If you choose to live large instead, you can live an upscale urban life for a fraction of what it would cost in a comparable sized city in a wealthier country. The most I've heard any self-employed person say they were spending in Vietnam was $2,500 a month, which included a luxury apartment with twice-daily maid and laundry service, a gym membership, and lots of socializing in clubs and nice restaurants at night. Numbeo.com says if you spend that amount here, it's equivalent to spending $8,500 per month in San Francisco. A better life for one-third the price.

Housing Costs

As in most countries, cities cost more to live in than small towns and rural areas, but Vietnam is a good value no matter where you choose to live. You can get a 900-square-foot apartment in the best area of Danang for around $600. Apartment prices can be half that in smaller towns, especially if you're content with the kinds of places most locals live in, but almost anywhere you can find something nice and reasonably roomy in the range of $300 to $800 per month. If you spend more than $1,000 per month, it's going to be a big multi-bedroom luxury apartment with a pool complex, a gym, 24-hour security, and probably a panoramic view.

James Clark and many other digital nomads who have settled in Ho Chi Minh City find that there's an easy network of short-term rentals to tap into upon arrival. "Every time I've returned, I've found a place within one day for a short-term rental. I'll book a guesthouse room for one night and the next day I've found a place," James says.

What you get for your money is generally quite good. "You can get your own private furnished one-bedroom apartment in District 1 where I am for under $500 that will be decent," he says. "That includes a maid who comes three times a week and does your laundry. All of them include internet. Electricity is never included though, which is $20 a month if you're not there much, three or four times as much if you have the air conditioning running all the time." He pays less now than when I talked to him for the first edition: $220 per month with maid service and internet included. He just pays the electric bill.

Halona pays a bit more in Danang, but for a more upscale place. "I have a large studio here that's on the river side of the city. I have a 4th-floor apartment that overlooks the river, a bridge that's lit up at night, the city, and mountains. There's a nice patio area with lots of sunlight and I have a full-sized refrigerator."

To put things in perspective, the crowdsourced site Numbeo.com says average rental costs in Ho Chi Minh City are less than one-fifth what they would be in San Francisco or London. So, if you're paying $3,000 a month for an apartment there, you can probably get something comparable here for $600.

In other cities, you can take your time looking around while sleeping in a value-priced hotel. Vietnam may just be the best accommodation value in the world for mid-range hotels. Western toilets, hot water, clean sheets, and fresh towels are pretty standard even in cheapie backpacker places running $10-$20 double per night. You'll say "Wow" more often than "Ugh" when opening the door to your room the first time. Rentals from Airbnb and the like are a great bargain as well, frequently $20 or less per night for somewhere clean, modern, and well-kept.

Food and Drink Costs

Most expatriates who don't try to live on a western diet or eat at fancy restaurants every day easily get by on a food budget of $300 a month eating very well. Some do it for half that and have a well-balanced, nutritious diet. "Overall, food is cheaper in Vietnam than Thailand," says Halona. "There's a lot of good fruit, vegetables, and seafood. You can spend $20-25 per week on groceries and eat great."

Figure on $300 to $500 a month for a couple if you're not on a strict budget and you frequent nice restaurants on a regular basis. This is a country though where you can get a big filling bowl of pho soup on the street for $1.50 in a central business district, half that in some other areas. If you spend more than $8 on lunch it was probably in a nice restaurant with uniformed waiters. "I'll go for a normal restaurant lunch with soup or a noodle dish that's maybe $2 and then later I'll go to a nice sushi place and spend $10" says James. "I go regularly to a vegetarian all-you-can eat buffet place that's around a dollar for rice and whatever vegetables you want to pile on."

Tropical fruit is a bargain, often $1 or less for a kilo. Parts of the country are at higher elevations, so there's a good range of vegetables too. This is one of the world's greatest producers of coffee, rice, shrimp, and multiple other staples, so prices on those are quite good if you go to the right stores. You'll pay $1 or less for a kilo (2.2 pounds) of rice, tomatoes, potatoes, peppers, or onions. Because of the French influence, this is one of the few Asian countries where you can get good, inexpensive baguettes.

This is one of the cheapest countries in the world for beer, which gives it a huge edge over Malaysia and Thailand if you like to tip one back on a hot day. Almost every day is a hot day here, so you'll be glad the prices are low. A big liter glass can be as little as 50 cents at a sidewalk *bia hoi* stand, with a bottled beer averaging a buck or less in a restaurant or bar. Dollar beers are the standard here, not the exception.

Sodas and basic coffees are 30-50 cents, though you can spend $2-$3 on a really good coffee at a specialized cafe. Fruit juices and shakes are 40-80¢. Ice cream and coconut popsicles can be a welcome treat in the heat and they're not much of a splurge at 50¢ or so.

A cocktail will run $2 to $5 in a bar. Rice wine and Russian vodka are inexpensive but vary greatly in quality. Foreign liquor here is about the same retail price as in the U.S., so you can drink your Jack Daniels or Tanqueray in a cocktail without breaking the bank. Wine is about the same price as you probably pay now as well—it all has to travel a long way.

Transportation
You can easily get by without a car in Vietnam unless you live in a suburban or rural area and need it for a commute or hauling groceries. Most of the population gets around on buses and motorbikes within the cities, so if you can get used to going with the flow, it's cheap and easy to follow their lead. If you don't want to buy a motorbike ($800 to $2,000), you can rent one for $100 a month or less.

Taxi rides range from 50 cents to $4 for most distances around the big cities, though it will cost more to and from the airport. If you pack light, James says you can get a Grab motorbike taxi to the airport for around $2.50. He recommends the taxi services Mai Linh and Venus Sun since they always use the meter.

Local city buses are 15-20¢ once you figure out the routes. To travel the long distance between Hanoi and Saigon will cost anywhere from $50 to $125 by bus, train, or plane. Shorter trips, such as the scenic three-hour train from Danang to Hue, are more like $3 - $5.

Although crossing the street on foot in Vietnam takes some getting used to because of the sea of motorbikes flowing around you, many neighborhoods are easy to navigate on foot. Some expatriates get almost everything they need in their local area, so their transportation costs are just occasional taxis and costs to leave the country on a visa run every three months.

Residents always cite cheap flight options to travel out of the country as one of the best advantages to living here. "Air Asia is kind of the backbone, but every country has their own budget airline. The ones based here are Viet Jet Air and Jetstar Pacific. Even just a week out I can get a flight to Bangkok for $100," says James. "If I plan ahead, I can get it for $50. I've picked up flights to Kuala Lumpur for $30 or $40. I've gotten domestic flights for $12 when they do one of the "$0 plus tax" sales here.

Healthcare
In a nutshell, Vietnamese healthcare is better than Cambodia's, but worse than Thailand's or Malaysia's. The system is government-run and tightly controlled, without the plethora of gleaming private hospitals dishing out medical tourism care that you find in some other Southeast Asian countries. This doesn't mean you'll get terrible care though: the government hospitals in the cities have modern machines and people who know how to run them. The doctors may earn a measly government salary, but that doesn't mean they're not well trained.

The main obstacle is often language. Some expats learn to hire an interpreter to bring with them to the public doctor (or get a favor from a Vietnamese friend who speaks English) because even counting that payment, the total will be less than a private clinic. It's not uncommon to pay $5 or less for a doctor consultation, about the same for many tests like an ultrasound or EKG, and less than $2 for an x-ray. An MRI can be a different story though, says James. "I was having some strange ongoing headache. I went to the western medical clinic here for $60. They said it was going to be $500 for an MRI and when my jaw dropped, they sent me to another location where it was $100."

Otherwise, his medical costs have been quite low. "I had a physical therapist here who got me back on my feet for $8 an hour—with acupuncture and massage therapy. I went to the dentist a couple months ago after way too long. He did a cleaning and x-rays for about $22."

You can go to the local clinic for super cheap but if you want better facilities and a foreign-trained doctor you pay more for a nicer place. If you need a doctor who speaks English, you will often pay more than that to go to a private hospital or outpatient center, though compared to your home country the costs will still probably seem quite reasonable. Hospitals in the largest cities are good enough now for most issues, but some foreigners feel more comfortable grabbing a cheap flight to Bangkok for major treatment or surgery since the service and communication there are some of the best in the world.

Other Costs
Vietnam is one of the best values in the world for fast internet if it's not included in your rent, with an average bill of $20 or less for a great connection. Mobile phone plans are equally cheap, as in $20 for unlimited voice and data or less for a pre-paid arrangement. James pays $8 a month on average.

Water can range from $4 to $20 a month depending on usage if you have to pay for that, garbage pick-up is a dollar or two a week if it's available. Cable/satellite TV starts at $4 and can rise to $25 with lots of premium channels. Bottled propane gas canisters for cooking and hot water will average out to $5-$8 per month.

It's inexpensive to get cultural stimulation in Vietnam. Admission charges at most museums are between 15¢ and $1.50. The outliers, such as the Hue royal tombs, still rarely top $4. Most cultural performances, even if geared to tourists, are between $1.50 and $5. The rare exceptions are grand operas or symphony performances in the big cities, often with foreign troupes on the bill. Still, they'll be a fraction of what you would pay for tickets in your home country.

A day of leisure won't cost you much in the coastal areas. "If you want to rent a chair at the beach around Danang it's maybe $1.50 to $3 for a day," says Halona. "You can sit there all day and order coconuts to drink from or food. There are hotels along the beach where you can get a nice lunch for $3 to $5 with a view of the water. Going to the movies feels like a bargain. It's around $3 for the movie, maybe $5 with popcorn."

As you'd probably guess just looking at the staff at your local nail salon, the Vietnamese have plenty of experience giving manicures and pedicures. Here at the source you'll probably pay around a dollar or two for either. Services like waxing and facials will be a few dollars, an hour-long massage $10 or less if you're not at a resort.

If you're running some kind of business and want to hire local programmers or designers, you won't spend a lot on that either.

With the average salary being around $400 a month, paying $800 a month could get you an A-level employee.

Visas
When you fly into Vietnam you can get a one-month visa on arrival. If you apply ahead of time though, you can get a three-month multi-entry visa instead. With that you just need to leave the country every three months to get a new one and start the cycle over again. Unofficially though, it's possible to renew it without leaving at all if you're willing to cough up some extra money. You can even pay a service to go take care of the visit for you.

With a one-year business visa, you can spend a whole year in the country without leaving—just checking in every three months at immigration. In most cases you either need to show that you will be employing locals, or you need to be sponsored by a local company to do a job a foreigner is required for, like teaching English or running the local division of an international company. You'll be expected to show a copy of your university degree and pass a criminal background check.

Others have claimed success getting a work visa for a freelancer/business owner just by showing sufficient proof of income that's earned in another country.

There's no retirement visa scheme here though and for now anyway, the only method for getting a multi-year visa is opening a company in Vietnam.

If you do have to go and come back, Cambodia, Laos, and Thailand are nearby and inexpensive to get to for a break. There are also frequent flight sales to Malaysia, Singapore, and Indonesia. Because of the plethora of cheap flights and the land connection to Cambodia, foreigners on temporary visas don't get too bothered about the need to leave four times a year, especially since the immigration authorities here seem content to let you do that indefinitely.

Downsides
What people usually picture as the downsides of living in a communist country don't turn out to be a bit deal here. There's far more surveillance, snooping, and rule navigation to deal with in the UK or USA than there is in Vietnam. You do have a lot of state-owned enterprises though (basically any company starting with "Vina"). This can stifle competition and keep standards low. There is some banning of certain websites and social media, but the government is really bad at it compared to somewhere like China.

Most foreigners figure out a way around the blocks in a few minutes and most coffee shops use some kind of proxy server to reroute traffic.

You can look around and see that capitalism is running at extreme speed here, so where you really feel the lingering effects of communism is the attitude that those who have more should pay more. It's often next to impossible to get old ladies selling fruit in Hanoi to give a white face a price that's even double what the locals pay—never mind parity. This gets a little better each year though as fixed-price supermarkets proliferate, and younger food stall owners find they get more repeat business by being more even-handed.

As mentioned in the healthcare section, most people go through a government-run, centralized system here that is perpetually underfunded. If you want the best equipment and an English-speaking doctor, you either have to pay a lot more at a private center or head to Bangkok. Having said that, the government did a terrific job in fighting the COVID-19 virus threat, with a fraction of the deaths of countries with equivalent populations in Europe. In contrast to the USA, they scored an A compared to an F in the much richer country.

Navigating the traffic in Vietnam's cities and trying to cross the street are both learned skills that seem insurmountable when you first arrive. From a vantage point above the streets in Saigon you can see a sea of motorbikes 1,500 riders deep, flowing around the smaller number of cars like a stream moving past the rocks. As a byproduct, noise and pollution are both a big problem. Environmental controls are lacking throughout the country. We stopped counting the dead fish in the lake in central Hanoi when we passed 50 the last time I was there.

Lastly, the further south you go, the hotter, muggier, and buggier it gets. Some people thrive on that kind of heat, but be advised that for part of the year it can routinely top 100F degrees, even in Hanoi.

For More Information
LivingInAsia.co
VietnamInsider.vn
MoveToVietnam.com
Vietnam-visa.com/blog/
ExpatExchange Vietnam forum
Search Facebook for apartment listing groups

Chapter 30:
Other Places to Consider

The country breakdowns that preceded this section are not meant to be a comprehensive list. They are meant to be a curated collection of places to consider so you're not overwhelmed with options. They were primarily chosen because of popularity, ease of residency, and overall value. There are certainly plenty of other countries where foreigners have settled down to live a better life for less money than they were spending before. I've included some info in this section for other destinations to consider for a half-priced life abroad.

If one of the following was on your short list before, by all means investigate further because it may be just the right place for you. After all, I added Albania, Georgia, and The Philippines in this revised edition after hearing from readers that they had moved there and found their perfect spot.

Indonesia
I'd love to live in Indonesia. I've spent months there on two different trips and it's a terrific country. It's basically a long string of islands with terrific beaches and snorkeling, it's quite cheap, and if you start getting tired of the heat you just go up into the mountains. I'm not alone: there are as many as 10,000 expats in Bali alone at any given time.

There's just one big problem: it's tough to get a visa to live here long-term. You either need to be working for a company that's giving you a work visa, to have an Indonesian spouse, or you're over 55 and have a decent income. Otherwise you are probably going to be leaving the country to renew your visa a minimum of six times a year. You also can't own property. In some parts of the country the internet is far from fast if you want to run a business online.

Coming for 30 days is no problem, plus you can pay a bit and extend that another month. Beyond that though, it gets complicated. The easiest way to live here is to be old and patient. There is special visa for retired people of 55 of older. You must show proof of income exceeding $1,500 per month, proof of health insurance, and proof that you're spending a sufficient sum on your housing: at least $500 per month in Bali, Jakarta or Bandung, at least $200 elsewhere. You also have to pledge that you'll employ at least one domestic worker on a full-time basis.

Some people manage to make it work though. David McKeegan and his wife used to run Greenback Tax Services from Bali, doing tax returns and advisement for expatriates. It's a virtual business with accountants around the world. They eventually moved on but were living a good life in Bali on a fraction of what they spent in Europe. "We had a three-bedroom house with two-car garage that we turned into an office. We paid about $14,200 per year in rent. Housing tends to be more western pricing, so that was the biggest expense, but just try to find anything like that within 60 miles of New York City! Each bedroom had A/C and its own bathroom. We had a nice yard with a vegetable garden, a swimming pool, and a place for the two kids to run around."

They paid $4 an hour for their babysitter/nanny and "she used to work at the Hyatt." Their housekeeper came six days a week for a salary of $70 per month, which was also the amount for the gardener and pool cleaner who came three days a week. "We had two different internet set-ups to be safe, which ran us $90 a month. Electricity was $200-$250 a month because of the pool and air conditioning."

They went out to eat a lot in Bali and it was not a big expense. At a nice tourist place on the beach, they would typically pay $25 for a family of four, including a couple beers. "Sometimes we would go eat at the night market and the total would be $3."

The big downside is the visa situation. "Every two months we had to fly to Singapore and back to renew our visas," David explains. "That's when we would do our doctor and dentists appointments and do a little shopping." It's a hassle, he says, "but the flight prices are reasonable if you plan ahead."

Stuart McDonald, who runs the authoritative Travelfish.org site on Southeast Asia, says you can go for years though if you arrange a "social visa" with an agency and follow the renewal rules properly. He's been living in Bali for nearly a decade with his family and for many of those years he only had to leave the country every six months. He would get a new visa in Singapore and go to immigration once every two months for a half hour or so in Indonesia.

"For that 'social visa' you need a local sponsor. In practice an agent can arrange this—in our case one of the housekeepers did it," he says. "In theory you need to be living in the same district as the sponsor; in practice, it doesn't matter. You must stay in the country for those six months though or start the process over. Plus, you can be denied at any time when you try to renew, which eventually happened to us."

Now he has to do regular visa runs like nearly every other person living on Bali, the big problem being that from there you have to do it by plane. When I talked to Stuart in 2020, he said, "I've made a trip to Kuala Lumpur airport 37 times now." Thankfully the flights are pretty cheap, and you can turn right around. As far as immigration is concerned, you can do this forever if you don't overstay or work, but it's a big hassle. (If you overstay, it will cost a fortune in fines.)

If you're in a popular expatriate spot like Bali, what you spend will depend a lot on how savvy you are. Stuart has this to say about the food options in his adopted home: "Where we currently live in Seminyak, I can get a simple noodle soup in the local *warung* for about 50¢. In the "tourist warung" market 100 meters away it is three times that and in the tourist restaurant, $3. Yes, six times the price for essentially the same meal (though the tourist restaurant dish will come with a carved tomato on the side)."

This is not a good place to live if you're a lush, Stuart advises. "If you're on a budget, don't drink alcohol! A small Bintang will cost anything from $1.75 to $2.50, a large one $2.50 to $4. While these costs may still seem affordable compared to grabbing a pint in your home country, they're disproportionally expensive compared to the cost of food and accommodation. Have a large Bintang with that *rendang* and you'll more than double the cost of dinner. Wine and imported spirits are taxed at a rate of close to 300%, so for those on a budget, best avoided. Expect a mixed drink or cocktail to cost $5 to $15 and a glass of imported wine slightly more. Local wine isn't all that good and the local spirit (arak) can be of very, very variable quality."

"Bali is not really a budget destination anymore," says Stuart, "especially South Bali." Go anywhere else in Indonesia and many of the prices drop in half, including meals and accommodation. But of course, you have more western food, more vegetarian food, and good coffee shops here so there's a trade-off."

Nepal
The Himalayas are home to 9 of the 10 highest peaks in the world and most of those peaks are in Nepal. The scenic effect is pure majesty. And with food and lodging costing about five percent of what they do in say, Switzerland, you feel almost guilty enjoying such a moving experience for so cheap.

More than snow-capped, five-mile high mountains will stick in your memory. The inspiring Buddhist and Hindu temples of the Kathmandu Valley and the Newari architectural styles are magical.

The people drift by awash in brilliant colors and jangly jewelry and you can get things hand crafted to your liking—from clothing to furniture—for unbelievable prices.

Like India, however, it's not for everyone as a place to live. Nepal's people have one of the lowest per capita incomes in the world, so the poverty is very real. If you pull out a brand-new iPhone and start taking selfies, you're probably flashing around something that costs more what a rural Nepali earns from 12 months of labor. Sanitation is deplorable, especially in the capital city, and thick smog is a serious issue there and in Pokhara. But when you get out of the capital and you're hiking or rafting through nature's splendor for a pittance, you realize that Nepal has a different kind of wealth and it's hard to miss home.

Few expats who can live anywhere live here though, for a variety of reasons. It's difficult to stay longer than five months at a time in Nepal unless you have a permanent job or have married a local. Some get a job with a local NGO for next to no pay just to enable residency.

This is also a tough country to live in if you need always-on fast broadband connections for running your online business. Even when I stayed in one of the best hotels in Kathmandu, the power went out at least once a day and the Wi-Fi would go out until the emergency generator kicked in and the signal reconnected.

Who ends up here? As an article in the VisitNepal.com site says, most fall into two camps. "Many of these expats are working for the giant organizations drawn to the country by the greatest contributor of Nepal's economy: foreign aid. But, then there's another side to the expat community. Yes, the old hippies from bygone days and the spiritual seekers—definitely some overlap with these two groups."

If you're looking for the absolutely cheapest place to live for a while and shore up your finances, Nepal may be your best bet. An experienced government worker will likely make under $100 a month, a maid or a gardener less than that. It requires a very skilled private sector job or a management job at a charity to earn more than $150 per month. So, there are expatriates getting by for $250 per month here and not feeling all that poor (provided they don't drink much alcohol). A couple spending $500 a month will be living an upper middle-class lifestyle. Come in receiving a typical U.S. social security check of $1,250 per month into your bank account and you could go from destitute in the land of your birth to deliriously rich here. (Ironically, the fattest fat cats in Nepal, the ones dining the most at the fanciest hotels, are working for international aid organizations. Get one of those jobs and you'll be sitting pretty.)

Bolivia

If the bureaucrats were more welcoming to foreigners, Bolivia would be an expat paradise. Prices are the lowest in South America, labor is cheap, and in places like Sucre, both the climate and the aesthetics are quite pleasant. Officially, you only need to show $1,000 a month in income—not carefully checked—to become a resident. Bolivia has been Venezuela's closest ally besides Cuba for a long while though: a distrust of foreigners and palpable anti-Americanism has lived on.

Because of the political track record, this is not a place where you want to buy something of great value: it's not unthinkable that the leadership will freeze or take your property, as it has already done with many private companies. There are more than a few wealthy Bolivians in Panama City who are stashing their money in a country they feel is a much safer long-term bet.

Getting permission to live here for a year or two is technically not hard on paper, but actually getting to the finish line of that takes superhuman patience. "The bureaucratic process is a complete nightmare" is how nearly every expat sums it up. It frequently takes people two or three years to get it done, as well as four figures in fees. But hey, you get 90 days on arrival while you're sorting out the mountains of paperwork and office visits.

If you're not looking to move here permanently, you can stay for 90 days and then move on to more welcoming pastures. I'm planning on doing just that one of these days: coughing up $160 for a tourist visa, finding a three-month rental somewhere chilled-out like Sucre, and doing some local adventure activities and excursions. I would imagine my wife and I could do it for $1,200 a month or less total and have a grand time. Then we'll travel to Peru, or Argentina, or Ecuador for longer.

Wendy Dale's parents moved to Honduras when she was in her 20s and that planted the seed in her head for moving abroad. A friend of her parents had a house in Bolivia out in the country that they said she could stay in anytime for free, so she took them up on it and moved into it for close to a year. "I was a freelancer in Los Angeles and the expenses were killing me, so that looked very attractive." She went from there to a place in the middle of Cochabamba with a better internet connection for $150 per month—"the most beautiful place I have ever lived in. That's a great place for expats, about a million people, with a university and a nice culture vibe." She spent seven years there, meeting her eventual Bolivian husband in the process. They moved to the jungle for a year to try that life out, then decided they couldn't deal with the lack of infrastructure, including poor internet access.

They eventually moved to the tourist town of Copacabana on Lake Titicaca. They bought a lot and built a small cabin on it to rent out. That was $10,000 for the land (500 square meters) and about $20,000 to build it, including furniture and appliances.

For rent they were paying $100 per month for a three-bedroom house with a yard. "Without tourists the town has maybe 5,000 people, so it's a bargain" she says. They spent $40 a month tops when running electric heaters and $4 for a propane canister refill. Since Bolivia is way behind its neighbors when it comes to broadband penetration, she was happy to finally have the option to pay $40 a month to get a fiber optic connection when it arrived in 2019.

"The nicest restaurant in town in Copacabana with wine and dessert will cost you around $60 for two. A two-course lunch in a local place averages $1.50. When we weren't traveling anywhere, we probably spent $600 per month on expenses in Bolivia. For $1,000 for two you can have a lot of fun. A seven-hour bus ride would cost $5 to $12 and hotels are cheap."

Uruguay
This is not the cheap destination it once was, and the Punta de Este beach region probably has the highest concentration of millionaires in Latin America during peak vacation times. Think of the coast here as the Hamptons for Latin Americans. Still, Uruguay is reasonable compared to many parts of the U.S. and Canada if you go elsewhere in the country (or come to the beach outside of high season). The capital Montevideo is certainly a less expensive place to live than Santiago or Rio—and is half the price of similar-sized San Diego, California.

It benefits from being a very liberal country in the traditional definition of the word. It's a "live and let live" place, with minimal regulations but strong privacy protections, low public health care costs and enlightened drug laws. The government wants to keep everyone safe and healthy, but it's not interested in acting like your mother and dictating how you live your life or who you marry.

When it comes to healthcare, this is one of the best values in the world. You get excellent care at reasonable prices, whether you're paying out of pocket or buying into one of the good-value insurance policies that covers most of your costs at private facilities. This is not a big country, so getting back to the capital for serious medical care is not an arduous task and provincial hospitals and clinics offer good care for routine issues.

The expatriates who live in Uruguay are generally not those trying to live on a shoestring budget, but rather those looking for a European kind of lifestyle at a much lower price than Europe. Think of this country as a more organized, better managed, and less melancholy version of Argentina. To make that step up, you'll need to spend maybe $3,000 a month as a couple instead of skating by for $2,000 across the water in Argentina. If that's within your budget, getting residency here is not complicated.

Once you apply for residency, you can remain in the country that whole time while everything is being processed if you'd like. You need to have a clean police record and the right vaccinations, but then as long as you meet the income requirements there's very little chance you'll be rejected—there's no quota on the number of immigrants and few hassles from power-wielding bureaucrats. There's no expressly stated income requirement, but some say the floor is $1,500 per month for a single person. Once you're approved, you have all rights a local does, plus you can import household goods duty-free. Once you've been a resident for three to five years (depending on marital status), you can become a full citizen and get a second passport.

Romania
Oddly enough, Romania has one of the highest average internet download speeds in the world. According to Speedtest.net, it ranks #5 in the world for fixed broadband. So, if you're running an online business and want a cheap place to hang while you ramp up, head to Transylvania. I loved my time traveling through that region and Dustin Overbeck liked Brasov so much he decided to base his business and his family there.

He and his wife were planning to spend three months there because of a business connection, then check out other spots in Europe. "After we arrived though, my wife found out she was pregnant," he says. "Plus, the first three weeks we were here we had such positive experiences with the people we met, the landlord, babysitters, and people in a co-worker facility I found, so we decided to stay.

A connection in the co-worker facility hooked me up with an immigration person to form a business. I met the attorney within an hour and within eight days had a business formed. I spent maybe €400 for the attorney and business formation. My wife and

I are directors and hired ourselves. After that we filed all the paperwork and got residency permits, which was maybe another €1,000 total for both of us. It all took only two months from start to finish. Then the renewal is much easier and cheaper a year later."

Their first apartment was right in the historic center, for €633 a month, furnished with all utilities and a regular cleaning lady, for a place of around 1,100 square feet. Then they moved to a bit smaller place, but still in the center, paying €500 a month including internet and TV. It's another €50-100 extra for utilities. Dustin spends another €80 a month for a co-working facility so he has people to collaborate with and doesn't have to have room for an office in his home. "We're probably spending a bit over $2,000 a month total," he says, "but that includes expenses related to our child, and taking language classes. Outside the city center you could probably do it for less than half that, but we wanted to be central and it's far less than we'd be spending in Wisconsin!"

If you're young and single though, you might prefer Bucharest. Vice.com praised its nightlife options with this summary: "It's a place where you can smoke indoors, a bottle of vodka costs a quarter of what it does back home and where the closing time is whenever the last person passes out."

Violeta Matei runs the site Bucharest Inside Out and has lived there for years. She says it's possible to live a fairly comfortable life there or in college town Cluj-Napoca for around $1,500 if you don't go out all the time. Other spots, including Brasov, have lower rents, so for $2,000 per month a couple can be in great shape. "In Bucharest, the average rental price for a 2-room flat (one living room and one bedroom) is 450 euros. For a large luxury apartment in the city center, however, you could pay 1,200 to 1,800 euros. In between, A 2- or 3-room apartment in a desirable area, well connected to public transport and close to nice restaurants, coffee shops, and museums, may cost between 450 and 800 euros."

Violeta notes that electricity bills can double in the hottest and coldest months but estimates utility expenses as €50 to €150 for most couples.

Public transportation is a bargain. You'll only spend a few euros to go five kilometers in Bucharest, the bus is around €0.40, and the metro is around €0.80. Uber is available in multiple cities. The train system is slow and antiquated though, so for most routes it's better to take a bus or fly.

While groceries are reasonable and have similar costs across the country, eating out here seems more expensive than it should be.

You don't get the bargain wine prices of Hungary and Bulgaria, nor the variety of cheap places to grab lunch. Expect to pay close to what you would in the USA for a pizza or steak, though if you stick to local dishes and what's in season, you can find a full meal for under €8 here and there. Baked goods are also available at attractive prices.

Just keep in mind you get a full-on winter here, to the point that there are several ski resorts open for months. The main downside though is the lack of long-term residency options. If you're already an EU citizen, it's easy. If not, you have to form a corporation, get a work permit, or enter into a contract with a charity as a volunteer. There's no residency option for freelancers, remote workers, or retirees.

Czech Republic
Until recently, it was tough for non-Europeans to get any kind of long-term residency in the Czech Republic unless you somehow lucked into a local job—and that seldom paid well. They eventually launched a type of permit for freelancers though that allows those earning money from elsewhere to stay on for a year or more—provided they pay taxes and buy health insurance locally. This technically isn't a visa; it's more like an overlay that gives your residency visa a longer life. So, it's the second step of a two-part process, then it makes renewals much easier.

With the *zivno* registry it is easier to qualify for a one-year, long-term residence visa, a stamp in your passport. Then there's a third step and you'll receive "a biometric, long-term residence card good for two years and renewable for another two." After five years, you can apply for permanent residency or citizenship and have a route to a European Union passport.

Prague can be pricey in the Old Town center that is normally thronged with tourists, but if you get a few metro stops or a bus ride away from there you can find reasonable rent prices for Europe, as in less than €800 for a furnished one-bedroom or studio, under €1,000 for a two-bedroom place. Once you get into any other city though, or the countryside, you can expect prices to be as low as half that amount. If you spend more than €1,000 per month outside of Prague, you will get something very nice.

The Czech Republic is the original home of pilsner and you'll drink some great beer here for €1.50 a pint or sometimes less. There's also a terrific wine region in the south of the country near Moravia. Very little of it gets exported and prices are attractive.

The average salary here is close to €1,000 and naturally that's higher in the capital city, lower in rural areas. That's a good bit higher than the other European countries I have profiled in this book though, including Portugal even, so to enjoy the continent's best-preserved capital city and its gorgeous castle-studded countryside, you'll need to up the budget a bit beyond those others. In Prague, the monthly living expenses should be on par with Lisbon's, but higher than in Budapest, Sofia, or Tirana. You can expect to live there on about half what it would cost in New York City, but if you move to a smaller city instead, half the price of Middle America.

Montenegro

When Brit Boone first visited Montenegro, he was struck by the beauty of the mountains and felt like it was a great land of opportunity. His first venture didn't work out, but he eventually started a travel company that brings tourists into natural areas and villages of the country for an authentic experience—at Meanderbug.com. The company also does some NGO work helping farmers. Since he has more than 70 partners in different areas, he has gotten a good handle on running a business there.

He and his wife spend €225 per month in the capital of Podgorica for rent and another €120 on their office. "They're both spacious and comfy" he says. He spent time researching the local market but says €300 to €600 is a normal apartment range for what you can find online, "though there are some international company people paying €1,200." He adds that electricity costs are high though and with window air conditioning units cranking in the summer, his bill has hit €150 to €200 at times for the two spaces. He says the internet speeds and service have gotten dramatically better since he moved there 7 years ago, and you can get high speeds over cable or fiber as long as you're willing to spend at least €40 per month. Outside of isolated hamlets in the mountains, cell coverage is good and inexpensive. You can get a Sim card for a couple euros.

He says eating out will cost €2 or €3 for a basic lunch, €5 to €10 for a nice place that's locally owned. He had just bought 10 pastries at a bakery for a meeting and it was €4.20. "There's a lot of good organic produce here and now a cooperative system to get it to market, so it's easy to get great fruit and vegetables for a couple euros a kilo." A good cup of coffee will cost a euro or two, a beer in a bar is around €2, and you can pick up a decent bottle of wine in a store for €3 to €10. If you pay €15 its going to be a world-class wine.

Montenegro used to be dominated by Russians, but after Montenegro's entry into NATO a few years ago, the number of Europeans started rising quite a bit and the Russian numbers are decreasing. The country is off the radar for most Americans, but it's worth looking into. Andrew Henderson from Nomad Capitalist owns property in Montenegro and says as long as you have hired good local help for the process, getting residency is straightforward.

"Basically, you need to buy any habitable property, and you should have at least 12 square meters of space for each person in your family (if they also plan to get a residence permit)," he says. "A decent, small apartment near the sea will cost anywhere from $30,000 to $75,000, and it will likely need a little renovation work. Once you have the title to a property in Montenegro, you can go through the procedures to obtain a one-year temporary residence permit."

Local salaries are low, around €400 to €500, but the official tax rate employers are supposed to pay is more than 60%. Brit says this is a laid-back culture, but people generally have a good work ethic and a positive attitude about facing challenges. "There's a full throttle approach to live," he says, "which I really appreciate."

The main downside of Montenegro is that the city-to-city public transportation system is not good. Many expats end up buying a car or renting one frequently. No rideshare services operate in the country, but a taxi across town in the capital will only cost a few euros.

There are a few other **European countries** where you could live a half-priced life fairly easily. Slovakia qualifies, even in Bratislava, though the winters can be quite cold. The country of Bosnia and Herzegovina is a tad warmer, next to Croatia and Montenegro. Turkey is in Asia apart from half of Istanbul, but if you can get past the dictatorship political system, it's a pleasant place and you can buy your way into residency by purchasing real estate. As I write this the local currency in Turkey is very weak, which means bargain prices.

Fiji

Are you dreaming of island life in the South Pacific? If you want to truly get away from it all and find your tropical paradise on a dot of land in the Pacific Ocean, then Fiji is your best bet. It's got enough land to have a real agricultural industry, it's populated enough to get imported goods by the container load (and fuel by full tankers), plus it has good air connections to the rest of the world.

Travel writer and guidebook author Chantae Reden has been based there for years and sometimes writes about her life there on her blogs ChantaeWasHere.com and the Salt Sirens. Here's what she has to say about life and costs on Fiji.

"Living in Fiji as an expat can be relatively cheap or extremely pricey depending on the level of lifestyle you want. If you want to live like a local, the day-to-day cost of living is much cheaper than living in the United States or Australia. For example, expect to spend around $1 for a fresh coconut, $2 for a heap of tomatoes, $1 for a head of lettuce, $2 for a heap of mangoes, $2 for a heap of eggplants, and $2 for a fresh pineapple. As Fiji is a largely communal society, fruits and vegetables are typically sold in a bundle. It's expected that you'll take the produce back to your home and swap any leftovers among neighbors. My partner and I spend around $20-40 per week on fresh produce. However, imported items like brand-name processed foods (cereal, snacks, cheese) cost about 50% more than what you would pay at home, as all of these carry the costs of import taxes and shipping.

Public transportation is also very affordable in Fiji. A 10-minute taxi ride around Suva (Fiji's capital) costs around $4 and bus rides start at $.25. A bus trip across the island of Viti Levu runs around $15 and takes about 4.5 hours. However, cars tend to retain their value and you will likely pay more to own a vehicle in Fiji than you would elsewhere. Because import fees are so high on vehicles, most expats opt to buy secondhand. When buying a car, I only looked at purchasing a Hyundai or a Toyota--the two most popular brands driving around the islands. While you might find a great deal on another brand, the poor condition of Fijian roads mean you'll probably break down at some point. Most mechanics won't have spare parts on hand to fix other brands of cars, meaning you'll foot the bill for shipping and import tax if you have to order a part from overseas.

Housing is where you'll find the largest discrepancy between value. If you live in a city populated with expats, like Suva, expect high, poor-value rent prices. Because most expats working in Suva have their rent subsidized by their employers, the cost of rent is inflated. A two-bedroom, one-bathroom apartment in a nice neighborhood on Suva's outskirts runs around $2,000 per month. You can find much more affordable housing almost anywhere else

Tim Leffel

on the islands because the prices are geared to locals, not corporate or government expats with a housing allowance."

African Countries

Africa is a vastly larger continent than North America, so leaving out this giant land mass looks odd. If you remove South Africa from the list, however, the vast majority of foreigners on the continent of Africa did not move there because of a lifestyle choice. They are there because they're working for a charity organization, an NGO, a religious organization, or the United Nations. The next largest group would be those who are getting paid well to relocate there (often reluctantly) for work: oil workers, engineers, hotel general managers, and those heading up local operations for international conglomerates such as Unilever or Deutsche Telekom.

Also, for a whole host of reasons, many countries in Africa aren't nearly as cheap as you would think they'd be. When you look at online cost of living estimators, the majority of countries on the continent that have sufficient data aren't any cheaper than small-town USA for a basket of living expenses. Sure, if you want to live and eat like a real sub-Saharan African you can do it for almost nothing. After all, 20 of the 25 poorest countries in the world are here. If you want to have even a few comforts and conveniences of home, however, you'll pay a huge premium for a nice bathroom, a modern kitchen, and the kind of school you want to send your kids to.

It's futile trying to find a local job in most of these countries unless it's for a foreign company or your state department. Broadband internet access is still hit and miss—when the power stays on. The jobless rates in some countries top 20%. (Leading to the boatloads of African immigrants that keep washing up on other shores.) Healthcare is far from ideal across the continent. At one point the World Health Organization said that "The risk of a child dying before their fifth birthday is eight times higher in the WHO African Region than a child in the WHO European Region." Of the 20 health care systems the WHO ranks at the bottom of their list, 18 of them are in Africa. (The others are Cambodia and Afghanistan.)

You also have some of the most corrupt and regressive governments in the world to deal with, especially if you're gay. Of the countries that still have enforceable laws on the books against homosexuals, more than 30 are in Africa. That means more of them there do discriminate than not. (Avoid Nigeria and Uganda

- 323 -

at all costs; you could get thrown in jail or worse just because of your sexual orientation.)

Former expat haven Egypt frequently sentences protesters to long trials and even death, while also jailing journalists who say anything negative against the government. Throw in lingering slavery, civil wars, and limb-chopping warlords in some countries, and urban Honduras starts looking like a walk in the park in comparison.

Writing off 50-some countries with one brush stroke is not fair though, of course, and there are indeed some people who move to Africa just to move to Africa. If you want to join them, dig in, travel overland, and do some research. Below are more details on my top recommendation where you can definitely live for less and still have some comforts—Morocco. Otherwise investigate Togo on the west coast and Madagascar off the east coast. I've talked with expats living in both those places who were quite happy with their decision.

There are some expats living in areas with lots of tourists in Tanzania, Kenya, and Botswana, mostly in the hotel or tour industries. If their expenses are covered, they can save a bit of money and have a wonderful experience. There are some independent foreigners living in Mozambique, Madagascar, Malawi, and Ethiopia because they like it there, as well as Tunisia up north when it's stable. If you've traveled to one of these and love it or have a connection that can help you get a tourism job, try it out and tell me how it went!

Morocco

The best overall value in Africa and with some of the best infrastructure on the continent, this is the place to get exotic without paying a fortune. With some judicious house hunting and a limit on how much alcohol you drink, you could squeak under the half price mark here in the main tourism centers or live more comfortably on that amount elsewhere. The per capita GDP is only around $5,000 per year and the average salary is less than $500, but prices are high in tourist areas just because...there are so many tourists driving up prices. Still, Numbeo estimates that the cost of living in Morocco is exactly half what it is in the USA and rents are 75% cheaper.

Be advised that English is often third or fourth on the list of languages though, even in the tourism sector. Arabic, French, and Spanish (in the north) are more commonly understood and French is the language of government and diplomacy. This is a Muslim country, so alcohol can be hard to find outside of tourist areas and is heavily taxed.

The country has some of the highest internet penetration in Africa and broadband is more prevalent than on most of the continent. Air connections are good, especially to Europe, and you can take a ferry to Spain. Medical care is decent in the cities, but poor elsewhere and you'll likely encounter a language barrier if you don't speak Arabic or French. Petty crime and property theft are nagging problems and the touts of Morocco win the international bronze medal for annoying schemers and scammers, just behind India and Egypt.

Foreigners are allowed to buy homes here and there is some financing available if you can pay 35 percent of the purchase price as a down payment and another 6 percent in various fees at closing.

You can stay up to 90 days on a tourist visa, but if you want to stay longer as a temporary resident you have to register within the first 15 days after arrival and apply for an alien registration card. If you can show sufficient means to support yourself, it should be granted after you jump through all the hoops. For a work permit, you need to show a signed contract from the employer and to live here as a freelancer you need to get a work authorization. Once you have that though, it's good for a decade.

Chapter 31:
Safety in Perspective

When your number comes up, statistics say it'll most likely be from something mundane like cancer, heart disease, or some other symptom of old age. That's how millions die each year. Almost half of all deaths are from heart disease and cancer. Normally around 56,000 die from flu or pneumonia in the USA, though the coronavirus more than quadrupled that number in 2020.

If it's an accidental death, you'll most likely die in a car crash. That's how 38,800 people died in the USA in 2019 and how 1.35 million died worldwide. That's despite the fact that driving is much safer than it used to be. That 39,000 number is down from more than 50,000 a year in the 1980s, despite more cars on the road. But it's still the equivalent of having a 9/11 terrorist attack every six weeks, year after year.

I'm not saying don't ever get behind the wheel again, but understand that hanging around your suburb and driving to work is more likely to get you killed than changing your address to Panama or Cambodia. If you do go abroad, you should worry more about bad drivers than you should about terrorists, cartels, or the danger lurking in dark alleys. According to the CDC, "Every day, almost 3,700 people are killed globally in road traffic crashes... More than half of those killed are pedestrians, motorcyclists, and cyclists."

If you're one of the 13.7% of people who still smokes, be advised that cigarettes cause an estimated 480,000 deaths a year in the U.S. alone. If you're obese and you light up regularly, your odds of dying early are already so high that on-the-ground safety shouldn't even be on your worry list. One of those two preventable things is probably going to kill you, not some random thug on the corner in a foreign land. Staying out of the hospital also helps. Some 200 people a day die from hospital infections; that's more than all the foreign violence in the world added together, including attacks on military personnel. Then there's the pandemic of 2020 that was still raging as this book went to press. Being around people not wearing a mask or maintaining their distance was far more likely to kill you than some scary narco traffickers in a foreign land. Until most of the world's population has been vaccinated and it actually works, this is your biggest risk of dying by far.

One potential cause of death is almost sure to decrease if you move out of the USA: the chance of getting shot to death. No country has a higher rate of gun ownership than the United States and only a few dots on the map have a higher rate of gun deaths. Most of them are either war zones or drug gang zones—which themselves are their own kind of war zone.

The number of Americans killed each year by firearms is only slightly lower than those killed in auto accidents: around 32,000 annually. For those between the ages of 15 and 19, this is the second leading cause of death after car crashes. More Americans have been killed by firearms since 1968 than in all of the wars we've fought in added together. So, living in an actual war zone could be safer than being in the wrong place at the wrong time in the USA. There was probably a random mass shooting the week you're reading this, no matter which week of the year it is.

Massive incarceration hasn't made a dent in these stats either. The USA only has 5 percent of the world population, but it has 25 percent of the world's prison inmates.

The truth is, your safety odds are better in most places you'll move to than they are in your current hometown, especially if you're American. Let's start there and *then* let's look at the real dangers and how to stay safe.

You Do Need to Be Smart
I'm not saying it's going to be an idyllic Eden where you're going, a place nobody hurts or robs anyone. Even Sweden, Singapore, and Japan have policemen solving break-ins and murders as we speak. We've seen scenes of deadly rioting and mass murders on every continent except Antarctica.

Although I'll talk until I'm blue in the face about how the drug cartels in Mexico have never targeted tourists, I do know people where I live who have had their houses robbed while they were out. A friend was hit in the head with a beer bottle and would have had his wallet taken if he hadn't swerved out of the way and ran. I'm in a safe city overall, but shit happens, especially in the wee hours of the night. In recent years, my state has seen a battle between rival cartels trying to control pipeline fuel theft, resulting in much higher homicide numbers. That kind of thing can come out of nowhere and turn a green state to red on the danger map.

There was plenty of crime to fret about in my former homes of Hoboken, Nashville, and Tampa in the United States though. There were so many lawn mower thefts in my neighborhood of Nashville that the neighborhood association made joke t-shirts about it and sold them as fundraisers. My garage and car both got broken into. When I lived in Hoboken, New Jersey, my license plates were stolen off my car the first month after arrival and I ended up replacing four broken car windows in four years from break-ins. Heck, I had two bikes stolen where I went to college in small town Virginia. I know plenty of people who have suffered some kind of incident abroad too, though thankfully I haven't myself except for a camera stolen 25 years ago in India. My most recent three years in Tampa were incident free, as have been my 6+ years in Mexico. Maybe my luck is turning. Or maybe I'm just getting better at keeping my valuables.

Crime happens everywhere. It's just the frequency and deadliness that vary. As I was trying to point out at the beginning of this Chapter, often your perception of what is dangerous is quite different than reality when you look at the odds. I've talked enough about my home country, but thuggery is rampant in England and Canada's crime stats would surely be higher if an estimated 50 percent of its property crimes didn't go unreported. The worst cities for pickpockets are in Italy in Spain, which are not exactly countries tourists avoid because of safety worries. Instead they avoid Mexico City, where your chances of getting pickpocketed are close to zero in the tourist zones.

To give you an idea of how low the assault or murder chances are around the world, Statistics Canada only lists eight countries where the five-year average of Canadians assaulted or killed is higher than it is on home soil. Only one in this book makes the list (Mexico), and barely. The worldwide average is 0.5 incidents per 100,000 people, compared to 1.2 at home.

For most people, living abroad is not going to be any more dangerous for you than staying home would be unless you're moving somewhere that is clearly a high-risk city. Where that's the case, I've indicated it in the individual Chapters as specific places to avoid. Spend some time on research to make sure, of course. Understand that you need to focus on specific towns and cities, not the whole country. The two largest cities in Honduras are teeming with drug gangs. The island of Roatan is not. Guatemala City is a place I don't even like spending one night in. But a town on Lake Atitlan? I wouldn't hesitate to move there.

There are some general trends to be aware of, however. In general, murder rates are highest in Latin America and Africa is next. Asia and Europe fare much better, partly because of a better-trained and less corrupt police force. According to a UN study, the Americas have a vastly lower conviction rate for murder, at 24 percent, compared to 48 percent in Asia and 81 percent in Europe.

Usually the places foreigners have gravitated to—especially retirees—are not high-crime areas. That's true in the USA and

Canada too. (Victoria, Scottsdale, and Palm Beach? Pretty safe. Detroit and St. Louis? Not so much.) So, find the message board or online English newspaper for that place you're considering, and you will probably get a fairly good feel of what's going on there, good and bad. Then spend some time there on a trial run and ask a lot of questions of locals about safety and crime if you're worried. Ask the old hands who have seen it all and ask a few newbies who just arrived this year. Pay attention to overall sentiment, not individual anecdotes. Our brains remember stories better than stats, but the stats provide a more accurate truth.

If all the residents say, "This place is going to hell," then at the very least just rent instead of buying. Maybe go back to the drawing board and look elsewhere. If the answers are neutral or positive, you're probably fine. If every bad story you hear is about something that happened to a friend of a friend two years ago, that usually means incidents are rare enough that everyone trades the same old tales of caution.

Don't do this in isolation, without looking at what goes on where you live now at the same time. What would be the impression of people thinking of moving to your hometown if they watched your local evening news every night? If they read your local paper? If they dug up the local homicide and robbery stats? What would you tell them to put it in perspective?

Apply the same sensibilities to where you'd be moving. Your town is probably just "the devil you know" and you're looking in fear at the one you don't know. Put the emotions aside and weigh them the same.

Petty Crime
If you live in a guard-protected gated community in the suburbs or you're in one of the safest areas of Canada or New Zealand, there's a good chance you'll be exposed to more petty crime where you're going. All the countries in this book have legitimate issues to worry about in their capital cities, though in the countrysides of the European countries you've probably got very little risk.

In some places there are pickpockets, in others there are house break-ins, in some spots you may hear about muggings or carjackings. The two best sources of news on this are going to be the local non-tabloid newspaper websites (sometimes in English, often not) and the local expatriate message board(s). Keep in mind both can make the problem look worse than it really is: newspapers everywhere seem to follow an "if it bleeds, it leads" policy and if two or three expats out of 1,000 have something happen to them, it's treated as a major trend and a cause for alarm. People forget that just as many incidents or more happened where they came from, but if it wasn't in their immediate neighborhood or happening to their friends, they ignored it.

Knowing what the problems are and how to avoid them will make you safer though. If there are a lot of pickpockets where you're moving, go out with less in your pockets and make sure those pockets are secured. If there are a lot of break-ins, get the right bars on your windows and invest in good locks or an alarm system. If there have been muggings at 2 am, don't make it a habit to stagger home drunk well after midnight.

Most expats will tell you they feel safer in their new country than they did in their old. Often statistics bear this out. According to the European Institute for Crime Prevention and Control, you're more likely to get assaulted in the USA or Canada as a visitor than in Mexico. In terms of reported crime, New Zealand, Scotland, Italy, and Ireland have higher assault rates than Hungary, Slovakia, or Portugal. The burglary rate is higher in Australia, New Zealand, England, USA, and Canada than it is in many countries featured in this book. So be reasonably cautious and savvy, but don't use safety as an excuse to stay put and keep struggling financially.

Getting Sick After a Move
When you move to another country, your stomach is going to encounter all kinds of ingredients and bacteria it's not used to facing. It's inevitable that you'll have a little adjusting to do. Whether you're headed to Thailand, Togo, or even Turkey, you probably want to give it a few days before you start diving into street food and market stall meals with full-on gusto.

After that though, most expatriates don't suffer anything worse than they would at home as long as they take normal precautions. After all, it's not like you're immune to this risk where you live now. The Center for Disease Control website says, "The CDC estimates that each year roughly 1 in 6 Americans (or 48 million people) get sick, 128,000 are hospitalized, and 3,000 die of foodborne diseases." The percentages are even higher in some countries where food safety laws aren't as strict or there's more risky food (like raw meat or raw fish) eaten regularly.

In developing countries, the biggest risk comes from untreated water and contaminated vegetables. You have to drink bottled or filtered water and wash your vegetables in an iodine solution. This is not necessarily a major inconvenience. Where I live in Mexico, guys deliver 5-gallon bottles of drinking water to my door two times a week for less than $2 each and I can buy iodine drops in any little convenience store. Some expats install a whole-house filtration system for their water.

In a poor country like India or Nepal that has lousy sanitation standards, you may have to worry about the meat as well. You'll need to seek out a butcher with higher standards and you probably don't want to eat anything with meat in it from a cheap restaurant. The first time I visited India and Nepal, I stayed a vegetarian the whole time. The second time I ate more meat, but only when we splurged at nice places with a good reputation. As a result, I never got sick in either country, which is a minor miracle. My wife got laid low for days though in Nepal with food poisoning from a cream sauce that apparently had unpasteurized milk in it.

This last round of mine in Mexico, I've gone nearly two years without any kind of stomach sickness or the runs. This is despite eating street food at least once a week, drinking fresh-squeezed juice regularly, and buying cut-up fruit in the market. Once your stomach fully adjusts, you're usually going to be fine.

The flip side of this is, most people end up eating a healthier diet when they go abroad. American fast food and packaged junk food has infiltrated nearly every corner of the globe now, but in most countries, they don't eat as much of it. And that processed food is not as cheap as eating what's been consumed locally for centuries already. I always lose 10-15 pounds in a few months after moving back to Mexico due to eating less junk food and walking more. When fresh fruit and vegetables cost a fraction of what they do in your local Tesco, Safeway, or Kroger, you tend to eat a lot more of them.

Chapter 32:
Working Abroad and Making a Living

In the first section of this book I wrote on the connection between how you'll support yourself and what kind of visa or residency permit that enables. I want to circle back to this subject though with some food for thought as you look to the future.

The best way to move abroad and leverage your first-world currency is to either be living off retirement funds from your home currency or to be earning a living remotely in your home currency—or a strong currency anyway. If you're getting paid in dollars, pounds, euros, yen, or Swiss francs, you're going to be in good shape almost anywhere.

It's far more desirable to take your portable job with you and get paid in dollars or euros than it is to try to support yourself locally in a country where typical wages are a quarter those of the place you left, at best. If you're trying to get a job locally, you've suddenly lost all your arbitrage benefits. You're not earning in a rich country and spending in a cheaper one. Instead you're doing what all the locals are doing: trying to scrape by on what typical local wages are.

There are ways around this of course, but most require specialized skills or enough capital to start a business. In the first case, for example, you could be a systems analyst or programmer working for a local company and because your skills and experience are on such a higher level than the local labor pool, you could get a higher salary or be made a team manager. Your salary may be lower than it would be in your home country, but it'll be high by local standards.

Or if you're a surgeon, architect, or experienced business consultant, again you may earn less than you could before, but since your expenses are so much lower, you could still be much better off in the end. Many executives get a posting abroad and then don't ever want to come back because their standard of living is so much higher. I once met an oil company expatriate living in Indonesia who got less than half his old salary but felt 10 times richer. He had a maid, cook, gardener, and nanny, plus a driver at his beck and call.

Running a business has long been an expatriate route that can be satisfying and downright lucrative. In many towns all over the world, there may be only a few hundred foreigners in town, but they often own the best coffee shop, the top restaurant, and the best boutique hotels. In many destinations it will only take you a few days to see huge service gaps in the local business landscape. When foreigners jump in and open a better hotel, a better bar, or a better bakery than what is offered already, they can do quite well in a hurry. The expatriates all flock there and then the trendy and wealthy locals follow. This requires some capital and the patience to navigate the local business rules (sometimes it's best to take on a local partner). The payoff can be close to a sure thing though if you've got enough capital and it's clear that demand is sufficient.

Here are a few common ways foreigners earn money abroad though if you don't see a path to earning a remote income in a hard currency.

Teaching English

If you don't have a portable skill, this is one you can pick up that's not a big stretch, assuming you're a native English speaker with a good command of grammar. When I was a young backpacker making my way around the world more than two decades ago, I got a TEFL (teaching English as a Foreign language) certification from Cambridge by doing a four-week course that involved both classroom lessons and live teaching practice. I did the course in Bangkok, but this program is offered all around the world and is widely recognized. Besides helping me earn a higher pay grade later, it also fully prepared me for whatever came at me in the classroom and made me a well-prepared teacher.

Armed with my certification, my now-wife and I taught in a suburb of Istanbul, Turkey on one trip, and then taught for more than a year on a contract in a suburb of Seoul, South Korea. The Istanbul gig barely paid enough to cover our expenses. The Korea one made us feel downright rich.

In much of the world, teaching English as a second language is something you do to get by, while in others it can be quite lucrative. Some expats make it a long-term career and do quite well. In general though, the most desirable places to live are not the ones that are going to pay you handsomely. The highest wages are in the Middle East and the richest Asian countries. For the countries in this book with the lowest cost of living, the locals simply can't pay the kind of money for classes that students can in Tokyo, Seoul, Dubai, or Taipei. On the other hand, you won't need as much either. The problem is that while East Asian and Middle Eastern countries often provide an apartment and cover your airfare over if you sign a contract, that's seldom the case in the rest of the world.

In the past few years, a sizable online marketplace has popped up to satisfy the demand for English teachers in China. You can teach lessons to students there via Skype and do it from wherever you choose to live. Just be advised that the hours can be very early or very late in the day if you're not based in Asia.

Your experience will vary, but in the destinations covered in this book, an hourly pay of $3 to $12 is the general range. That's a wide range, yes, but even at the high end you're not going to be living large, especially if they can't guarantee you enough hours to make it a full-time job. If you have lots of experience you can bump that up by teaching at a university or by teaching business English classes that get paid by the company. You could get up to a range of $2,000 or $3,000 a month and be doing well. Those jobs generally go to people with lots of experience though. You can increase your pay by lining up private lessons, but that takes some time to build.

Some of the people profiled in the country Chapters started out as English teachers, while some did it for more than a decade and are still at it. It's a rewarding job and you end up with a large social circle right away, so it can be a lot of fun. Just understand that your pay will be limited by the locals' salaries, so it's not a way to live significantly better than a middle-class local.

If you're really short on funds, the best route may be to pack this book and go teach for a year or two in a rich country, socking away lots of cash for later or paying off your student loans. Then go live where you really want to live, having enough of a cushion to get you by while you figure out next steps for income. (If you want to keep teaching elsewhere, or online, you'll now have experience and hopefully a recommendation letter.) To give you an idea of how this can work, my wife and I worked our butts off in Korea teaching a little more than a year and put more than $30,000 in the bank. In 1990s dollars. It was the richest I ever felt in my life: we traveled a lot around Korea, ate out whenever we wanted, and still saved a small fortune.

In terms of resources, the *Teaching English Abroad* book by Susan Griffith is great and Dave's ESL Cafe is a great gut check online. Both have been around since before I started teaching in the late 1990s. You can also find info on local expatriate message boards, on the local Craigslist site, and country-specific sources. Really though, unless you're going to work for the JET Program in Japan or something else that has a well-established recruiting system in your home country, it's best to just show up and start looking around. Often what you see on paper or online bears no relationship to actual conditions on the ground. Your main concerns when taking a job with an English school are financial stability, number of hours you'll get weekly, and the pay rate—in that order. There's no point in taking a $30 an hour job in Korea if they school's going to stiff you out of your pay a month after you've started.

On the plus side, these are pretty easy jobs to get, especially if you have a college degree, and many governments will look the other way if you're teaching English while on a tourist visa. (Bangkok's ESL industry would collapse if their teachers all required work visas.) From Buenos Aires to Guadalajara, Marrakesh to Yogyakarta, you can probably find a job teaching English if you are patient, persistent, and presentable. Just don't expect that to happen in India, Nepal, or the Philippines—anyone educated already speaks your language.

Selling Real Estate

I'm mentioning real estate sales in passing because from Mexico down through South America, if there's a community with 100 or more foreigners, you'll find at least one English-speaking foreigner selling real estate. You'll also find foreigners involved in holiday destinations like the Algarve of Portugal and Phuket in Thailand. Most of these countries have looser qualification requirements than you have in more developed nations and half the time you don't even need a license or certification to broker property deals. There are downsides to this of course—no qualifications mean no recourse when something goes wrong, no governing body overseeing practices.

If you're good at this kind of thing though, it means there aren't many barriers to entry if you want to join an agency or start one of your own. Since real estate is a low-overhead, commission-only business, it's something you can start without having much capital or join an existing office investing nothing but your time. For obvious reasons, it helps to know the local market and the local language, though some have managed to blunder through without either...

Freelancing

In these times when so many jobs have been forced to go remote, employers are realizing they don't have to have so many physical bodies in expensive office buildings after all. They can get most of what they need done through e-mail, phone, and video calls.

If you have a skill that is worth paying for, there's a good chance you can get paid for that skill wherever you choose to live. Or you can learn a new skill and start going after clients. To see how varied these opportunities can be, scroll around Fiverr.com and Upwork.com and see what companies are already paying for. The obvious ones involve online tech work, writing, graphic arts, and transcription, but there are literally thousands of gigs posted and taken every week. If you already have contacts you can pitch to and industry experience, it's even easier.

You may have noticed that a lot of interviewees featured in this book are freelance writers, editors, teachers, or coaches. It's because people in those lines of work can easily transition to working remotely and not miss a beat. It was also easier for me to find them though because their work is public. There are thousands of others I didn't talk to who are website designers, systems analysts, translators, transcriptionists, researchers, customer service agents, and sales reps. The possibilities are nearly endless.

Running a Business

When it comes to running an expat business, you can find some good entrepreneurial stories almost anywhere you pick for a trial run. It usually goes something like this: "I noticed that other expats kept complaining that there wasn't a good [insert product or service] here and that they'd gladly pay top dollar for it. I did a little market research, rented out a place, and started offering it. The business took off quickly now we're expanding."

There is the inevitable risk any small business faces, so you probably don't want to invest your life savings in this endeavor, but I'd guess the chances of success are far better than in your home country because it's easier to do research and test your target market. It's also less expensive from a capital standpoint and there's less competition. Where I live in Guanajuato, we probably only have about 500 foreigners living here most of the year. But expats own the two best bakeries, the best coffee shop chain, most of the ethnic restaurants, and a few of the top high-end restaurants. Expats also own the best walking tour company (mine!), the top high-end real estate agency for investors, and some of the best multi-unit Airbnb operations. It's not that foreigners are necessarily better at business than the locals, but they often have more capital to work with and know better how to reach their target audience to get the word out. They often put good customer service higher on the priority list as well because they come from a country where it is standard.

When Charles Vassels landed in Malaysia and was trying to figure out how to turn his interests into a job, he noticed there weren't any donut shops in the big city of Kuala Lumpur. It seemed to him that if you were the first one, you could do pretty well. He called up a donut machine manufacturer when he was back in the USA and found out it was $5,000 to buy one. "I had them send it to Malaysia, my Chinese girlfriend and I rented some space, and the next thing we knew we had a successful donut shop. I asked myself, 'Can it really be this easy? Can you just step off a plane and start a new life with a new business?'"

His background was in product design though, so he kept looking for opportunities in that area and in film production, where he worked before, but wasn't able to make it happen quickly. "So instead I took advantage of the blank slate, the ability to be a pioneer." Eventually he sold the donut shop and started other companies, one doing product design and another producing forms used in courts in California, made in Malaysia. He got to the point of having 20 local employees.

Charles and many like him have followed a simple path to success: meet a demand that isn't being filled, but start off small enough that you aren't betting everything you have. Follow the lean startup model in testing the market to see if your hunches are correct. If they are, you can expand into a larger space, a second location, or a larger regional area. Just keep in mind you will probably spend as much on lawyers and business license fees as you will on the first few months of rent. And in some countries with very strong labor laws, it's next to impossible to get rid of a lousy employee just because they're lazy. Take your time hiring good people instead of snatching up warm bodies. Get lots of local advice from other expat business owners before taking the plunge and you'll have a lot fewer headaches later.

Your Own Virtual Business
As I've said several times in this book, the ideal situation when moving from a rich country to a poorer one is to keep earning money from a rich country. Money in your bank account has no borders. If you can pull it out in a place where you don't need so much of it, that's the true "half price life" dream.

This is also the path for those who want the minimum amount of bureaucracy. Many digital nomads simply bop around the world on tourist visas, never even bothering to get permanent residency anywhere. Since they're adding to the local economy instead of subtracting from it, nobody in government is usually going to bother them unless these people start running afoul of local laws.

If you do apply for residency, in most countries you'll be welcome to come stay a while as long as you can show proof of sufficient income. That "sufficient" number is sometimes much higher than what the average local lives on and it varies from as little as $400 a month to as much as $3,000.

There are as many different virtual business opportunities as there are people reading this book. If you go to Flippa.com or EmpireFlippers.com you'll see all kinds of them for sale. If you have a little capital (sometimes less than $1,000) and some basic tech skills, you can skip a lot of building time by buying something already up and running that is generating cash flow. Many people do quite well being solopreneurs, farming out their skills in web development, coding, technical writing, or translation—nearly any job that can be done remotely is a candidate for that. Some get to a point where they have more work than they can handle, and they need to scale. The next thing they know, they have three or four virtual employees or additional freelancers.

I spent a lot of time on this subject in an earlier Chapter of this book, so refer back to that for specific idea generators. Just know that the world is full of online opportunities for those who can meet a market need. Assess your skills, be observant, and be attuned to where what you can do intersects with what people are willing to pay for. Whether you need to earn a full-time living or just supplant what you're getting from investments or retirement funds, you can probably find a way to earn what you need without working for low local wages.

Chapter 33:
Taking Care of Details

As Charles Vassels, an American living in Malaysia says, "Many people dream of this kind of life, but they don't have the guts to really do it. They don't take that step to get on a plane and get off in another country where they don't know anyone."

The big leap to actually getting on that plane and moving abroad seems the scariest, but it's really the end of the checklist. Unfortunately, at times it may feel like there are a million things you need to do before that point. The more you put plans in motion, the more you discover.

Many books on moving to a specific country will give you some kind of checklist for what you should be taking care of one year ahead of time, six months ahead of time, three months out, and the week before you leave. Since I'm covering so many places that appeal to so many different kinds of people, I'm not going to try to repeat that here. I do link to some examples in the Resources section though where you can find these checklists. You need to have some kind of to-do list and it's going to be a long one. Consider the list you would have for moving to another state or province in your own country, then double it. If you're a couple and one of you is more organized than the other, designate that person as the checklist maker and paper gatherer. Otherwise you may never get on that plane. You certainly won't get a residency permit.

You will discover other tasks besides these big ones below that you only have to deal with every once in a while, like taxes and voting. Yes, you probably still have to pay taxes but yes, you can still vote from abroad. If you have a permanent address in your original country, you can request an absentee ballot and vote for everything, including local races. If you don't, you can still vote in national elections via an oversees ballot unless you have renounced your citizenship. Just plan ahead to get it done.

Here are the broad categories of steps you'll need to take to prepare.

Storage
Unless you sell absolutely everything, you'll need to figure out what to do with your stuff. I'm a strong advocate for making a clean break, but some people are willing to spend money to get things shipped to where they're moving to. The more expats there are where you're going, the easier that will be without sending an

entire container load. Otherwise you're limited to what you can fly with and ship via a service like DHL.

If you leave some things behind, for sentimental reasons if nothing else, you'll need to store them somewhere. If you've got a relative with some garage or attic space, great. Otherwise you'll probably need to hire space in a storage facility and add a monthly fee to your living expenses. Obviously, you want to get rid of anything not essential or important because the more space you need, the more it's going to cost you. If you're storing your things in a hot place, you'll probably also need to pay for climate control.

Renting out a home you own instead of selling it can alleviate some of these issues. If you can cover your expenses or ideally make a profit, it might make sense to rent out your place and rent where you're going so you can hang on to furniture and decorative items. If you rent it as an Airbnb place, you can even leave all your dishes, towels, and decorative items. Then you still have a place to come home to when you want—another reason for not jumping into home ownership where you're moving to.

Mail
You'll need to move everything you possibly can online for bill paying and updates, like paying credit card bills, getting back statements, and paying taxes. You'll probably still need to maintain an address in your own country though, both to have a place for lingering mail to go (like with those remaining utility bills that aren't online) and to avoid hassles from your financial institutions. For taxes and credit cards, at a minimum, you'll need a "permanent address" in your home country. You can have a mail address that forwards to you overseas, or even just scans your mail, but a more practical approach is to use a relative's address so they can alert you when something fishy or urgent comes in.

There are also services that will receive your mail for you, and some will scan it so you can see what you got online. You can then have them trash or forward the physical copies. If you need to set up residency in the USA, several people I know have set that up in South Dakota, for example, using a service there specifically meant for people roaming the USA in a recreational vehicle or roaming the world without a fixed address. There are similar (but more complicated) ones in states with no sales tax like Nevada, Texas, and Florida. Many residents of San Miguel de Allende use a service where they have a United States mailing address in Laredo, Texas and a guy actually drives up there twice each week to bring everyone's mail down to central Mexico. If you want to keep a voting and driver's license address though, a simple mail drop won't cut it.

Don't forget to alert everyone you get mail from of the new address as your forwarding order will only last 6-12 months depending on the items. This is especially essential for tax documents since those are still mostly sent by mail. For recommedations and more detailed info on this subject, search "mailbox" at CheapestDestinationsBlog.com.

Phone and Keeping in Touch
You may think that when you move out of your home country, you won't need a home country phone number anymore. Unfortunately, the modern "two-factor authentication" world has made that impossible. You'll need to maintain some kind of home country number to avoid pulling your hair out. Ideally, it's one that can still receive text messages since that's far easier than getting an automated call every time you log into your bank account or go to pay a credit card

You also might want to give friends and relatives who aren't very tech-savvy a way to call you. (For the more savvy, they can use WhatsApp, Facebook Messenger, or other apps.) There are services such as Google Voice, Number Barn, and Ting to tap into, you can get a "burner phone" pre-paid service just for this purpose, or you can actually hold onto your existing phone plan if it still works in the country you'll be living in. I still use my US T-Mobile account for my family of three, for example, because it's a good value and it treats all of North America as the same country—no extra charges. I have free data roaming almost anywhere in the world, so it's worth paying a premium to keep it as a travel writer.

"We ported our existing mobile numbers to Google Voice, but we also got US numbers through a service called Ting," says Mary Anne Machado, who moved to Queretaro, Mexico with her husband. "Each line has a base price of $6 per month, and you pay for the minutes/data you use. So, when we're in Mexico we will probably never use them, but they are additional numbers we can add to our profiles for US banks, etc., just in case Google Voice doesn't work. Plus, we each have a 'real' phone number for visits back to the USA."

The expatriate life is far easier than it used to be when it comes to communication. By paying a few bucks to voice-over-IP-services like Skype or Google Voice, you can talk for hours with your relatives if you want. With Facetime or Zoom you can even see each other. Nearly all cell phones now let you call over Wi-Fi, but you can also set up a phone number in your own country that will ring to your laptop or smart phone. You can transfer files by Dropbox or Google Docs and easily share photos on social media.

Some of these services are free and none of the paid ones costs all that much or will be difficult. But international communication is one most important thing to put on your to-do list.

If you want to stream video or audio, you might want to set up a proxy service as well. This allows you to tap into an ISP in your home country, so it still looks like you're there. None of them are perfect or foolproof (and sometimes Netflix has a better selection abroad anyway), but some of the most widely used are TunnelBear, ExpressVPN, PureVPN, and Hotspot Shield. These run anywhere from $3 to$10 per month.

Finances
There are things you need that you probably haven't even thought about when it comes to financial instruments. Do you have a credit card with a chip instead of just a magnetic stripe—or these days a touchless version? You might need that where you're going. Do you have a credit card that doesn't charge a foreign transaction fee? You'll pay a lot more if you don't. Do you have a bank account that will allow you to withdraw your money from an ATM without getting dinged for $4-$5 every time? Over a year, this can make a huge difference. (In general, credit unions and the cash accounts of brokerage companies are the best bet for this.) Don't forget bank alliances that can save you money: your current bank may be connected to another one in your destination country that will allow you to withdraw money at no cost.

You want backup plans in all these cases too. If one debit card gets eaten by a machine or lost, you will be glad you had a second one, preferably to a different account. If one credit card gets denied, which happens all the time for no good reason, you want to be able to pull out a second one. In some places Visa is not common but MasterCard is, so you want both. Maybe an Amex too for good measure.

Ideally you want to have several bank accounts (easier if you're with a spouse) and you want to be able to transfer money between them. Unless you have six figures sitting around in cash accounts, you're probably going to need to move money around now and then. You may want to have accounts with PayPal and even TransferWise for international transactions online. Even in the 2020s, it's often difficult for me to use a U.S. credit card to pay for something online in Mexico—even for bus companies, airlines, or huge operations like Mercado Libre. If you're running any kind of business or are a freelancer, having a PayPal and/or TransferWise account will enable regular transactions with people in other countries. You can connect this to a bank account to transfer in and out. If you live in Argentina or another country with bank restrictions, you may need to use Xoom or Western Union sometimes.

Healthcare
There's usually no rush to line up health insurance abroad like there would be if you were moving to the super-expensive USA, but you'll probably at least want to do a little research if you're not going to self-insure. You also want to have all the details on your prescriptions if you take meds regularly, including the actual drug name and dosage, not the brand name.

You are often better off setting up insurance after arrival because you can use a local broker in some countries and get feedback from others on what they are using. You'll probably either be on a local plan specific to your new country or on some international plan that covers you when you travel as well. A high-deductible "catastrophic" plan will run a couple anywhere from $1,500 to $5,500 per year depending on age and whether it includes the USA or not. If you have to return to the U.S. for more than two weeks in a year, that can easily double the rate. This doesn't apply if you're from a country with a national health care plan, such as, well, pretty much every other developed country in the world. It also doesn't apply if you're American and are old enough to be on Medicare and you plan on returning for serious procedures. See the Resources section at the end for companies offering expat insurance.

You'll probably find that all this detail work is relatively easy to cross off your lists. It's just time consuming to set up. What you really have to worry about is the emotional part...

Chapter 34:
The Resistance You Will Face

"If you limit your actions in life to things that nobody can possibly find fault with, you will not do much," said author Lewis Carroll

In 1902 another author named Owen Wister published a novel called *The Virginian*. It is widely credited as the first true "western" and had a huge influence on a whole class of books, movies, and TV shows that followed. Although this launched Wister's writing career and he spent the rest of his life publishing other books and living a life of celebrity, he never wrote another western. This fact is glossed over without any explanation in most biographies, but apparently it was a scolding from his mother that was the reason. She reportedly thought it was beneath his talents to write that kind of trashy story and she reprimanded him for the frequent violence in the book. With that one rebuke, Wister stopped doing what had broken new ground and returned to doing "normal" writing again.

He went on to write four more novels, 11 non-fiction books, and a large body of short stories. It is that one revolutionary book that Wister is still known for today though. None of the others came close to selling the 200,000 copies *The Virginian* did its first year. Five movies and a TV series have used that book as the basis of their story, and it has never been out of print.

When you do something that seems different or radical to others, you can expect lots of resistance. Perhaps even contempt. A whole mix of emotions erupts when someone else freely embraces a drastic change. So, when you excitedly announce your plans to move abroad, your mother may not approve. Don't expect your friends and relatives to be universally excited for you either. Some will get downright hostile. To your face or behind your back, you may be called a deserter, a runaway, a slacker, a coward, a communist, a kook, or worse.

If the TV news channel you watch all day keeps telling you that you live in the greatest country in the world and everyone wants to be live there, sooner or later you start believing it. In an article I read about the ten most popular countries for Americans moving abroad, the nasty comments underneath it included gems like this.

"I ALREADY LIVE IN THE BEST COUNTRY IN THE WORLD WHY WOULD I WANT TO GO ANYWHERE ELSE!! EVEN AT OUR WORST WE ARE WE ARE BETTER THAN THE REST!!!" (Typos corrected, screaming capitals left.)

"Well now anyone who is on the run from the Law knows where they can ESCAPE to, as you put it. Bye, maybe we can empty the prisons and send them to these places."

Read any article online about moving abroad and you'll find a large number of comments that are hateful, paranoid, ignorant, racist, or just dead wrong. Most of the people writing them haven't traveled out of the country or if they did, it was on a safe and predictable cruise ship. They ignore the troubles in their own town as if they don't exist but proclaim to be experts on all the troubles you are bound to encounter if you go live in Mexico. Hey, they saw it on TV.

While the rah-rah USA types are the worst, you'll also get strong resistance from people you are close to if you're moving from Manchester to Porto or from Toronto to Trujillo. Some cultures are more open to moving abroad than others, especially if you're only doing it six months a year, but that doesn't mean your blood relatives and close friends are going to be thrilled that you're abandoning them and will be eight hours away by plane. Many will be legitimately perplexed.

The Emotions Behind Resistance
If you understand why people are not happy about your grand plans to move abroad, it gets easier to deal with the criticism (or wall of silence). Then you can just say, "Excuse me, there's someone over there I need to talk to" when someone starts criticizing your plans instead of getting red in the face and telling them off. Here are a few reasons behind the resistance.

1) They haven't traveled much.
Most people who don't understand why you would take off and travel around the world for a year or move to another country haven't spent much time outside their own country. (In many cases, that's a good thing for the rest of the world.) If they have traveled internationally, it has been on a secluded ship, in a secluded resort, or a very tightly organized tour. They don't know much about real costs and they probably don't believe things are as cheap where you're going as you are telling them. Or they think if your rent is $250 a month, then you must be moving to a cave with dirt floors and no indoor plumbing.

2) They're envious because their own boring life is all mapped out.

"Going on an adventure" is a depressingly rare event for nearly all the adult population of my home country. Vacations are strictly planned. Time off work is a too-rare commodity that can't be spent spontaneously. The race for more stuff and more money to pay for bloated health care and university systems saps the life out of most people who have managed to land a good job and keep it. Ask them how their life will be different in five or ten years and they may not be able to think of anything. Or they'll just say something weak about a hoped-for promotion, retirement, or their kids going to college.

For a majority, the closest they'll get to an adventure is having an illicit affair with a co-worker or staying up all night "getting crazy" at the next convention in Vegas or Orlando. They are slaves to routines, commutes, the kids' activity schedules, and the big-screen TV. They'll say, "I wish I could do what you're doing" but will have plenty of the usual excuses as to why they can't. It's all mapped out, pre-ordained, set in stone. They have responsibilities. There are two car loans to pay off, a big mortgage to keep paying, promises to keep, ladders to climb, plus they just got that new riding mower for the lawn...

They're in a jail of their own making but they don't realize they have built it themselves.

You represent a threat because you're showing them it doesn't have to be that way. And that's as scary as the revelation in *The Matrix*. Every time you tell them about your adventures abroad, it's going to be a reminder of what's on the other side. The life they may have dreamed of before they donned so many shackles and chains. They won't tell you all this. They might not even be able to see it and verbalize it. But you may be making them feel some negative emotions without you even knowing it.

3) If you're leaving, that means this place is not perfect

If you're in some kind of membership club and people start dropping out, that makes you wonder what's wrong. If the star performers in your company start taking jobs elsewhere, you're going to think that's a bad sign. You may feel like a sucker for still being there.

If someone tells you they're moving away from where you live and that they think this whole lifestyle they've been living in your town is not the best they can do, how's that going to make you feel? If they moved away to Silicon Valley because of a great job offer, that's perfectly logical, but to move abroad just because there's a better life somewhere else? That's...well... "different."

Some will just think you're nuts, and they'll feel okay because you're obviously off your rocker. Some will feel envious and maybe a bit bitter (see #2). Others will start wondering if this club they thought was perfect may not be so great after all. This life they've been told to pursue, the one that's supposed to represent fulfillment, is not feeling so fulfilling. Now you come along saying there's a way out and you're hopping on a plane to take it.

Maybe they had a nagging feeling that this land of opportunity they're in is not so full of opportunity anymore, that getting ahead financially is getting tougher every year. Now you're regaling them with tales of half-price living in a place with better weather and less stress. They might be happy for you, but you're not making *them* happy. Because they're stuck in this place that's looking a lot less perfect now. You just shined a bright flashlight on the troubles.

Empathy and Strength
You don't want to hear your mother say, "You're an idiot for doing this and you should feel guilty for leaving me."

But then again, hearing "We're so happy for you" while seeing a dark cloud pass over her face is not so great either.

Understand that your radical decision (in their eyes) can spur heavy emotions and soul-searching, no matter how much that person knows you're going to have an amazing time. You'll be told you're an idiot, people will say, "See you back here in six months!" with a laugh and a pat on your back. Just smile, keep making your arrangements, and then post lots of photos seven months later.

Understand why you may meet resistance and don't let it get you down. Understand their position, but be extra resolute about yours. This is your life and doing what other people tell you is "normal" is probably going to put you on a treadmill that's not going anywhere. It's your decision to make and it's a good one, so lock the storage shed door and go!

One good solution to all this if you're not getting much support on the home front is to find new people to talk with. Join up with groups of like-minded people who are thinking of moving abroad or are already doing it. My Cheap Living Abroad groups are a good solution of course, but you can also find destination-specific message boards and Facebook groups to drill down further and make new friends where you're going. If nothing else, being around these people instead of the ones that don't understand will dissipate this feeling that your decision is crazy or radical.

If you're one of the lucky ones, your friends and family will be supportive and will even come visit now and then. If not, don't take it personally. Just spend more time with the people who understand what you're doing or have already done it themselves. There are millions and millions of you already, so don't let anyone make you think you're an oddball.

Chapter 35:
Family Considerations

Wherever you end up moving to, there will be foreign families living in that country. Sure, there may be more empty nesters, retirees, and young English teachers, but plenty of families move abroad for job transfers, proximity to relatives, a slower pace of life, or cost savings. A family can live anywhere other expats can live: children are everywhere of course. There's one major factor though that can limit your choices: schooling.

If you're the kind of patient, educated, meticulous parents who can pull off home schooling for years on end, you'll have it easier. You can get all your lessons and meet your home state or province's requirements online, just as if you were home schooling back in that location. This takes lots of up-front preparation before leaving and your child has to be the type that can thrive outside a classroom environment though. You'll also miss out on some of the language immersion benefit that comes from mixing all day with local children. When you factor in the ability to live anywhere and make your own schedule though, the parents that go this route are usually happy with it.

For everyone else, the local school situation is going to be a big factor in where you can and cannot live. Sure, there will be local schools almost anywhere you would choose to live. You can't assume they're going to be good schools though, and they will likely be in a foreign language if they're not private international ones. The public schools may not be anywhere close to the standards you're used to, and the classrooms may be overcrowded.

Within a country or even within the same state in that country, the number of foreigners or wealthy businesspeople can make a huge difference in the choices. Where I live in Mexico, for instance, my daughter went to two different private schools, which after initial fees carried a very reasonable cost of $300 or so per month. Classes were in Spanish only though, and there was no English language option. We wanted this for her, and she adjusted fine, so it wasn't a big issue, but some children really struggle if they don't have a good language base already.

Just an hour and a half away in San Miguel de Allende, however, there are several schools with bilingual classes and one accredited international school in English. If we lived in the industrial "shoe capital of Mexico" an hour in the other direction in Leon, we'd have even more options. In Guadalajara or Mexico City, we could choose from many elite international schools affiliated with the International Baccalaureate program.

Keep this dynamic in mind when considering family locations if you are not going to home school the little ones. In general, capital cities and industrial cities will have plenty of options. Smaller towns and secondary cities though—which are often more desirable places to live—may not have more than one or two options. The best ways to find out are to seek out other parents already living there to get info, as well as visiting prospective locations in person to pound the pavement and see the possibilities for yourself. Also check into tutoring options. For a fraction of what you would spend at home, you can probably get a private tutor to help your child in subjects he or she is having trouble with, at a slower individual pace. (We hired a math one for a year at one point.)

Don't automatically assume your child will quickly pick up a new language and make new friends immediately. The common assumption is that children are sponges when it comes to languages, but that's often an oversimplification. Sure, they pick it up faster than adults, but it still takes months to get to a halfway reasonable level of fluency. The older they are, the tougher the classroom vocabulary: imagine taking history, science, civics, and math in a language you barely comprehend, at a high school level! Do everything you can to get them past the basic language level before they step into the classroom and face a sea of unfamiliarity. It's tough enough moving to a new country with a different culture. Add in language difficulties and different customs and it can be emotionally trying to say the least.

Once they get through it though, the payoff for the rest of their life can be substantial. No matter what field they go into, having a second language is a big plus (especially if it's a commonly used one) and that experience of adapting to new challenges is great preparation for the demands of the modern workplace or of building a business.

English or Not for School
At the risk of generalizing, the more useless a country's language is outside that country, the more likely it is that the elite private schools will be run in English. In Thailand, for example, Chiang Mai alone has six international schools and several more with bilingual programs. The choices are even greater in Bangkok, though naturally they decrease in resort areas where there is not as much of a business reason for them. With Thai being such a

limited language internationally, a lot of business is conducted in English and most education administrators you deal with will speak English well.

In a country like India, Nepal, or Malaysia, English is already the language of politics and business, so it will be quite easy to find a school with classes in English.

In other countries, especially Spanish or French-speaking ones, get ready for immersion unless you want to shell out high rates for an elite private school.

We were parents that actually wanted that local language schooling. We felt we were giving our daughter a huge leg up in the world by giving her the means to become truly bilingual. But some kids really struggle with this, so evaluate your situation closely. Just as your home neighborhood where you are now may be influenced by the school options, the case may be the same when you decide where to move abroad.

Domestic Help

I mentioned earlier that it's generally quite inexpensive to get a private tutor, something that's especially true in university towns. In many of the countries profiled in this book, there's a long history of quality domestic help in other areas, so parents can get assistance in the form of a nanny, housekeeper, a tutor, and even a daily driver for very reasonable rates.

The price for these services can seem ridiculously low in your home currency and in some cultures, you're looked down upon if you don't hire as much domestic help as you can afford to spread a little of your money around. In a country like Indonesia, it can even be part of the residency visa requirement.

Figure out what the local rates are from others but don't be afraid to pay a bit more for reliability and trust. Our rule of thumb is to pay someone good at the top of the local rate for these services, but not to overpay so much that it upends rates for the local homeowners and creates resentment. You don't want to price the locals out of their own market and be despised as "that rich foreigner" who is marching in and raising expectations.

Keep in mind that many countries have a mandated year-end "13th month" bonus you are required by law to pay domestic workers, whether they live with you or not. Put it into the budget for December.

Diversions

"This is a rapidly modernizing country with all the things kids love: shopping malls, great movie theaters, amusement parks, and big swimming pools." That's what one moving abroad publication said about Thailand, but it could also apply to Malaysia, Panama, Mexico, and others.

Unless you're moving to a very rural area, there will plenty for your kids to do. If they're in school, they'll probably get invited to all kinds of local social events with other kids. You probably won't have a problem finding a playground or a pizza shop. Plus, you can probably get some version of the streaming services and TV channels available in your own country. In other words, whether your child or children will be able to stay entertained is probably the least of your worries.

Books

You'll want your child to keep reading, but there probably won't be the big selection of English books you're used to. There are some anomalies like San Miguel de Allende or Oaxaca in Mexico where there's a big English library. Some bookstores in India have a great selection of new English books and some resort towns have a lot of used ones. Often printed books will be more expensive abroad than they are in your home country, however, even if Amazon is available.

You should probably expect to get a Kindle, tablet, or Kobo for your child so you can download books over Wi-Fi wherever you happen to be. If they're at picture book age, an iPad or large Android tablet is a better choice because of the graphics.

Diet

If there's a vegetarian in the family, you'll have a much easier time in the Asian countries featured in this book than the others. Residents of developed countries are spoiled for choice and they forget (or don't know) that this wasn't always the case. Being a vegetarian in the 1950s in the USA or Canada was no picnic and that's how it still is in much of the world. If you are a local and don't eat meat, it's usually not by choice: it means you're too poor to afford it.

In India, however, it's a religious choice for a large portion of the population, so especially in the south, it's easier to be one than not. (And this lessens your odds of getting sick.) Because there are so many ethnic Indians in Malaysia, it's the same story there, in the western half of the country anyway. In Nepal, Thailand, Bali, and Vietnam it's relatively easy to eat vegetarian in cities and where tourists gather, especially if you have a phrase book or translation app for situations where nobody speaks English.

In other places, if you're not too strict about it, you'll have choices, but if you are a strict vegan, you'll be doing a lot of your own cooking. Even in Vietnam, they use fish sauce for flavoring. In Latin America, your refried beans, empanadas, and tamales may contain lard. The beautiful salads you order in Bulgaria will be covered with grated cheese and everything comes with yogurt. In any of these places though, after you've lived there a while, you'll find your favorite spots that can accommodate your special requests.

If you have an intolerance to lactose, gluten, or nuts, don't be surprised if nobody knows what you're talking about in your new home. In the U.S. especially, these issues are either over-diagnosed or caught more often—depending on which medical study you read—but in the rest of the world they're treated more like "my kid has digestion problems."

Otherwise, anywhere you go you're going to have the normal picky kid issues where your little one doesn't want to touch all those strange things on the plate and it's a battle to get them to expand the culinary horizons. Many expats find the best approach is to take it gradually, mixing in the new with the familiar. Often you can find something that's semi-familiar, like chicken satay, breaded chicken breast, or corn dogs that will do in a pinch. Some families force their kids to try new things in restaurants, then cook what's more familiar at home. It's pretty easy to approximate what they're used to in most of the world these days, though you may find certain spices tough to find and certain ingredients to be more expensive. Those are the things you ask friends and family to bring when they're visiting, or you buy when traveling elsewhere.

In general, moving abroad with kids is only slightly more difficult than moving abroad without them. Get the schooling sorted out and the rest will fall into place eventually.

Chapter 36:
Caveats and Legalese

You've reached the end of *A Better Life for Half the Price* and I hope you've found it useful. If you've joined one of the Cheap Living Abroad groups, we'll keep exploring the advice and topics in here. (See CheapLivingAbroad.com.) You can read my weekly articles on the Cheapest Destinations Blog (CheapestDestinationsBlog.com).

If you enjoyed this book, I'd be grateful if you'd do me one favor: leave a review on Amazon or Kobo. That helps it show up in front of other readers interested in making a move.

Before making big decisions about this move abroad, remember that I'm just one person; you should recheck what I tell you before making a life-changing decision.

I'm not a lawyer, CPA, tax advisor, financial advisor, or doctor. I'm just a guy with a bachelor's degree from university, a blog, and a few books with my name on the spine. I am a journalist only, so consult with a professional who has letters after his or her name before making any major legal or investment decisions. The information presented in this book is a collection of advice and opinions from a person who has lived abroad and talked to a hundred+ others doing the same, but none of it is guaranteed or insured to be without fault. Nothing in this book should be construed as legal, financial, or medical advice that should be taken without secondary verification.

Also be advised that prices, tax laws, visa requirements, and exchange rates are in a constant state of flux. Anything written in these pages is subject to change, so always verify key items before basing a decision on them, especially something so important as where you are going to live. All attempts have been made to ensure visa/residency information was correct at the time of writing, but it's especially important to verify this information with your local consulate or embassy—or the people living where you want to live—before proceeding.

As I have stressed many times, some people are not cut out for a move away from the land of their birth. The best way to ascertain this for yourself is to travel widely and do a trial run in your potential target(s). Reading 100 books and message boards is no substitute for having feet on the ground for an extended period and living like a local instead of a tourist. Please invest the time and resources to see if what looks good on paper is really a good match for your wants and needs. That's part of the fun anyway, so enjoy it.

Happy trails!

Chapter 37:
Resources for Living Abroad

This is by no means an exhaustive list of resources and things are bound to change, so these are not hotlinks. You'll want to check the CheapLivingAbroad.com/resources website page to get the most current version and just click on links. Here's plenty to keep you busy though as you research your plans to live a better life for less money.

STAYING IN TOUCH
Keep reading updates from me at CheapestDestinationsBlog.com, at the Facebook page for that site, and on social media. I'm @timleffel on Twitter @globetrots on Instagram, and Tim Leffel on YouTube.
If you want some extra guidance or one-on-one consulting before your move, see the upgrade options at CheapLivingAbroad.com.

EXPAT/LIVING ABROAD WEBSITES
International Living (internationalliving.com)
Live and Invest Overseas (liveandinvestoverseas.com)
Escapeartist.com (escapeartist.com)
Transitions Abroad (transitionsabroad.com)
Retire In Asia (retireinasia.com)
South American Living (southamericaliving.com)
Viva Tropical (vivatropical.com)

EXPAT FORUMS AND BLOGS
Expatexchange.com
Expatfocus.com
Internations.org
TheProfessionalHobo.com
NomadFlag.com

EDUCATION
International Baccalaureate Schools Directory (ibo.org/general/who.cfm)
WaldorfEducation.org

HEALTHCARE AND HEALTH INSURANCE
CDC-Centers for Disease Control (cdc.gov)
IAMAT.org to find English-speaking doctors
World Health Organization (who.int)

AllianzTravelInsurance.com
SafetyWing.com
Worldnomads.com
Sevencorners.com
HealthcareInternational.com
AetnaInternational.com
CignaGlobal.com
Bupa-intl.com
Geo-blue.com
Axa.co.uk/healthcare/international
AllianzWorldwideCare.com

MAIL
Search "mailbox" on my CheapestDestinationsBlog.com for current services

MOVING SERVICES
JustMovers.org
ReallyMoving.com
ExpatFocus.com
WORKING ABROAD
TEFL.com
Search jobs at the U.S. State Department (Careers.state.gov)
USAID.gov/careers
ESLcafe.com/job-center
French Foreign Legion recruiting (legion-recrute.com)
Peacecorps.gov
MilitaryBases.com
Upwork.com
Indeed.com
Monster.com International (Monster.com/geo/siteselection/)
Also check industry-specific sites that match your skills, such as JournalismJobs.com

STUDYING ABROAD
Transitionsabroad.com
VISA INFORMATION
State Department – US Passports and International travel (travel.state.gov)
UK Passports and International Travel (gov.uk/browse/abroad)
Canada Passports and International Travel (travel.gc.ca/travelling)
A Briggs Passport & Visa Expeditors (abriggs.com)

Travel Visa Pro (travelvisapro.com)
Visa HQ (travelvisapro.com)
CIBT Visas (cibtvisas.com)
EmbassyWorld.com (embassyworld.com)

PRICING INFO
Numbeo.com
CheapestDestinationsBlog.com
Priceoftravel.com
NomadList.com
Expatistan.com

COUNTDOWN LISTS
Medical checklist article (expatexchange.com)
US State Department moving abroad checklist (state.gov)
International Relocation country breakdown at
ExpatExchange.com
For UK residents: Expertsforexpats.com/relocation/moving-abroad-checklist/
ClockworkRemovals.co.uk
Search "moving overseas checklist" at Suddath.com

TAXES AND DOING BUSINESS
Doing Business guidelines from the World Bank
(doingbusiness.org)
World Economic Forum (weforum.org)
CIA World Factbook (cia.gov/library/publications/the-world-factbook/)
Sovereignman.com
Flag Theory (flagtheory.com)
Nomad Capitalist (nomadcapitalist.com)

PETS
Search "Pets" at ExpertsForExpats
Search "Pets" at any expat forum site
ipata.org/
PetRelocation.com
USDA pet relocation section: Aphis.usda.gov/aphis/pet-travel

HOUSE SITTING (for a trial run)
TrustedHouseSitters.com
MindMyHouse.com
HouseCarers.com

Also search for ones in individual countries

MISC.
Global Property Guide (globalpropertyguide.com)
FreedomHouse.com (human rights and state oppression rankings)
ConvertIt.com (currency, measurement, time zones, & more)
XE.com (exchange rates)
ExpatExchange.com
EscapeArtist.com
ExpatFinder.com
Tropical MBA podcast for online entrepreneurs (tropicalmba.com)
SmartPassiveIncome.com
ZeroToTravel.com podcast
ExpatMoneyShow.com podcast
Nomadtopia podcast

Acknowledgements

I have a lot of people to thank who have kept my writing and publishing business thriving for a decade and a half, including my wife Donna, my associate editor Lydia, and my assistant Paty. Without all the readers on my various websites and those who have bought my books, I'd be bored and annoyed in a cubicle somewhere in my home country probably, so thanks.

This book would not be possible without all the interview subjects who graciously offered their time to be interviewed, as well as the other travel bloggers living abroad who helped me fill in the blanks. Thanks to Numbeo.com for providing good crowdsourced gut-checks and those chiming in on expat sites with solid numbers on living expenses.

Thanks to my recent college grad daughter Alina (with a writing degree!) for the proofreading help. Thanks to Nyári Zoltan for the book formatting work

Last, thanks to everyone who bought the first version of this book or the advanced packages to turn their plans into reality. Especially if you left a review on Amazon!

Made in the USA
Coppell, TX
13 September 2023

21570271R00203